From Nation to Diaspora

Samuel Selvon,
George Lamming and the
Cultural Performance of Gender

Curdella Forbes

The University of the West Indies Press
Jamaica • Barbados • Trinidad and Tobago

University of the West Indies Press
1A Aqueduct Flats   Mona
Kingston 7   Jamaica
www.uwipress.com

09 08 07 06 05   5 4 3 2 1

CATALOGUING IN PUBLICATION DATA

Forbes, Curdella
From nation to diaspora : Samuel Selvon, George Lamming and the
cultural performance of gender / Curdella Forbes
p. cm.
Includes bibliographical references.
ISBN: 976-640-171-3

1. West Indian literature – 20th century – History and criticism. 2. Selvon,
Samuel – Criticism and interpretation. 3. Lamming, George – Criticism and
interpretation. 4. Culture in literature. 5. Gender identity in literature.
6. Masculinity in literature. 7. Nationalism in literature. I. Title.

PR9210.F67 2005   810.9.9729

Cover illustration: Lilian Sten-Nicholson, *Fire from Within – Desperadoes*
(oil on canvas, 1989, 100 x 190 cm). (Painted to Despers' 1987 "Panorama"
rendition of Kitchener's "Pan in A Minor".) Reproduced by courtesy of
Lilian Sten-Nicholson. Photograph by Alicia Roche.

Book and cover design by Robert Harris.
E-mail: roberth@cwjamaica.com

Set in Adobe Garamond 11/14 x 24
Printed in the United States of America.

From Nation to Diaspora

For my parents,
Ionie and Sebert

Contents

Acknowledgements

THE RESEARCH FOR COMPLETION OF this book was made possible by a Principal's Fellowship from the University of the West Indies, Mona. I thank the university for this invaluable assistance.

The universities of Hull and Birmingham very generously made their library holdings available to me and provided assistance whenever I needed it. Special thanks are due also to the staff of the West Indies Collection, University of the West Indies, Mona, for their always sterling work and unstinting assistance.

This book is based in part on my PhD dissertation; acknowledgement and thanks to the supervisor of that project, Professor Edward Baugh.

I wish to acknowledge the many friends who in various ways assisted me throughout this project: with advice, encouragement, accommodation, information, prayers, incantations. The contribution of friends can never be measured. Thanks to Victor Chang, Norval Edwards, Joan Miller Powell, Pauline Hanson, Fay Davidson, Burchell K. Taylor, Thelma Brown, Melvia Bullock, Conrad James, Ruth Minott Egglestone, Gertrud Buscher, Michael Cooke. My particular appreciation to my niece Angella Brown, for her patient, graceful help in last-minute searches for records I had stacked away too neatly or too untidily to be able to find on my own.

Versions of sections of the book appeared in previous publications as follows:

From material in chapter 2: "Revisiting Samuel Selvon's Trilogy of Exile: Implications for Gender Consciousness and Gender Relations in West Indian Culture", *Caribbean Quarterly* 43, no. 4 (December 1997): 47–63.

From material in chapter 1: "Tropes of the Carnivalesque: Hermaphroditic Gender in Slave Society and West Indian Fictions", *Journal of West Indian Literature* 8, no. 2 (April 1999): 19–37.

From material on *The Emigrants* in chapter 5: " '. . . and the dumb speak . . .' : George Lamming's Theory of Language and the Epistemology of the Body in *The Emigrants*", special Postcolonial Issue, *Literature and Psychology: A Journal of Psychoanalytic and Cultural Criticism* 48, no. 4 (Winter 2001–02): 6–32.

Introduction

The Necessity of Gender
Selvon, Lamming and the Re-imagination of Culture

THIS BOOK IS A DISCUSSION of gender in West Indian culture. It undertakes the discussion through a revisionary reading of gender in selected novels written by Samuel Selvon and George Lamming from the 1950s to the 1970s,[1] the period in which nationalism in the West Indies (that is, the anglophone Caribbean) reached its highest level of consolidation. The book locates Selvon's and Lamming's representations of gender within the discourse of nationalism, the primary mode in which the West Indies has thought about itself since the early decades of the twentieth century. The discussion suggests how Selvon's and Lamming's texts point towards issues within the discourses of diaspora and postmodernism, the major paradigms that, from the last three decades of the twentieth century and increasingly in the twenty-first, have begun to shift nationalism from its central place as the shaping force by which West Indianness is imagined.

Part of my argument is that the nationalist representation of West Indian gender – taken as a collective cultural phenomenon of which Selvon's and Lamming's representations form a part – highlights a complex and unusual scenario for which a new vocabulary needs to be found. Diasporic and postmodernist discourses have drawn on the nationalist representations yet, like feminism, have fallen short of providing this necessary vocabulary for speaking about West Indian gender. An attempt is made to point towards the terms of such a vocabulary (which essentially has to do with a more adequate epistemic perspective) and to examine its implications in the historical setting from post-Columbian colonization and slavery to the twenty-first-century context of globalization, within which Selvon's and Lamming's fictions resonate.

I use the term "revisionary" to mark the fact that the book applies gender as a paradigm of reading to texts that for most of their existence were, *in practice,* considered to have been already "definitively" read by the frames of nation and its related constructs such as class, race, colour and language, which characterized West Indian reading throughout the decades of nationalist ascendancy. "Revisionary" implies not just different interpretations, but a different episteme. That is to say, reading through the lenses of gender is a way of reconceptualizing both the fictions and the fundamental issues with which the fictions have been seen to concern themselves; these include not only social constructs such as those listed above, but also issues about the nature and goal of writing, specifically West Indian writing, and the issue of the identification of the West Indies itself as a cultural space.

The location of Selvon's and Lamming's fictions in nationalist categories of criticism is a main reason why, up to the very late 1990s, no thoroughgoing examination of gender in these texts was undertaken, despite their engagement with gender as part of the very world view they proffer. A beginning recognition of gender discourse in West Indian men's writing emerged in the 1980s (for example, Paquet 1982, Campbell 1983) and the mid-1990s (notably, Gikandi 1992 and Nair 1996),[2] but it was not until works such as Belinda Edmondson's *Making Men: Gender, Literary Authority and Women's Writing in Caribbean Narrative* (1999), A. J. Simoes Da Silva's *The Luxury of Nationalist Despair: George Lamming's Fiction as Decolonizing Project* (2000) and Sandra Paquet's *Caribbean Autobiography: Cultural Identity and Representation* (2002) that major discussions of this subject appeared in the literature. Although Edmondson's is the only one that makes gender its primary focus, all three of these texts fracture traditional readings, showing how in different ways particular men's texts sought to figure the nation "in the gendered terms of male privilege and dominance" (Paquet 2002, 86) and how in doing so they often failed to adequately represent women's oppression and even sometimes created structures of such oppression through their narratology.

Not surprisingly, given his outstanding preoccupation with gender as a major battleground in his narrative-ideological discourses of liberation, Lamming features prominently in these postnationalist revisionings. Selvon, on the other hand, is scarcely ever mentioned, no doubt because of the low-key, seemingly more "naturalistic", less polemical style that functions to disguise both his gender discourse and the immersion of his characters in nationalist imaginings. This "disguise" notwithstanding, it remains surprising in an era so preoccupied with gender issues that in none of the major post-1970s texts on Selvon's work is this subject given more than cursory attention. These texts include Shusheila Nasta's edited collection of critical essays (1988), Wyke (1991), Looker (1996), Salick (2001) and the 1996 *Ariel* special issue dedicated to Selvon's memory two years following his death. In Wyke, Looker and Salik, gender is not even mentioned; in a couple of essays in Nasta's collection (which mainly covers critical responses prior to the 1980s), as well as two interviews in the *Ariel* issue, gender occupies a small place as one among several topics of discussion.[3]

From Nation to Diaspora seeks to fill some gaps in West Indian discussions of gender in literature. These discussions have tended, in practice and sometimes in theory, to conceive of gender in terms of women's issues. Simoes, Paquet and Edmondson represent a significant shift to a more inclusive evaluation, in that they examine the implications of the "gendered nation" for both men and women, and Paquet (2002) and Edmondson in particular go beyond this to show the paradoxical transgressions between masculinism and feminism in the literature. However, all three stop short of advancing a comprehensive episteme by which to describe West Indian gender outside of the deadlock of oppositional masculinist/feminist discourse. There has also been a tendency to assume, a priori, that male-authored fictions, particularly those before the 1980s, propagate a negative representation of women, whether through "silencing", recuperation or deflation. Undoubtedly there is an almost exclusive preoccupation of (male-authored) fictions from the nationalist period with male protagonists and a concomitant concern with the crafting of men's identities in the context of social and national evolution. But it is also true that the nature of language, the reader and the social fabric from which the artist creates metaphor are such that every text is a site of dynamic, contested meanings in which even the intention of silencing, recuperation or deflation, if it exists, may be problematized. The discussion, then, is concerned not only with overt textual ideologies of gender, but also with the subtextual representations which may variously support, transgress, subvert, question or otherwise problematize the overt ideologies. The ways – positive, negative, contradictory and paradoxical – in which these trammel gender representations in the male-authored texts, Selvon's and Lamming's in particular, are seen as giving complex insights into the West Indian gender scenario and world view as a whole.

"Gender" in this book refers to the entire complex of social relations mediated by this construct. It is defined first as the allocation, investiture, assumption and performance of social roles and identities based on biological sex, but second by the use of biological sex as a trope for identifying types of social and political processes and systems. This second application is particularly important in a discussion of texts produced in the nationalist setting, since inevitably in this context we confront the idea and critical implications of the nation and its instruments and symbols as gendered entities. The book's underlying frame of reference is the idea of history as both socio-political process and representational praxis. Thus an understanding of the reasons – social, political and literary – why gender remained almost completely unread in West Indian fiction prior to the 1980s and why, being read, it is applied as a critical and epistemological category to emerging fictions almost to the exclusion of previously existing fictions is important to the attempt to place Selvon's and Lamming's gender representations across three distinct yet overlapping discourse practices, two of which are asynchronous with their work.

Nationalism, the first of these discourses, is also the most important, since it dominated West Indian thought throughout most of our active life as modern and emergent modern polities – that is to say, throughout most of the twentieth century – consolidating currents that arguably began to make themselves felt even from the nineteenth century. The era of West Indian nationalism may be traced in two phases: first, the drive towards self-government in the first half of the century, and second, over at least the next three decades, the independence and post-independence struggles against the colonialism which after independence still dominated the territories in all but political name. The West Indies in this period may be described as a region in search of itself, so that the crucial issues as seen by intellectuals were freedom, identity, race, class, colour, society and the implications of these for the nation. "Nation" meant the distinctive political and cultural identity both of individual territories and of the region as a whole, the search for the latter being most clearly seen in the movement towards West Indian Federation in the 1950s, and to an extent in the continuing existence of the Organisation of Eastern Caribbean States.[4]

The nationalist period saw literature being drafted into the service of the struggles towards political independence and cultural sovereignty. Two generations of West Indian literary tradition have firmly anchored the ideology of nationalism as the paradigm by which we have interpreted and assessed our creative literature. From the 1950s to the 1970s, reading of West Indian fictions in the academy was directed to the specific enterprise of "making" the West Indian literary canon, and for three decades the West Indian readership exposed to the academy's canon-making efforts read West Indian fictions by the conventions, ideologies and expectations indicated by the canon makers.[5] The enterprise was made easier by the fact that many of the creative writers were themselves ardent nationalists, who, in interviews, essays and other forums, were in the habit of linking their creative work to their nationalist world views, so much so that in the West Indian academy a strange kind of fallacy of authorial intention developed in reading – the equation of meaning in the text with the author's expressed views in other contexts.

Inevitably, given the nature of nationalism as an intrinsically totalizing world view, the focus was on those issues that affected the societies macro-cosmically, with a concomitant "unreading" (by which I mean to suggest both dismissal and failure to notice) of the microcosmic differences, processes and relations upon which the integrity of the societies had to be founded. Indeed, all "right-thinking" West Indians were expected to allow national imperatives to take precedence over individual, subcultural and sectarian interests. It was in this context that gender remained unread, even though it was being inevitably and in some cases deliberately and ideologically written in the fictions. (Its inevitability has to do with the fact that gender is a condition of being male and female in the socially constructed world as we know it, that is, part of the inescapable phenomenology of the social world and its representations. Thus every writer inescapably writes gender.)

Women, who are generally seen as the persons most concerned with the reading of gender, appeared to subscribe to the gender-erasing imperatives of the nationalist movement, as did women elsewhere in comparable societies and contexts.[6] This is important: some feminists have accused the male-dominated academy of ignoring women's issues, but it must be acknowledged that women to some extent acquiesced in this "silencing". The times were exigent, the large outlines of the socio-political world were being made anew and the collective excitement which suppressed other considerations was altogether understandable, and no doubt inevitable, as it usually is at the beginning of all movements of resistance and identification.

The fact that nationalism aims to totalize, insofar as it seeks to bring disparate elements in a society under the single umbrella of nation (Benedict Anderson's "imagined community" [1991]) along macrocosmic indices such as race, culture and language, has of course been problematic even along these very indices. Racial and cultural differences within the populace are elided or succinctly rationalized into a singular rhetorical representation of the nation as One. Similarly, we accepted our designation as the West Indies, the English-speaking Caribbean, but increasingly began to acknowledge and celebrate our linguistic diversity, which included the unprecedented (Creole) languages we had forged at the cutting edge of linguistic denudation and imposition. For the most part (the main exceptions being Trinidad and Guyana, with their large Muslim and Hindu populations), we designated ourselves "Christian countries", but a vast unofficial underbelly of diverse religious and magical practice characterized our day-to-day living and sensibility. In fact, Christianity elicited much rhetorical (as opposed to practical) suspicion and disapproval, as one of the colonizer's most devastating tools of oppression. We knew we were "different", requiring different modes of self-analysis and self-identification, yet in the vulnerability of our situation, finding ourselves adrift and called to name ourselves in the midst of Western modernity, we embraced the Western category of nationhood, with all its attendant singularizing paraphernalia. Ironic tensions, or at least challenging paradoxes, are bound to arise where the very pluralities of race, ethnicity, religion and language are the ground on which a unique nationality, different from those of the totalizing colonial master, was fought for and celebrated.

Perhaps these tensions and paradoxes are nowhere more clearly seen than in the doctrine of creolization, posited by generations of nationalists as the unique mark of West Indian national identity. Creolization is in itself a fluid, various and sometimes nebulous, always controversial concept, but no matter its variations, the basic principle of its earliest formulations was that the vast complexities of difference in the West Indies merge or are merging to form an ultimate synthesis: out of many, one – though, significantly, a heterogenous one. In the ideology of creolization, the contradictions of democracy as a modernist world view become apparent. In most territories, and in West Indian intellectual thought as a whole, the principle of equality among various groups, religions and languages is problematized by the principle that the national synthesis should privilege the majority, and particularly in a context such as ours, where the majority – in this case the black West Indian poor – has traditionally been denigrated and marginalized.

The result of this democratic principle in our self-representations was that the West Indian nation was typically iconized in terms of the culture and face of the black peasant majority (later, perhaps, the black proletariat, as images of urbanization began to replace the rural smallholding in the nation's imagination). The unspoken idea was that other races and social groups, their presence and equality being implied in the rhetoric of West Indian plurality and difference, were to assume themselves to be represented in this icon. The assumption was to apply to women in another way. The iconic face of the nation was uncompromisingly masculine and male, drawn as it was through historical texts in which it was men who were principally named, through the discourses of an academic world dominated by men, through public political platforms on which male figures loomed large and, of course, through the linguistic hegemony of the pronoun "he". The rhetoric of nation assumed a single gender, into which all were subsumed. But the net effect was to occlude the huge and active involvement of women in the crafting of political freedom and national identity and to disguise the astonishing traumas, poignantly illustrated by Selvon and Lamming, that men encountered in the process of acquiring the type of masculine identity the ideology of nation assumed or seemed to demand.

Continuing racial tensions in territories such as Trinidad and Guyana, which have almost equal mixes of Afro- and Indo-West Indian populations, are only one sign that creolization, despite being a reality (though to varying degrees) as a cultural phenomenon, cannot be conflated with the political imperative of (distributive) equity, which all too often the doctrine of creolization is used to evade. These tensions also have to be viewed against the background of the fact that the early discourses on creolization tended to anchor themselves in a black/white dichotomy in which the main racial and cultural groups seen as participating in the creolized blend were blacks and whites. That is, other racial and cultural groups tended to be relegated, consciously or unconsciously, to the margins of that discussion. This does not mean that these groups were "silent", any more than women were – the racial upheavals in Trinidad and Guyana, particularly the latter, at the height of nationalism are well known, and it may well be argued that these arose out of the very fears nationalism engendered in the Indian population.

In other territories, it was the intersection of class and nation, rather than of race and nation, that was the more visible sign of conflict, and, particularly in the earlier decades, colour was almost invariably linked to class. The presence of gender at the intersection of all four (nation, race, colour and class) may have been hidden in the overarching rhetoric of nation-making, but it was most certainly visible in the day-to-day experience and cultural representations of the societies: in discriminatory work conditions, in unequal educational opportunity,[7] in the society's songs, proverbs, stories and performances, Selvon's and Lamming's work among them.

The issue of black-white racial discourse obviously relates to the fact that West Indian nationalism began, necessarily and inevitably, as an ideology of opposition and reply to British colonialism. This fact, again ironically, served to erase or delay other concerns and to focus our search for a national identity directly on Europe's actions: in other words, and more bluntly, Europe spoke, we replied. In the literary academy, the fledgling national literature became part of the paradox of simultaneously asserting nationality and celebrating difference and space for the contention of voices. As becomes clear from a reading of Kenneth Ramchand's seminal *West Indian Novel and Its Background* (1970) or of C. L. R. James's pronouncements on the issue (1965),[8] the overarching frame in the list of criteria for a novel to be considered West Indian was whether or not the work contributed to an "authentic" and "responsible" representation of the West Indies as a national cultural entity.

And while the framework was expansive and fluid enough to include works which arguably displayed no overt concern with nationalist principles – and the fictions of V. S. Naipaul, Samuel Selvon and Wilson Harris, as well as the early poetry of Derek Walcott, may be included among these – it is instructive that several critics castigated writers for not being nationalist or "political" enough. Selvon was on more than one occasion taken to task for this very "lack", as were John Hearne and Michael Anthony; the disaffection of some with Naipaul's ideologically negative position on the region is legendary. Harris and Walcott early set themselves against much of the methodology of literary nationalism, arguing against it as "documentary" reading and writing (Harris 1967, 140–59) and as writing tyrannized by the facts of history (Walcott 1974), where it needed instead to be fired – and freed – by what could be loosely described as the visionary power of imagination.[9]

What all of this fierce debate suggested was that even while as true historicists West Indians believed in dynamic links between literature and society and saw attention to these as a sacred responsibility, the tensions between political demand and literary vision – between cultural and political nationalism – were making themselves felt. Literature as self-referentiality and literature as reply to a Europe that did not even care to listen were part of the terms of the conflicts of emergent nationhood. And the fierceness of the debate both underlines the fact of the hegemony nationalism exerted on West Indian thought and prefigures its displacement by other paradigms.

Within the nationalist paradigm, language – or, more specifically, linguistic opposition to the colonial insistence that English (and the British version at that) was the language of acceptable expression for West Indian writing – became an increasingly important critical category. C. L. R. James and Roger Mais were valorized not only for their unapologetic representation of West Indian (Trinidadian and Jamaican) yard culture, but for their "authentic" representation of the people's idiom. V. S. Reid and Samuel Selvon were celebrated for their attempt to forge a literary idiom which captured the nuances, rhythms, sensibility and ethos of West Indian speech. As the West Indian academy matured in self-confidence and familiarity with its own literature and moved, albeit slowly and fragmentarily, away from the Euro-American New Critical tradition of reading in which it was initially inured,[10] the emphasis on language as a sign of the break with colonialism expanded to encompass a concern with iconoclastic form and structure.

By the 1980s, instances of what some would term "postmodernist" form in the work of novelists such as George Lamming and Wilson Harris, who had often been pilloried for being "too difficult", began to be recognized as one more unique feature of West Indian writing. The advent of Erna Brodber (*Jane and Louisa Will Soon Come Home* [1980], *Myal* [1983], *Louisiana* [1988]), with her extraordinarily unconventional novelistic style, is important. Brodber's first novel, *Jane and Louisa Will Soon Come Home,* by the author's own account started out as an ethnographic case study, and it bears the marks of that interdisciplinary connection both epistemologically and methodologically. The style is eclectic and complex: fragmentary, marked by various strategies of interiority – stream of consciousness, dissolution of narrative hooks and event boundaries, structural, formal and linguistic obfuscations in the pattern of West Indian speech culture and performance culture – to the extent that the text may well be said to problematize the idea of what constitutes a novel. Brodber's text, widely acclaimed in a climate ready for it both as a woman's text and as a structurally iconoclastic text, is indicative of her style in the succeeding novels. More significantly for this discussion, it prompted comparisons with Lamming's novelistic style, suggesting that a process of revisionary "looking back" at the older fictions was taking place, though not as yet from the perspective of gender (see, for example, Cooke 1990).

Some critics in the womanist/feminist academy, quite mistakenly, identified the kind of writing that Brodber may be said to exemplify as an essential mark of femaleness, or women's writing (for example, Covi 1990).[11] While the fallacy of this view is clear from the work of Lamming, Selvon and numerous other writers, both West Indian and non-West Indian, the discussion does bring into focus a characteristic factor of much of West Indian fiction, whether male- or female-authored: namely, that West Indian fictional style is more in keeping with traditional ideas of "femininity" than with ideas of "masculinity" (and this despite the fact that some writers and politicians – the latter arguably fictive speakers – have been lauded for their "masculine prose" [Nettleford 1971]).[12] That is, if femininity is associated with the circuitous, the arcane, the refusal or "inability" to stick to the "straight and narrow" of logical progression and instead to follow diversions, loquacities and obfuscations and to effect fusions of disparate elements such as the poetic and the theoretical, then it may be said that the ideologically feminine characterizes West Indian writing, both literary and discursive.

And yet, both within the collective body of the literature and within individual texts, there exists an in-betweenness, a "dance" between a range of iconoclastic and traditional forms, so that the gendered body of West Indian fiction may more easily be termed hermaphroditic than feminine. Either designation recalls the historical factors that have made the West Indian experience of gender a curiously liminal thing: the colonial exemption of the slave population from the social categories of identification within which socially sanctioned gender is predicated; the continuing construction of the West Indies in exoticized tourism advertisements as what might well be termed "a certain kind of woman"; the continuing voyeuristic discourses that construct the black male as at best a lesser kind of manhood; above all, the West Indian capacity to self-construct in varying obfuscatory guises, gender included – and this as a direct response to slavery and colonization. In other words, gender in the West Indies shares the anomalies and paradoxes of the entire West Indian experience and inflects the literature and the ways in which we might speak of the literature as surely as do race, class, colour and language.

It is fairly recently that the idea postulated above, of the text as a gendered entity, has entered Caribbean literary discourse, and it is important for the present discussion that such an idea bears the marks of a postmodernist influence (see, for example, Benítez Rojo 1996, 23ff). One factor that emerges out of the revisionary reading undertaken here is that both together and individually, Selvon's and Lamming's work in gender at the height of the nationalist period conjures a West Indies – and by extension a Caribbean – that bears remarkable resemblance to indices that are now commonly recognized as postmodern. An important issue that this book addresses is whether this means that the Caribbean or Caribbean fiction – and, by extension, Caribbean gender representations – can be seen as either an anticipation or a prototype of the postmodern. It also raises the issue of whether an affirmative answer to these questions displaces the nationalist tradition by participating the Caribbean into Western or globalized epistemes or instead suggests the Caribbean, including its nationalistic face, as a space of ur-modernity, as is implied in Lamming's description of West Indians as the "most cosmopolitan [people] in the world" ([1960] 1992, 37).[13]

It is important that the nationalist concern with literary form and structure referred to above, which continued into the 1980s – in some territories arguably the beginning of a postnationalist era – was not purely of the type that characterizes the New Critical tradition. For nationalist literary ideologues began to recognize that West Indian literature was attempting what might be termed "redefinitions" of the concept of the novel, in keeping with a sense of the unique cultural realities that separated West Indian aesthetic expression and reception from its canonical British counterparts.[14] Creative writers writing as literary critics and as theorists seeking after "indigenous" form were among the first to pay attention to these features and to suggest their radical significance. Sylvia Wynter, in 1971, without any apparent influence from Mikhail Bakhtin, pointed to the West Indian need to exploit the intrinsic subversive potential of the concept "novel", which she saw as having arisen out of contradictory currents – traditionalizing/orthodox and heterodox/revolutionary. Similarly, Kamau Brathwaite's excursions around the idea of the West Indian novel as a jazz novel (1967) sought in effect to name the West Indian novel aesthetically as a novel of improvization and diversion and rhythm and sound, or of music and orality. In an interview with Caryl Phillips (1997a), Lamming speaks of his constant attempt throughout the 1950s to 1970s to trouble the idea of what a novel is and to create a uniquely West Indian version of the form. Wilson Harris's arcane applications of metaphysical thought to creating form and structure are theorized in his essays of the 1960s as well as exemplified in his symbolic, stylized fictions.

Postcolonial critics and theorists have long sought to give a name to the iconoclasm of form which they early noticed not only in West Indian and Caribbean writing generally, but also in the writing of the rest of the two-thirds "postcolonial" world, which shares a similar history and a similar imperative to "speak differently". One designation that has been used is "Third World Novel".[15] But arguably, "iconoclasm" is no longer an appropriate term by which to describe the differences between West Indian literature and English canonistic traditions. For one thing, four decades into the experience of independence, West Indian literature inhabits a context where both national life and cultural production are less and less grounded in the ethic of opposition and reply to European colonization, and more and more based on two crucial indices: one, an ethic of self-referentiality, within which the postcolonial/postmodernist word "difference" sits more easily than "iconoclasm", which comes implicitly invested with an oppositional loading; and two, the idea of diaspora, which inserts a larger reference to the context of "inhabiting abroad" within which growing numbers of our writers find themselves.

The decline of opposition and reply as the organizing dynamic of nationalism coincides with an attenuation of the nationalist imperative itself. It is within that context of attenuation that the emergence of gender reading is located, though it has emerged as another facet of nationalism rather than more radically as an alternative critical and epistemological construct. A wide range of local and regional shifts which impact on each other in various ways may be cited to explain the decline of West Indian nationalism both in the general political arena and in intellectual, including literary, discourse. Among these is the fact that the macrocosmic concerns with which readers in the academy were preoccupied have by and large been either resolved or reconceptualized. (Naturally, there are wide variations across territories, but a general trend seems to be applicable especially among the larger countries.)[16] As the former colonies have settled into the experience of over two decades of independence and the colonial problem has given way to the problem of psychological and economic neocolonization from the North American mainland, society and societal concerns have been redefined in economic (as opposed to political) terms.

Structural adjustment models of economic growth in the 1980s, family fallout from mass migrations in search of economic betterment, and disillusionment with generalistic and political solutions based on the poor performance of the homegrown politicians and bureaucracies have also moved West Indian consciousnesses more towards individual solutions and microcosmic processes and have opened up space for the emergence of sectarian interests that were formerly elided or downplayed under the totalizing nationalist imperative. This is true not only of literary criticism, but also of the literature itself, though the extent of the shift in the latter has been less dramatic than in the former – not surprisingly, given that, as noted before, literature always concerns itself with microcosmic processes, political exigencies notwithstanding. Indeed, the very possibility of a revisionary reading such as is proposed here is that much existed in the fictions of the nationalist era that was suppressed in the academy's reading at the time.

The sense of a greater freedom to express individual and other non-macrocosmic concerns may be marked by the advent of novels such as Colin Channer's *Waiting in Vain* (1999) and *Satisfy My Soul* (2002), which concern themselves with the private world of sex and romance. These novels arguably have more in common with American pulp fiction and the Hollywood soap opera than with the generality of West Indian fictions. The greater freedom is possibly also marked by the individualistic fictions of Jamaica Kincaid, who, while exploring the problematics of being West Indian, almost invariably moves her protagonists towards personal solutions that seek to dismantle the idea of a collective destiny that had been posited in the texts of arch-nationalists such as George Lamming, Andrew Salkey, Earl Lovelace and Kamau Brathwaite, and more recently in the work of Erna Brodber, Merle Collins and Marlene Nourbese Philip, not all of whom necessarily write as nationalists but all of whom share the nationalist commitment to communal perspectives.

Emergent sectarian interests include the assertion of Indo- and Sino-West Indian ethnic difference, subtly challenging the classic narratives of creolization, as in the fictions of Lakshmi Persaud, Cyril Dabydeen and Willie Chen, the poetic memoirs of Easton Lee and, more problematically, Patricia Powell's imagining of female Chinese experience in her novel *The Pagoda*.[17] White West Indians and West Indians of mixed race write of their own place in the nation, clearly expecting to be given a hearing in a way they might not have expected in the more fraught climate of the 1950s, 1960s and even 1970s. Michelle Cliff, in her novel *Free Enterprise* (1993), unapologetically invents a genealogical etymology and a series of narratives of the "*gens inconnu*" to record her vision of the contribution to liberation by West Indians of mixed African and European race. Mixed-race West Indians are often discursively presented as "house-slave Ariels" – self-seekers who aligned themselves to Europe in the post-Emancipation era and beyond, and who enjoyed the privileges of class and colour compared with their black counterparts. With the latter, Cliff asserts racial connection, shared action and shared space. Lawrence Scott's 1993 novel *Witchbroom,* with both grace and daring, proffers an ethic of racial forgiveness as an alternative type of militancy to the antagonistic brand that characterized the height of nationalism. Scott's attempt is neither to minimize the culpability of the white race to which he belongs nor to refute the necessity of the earlier antagonism. Rather, it is to explore the depredations, contradictions, paradoxes and collusions that have produced a shared history, a shared anguish and an increasingly shared peoplehood, and to suggest that this sharedness makes different demands of West Indians than it did in the not-too-distant past. And critic Evelyn O'Callaghan (1993) argues for the inclusion of early white women's texts that traditionally have been left out of the category "West Indian".

These shifts are in stark contrast to the sense of racial isolation suffered by Jean Rhys's protagonists, written in an earlier historical period, or to the suspicion with which Derek Walcott's unapologetic embracing of the European side of his racial heritage was received – and they are taking place side by side with the paradoxical fact that horrendous problems of race, class and colour still striate the West Indian socio-political scene. Interestingly, Scott's novel also, consciously or unconsciously, suggests an idea of creolization that works against the classic theories of creolization. Through his narrating character Lavren, a creature of indeterminate race, origin, culture and gender, the novel suggests the West Indies as sets of agglomerations whose most definite reality, even in future terms, is indefinition (in-betweenness, suggested by Scott's term "hung between"). The idea of a synthesis of differences begins to break up and to give way to an idea of suspension, of commas in a narrative whose fundamental principle is that it has no dénouement either as ideal or as possibility. This is also an idea of carnival admixture and contention rather than fusion. It is an idea that in 1992 was already being theorized by Antonio Benítez Rojo (1996), who envisioned the Caribbean in terms of carnivality and supersyncretism that opened the Caribbean out to the postmodern world. More obliquely, Édouard Glissant (2000) also implied a less nationalistically bound approach to creolization in his particular understanding of the accommodation cultures must find with one another in an increasingly globalized world.

In 1998 and 2001 respectively, the appearance of two collections of essays, *Caribbean Creolization: Reflections on the Cultural Dynamics of Language, Culture, and Identity,* edited by Kathleen Balutansky and Marie-Agnés Sourieau, and *New Caribbean Thought: A Reader,* edited by Brian

Meeks and Folke Lindahl, indicated further growing shifts in the definition of creolization. The essays taken together suggest a movement towards a sense more of complex accommodations than of mergings, and towards a greater *present* sense of the rest of the world as involved in Caribbean (including West Indian) self-fashionings. Such shifts have direct bearing on the issue of what kinds of (creolized?) gender identities we perceive the West Indies, and by extension the Caribbean, to be fashioning, or needing to fashion, in the complexities of the times. They also have bearing on the kinds of analyses we make of gender in West Indian fictions: for example, into what kinds of dialogue with the present time do representations of gender in Selvon, Lamming and other nationalist-era fictions invite us? Are these gender representations of a West Indies radically different from the West Indies of the present, or are they stages on an inflecting, creolizing continuum?

Part of the paradox of West Indian nationalism had been, on the one hand, its espousal of the arcane, the unknown, the mythic and the fragmentary as part and parcel of what separated the West Indies from the totalizing linearities of knowledge associated with colonial Britain and, on the other, its groundedness in logico-cognitive epistemes and ways of conceiving its own liberation. Erna Brodber and Nalo Hopkinson, writing in the late 1980s and 1990s respectively, are perhaps the first two West Indian novelists to take the idea of a different episteme of liberation really seriously. Hopkinson's *Brown Girl in the Ring* (1998) posits West Indian folk magic not merely as the people's belief system, but also as her text's epistemology of liberation. Brodber does the same with religion but goes two steps further than Hopkinson. First, she includes Christianity – denigrated in orthodox literary nationalism – in her mix of liberating religious practices. Second, in her novel *Louisiana,* she explicitly replaces the humanism of the nationalist agenda with a deistic spiritualism as the ground of revolutionary action. That is to say, in Brodber's epistemology, not human thought or action but divine agency becomes the source of liberation. And like Scott (though here in the context of black-on-black and gender relations), Brodber embraces an ethic of forgiveness – a different kind of militancy – in place of the anguished, retaliatory militancy of earlier years.

While it is true that socio-political currents do not account for all a writer's choices, it is also true that these are positions that writers of an earlier generation might have found embarrassing to espouse, especially in the context of the fierce antagonism and humanism of nationalist thought. It is also true that such positions find easier accommodation in a context where West Indians live more comfortably with one another and with the world, and where they feel they have moved to a more complex stage in their political and social relations, despite continuing frictions. At the same time it must be recognized that the seeds of possibility for these new positions to emerge were always present, given the West Indian psychic and cultural acceptance of plurality and difference which asserted itself even within nationalism – and this again may be seen as simply one more of the region's huge investments in paradox.

Not coincidentally, every one of the recent fictions mentioned above is marked by an ideological commitment to the treatment of gender as a theme, in ways that distinguish them from most of the earlier fictions. The difference is not in the fact that gender is treated, consciously or otherwise, but in the fact that it comes invested with an activist attention to issues of justice, equity and reconciliation in the context of gender relations. This attention, while not absent among fictions of the earlier period, is not nearly as widespread *as a primary commitment*. The older fictions are perhaps more concerned with socially realistic representations of gender as self-fashioning. Yet there are writers, Lamming among them, who are fiercely ideological about gender in ways reminiscent of the later novelists.[18] Brodber's spiritualist epistemology directly influences a community-based, inclusive concept of gender which effectively de-links gender from biological sex; at the centre of Hopkinson's folk liturgy is a strong feminist assertion of women's power; Scott problematizes the idea of West Indian gender as a form of indeterminacy, paradox and potential equity, linking it to his concept of the West Indies as a carnivalesque society. In the present political climate, which privileges gender reading as an activist project, the idea of gender as a site for radical militancy is marked in a range of fictions by Michelle Cliff, Dionne Brand and Jamaica Kincaid. The same currents which privilege the ideological espousal of individual(istic) and sectarian projects, as well as "other" ways of seeing, are the currents which push towards the writing and reading of gender in activist ways.

The emergence of West Indian women in professional and leadership positions – the results of changes in education and economic patterns – and the increasing production of literary works by women are other local and regional factors that fuelled the activist gender criticism which reached a kind of high point in the 1990s. And yet the reading of gender during this period cannot be seen as a displacement of nationalism, as several womanist/feminist critics in the academy sought, in a sense retrospectively, to enlarge the input of women writers in the nationalist struggle. That is to say, while gender critics may be said to have posed the most far-reaching challenge to the nationalist critical agenda, many proposed gender as an additional nationalist theme rather than as an alternative epistemology. From this perspective, women's fictions were read as the expression of women's particular gendered experience of the same socio-historical categories of race, class, colour and identity in the context of colonization read in the men's fictions, where this experience is seen as having been before encoded in silence. Evelyn O'Callaghan's *Woman Version: Theoretical Approaches to West Indian Fiction by Women* (1993) and the prefatory and introductory material as well as the essays in the landmark womanist/feminist collection *Out of the Kumbla: Caribbean Women and Literature* (Boyce Davies and Savory Fido 1990) are typical of such a continuing nationalist stance.

It is true that womanist/feminist nationalism came to be intersected by more "diasporic" perspectives, evidenced in works such as Carole Boyce Davies's *Black Women, Writing and Identity: Migrations of the Subject* (1994) and Isabel Hoving's *In Praise of New Travelers: Reading Caribbean Migrant Women's Writing* (2001). But even in diasporic frames, a nationalist focus is not absent. Edmondson's landmark text (1999), for example, provocatively locates diasporic Caribbean women's writing as extensions of (masculinist) nationalist paradigms, and Hoving recognizes nationalist imperatives in much of the work she discusses. Marlene Nourbese Philip's wonderfully nuanced collection of essays *A Genealogy of Resistance and Other Essays* (1997), in which she crafts her "*i-mage*" (43) of the resistant black New World Caribbean West Indian female poet, draws as much on the canonical tropes established by male cultural nationalists as on her own linguistic theory and diasporic formulations. As a parallel example from a male-authored text, Benítez Rojo's *Repeating Island* ([1992] 1996) examines gendered textualities from a position that marries Western postmodernism and Caribbean nationalism.

The varied grounding of much gender-focused reading in the anti-colonial tradition of nationalism suggests that the latter has at different times been seen either as the major energizing frame within which to locate new fictions or as a crucial point of departure which gives context to the fictions and is in turn problematized by them. This is important, for it indicates that despite shifts into discourses of diaspora and postmodernism, and despite concomitant dissociations from nationalism in favour of transnationalism and "borderlessness", some critics and theorists perceive and seek to close a gap in the dialogue with the (albeit recent) past. So there is one body of work that sets out to close that gap by inserting recent women's fiction into the pre-existent paradigm and another, barely emergent strand of discourse, signalled by Edmondson's text, which sets out to bring the older men's fictions into dialogue with emergent paradigms. *From Nation to Diaspora* belongs to the latter strand. Both enterprises suggest the existence of a continuum in West Indian experience and West Indian literature that is often occluded by the emphasis on the diasporic.

The diasporic focus in Caribbean gender studies is of course at one level merely indicative of the global factors that militate against a classical nationalist positioning. Globalizing perspectives are the product of hugely complex interactions among events and trends that have marked the last forty years of "First World" and megabloc societies – among these, of course, the post–Berlin Wall and post–September 11, 2001, reordering of inter-national relations, the "redefinition" of traditional institutions such as family and sexuality, and shifts in the mass migration of political and economic refugees from the former colonies to the "mother" or "father" countries. All of this has spawned various mutating foci on "minority rights". An important phenomenon of this period has been the insistent emergence of voices of the "Fourth World": those minorities, such as women and "not-men",[19] who exist in various states of submergence in all societies, cutting across First, Second and Third World designations (obsolete as these now are, post–Berlin Wall). Societies have been pushed into a somewhat agonal searching of their microcosmic processes and relations in an effort to form a more equitable structure in which all individuals, cultures and subcultures have an equal chance. In a sense, there is an assertion of the individual, the subset and the group, and concomitantly an attenuation of the overarching national. These movements, part of the reason for the emergence of the terms "postmodernism" and "postmodernity",[20] signal changes not only in how the world is organized, but also in concepts of knowledge within the world.

At the same time, the monologic imperatives of economic imperialism – expressed in the free market, the doctrine and practice of globalization and the formation of exclusivist trade blocs – exert a pressure against these dynamics of change and responsiveness to multiple voices. Within societies such as the United States, the situation is especially paradoxical, as the lobby for greater individual and sectarian freedom exists side by side both with an aggressive nationalist-imperialist foreign policy that deracinates men of other nationalities and with the lobby for greater government responsibility and legislative intervention in domestic matters, at the cutting edge of which gender first confronts us. All of this has become an integral part of West Indian/Caribbean experience, both through the increasing efficiency of communication technologies in disseminating the experience of worlds into each other and through migration, by which West Indians/Caribbeans increasingly become part of what might be termed a "global personality". (I use "global personality" here not to mean an erasure of national and other group or individual characteristics, but rather to put a name to an *idea* of shared consciousness – an idea which is in effect a composite construct, similar to the notion of the "average man".) This "global personality" is reflected not only in the contemporary West Indian and wider Caribbean interest in gender, but in the type of gender positions taken up by West Indian literary artists of the late twentieth and twenty-first centuries.

That gender in the Caribbean is linked to migration is something of a given. Most of the racial, ethnic and cultural groups that now make up the Caribbean arrived here through voluntary or forced migration, which unmoored their members from their original gender roles and identifications in varying and significant ways. As noted above, the Caribbean has continued to be a migratory region, with its own diaspora now across the globe, though particularly concentrated in Europe and North America. In a context where they had to chart their own landmarks – Columbuses in reverse – and where they found no predisposed spaces of accommodation to receive them in the putative "parent" countries, West Indian writers of the 1950s to the 1970s who migrated in order to write saw themselves as exiled members of a national entity geographically located in the Caribbean Sea. The literary critics agreed, to the extent that exile and displacement became tropes by which we read our migrant literature and much of the literature set at home. Selvon's London quartet and Lamming's *The Emigrants* (1954) and *Water with Berries* (1971) are among the fictions that graphically and painfully represent some of the effects of this sense of exile on gender consciousness among West Indian migrants in the nationalist period. In an oblique variation on the theme, Lamming's *Natives of My Person* (1972) examines, with a similar sense of mourning, the role of gender in the colonial/imperial migrations that shaped the Caribbean.

The migratory trends of the late 1970s to the 2000s have exerted a different kind of influence on West Indian literary discourse. New generations of more "savvy", more educated and skilled West Indian migrants arriving in the North American and European metropoles (many of them establishing places in the academies of the north), acquire confidence from the landmarks laid by the earlier migrant generations, the protection afforded by the presence of pan-Caribbean as opposed to merely West Indian communities, and the "postmodern" conditions in which they find themselves and to which they have also contributed. Many have felt more entitled and more politically empowered to assert their sense of equal contribution and therefore of "belonging" – their equal right "to be there", as it were. Not infrequently, the feeling of right and "belonging" ("right to place") is shared and, even more so, experienced by the second-generation children of migrants, born or brought up in the metropoles; these, whatever their cultural and psychological connections to the West Indies or their sense of alienation from their countries of birth, in practice know no other place but the country of their birth to call home. The net effect is that not only nationalism but also related issues of exile and geographic displacement, while not absent, are no longer the distinguishing marks of West Indian fictions of migration or the literary discourses of migrant West Indians.

It is here that the more ameliorative concept of diaspora and concomitant issues of relationality and globalism have begun to enter the conversation. Mourning, which once became Electra, increasingly shares place with celebration, militant discourses of appropriation and carnival contention, as those who have left the Caribbean home space either no longer leave with the intention of return as their very ground of possibility for hope, or leave feeling that leaving is a choice not a forced conscription, or leave knowing that improved transport options, globally accessible communication technologies and greater economic possibilities allow them to keep in touch with or return home with relative ease, or leave actively deciding that the new place will become "home", or find that the option of "belonging", however Janus-faced or psychologically "in-between", is an imperative of success in the metropole that is "home".

The fact that these new perspectives often (albeit sometimes ironically) are more easily acquired when one has privilege – the privileges of class, race, colour, access and education which exclude large numbers of migrants – raises the question of whether some migrant writers who take a celebratory approach may not be out of touch with the majority of their fellow Caribbeans in diaspora. Whether or no, the perspective that I refer to as "diasporic" certainly points to an important change brought about by its proponents. Out of their often paradoxical settlement, established community and negotiation of space and identity in the metropoles, new questions arise around the issue of Caribbeanness – questions about its essence (what is Caribbean?), about its "whereness" (is it any longer a geographical space?), its plasticity (is it something fixedly identifiable, or is it whatever it is made to be in the complex negotiations between diaspora and host nations?), its connectedness (for example, what does one make of the putative dual nationality of Caribbean people abroad and of second-generation Caribbean people in diaspora?). These issues are central to the two essay collections mentioned above, and they have been raised in other contexts by Caribbean thinkers as diverse as arch-nationalist George Lamming (Birbalsingh 1996a; Lamming 1995; D. Scott 2002), "diasporic" feminist/womanist Boyce Davies (1994) and postmodern Caribbeanists (or Caribbean postmodernists) Glissant (2000) and Benítez Rojo (1996). Whatever the answers, undoubtedly there is in the lives of migrant West Indians an enormous amount of flux and negotiation between "Caribbean/ West Indian" values and those of the metropoles. In conjunction with intra-regional factors, the impact of this conglomeration of influences on the West Indian writing of gender and the related theme of sexuality has been quite marked: open, celebratory treatments of homosexuality by Michelle Cliff, Patricia Powell and Dionne Brand;[21] of sexual pleasure Hollywood-style by Colin Channer and Oonya Kempadoo; of culturally eclectic gender identities by writers such as Scott, Cliff and Brodber.

To a large extent, the shift towards a "diasporic" perspective and the pressure it exerts against a nationalism conceived in terms of boundaries (including, fundamentally, geographical ones) has been not just a result of "new [West Indian] thought", but also a direct product of the literary global marketplace. A fledgling and scarcely known literature in the 1960s, West Indian and, more so, Caribbean literature have rapidly become one of the major – though consistently obscured – cornerstones on which postcolonial studies has rested.[22] The idea that postcolonialism has in turn been inducted or co-opted into the Euro-American academy has long been commonplace.[23] Much of the aura of celebration that surrounds West Indian and other Caribbean writing is derived from location within these discursive fields: diasporic studies, postcolonialism and postmodernism, which generally valorize "Third World" resistance, whether textual or cultural, as effective subversion of (neo)imperialist enterprises. Thus, while the West Indian writing of gender and other issues in the context of migration has undergone changes based on the artists' own perception of their changing relation to the world, it is also true that displacements such as the incipient displacement of nationalism being discussed here have been affected by the globalizing perspectives of literary discourse. These may function to obscure or exaggerate aspects of individual writers' representations. The discussion of recent fictions in chapter 6 suggests that West Indian novelists' perspectives on gender in diasporic spaces are varied, complex and often as troubled and mournful as those of the nationalist period.

Obviously, the need to define West Indian gender more comprehensively in our critical practice is not merely an issue having to do with the complexities of connection with the rest of the world. It is, more so, an issue that has immediate critical significance for the West Indies of the twenty-first century. A particular urgency has been brought to West Indian gender discourse on the home front by the very migration trends that have led some to celebrate our integration into this "global personality" of which I speak. West Indian migration has produced, for example, a generation of West Indian "barrel children", who may not even be able to speak of the ubiquitous nurturing grandmother/matriarch, as parent-figures of both sexes are increasingly absent in the metropoles and parenting is increasingly done by remittance, so that children's gender development is seen in some territories as imperiled. While much of the literature portrays West Indian people successfully "playing gender" for advancement in the cities of the diaspora, the voices of these children seem to resonate a counter-discourse against too unequivocal a celebration.

The increased activity of women in the fields of business and commerce as a result of their superior education compared with their male counterparts, side by side with the continuing anomalous discrimination against such women in the workplace, has added to the tangle of problems to be resolved, and points to the need for a continuing militant feminism as one strand in the complex of responses to be desired. The apparent growing deracination of men and boys in some West Indian societies in the context of societal violence, drug use and dislocation has become part of the interplay of factors affecting gender relations and familial institutions. The link between diasporic drug culture and the international representation of West Indian (particularly Jamaican) masculinity in terms of the "yardie" and the "deportee" adds to the problem. All of this has contributed to a sense of crisis in some societies and refocused attention on the socialization of West Indian men and women, suggesting the need for explanation and evaluation. At the same time, day-to-day awareness and a growing body of research have suggested that a "necessary kind of woman" has begun to emerge in the West Indian context and that more equitable gender behaviours among men are at work in the society.

The issue is how to draw these disparities together in our analyses of our societies. Crucially, since the discourse and representation of nationhood have traditionally been gender-focused, implications arise for the terms by which we may reconceptualize the idea of nation in this context of flux in which West Indian nationalism comes up for question. The issue of gender, then, is fundamental to any comprehensive analysis of West Indian society in the present century. Clearly, as historians, sociologists and a small but growing number of literary critics such as Edmondson and Simoes Da Silva have recognized, the idea of gender as women's issues will not serve.[24]

In light of all the foregoing, what does this book attempt? First, this revisionary reading of Selvon's and Lamming's fictions attempts to provide additional insights into how we have understood our societies at the level of gender roles, performances and ideologies; how these writers have allocated or orchestrated such roles and performances; and how they have constructed, seeded and, by extension, perpetuated or interrogated such ideologies. Second, the book attempts to locate its reading of Selvon and Lamming within the historical context of nationalism in which they were produced, and within the context of the historical influences and periods that had an impact on the West Indies in the nationalist era. That is to say, of equal importance with the more immediately "literary" concerns is the examination of the texts in light of their resonances with representations of gender in the wider West Indian society. Part of the overall aim is to suggest the power, even the possible authority, of fiction as an aspect of social relations, as well as its mutually constitutive relation to other aspects of social relations. These artists were engaged in live debate with and within a specific social current, and so were part of the production of a living, contemporaneous history and identification of the West Indies.

I also explore ways in which writers of the nationalist period may have anticipated, in their gender representations, the issues of diaspora and postmodernism as discussed in this introduction. Quite apart from the obvious rationale provided by the fact that diasporic discourse poses a challenge to nationalism, the exploration of diasporic linkages seems logical given that Selvon and Lamming deal with gender as a feature of home and also as a feature of migration – both out-Caribbean migration to the centre and migration from the centre to the Caribbean.[25] In this context, comparison with current diasporic treatments, though necessarily brief and generalized, should yield insights into changing and continuing West Indian gender realities. I look at postmodernism in light of the fact that the Caribbean text and Caribbean culture as a whole have become a site of appropriation for postmodern theory. The Caribbean (and this explicitly or implicitly includes its gender) has been argued as a prototype of the kind of identity and relationality to be desired by the globalized "postmodern" world (Benítez Rojo 1996; Glissant 2000; Ledent 2001). The Caribbean text is seen as metonymic of this. The issue of grounds on which such identifications are extrapolated from the type of texts and the cultural moment being studied, and how the texts form a continuum with diasporic representations in creating such grounds is taken in consideration.

The idea of a postmodern tradition in Caribbean literary art becomes more interesting as it has also been posited that, rather than there being such a tradition, the "postmodernist" moment in Caribbean writing was heralded by its women writers. Gikandi argues that women's writing marks a new phase by its "increasing" recourse to "postmodernist narrative strategies" that radically revise the modernist project of the male (nationalist) writers (1989, 19). His discussion suggests that the epistemes and vocabularies of postmodern theory enable the effective criticism of Caribbean women's writing whereas a different kind of episteme and vocabulary is needed for Caribbean men's writing. Clearly, these various positions raise important questions for Caribbean intellectual thought in the future. Gender theory and criticism are obviously implicated, but so is the issue of the terms of reference for West Indian identity in the twenty-first century, as well as the West Indian relation to the rest of the world, particularly since West Indian literary criticism has never separated between literature and society. The point is not simply that texts participate asynchronically and diachronically in the construction of socio-political reality, but also that gender is part of a larger complex of socio- and geopolitical relation in the world.

These problematics of identification are linked to a fourth concern of the book, which is to raise the issue of an alternative trope and vocabulary for speaking about West Indian gender, both descriptively and in ideological terms that might suggest an activist praxis for addressing West Indian problems of gender. I suggest the trope of hermaphroditism as a starting point but go on to show that it is ultimately inadequate as an indicator of how we might address problems of gender. The trope as I use it has sufficient breadth to point to the inescapability of relations with the global world, but it resists an easy reduction of West Indian identity into global terms: its primary genealogy is within West Indian historical experience itself, and as such it carries within it markers of historical pain that remind us of particularized difference. It also carries reminders of the fact (already discussed) that diasporic celebration is only one side of the coin of West Indian migrant reality – that many migrants are outside the pale of privilege and opportunity, which facilitate an embracement of the terms of postmodernism or globalization. But it is that very rootedness in the debilitating historical that limits the capacity of the trope of hermaphroditism to point towards a future of problem-solving that effectively takes into acoount our particularized situations and new terms of relation with the rest of the world. There are in the end no easy answers to the questions that are raised; this book sets out simply to consider their implications for a new vocabulary of West Indian gender.

In chapter 1, I draw on historical documents, sociological research and literary texts to construct a necessarily cursory picture of aspects of gender representation in slave society, post-Emancipation society and the nationalist period, both at the public level and at the more microcosmic level of domestic and individual gender relations. My aim in making this drawing is to create a map of gender realities in the last thirty years of the nationalist period (1950s–1970s) in light of the primary concern with elucidating the sociological problematics of gender in this period, the period in which Selvon's and Lamming's fictions were written. While slavery and its aftermath are seen as major influences on the nationalist gender scenario, the book does not in any way look for historical continuities as the only given. It seeks to clarify and respond as well to patterns of disjunction, discontinuity and rupture which are characteristic of West Indian historical reality.

I conceptualize the relevant history in four broad periods: slavery, post-Emancipation (spanning 1838 to the beginning of the twentieth century), a "watershed" period from the turn of the century to the 1920s, and the period from the 1930s to the 1970s, spanning the movement towards self-government, the independence movements, actual independence and the consolidation of nationhood. This last period, which has been the largest segment of West Indian existence as a political entity and the source of its most influential literary and intellectual thought, is what I term "nationalist". Because the scope of the discussion does not allow for a comprehensive historical survey, I have opted to explore the broadest general resonances between the 1950s to 1970s and the years that preceded them. Since the first two decades of the twentieth century are envisaged as a watershed between Emancipation and nationalism, showing the influence of the former and containing the seeds of the latter, I do not allocate the first twenty-year span of the twentieth century a specific section in the discussion, rather referring to it where necessary for comparison and reinforcement. Similarly – again for ease of focus in a necessarily limited survey – most of the fictions to which I refer in chapter 1 are fictions produced in the same thirty-year span as those by the two writers to be examined. In that context, then, my focus on the first two decades of nationalism is only glancing.

In any discussion, choices have to be made concerning what to include and what to omit. In order to keep the book to a reasonable length and also in keeping with the admittedly imposed (and, for that reason, debatable) periodization, I have omitted texts which may be relevant to the issues discussed but which were either written outside of the designated period or would not necessarily add new parameters to the discussion. Chapters 2 and 3 examine gender in three of Selvon's migration, or exile, novels and in two of the novels set in Trinidad. Chapters 4 and 5 examine gender in three Lamming novels set in the West Indies and in two of the migration novels. In each case, the relation to social context discussed in chapter 1 is explored.

Chapter 6, the conclusion, summarizes ways in which nationalist-era representations point towards a new vocabulary for speaking about West Indian gender. Through a brief discussion of gender in late-twentieth- and early-twenty-first-century migration fictions, the conclusion also reflects on the implications for the West Indies of similarities and differences between nationalist and diasporic perspectives. I then bring all this into the ambit of recent thinking about how Caribbean identity (by implication also gender identity) resonates within postmodernist thought. I explore the issue of what claims can be made on the basis of such resonances in the troubling context of globalization and the post–September 11 "war on terrorism". If the latter in particular functions to confound all concepts of difference as imagined privilege and to reorder the world more solidly along the lines of its traditional tendencies, between Manichean polarities of national selves and migrant bodies, it may also be said that the former with no less force/fulness serves to distinguish along systemic economic indices, between societies of men and "anti-societies" of "not-men". The question is raised of whether and to what extent applications of Western theory to the identification and analysis of West Indian subjects can occlude processes of subjection.

It remains to be emphasized that the concern of this study is with ideologies of gender as distinct from representations of women, and that the examination is of the entire complex of social and political relations mediated by gender as portrayed in the fictions. I make a distinction between sex, which is biological and understood as being either male or female, and gender, which, though based on sex, is a social construct which may vary across societies and historical periods within societies and within which the complex of roles and identities is fluid and subject to change. Further, gender is not restricted to persons but may be extended to acts, representational forms and institutions.

The terms "male" and "female" refer consistently throughout the book to biological sex, while "masculine" and "feminine" refer to gender. "Feminine" is not automatically linked to "woman" nor "masculine" to "man": the texts I examine, and my own concept of these categories, particularly as they are manifested in West Indian lived experience, constantly and in various ways problematize the application of the terms "masculine" and "feminine" to the sexes. The discussion critiques both the traditionalizing patriarchal tendency to preserve the sex-gender link and a traditional feminist approach that preserves this Manichean divide while seeking to attack it from within. Both tendencies are shown to be in constant conflict with concepts and lived realities that effect their interrogation.

In the conceptualization used here, gender is determined both ideologically and experientially, so that conflict may exist between ideology, which is received through indoctrination, and lived reality, which is received through the gamut of experiences of which ideology may be only a part. Where such conflict exists, the gender role the subject chooses to perform will depend on the relative strength of competing external or internal forces, but I incline to the view that lived experience tends to supersede ideology, whether at a conscious or a subconscious level. Also, gender is conceptualized not only as allocation, investiture and assumption of role and identity, but also as role and as performance. Extrapolating from West and Zimmerman's (1991) formulation of "gender" as an active verb, the idea of performance suggests that an individual may choose for whatever reason not to "do" the gender she or he is assigned (Lipsitz Bem 1993).

Throughout, I refer to the collective human subject by the pronouns "she" and "her". Where the context requires, "s/he" and "him/her" distinctions are made. The terms "Caribbean", "West Indian" and "West Indies" are used together throughout the book: "West Indies" and "West Indian" refer specifically to the anglophone Caribbean; "Caribbean" or "West Indian/ Caribbean" is used when factors relevant both to the West Indies and the rest of the region are being discussed.

Chapter 1

Representations of Gender in the Nationalist Period

Images, Foundations and Performances

From Slavery to Independence:
Suppressing the Hermaphrodite

THE SOCIAL CONTEXT IN WHICH Selvon's and Lamming's representations of gender were produced, and within which they became a constitutive element, was an extraordinarily complex one. West Indian society, then as now, held in contradictory and transgressive tandem a number of cultural and socio-historical influences dating back to the experience of slavery and Emancipation. In gender as in everything else, enormous complication arose from the basic mismatch between the populace's lived experience (from slavery, Emancipation and onwards) and the official dogmas that were systemically entrenched through formal education. On the one hand, gender experiences were deeply inflected by socio-economic realities that constantly shifted the authorities associated with masculinity between male and female members of society. As a direct result of this, West Indian society has been variously described as "matrifocal" and "matriarchal", the latter in the face of clear evidence to the contrary (for example, Miller 1991b). On the other hand, vestiges of the colonial education system in the form of ideas of the male as breadwinner, household ruler, public authority and social pioneer were valorized. This ideology continues to mediate West Indian thinking despite its increasing distance from lived reality, which shows, among other contradictions, over 40 per cent of households being female-headed, females outnumbering males at all levels of the education system and women holding occupations in most of the fields traditionally associated with men. Serious psychological conflicts and disjunctions occur at the site of these contradictions. In fact, it is not far-fetched to suggest that much of West Indian misogyny and spousal violence have their roots here.

The nationalist period, concerned with the exigencies of attaining political independence and, concomitantly, shaping distinctive national and regional identities, focused the gender contradictions in very specific ways associated with periods of crisis in general and with the West Indian and political nature of the nationalist crisis in particular. ("Crisis" here indicates a point of critical change – in this case political change – and the sense of urgency associated with it.) Addressing large-scale (macrocosmic) concerns in a colonial society, the nationalist movement was marked in the public sphere by totalizing discourses, including those of gender. Public political discourse and its metaphors created the nation as an iconic masculinity – that is to say, in the image of a man. The image was reinforced by the literati: the fictions produced from the 1950s to the 1970s exhibited an almost exclusive concern with male protagonists, depicted in an exigent search for identity. That was not in itself a sign of misogynistic attitudes; more endemic than any concerted attempt to "inferiorize" women was a tendency to pay less attention to the development of female characters as psychological constructs. This was as much a function of inherited ideologies about writing (the idea of the single protagonist, often preventing full development of other characters), which West Indian writers had not totally broken away from, as it was a function of anxiety about masculine becoming. In its turn, the anxiety was arguably the direct result of the pressures placed on men by nationalist demands.

It is true that female characters sometimes appeared, implicitly or explicitly, as various images of male desire: the much-vaunted, fetishized "Mother"; the golden-hearted prostitute; the absent presence in the background of action; the abrasive, loud-mouthed shrew providing entertainment but also disturbing the peace. A widespread representation which transected many of the others was the strong, resourceful female who nevertheless either was not quite as strong as the male or became weak in relation to him. This was only one sign, among many, of the continuing tension between lived knowledge and ideology as desire. The latter was patriarchal desire in distinctly (Western) middle-class terms: as independent nationhood became more and more a possibility, the West Indies came more and more to imagine itself in the likeness of Western bourgeoisie that the idea of nation carried with it. As Rhonda Cobham's 1990 essay on the literary representation of women in nationalist Jamaica shows, across the West Indies such images appeared as much in the work of the few women who published as they did in men's writings, giving point to the fact that gender attitudes are not neatly distributed according to sex and that women also shared in the nationalist imaginings.

At another level, such images of women in fiction could be read as an old wolf in different clothing – mere transmutations of male anxiety and other paranoias which had been hidden in the subtexts of writers from the 1900s through 1940s, the period before nationalism had reached its full ascendancy. These writers had paid more attention to the creation of female protagonists, but arguably as a means of deflecting female threat. H. G. DeLisser and Thomas MacDermott, between 1904 and 1921,[1] created black working-class female protagonists who displayed strong characteristics of independence, resilience and a certain self-empowering iconoclasm. The portrayals were no doubt influenced by the visibility of aggressive cadres of young black women "invading" the urban economic space in order to create opportunities for themselves, especially in the wake of male emigration to Puerto Rico and the Panama Canal and economic fallout from the First World War. But the fascination overlying these portrayals arguably speaks more of a privileged (and therefore threatened) outsider's unease than of an unequivocal admiration. Such unease may have been class- and race- as well as gender-related (DeLisser and MacDermott were upper-class and white). DeLisser's texts in particular are marked by a tendency to ridicule the speech and behaviour of his protagonists, suggesting an attempt to neutralize the perceived threat by his strategies of representation.

Claude McKay's *Banana Bottom* (1933) is a far more unequivocally positive representation, but even a text such as C. L. R. James's *Minty Alley* (1936), which celebrates the varied and complex abilities of working-class women, is flawed by an unconscious male middle-class position of superiority. This position is represented in the lower-middle-class male protagonist, who, audience-like, looks in on the yard where the main "actors" are working-class women, with whom all his relations are relations of influence. The outsider-voyeur gradually becomes confidant-messiah, the women deferring to his superior education, status and "position" as a man, while he continues ultimately inviolable, held apart from the yard's basic culture. Clearly, equivocal attitudes to women arrived neither with the independence thrusts of the 1950s nor as a function of the emphasis on male protagonists. Rather, as argued later in this chapter, what seems to have marked the 1950s was the increased public visibility of anomalies in the construction of masculinity and femininity, and a greater investment in the construction of masculinity, particularly when aligned to maleness, as a public resource.

The representation of the nation as an iconic masculinity was, paradoxically, in many ways a re-staging of the performances by which Britain had played out its imperial identity in the colonies. Like its predecessor, the nationalist iconization of masculinity exhibited fissures and contradictions, some of which were internal to its logic, others of which appeared via their inevitable contestation by contradictory currents in the society. This emergence of the nation as colonialist re-staging is unsurprising, both because of the inevitable psycho-cultural trammels left by the colonial experience and because the (again inevitable) couching of the nationalist movement in terms of opposition and reply to the colonial establishment already marks it as an extension of the colonial paradigm.

The contestatory transgression of the masculinist icon by the vast underbelly of the people's lived reality was also inevitable, and showed the extent to which those who sought to shape the nation as political entity were out of touch with the very "folk" they sought to represent in that icon. The people's lived gender reality was, in its turn, remarkably similar to the slave's challenge against the master's gender categories on the plantation. This challenge, in overt and covert forms, appears in the documents of the plantation period as what might be described as a liminal category: transgressive, visible yet unseen, subtly hidden and publicly masqueraded. But in the slave's challenge were planted the seeds of an alternative identification of the twentieth-century West Indian nation, a fact which went unrecognized in the nationalist period – a time when its revolutionary potential might have given a different shape to West Indian political history.

Slave society fielded major dislocations between private and public life and identity – dislocations caused in part by the master's assumption that the slave was, in Orlando Patterson's famous phrase, "socially dead" and therefore "outside the *mana* of the gods" (1982, 2). To be socially dead while being yet alive meant to occupy the space of the liminal, neither here nor there, this nor that – a kind of shifting comma of possibilities on a dimension at once outside and within known reality. To be socially dead meant to have no gender, if we define gender as the allocation and investiture of social roles and responsibilities based on biological sex. The slave, though most categorically sexed (the investment in the slave's sex was the (re)productive basis of the slave economy), could not have been allocated any form of social role in a society in which s/he did not socially exist. The slave's existence was economic, commodified. The fact that it was primarily in the body of the female slave that the economic investment in slavery was located was not a form of gender differentiation, but rather a form of sex differentiation, which created the female slave as a brood mare – in this context, an analogue of the machine part of a production line.[2]

Yet it is true that actual practice contradicted the slave's ideological "genderlessness". Some contradiction arose from the master's inability to keep the lines of relationship clear. Frequent cohabitation with female slaves, especially those of mixed blood, and the fact that the slave was often offspring or a trusted member of the household – or both – resulted in "emotional slippage", so that the lines between (gendered) human and ("merely" sexed) slave were constantly blurred. That is to say, the master's ideological position was often betrayed by feeling, which recognizes the other's humanity. There may also have been instances when the master, in the absence of other precedent, reverted to his experience of gender in his home society, as a way of regulating plantation society. The exclusive allocation of males to skilled labour (artisanships) may have been an example of such reversions. It constituted a kind of involuntary admission that the slave was capable of becoming a man.

The abolitionist movements of the nineteenth century were also a complicating factor. These focused on the treatment of female slaves as a major plank in their argument against slavery as a degenerate institution. The response of many slave owners was to valorize the hitherto degendered female slave as the essence of fertility, kindness and other nurturant "feminine" qualities. This of course was a means of countering any suggestion that female slaves were badly treated or negatively viewed, and by extension a means of preventing abolition on those (or any) grounds. But it also carried the self-subverting risk of creating the female slave in a human image. In effect, then, the economic enterprise of slavery carried contradictory elements that fissured its gender representations not only at the level of lived reality, but also at the ideological level. Even so, the fact of the slave's continuing absence from "society", rooted in the legal status as chattel property, or "livestock",[3] meant that the slave was, by the definition of gender used here, ungendered in the master's overarching categories.

But the subversive power of the slave's liminality appears in the oxymoron of freedoms which s/he occupied. First, liminality establishes the slave's capacity for independent as opposed to controlled movement across the systems of exchange – in some things, the slave, being considered absent (from humanity), simply was not noticed. Second, it inscribes the slave's almost total freedom from existing social institutions and, concomitantly, the almost total freedom to create independent institutions, uncontrolled by "the *mana* of the gods". "Almost" is important: it inscribes limits that are within the condition of liminality itself. Liminality suggests the slave as a kind of Unconscious, free from restraint but also inexorably mapped in the fears, desires and repressions of the master society. By the same token, the slave's self-creations, rooted in desire, are transgressed by the master's projected fears, desires and repressions. Both psychic and representational distortions of self may result. Finally, the rigidly policed propertyhood of the slave curtails and sends underground the alternatives constructed in the paradoxical space of freedom. There is then a dimension of entrapment within the liminal space, the most powerful aspect of which is some amount of psychological acquiescence in the "master" representations by which one's social death is effected. Even so, the available cleared space of freedom conferred by exclusion from the master's institutions allowed the slave to construct the radical gender representation by which s/he was able to oppose the master's performance of iconic masculinity.

"Iconic" describes the identity against which the slave contended insofar as it was, visibly and symbolically, a Man[4] who had the freedom, privilege, authority and power of the slave master. The slave master was not only the sign of his own individual authority, but also the personation, metonymically, of plantocratic authority and, by extension, of imperial colonial authority. Every institution was male-dominated, and dominated by men who were very careful to display a particular type of authority that would keep the slave and slave society in place. That is to say, the visible, stable identity (behind which was the face of mercantile capitalism) was a particular masculinity which was personal, social, civic and political, but in the end utterly public, since even in its personal face it was accessible to the slave only as spectacle/spectacular authority.[5] So powerful in its reach was this "played" (spectacular) masculinity that the few slave-owning women arguably became subsumed within it as assistant masculinities. Poor whites, both male and female, shared in its aura, and appeared more as having fallen from than as being completely outside its grace.

The records of the time indicate how carefully this iconic identity was played. Across a range of narratives which include the journals of Lady Nugent (1839), wife of a governor of Jamaica during the nineteenth century, the planter Matthew Gregory "Monk" Lewis (1861), and the peripatetic visitor-voyeurs F. W. N. Bayley (1830) and Bryan Edwards (1801), images of the plantocracy's self-making "personation[s]" (Bayley 1830, 45) display themselves. Their performative nature appears in the endemic stage language, the audience-gaining strategies, the voyeuristic posturings and the governor's military progresses around the island – grand ritualizations of imperial power enshrined in the militia's show-dressed, masculine body. The institution of the governor's progress as *spectacular* display of the empire's metonymic body continued well into the twentieth century, and was clearly for the benefit of the liminalized, unacknowledged audience – the slave, the ex-slave and their descendants. Yet the spectacle of empire was never more powerful than when it was displayed upon the body of the slave himself, as, for example, in the hierarchical costuming of the driver in symbols of office (staff, topcoat and whip). The slave-driver as object lesson lived at the heart of schizophrenia: at once the sign of his own genderlessness and the authoritative violence of imperial masculinity.

The slave brought to the war against the master's display a gender representation that may be described as hermaphroditic. This description is a way of troping the level of male and female participation in anti-slavery resistance and the specifics of the gender-type performances which it involved. In the struggle against the institution of slavery, the slave population – regardless of sex – showed equal involvement. While, with the exception of Jamaica's famous Nanny of the Maroons and Barbados' Nanny Grigg, we have no records of women actually leading military engagements, we do know they were ferocious inciters, an active part of the camps and a formidable intelligence network in such engagements, the latter especially because of the strategic placing of some of them in the Great Houses. We also know that men and women employed similar methods of underground resistance, such as poisoning, obeah and pleading physical indisposition, though biology dictated that the latter was used more widely by women.

The slaves often cross-dressed in carnivalesque plays on free days, or "days of jubilee", men playing women's parts and vice versa, in coded, parodic challenges to the master's identity and the "identities" they had been assigned.[6] The practice continued into Emancipation, and was a source of great trial and tribulation to the colonial authorities, who constantly sought to suppress the post-Emancipation carnivals in which "herds" of subversive "male and female bodies" (Pearse 1956, 188) paraded in the streets, too visibly and too defiantly for imperial comfort. The slaves' composite body in such masquerades constituted a vociferous counter-narrative to the narrative of the masculine, imperial conqueror. Indeed, their dramatic narratives, played in and through the cross-dressed body, included fictions about European kings forced to contend for authority (Nugent 1839, 42).

The narrative produced by the slave girl Mary Prince ([1831] 1997) is instructive as an example of how slave women might have seen themselves. The details of Prince's narrative highlights it as a woman's narrative – that is, a narrative of what it was to be female and slave in that society – yet Prince displays an almost "genderless" perspective when she declares that the narrative is not only to show her own sufferings but the sufferings of all her race. Prince's narrative then stands in the collective tradition of these public stagings of identity, and she enters the arena of public discourse both in her identity as a female slave and in her identity as an inhabitant of the liminal space where, for the purposes of resistance, only a single, "unified" gender could be allowed. The two identities were distinct yet unseparated.[7]

The whole point is that the exigency of crisis and exclusion within which all the slaves were placed left no room for gender differentiation in the public arena of anti-slavery resistance. The situation was no doubt quite different in the slaves' private domestic and other relations among themselves. For obviously, the slave inhabited two parallel worlds: the visible one of the planter's authority and the liminal world of the slave's other Otherness, within which was constructed an alternative society, no doubt with its own gender and other social categories. Thus the complete picture of the slaves' gender representations included not only those which were interruptively staged inside the boundaries from which they were excluded, but also those which characterized the community the slaves constructed among themselves and which remained in the liminal space as the slave's hidden, unread(able) lives. This latter type of representation was for the self and the inner community, and in this sense constituted not opposition and reply, but first speech, free agency. What this means is that while the slave's self-representations were inevitably a response to the condition of slavery, they were by no means necessarily a reply to the slave master. To argue otherwise is to negate the eidetic humanity of the slave, for the figure in an unbending posture of opposition and reply is essentially only a slave, humanoid, never human.

Equal involvement in resistance, the public performance of dual gender in mutual cross-dressing, the rhetorical lack of differentiation between men and women in the cause of freedom, and a hidden, private life that frustrates outsider attempts to allocate gender – these are the grounds on which we may extrapolate a connection between the hermaphrodite's and the slave's physical presentation and place in society. The biological hermaphrodite becomes an arcane presence through a sexual identity that is not only ambiguous but also hidden, since often only one set of the contradictory genitive organs is exposed. It is therefore possible to speak of hermaphroditism as a condition of mystery and recalcitrance (since only what comes to conscious light can be contained). This means it is potentially transgressive and subversive. Indeed, it is already transgressive by virtue of being outside what is sanctioned and known. Its basis in duality, the fusion of "natural" separates, allows it to describe, in a way more traditional constructs cannot, the slaves' public gender (re)presentation, which was essentially syncretic, transgressive and subversive.

The hermaphrodite is an endemic paradox, etched in contradiction in many guises across societies. In ancient societies, s/he elicited horror, bewilderment and contempt. Made to bear the sins of the community for reminding the community of its own imperfections, s/he was taken outside the city walls and burnt or left to die. Yet in several Eastern and Greco-Roman myths, the hermaphrodite is linked to divine and metaphysical principles: here s/he is envisaged as the self-engendered offspring of a one-parent god or goddess. In some existing traditional societies, such as Native American and New Guinea societies identified by Cucchiari (1991) and Porter-Poole (1991), performing hermaphroditism through dress is a way of selecting ritual religious leaders. Among other groups it is a practice by which persons choose to inhabit ambiguous identities for social kudos (Whitehead 1991). Across several cultures, the hermaphrodite is the figuration of the principle of paradox, representing not only radical heterogeneity, but also the tensions and matrices between hetero- and homogeneity.

In Greco-Roman mythology, which I cite first because this is where the term has its origins, the hermaphrodite is not only the fusion of sexes and genders, but also the offspring of two polyglot gods, Hermes and Aphrodite. Hermes is in a very real sense the expression of the creolizing principle by which the slave learnt survival. The arch-messenger, bearer of good and bad news, he is also saviour and trickster; god of wayfarers and roads, thieves and entrepreneurs, the phallus and the stone, the lyre and the lie – a mixed rag-and-bone patronage by which he is revealed as a principle of irony and transgression. If Hermes is the arbitrary fusion of disparate forces, Aphrodite may be said to represent the principle of fissure in monoglossic traditions. Aphrodite is simultaneously the goddess of marriage and family – both of them traditionalizing and stabilizing institutions – and of free erotic love, which connotes an abandon significantly at odds with stability and institution. Aphrodite's connections with the sea (wife of Poseidon, rising magically from the Mediterranean foam) also suggest her as a protean figure.

The concentric circles of signification of which the hermaphrodite is capable are more fully implied in the way the myth describes the second birth of Hermaphroditus, the son of these two polyglot gods. Hermaphroditus's body, already the product of fusion between the two, becomes a site of double and ambiguous sex on which no clear gender can be mapped when he fuses with the nymph Salmakis to produce a new body with twinned genitalia (the phallic vagina, the vaginal phallus). The hermaphrodite then makes out of fissure a cohesion, fusing radical contradictions in a circle of dynamic tension which in effect cancels out cohesion. Both creativity and latent destruction are subsumed in this open predicate of fusions and their opposites.

The body and signification of Hermaphroditus seem a fitting way to characterize the gender of the resistant slave group, both because of the radical unease provoked by both in society and because the slave's psyche was so much the site of multiple gender performances that blurred the lines between men/masculine and women/feminine. These performances laid the traces of gender consciousness in later West Indian society. They cannot be described simply in terms of androgyny, which is an officially sanctioned and therefore sanitized (unthreatening) category. Moreover, androgyny points to a harmonious fusion of opposites, hermaphroditism to a greater range of possibilities, both positive and negative, than mere Manichean opposites. In the end, androgyny as a descriptor does not encompass West Indian historical realities – nor the sense of complexity inherent in the West Indian experience of the transgresive and the syncretic.

Hermes, Aphrodite and Hermaphroditus, taken together, bear striking resemblances to certain West African figurations of the divine, which is not surprising given the derivation of Greco-Roman mythology from West African mythology via Egyptian adaptations (B. Davidson 1984; Henriques 1974). Significant among these figurations are the multiple guises of Esu, the god of paradoxes, who appears variously as Legba and again as Elegbara. Hermes and Esu-Legba are identical in signification, with the exception that whereas Hermes is uncompromisingly male, Esu presents an ambiguous sex-gender in keeping with his overall signification as the metaprinciple of paradox.[8] Esu, Hermes, Aphrodite and Hermaphroditus are morphological expressions of an intricate philosophical construct: an idea of ultimate "speechlessness", the inability of the sign to signify single, definitive truths and therefore the absence of a base on which to declare hierarchies of humanity or knowledge.

Representation then in a sense becomes only an attempt, never an accomplished fact, since no representation can fully pin down the thing being represented: the thing recedes in paradox and also in absence, since only its absence produces the need to represent it. Any "true" representation, then, must hedge itself in paradox and self-reflexive questioning. These are ideas that subsume much of nationalist West Indian thought, particularly George Lamming's, and appear more explicitly in recent Caribbean and Western postmodernist theories (see chapter 6). (Their place in nationalist thought, which is teleological in intention, is only a sign of West Indian paradox.) In the present context, what is questioned by these morphological constructs is the linear definition of abilities, qualities and behaviours based on biological sex as sign.

Interestingly, the Caribbean figure of Anancy, who represents various transmutations of the West African trickster god, shares many characteristics with Hermes and Esu: contradiction implied in his double tongue and his steely strength underneath apparent vulnerability; the concept of representation, that totally impossible possibility, signified in his persona as a spinner of tales; the paradox of gender subsumed in his presentation as a spider-man, a man who weaves. In his mythic personae, Anancy, like Hermes, is uncompromisingly male. But his capacity for gender transgression is latent in his taste for costuming and ventriloquism as disguise. This capacity becomes quite explicit in the practice of describing anyone who displays his trickster qualities as "Anancy self", regardless of biological sex.

The Indian population which arrived after the beginnings of this seething chaos in which the society was formed had their own experience of liminal gender codification, in both Hindu and Moslem culture. Both cultures have a long tradition of transgenderism, represented in modern times in the Indian and Pakistani *hijra* – communities of eunuchs, transsexuals, transvestites and hermaphrodites who become living symbols of the contradictions of reverence and terror associated with these liminal categories. *Hijras* are important performers of blessing at societal rites of passage yet are deeply feared and reviled. In Hindu cosmology, Lord Brahma the creator god is a kind of hermaphroditic figure, part *purusha,* male principle, and part *prakriti,* female principle. The twinning of the sexes speaks radical terror through the figure of the goddess Kali in her simultaneous guise as terrible mother and all-devouring man of the abyss, signifying the destructive principle in the universe. (The destructive hermaphrodite in the female figure aptly describes society's sanctions against female masculinity.)[9] As active agents in the creolizing gender process (discussed later in the chapter), Indo-West Indians could well have been influenced even at unconscious levels by such discursive signs.

A sense of the human world as paradox within which gender is inflected is suggested in other narratives which influence the West Indian psyche at conscious and unconscious levels. The Esu figurations are part of a West African myth of origins. Biblical narrative also presents concepts of human origination that embed a radical gender ideology. The Adamic prototype is described as hermaphroditic in a peculiar way: Eve, hidden inside Adam, appears not as the product of phallic (masculine generative) activity, but as an incubated complete person with separate biological sex. She is not "birthed" but rather appears, and her appearance is described not merely as a necessary separation (fissure) but as the coming to material visibility of the (hitherto hidden) principles of duality and fusion, encoded as a liturgy of marriage: "Therefore shall a man leave his father and his mother, and cleave unto his wife, and they shall be one flesh" (Genesis 2:24).

This is reinforced by the commandment to multiply, replenish, renew and exercise authority across genders and generations, which is given equally to both (Genesis 1:28). The implication of Adam as womb (incubator) and Eve as "wombed human" continues the idea of paradoxical fusion, which is again reinforced in the fact that neither is a half-being: the fusion is between two complete beings, who therefore continue to remain separate within fusion. The possibility of creation from such incompatible elements as clay, word and flesh figures the space and the mystery of the connection among materiality, spirit and sign. Again the idea is suggested of an ontic gap, a kind of cognitive "black hole", that defies closure by way of Manichean knowledge, interpretations or identity prescriptions based on these. In sum, the slave's gender representation in the public sphere of resistance, insofar as it can be described as hermaphroditic, seems to return to an idea of nascence, of what is possible outside the boundaries – on the edge of chaos, at the point of emergence from chaos and at the point where the gods, who inhabit all possibilities, seem to live.

By presenting in the public sphere an iconic masculinity as symbol of the nation, nationalism erased the majority of the populace, whose gender experience was closer to the slave norm, as much as the slave master had done. But where the slave master's iconic image could be described as a fissured face, the image of the West Indian nation was more precisely a hydra, a head with competing faces. The essential difference had to do with who was to be represented: not a single "lordship", but a unified body out of a complex mix of races, cultures, classes and colours which were often oppositional and even hostile to each other yet which were the products of a common colonial experience, and which were to have equal stake in the new polity. In this context, it is not surprising that the politics of the nationalist period became highly conflictual.

Man of Speech Speaks the Torn Messiah

In public discourse – specifically on political platforms and in the intellectual arenas in which the collective identities of nation-territory and region-nation were invented, played and described – there was no real certainty as to how the nation was to be represented, except that it was to be uncompromisingly male/masculine. This became clear at the level of both speaker and speech. First, the apologist for nationhood on the public political platform was usually a man, who attained an iconic messianic status of such proportions that it might not be far-fetched to suggest that, in the people's imagination, he was the figuration of the nation itself. The iconic, messianic status of political leaders such as Eric Williams in Trinidad, Grantley Adams in Barbados, and Norman Manley and Alexander Bustamante in Jamaica has become a matter of general acceptance, even proverbiality, in West Indian discourse. It was attested to in cognomens such as "Father of the Nation", "Saviour of the Negro", "Chieftain" and "Moses the Second" – titles very clearly linked to their and their followers' feeling that they were counter-masculinities interrupting the masculinist-imperialist discourses of the colonial power and creating the image of the West Indian nation in their individual persons.

A political speech by Norman Manley gives the following illuminating overview which shows the linkage between masculinist messianism and performative representation:

> We . . . can remember, that Governors when they arrived here proceeded on a grand tour of the island wearing the fantastic colonial uniform designed for no other purpose than to impress the natives with the magnificence of the rulers from abroad. From one end of the country to the other they used to take themselves around with high ceremony, and give promises of what, as representatives of the king, they were supposed to do for this unfortunate island.
> . . . It was very necessary that there should arise a man who might be regarded as ideal in politics, a sort of John the Baptist, telling what was to come. That man made it his particular task to reduce the official to his proper status in this country. And in his own character and temperament he was an absolute incorruptible. (Manley 1971, 114–15)

Clearly, here the black man (Manley's reference is to J. A. G. Smith, Sr) appears as the "ideal" messenger of a new, quasi-religious dispensation. In the theatre of proclamation, the governor's imperial costume was no match for the black man's camel's hair and wild honey. Manley's speeches are generally larded with references both to the performative nature of the politics of the period and to the iconic status and authority of the men who led the political parties "controlling between us . . . the majority of the people in Jamaica" (1971, 282–83). Some of these references are almost uncannily reminiscent of passages in Bayley's and Long's narratives, which constantly image imperial masculinity and contenders for its space in terms of performative dress (for example, Bayley 1830, 45).

It is instructive that Nettleford, editing the 1971 collection of Manley's speeches, praises Manley's "masculine prose", refers consistently to "men" and "man" as the primary subject of discourse, and entitles the People's National Party's twenty-first-anniversary speech, "In the Year of Our Manhood". (Interestingly, Dawes, writing in 1955, praised the "masculine prose" of Roger Mais. It seems that the term may have been in some currency during the period.) Selwyn Cudjoe in his introduction to a similar collection of Williams's political essays (1993), emphasizes Williams's *glamorous* linguistic theatricality as part of the basis on which he became a founding father of the nation: "In a land where *picong* was king, Williams, versed in this art form, proved to be one of the reigning monarchs" (40); "His was part of the founding discourse of the nation" (102). Party loyalists, drunk on Williams's linguistic brilliance, were known to shout "Giant! Master!" after the great man had spoken. The masculinity of nationhood, which the people colluded to shape, was individualistic, charismatic and powerful, an image of manhood linked not only to authority (official force), but also to power (influence voluntarily accorded).[10]

The popularity, even fetishization, of these leaders is an indication of the psychic (con)fusions carried over from slave society. In most cases, at least in the larger territories, the leading politicians were members of the middle and upper classes by birth, by education or both. Many had been to England for tertiary education. It is interesting that the thrust towards nationalism was orchestrated by men of these groups that by social, political and/or educational experience were more attuned to the systems by which Europe governed itself and crafted its own nationalisms. The fact that it was the men of these groups who were most visible in public life had obviously to do in part – but only in part – with the fact that up to the 1960s, women's education, in keeping with European patriarchy, socialized women into caregiver and "nurturant" professions rather than public political roles (Senior 1991).

The combination of class dominance, ideological indoctrination and predominant male visibility was underpinned by the emphasis on Westminster-style rationalistic debate (the logocentric shaping of the word learnt in the academies of the fatherland) as one instrument through which national identity was to be shaped and signified. All of this established at one level conditions for the representation of the nation as an iconic masculinity in an Anglo-Saxon (or perhaps, more accurately, "Afro-Saxon") mode which was extraordinarily attractive to a colonized people. The messianic leader was someone whose physical presence was an assurance that Prospero's language and modes of government – signs of civilization – could be attained by the slave's descendant. It was a way of legitimating ourselves, through a double process of vicarious possession: the people rose in status by one channel if the (middle-class) political representative was coloured, and by another channel if he was black. This is no different from the process by which the slave inhabited status by playing the master in the mimicry of masquerades.

Literary artists of the period who lent their support to the political image included Roger Mais and V. S. Reid. Reid's novel *New Day* (1950) valorizes the messianic image of the middle-class intellectual and portrays men as the sole participants in the Jamaican political tradition. His aggressively masculinist fiction imports a version of this ideology into his presentation of the urban working classes, the class most unlikely to field masculinist gender division in actual reality. Mais's working-class female characters, without exception, are pathologically dependent on men, his working-class men sociologically overdetermined, particularly in his earliest novel, *The Hills Were Joyful Together* (1953). The two later novels, *Brother Man* (1954) and *Black Lightning* (1955), show a progression away from this unconscious middle-class bias in the portrayal of male characters, but the portrayal of female lack remains uncompromising.

In Barbadian texts such as Lamming's early *In the Castle of My Skin* (1953) and Austin Clarke's memoir *Growing Up Stupid under the Union Jack* (published in 1980 but portraying colonial Barbadian society), it is the role of the colonial education system in fostering male supremacy in the public space, and by extension these writers' collusive stance, that is highlighted. This is not surprising given the foundational role of education in Barbadian strategies of independence and the fact that boys' education and future participation in public life were invested in while girls' education and female capacity for political action were downplayed or sidelined.

Yet Lamming later became an extraordinary voice of interrogation of the very movement in which he was a dominant voice. In seeking to reinscribe at the public political level of signification the more complex gender experience which remained among "the folk" who were also the object of his commitment, Lamming registers the most severe critique as well as the most compassionate understanding of the class and gender posturings of the native bourgeoisie and political directorate after Independence. The 1960 novel *Season of Adventure,* through whose female protagonist is figured the Oedipal crisis of the nation growing towards "masculinity", is a remarkable example of Lamming's developing sense of West Indian gender realities. Here Lamming comes close to dismantling the masculinist figuration of nationhood, even though even his representations are ultimately circumscribed by that figuration.

One of the most powerful and enduring masculine images of the nation ever circulated in nationalist discourse is Lamming's representation of Shakespeare's Caliban ([1960] 1992) as a counter-masculinity speaking against Europe's hierarchical figurations of manhood. Caliban in academic circles replaces Anancy as the folk hero; both possess the capacity for subversive action and subversive speech, which are the signs of their power, even while they lack authority (official power-status in the colonial scheme), but with the distinct difference that Caliban possesses not only his own Creole speech, but Prospero's English as well. For Lamming, the ability to speak from within Prospero's language is paradox – a sign of potential schizophrenia, but also a sign of insurrectional capacity and potential authority. Caliban is essentially the slave emerging out of slavery into nationhood, which for Lamming is synonymous with the entry into (free) speech.

The Caliban trope is extraordinarily powerful, especially in its capacity as refiguration. The extent to which it has been appropriated by both male and female intellectuals across the Caribbean and Latin America indicates how widely it is seen as conveying a particularly New World colonial experience to which no particular gender can lay claim. Of course, one reason for Caliban's popularity in academic circles is that he is an intellectual. But female academics' appropriations of Caliban also point either to the willingness with which women allowed themselves to be co-opted into the single-sex, single-gender ideology or to a "masculinity" which West Indian women perceived in themselves.

Lamming's theorizing of Miranda, in *Water with Berries* (1971) and *Natives of My Person* (1972), has scarcely been addressed in critical discourse, and no female counterparts of Caliban have been produced. Brathwaite's revaluation of Sycorax's speech as the foundation of "nation language" has not been applied at the cutting edge of critical discourse, including discourse on nation language itself, even though an investment in Sycorax as the symbol of Caribbean languaging has several obvious advantages, not the least of which are a diminution of Prospero's ascendancy and a revaluation of the female. Prospero is, of course, a fact of history that will not go away, but the issue is how to find concepts and practices of language that acknowledge this fact and give it its proper place in the linguistic equations within which West Indian identity is predicated. It may be that Brathwaite's position is somewhat extreme, but outside of the latent opening provided by his Sycorax, the anomalous gender implications of how the equation is formulated within the Caliban trope remain unaddressed, except by Edmondson (1999), with reference to women *writers*, and before her by Sylvia Wynter, who in 1990 argued that the failure to locate "Caliban's woman" is part and parcel of "the new [world] secularizing schema by which the peoples of Western Europe legitimized their global expansion" (1990, 361–62).

The fetishized Caliban in academic discourse highlights another problem of nationalist political leadership. Contradiction existed not only between the lived reality of the society and the image of the nation as figured in the person of the leader, but also within the image itself. For the leader was also expected, implicitly or explicitly, to demonstrate aspects of masculinity valorized in folk culture. Significantly, he had to be a man of speech in the people's idiom: *picong,* hybridization of registers, self-aggrandizement, circumlocution and diversion. The mode of the tea meeting, the calypso, the dub version, the chantuelle, the Midnight Robber and the deejay, it was an iconoclastic speech completely inimical to colonial orthodoxy. This partly accounts for the immense popularity of politicians like Williams, Michael Manley and Alexander Bustamante, who were versed in the people's idiom, and the lesser fervour with which people greeted Norman Manley, whose command of the Queen's register was legendary but whose self-aggrandizement and facility with Creole speech were lacking or non-existent.

This aspect of identity was crucial as an obverse side of the subversive continuum begun in slavery: language not as space shared with the master (the exact appropriation of Prospero's tongue), and in that sense a means of coming to terms with feelings of inferiority, but as the space of one's own first speech and self-signifying, unintelligible to the (eavesdropping) outsider's ear and endlessly capable of expropriation. Such speech was a large part of the charismatic aspect of the leaders' authority, which was already in contradiction of the more Afro-Saxon side. The contradiction begins to indicate the schizophrenia the West Indian nation inadvertently imposed on its leaders. Westminister-style politics purportedly called for transparency of speech and action; "the need for transparency in politics" in fact became the fashionable cry whenever the native politicians were seen as having become corrupt. Yet the man of speech in the West Indian mode must be a man of occlusions, obfuscations and dazzling amorphous self-aggrandizing linguistic display. What is doubly interesting is that the linguistic qualities of the man of speech are, in Europeanist orthodoxy, distinctly feminine qualities.[11] And at least one ninetheenth- century listener found the St Lucian vernacular, the *kweyól,* to be that worst of disgraces, "the French language, stripped of its manly and dignified ornaments, and travestied for the accommodation of . . . toothless old women" (Breen [1844] 1970, 105).

Man-of-speech performance is related to crablike action, a recurrent metaphor in Lamming. Rooted in guerilla activity, it is the avoidance of the direct way, to which Edward Long (1774) unwittingly referred when he contemptuously declared that no slave was intelligent enough to draw a straight line. Westminster politics, as West Indians understood it, toed the straight line in lip and limb. It involved both a factual logic of speech, action and analysis, which was its own morality, and a linearity of process and protocol, by which the Manichean division of opposites was enshrined in the two-party system and in which the abstract laws of supply and demand formed the basis of economic policy. The West Indian ideology of masculine speaking evokes Anancyism, for which many of the most populist leaders were famous. Anancyism – the ability to rob, surreptiously defeat and *samfie* or *mamaguy*[12] – is already contradictory, being a quality both endlessly celebrated and frowned upon in West Indian society, depending on who is at the receiving end of the spider-man's action.

The tensions between the two sides of the leader's image were never resolved: the widespread accusations of corruption which marked the decline of messianism in the 1980s arose out of factors such as distrust of Anancy's tongue, which said one thing and meant the other; and the perception that speech which was not to be trusted was in fact being accompanied by dishonest action. Where dishonest speech and action had been perfectly acceptable against the slave master, in national relations subversive speech was for the purposes of entertainment, bonding, belonging and identification. The nationalist leaders were seen to have debased the tradition (of man) which they were expected to uphold. The people therefore felt a growing alienation from the political process; this ultimately translated into hostility between the man in the street and the man of politics, soon to be considered also imperialist.

The irony, of course, has to do with the question, which identity is rejected? Is it the man of Westminster's categories, or the Anancy of West Indian culture? For in their investiture in one person, the lines become blurred, and the populace confronts and rejects its own identity at the crossroads of transgression between the master's categories and the slave's answer. In the context of nationalist society, neither seemed to work, as the ground on which fusion could be effected (since, as the West Indian Creole languages already show, there is in the end no such thing as the irreconcilability of grammars) appeared endlessly elusive. Perhaps the missing link was that the problem of a West Indian grammar of morality – etymology, context and principle – was never really addressed.[13]

At the same time there was the issue of a kind of almost unspoken malice. The politician was an object of suspicion by virtue of his superiority, which was read in terms of his possession of the master's language and spaces of representation (Assembly, Parliament and Cabinet). Yet he was the people's servant and therefore the possessed. At any given moment he could be recuperatively "devoured" by the populace. The particular virulence with which West Indians criticize politicians may be as much a function of this suspicious and counter-despotic malice as it is a function of the politicians' moral failure. The people's linguistic decimation of the politician finally assures him that they can at any moment expose his posturings and his lack; Creole cursing attacks Westminster masquerade. West Indian messianism may well be the reversal of, and therefore the complete entrapment in, the dialectic between the slave and the iconic Man who "governed" the slave. The dance around the slave master is substituted by the dance around the messiah, who is now also blood and cultural kin, and therefore the site of seriously problematic cathexes. We are already rejecting our self/selves even as we are seeking it/them.

Sylvia Wynter's fictionalized portrayal of the messianic Bedward religious movement in her novel *The Hills of Hebron* (1962) is of particular interest to our discussion, both because it is a female writer's critique of messianism and because it is Wynter who elsewhere articulates the most cogent critique of the absence of "Caliban's woman". *The Hills of Hebron* vividly illustrates the investment in religious messianism of which political messianism was a paradigm and the extent to which the man of speech was an integral part of the messianic persona. But the novel proves curiously disappointing in its espousal of a problematic social materialism akin to that of Roger Mais. Wynter's portrayal of the rural working class as impossibly locked into a syndrome of dependency which spawns the messianic movement is at odds with her simultaneous project to show the same class as agent of resistance. In the end, her rejection of messianism functions not as a critique of political nationalism founded on this construct, but as a critique of the religious manifestation of messianism among a peasant class whom she presents, except for the leaders, as being almost completely in a position of victimization and objectification, and in which they psychologically collude.

Wynter's rejection of messianism also causes her to focus on and therefore highly privilege the male protagonists within whom the messianic impulse resides. This already causes the female characters to take second place, where they are further diminished by being helplessly locked into a total dependence on the men (the dependency being a way of showing the pernicious nature of messianism). This negative image remains despite the dominant female figure of Miss Gatha, who for a brief period in the absence by default of a male leader and in view of her economic power, takes on the role of the community's messiah. In the final analysis, Wynter's gender discourse is as problematic a "forced representation" of the folk (that is to say, a representation in which folk figures are made to "perform" according to a preconceived, if well-meaning, middle-class script) as are the fictions of other middle-class writers such as C. L. R. James, Orlando Patterson (*The Children of Sisyphus*) and Mais.

The problem of Wynter's text reminds us that not only the image of individual leaders, but also the representations in the *discourse* of nationhood exhibited contradictory faces. Contradiction arose in the attempt of the nationalists to craft an image of the ideal West Indian citizen as educated and rationalistic. Education was critical not only because it was seen as the process by which the poor would attain a better stake in the society, but also because it was seen as the cohesive force that would transcend divisions of race, class, colour and competing interest. But the nationalists sought also to represent this ideal, educated West Indian citizen iconically in the image of the black male peasant or proletarian (indicated in the many references to "the black man" in political discourse), who by virtue of numerical dominance and historical disadvantage was seen as representative of the composite entity.

One anomaly of course had to do with the fact that even well into independence the black peasantry/proletariat in most territories had the least access to rationalist education and arguably lived a tradition in dynamic contradiction to rationalism. Another had to do with race. The problem of emphasizing the culture of the racial majority in order to procure and represent national oneness was never quite resolved. Because of the race issue, the movement towards national unity (in the sense of a political *rapprochement* across races) was delayed in those territories such as Trinidad and Guyana, which had large Asian populations; and in Guyana especially, the situation was sometimes explosive. Racial tensions erupted around the issue of Indian representation in particular, as Indians felt they were being left out of the cultural and political equation in this "melting-pot" nationalization in which blackness and creolization in black modes were the collective symbols. In these territories the face of national representation was split (between Cheddi Jagan and Forbes Burnham in Guyana, and between Eric Williams and a number of Indian leaders in Trinidad).

The problem of lag between official ideology and lived reality was apparent also in the distance between the nationalist agenda and the preoccupations of the working classes, who from Emancipation had tended to emphasize social and economic advancement and, at least in some territories, to delay, even resist, political unification/federation as a sign of threatening, essentially re-enslaving authority. The fact that the first great wave of migration of working-class West Indians took place at the height of nationalism is arguably a sign of the different agendas of middle-class nationalists and the mainstream of the people: the one was more political, the other more economic. The intelligentsia of the middle and upper classes tended to migrate temporarily, in search of educational advancement, by which they hoped to assist in national development on their return; lower-class West Indians were often more concerned with individual or familial survival, and more often than not were unable to return.

The 1970 Black Power uprising in Trinidad and the rise to prominence of the Rastafarian movement in Jamaica during the nationalist decades may be evidence of the fact that some working-class men felt themselves completely distanced from the nationalist project because of continuing economic and cultural subjugation. Rastafarianism began in 1930s Jamaica and continued to flourish in the 1950s, despite numerous attacks by the colonial establishment (see, for example, Smith, Augier and Nettleford 1960). By the late 1970s, it was beginning to export itself to other territories and, via the music of Bob Marley in particular, to the metropoles and the Caribbean diaspora abroad. The movement, as one subgroup answer to colonialism, separated itself from nationalism in favour of a "back to Africa" ideology. Rastafarianism as a black counter-masculinity was demonstrated in particulars of dress and body play (beard and dreadlocks) as well as in a different lifestyle. (This statement is not meant to suggest that women were not involved in Rastafarianism, but rather highlights its origination in male projects of self-empowerment.)[14]

Throughout the 1970s, a significant amount of reggae music, under the influence of the Rastafarian world view, expressed working-class rejection of everything for which the political directorate was felt to stand, even after Independence.[15] Many found this stance attractive because it placed "the black man" in a central position. "Babylon" in reggae lyrics became the icon of Europeanist masculinist imperialism, within which the political system espoused by mainstream nationalists was seen as being hopelessly inured. If Haile Selassie was the (masculine) image of god, Marcus Garvey, as a militant "back to Africa" advocate, was the image of (the) man with whom Rastas most closely identified. Rastas displaced iconic political messianism by splitting and deploying their gendered identity among Selassie, Garvey, the "I" of the individual male masculine subjectivity and the "I and I" of the Rasta community.

The fact that Rastafarianism had to do primarily with types of man appears even more clearly in the 1990s, which as Joseph Pereira (1998) points out, have seen the transmutation of "Babylon" from the negative iconization of an immoral system of men to the negative iconization of one symbolic man – the Pope. (Of course, this iconization of the Pope had its antecedents in the anti-Christ warnings of the Protestant Reformation and indeed in the theology of current sects such as the Seventh-Day Adventists, but its rearticulation in the evolution of Rasta music theology is worth noting.) Rastafarianism, then, led the gender representations of a whole underclass of men who staged themselves in radical defiance of the fissured national masculinity, much as the slave collective had done against the colonizer's self-representation. Not the least significant of their radical moves was the invention and characteristic use of a Creole speech version which mixed several vocabularies – royalist, priestly, biblical and idiosyncratic. Based on strategies of substitution, inversion and subversion, Rasta speech opposed itself to existing Creole registers and to the standard English of the Parliament. The Rasta was clearly another man of speech, firmly within the resistance tradition which Brathwaite (1971) succinctly terms the "(mis)appropriation of language".

Brathwaite and Lamming (particularly the former), in propounding their theories of language, had a very good understanding of the role of performative speech in West Indian culture, as did Selvon in his privileging of carnivalesque creole speech in his London novels, Earl Lovelace in his celebration of carnival in *The Dragon Can't Dance,* Austin Clarke in his structuring of standard English prose on a transformative foundation of Barbadian speech rhythms and, in a different way, Walcott in his celebration of folk iconoclasm in *Ti Jean and His Brothers.* (Arguably, Ti Jean's triumph over the Devil comes from his refusal of the linguistic categories by which the Devil sets the terms of discourse and the parameters of what is to be seen. This implies Walcott's concept of the West Indian artist's responsibility as "Adam" – the namer of things.) Brathwaite's theories, rooted like Lamming's in an understanding of language as the motivating force and heart of all political relations, recognized the revolutionary potential of the folk use of language in national representation and political practice at the highest levels, hence the former's use of the term "nation language" to designate consciousness arriving out of folk speech. As we have said, a major problem of nationalist imagining was in assuming the folk as a single gender.

The man of speech was one folk masculinity that fissured the nationalist icon. Another was the "village ram", who was completely *de trop* in official nationalist figurations and whose behaviour was in fact actively discouraged in demographic planning. The criterion for this identity was sexual prowess, with corollaries of prolific fatherhood and sexual authority over many women. The greater the distance from social and economic authority, the greater the investment in sexual authority. Rastafarianism is an interesting phenomenon in the way it sanitizes this form of masculinity: in Rasta cosmology, sexual power has divine connections, and prolific but responsible procreation signals obedience to the biblical commandment, "Be fruitful and multiply".

Masculinity as authoritative, prolific and prodigal sexuality was a contradiction in that, while moral rectitude was expected from the holders of public office, there was also tacit acceptance, sometimes even hidden celebration, of well-displayed sexual prowess by men of this category. (It is in fact inconceivable that a West Indian politician could be indicted for sexual indiscretions, despite unceasing complaints that national life is fractured by the immorality of politicians.) This is a marriage of contradictions similar to the marriage of Creole speech/action traditions and Westminister protocol, and further complicates the image of masculinity that West Indian society crafted for itself and held up to its own gaze. Here was a kind of transmuted replication of the slave master's taboo against the irresistible sexuality of the slave, which under the master's transgression produced "another kind of being" whose body was *créolité,* the paradox of the fusion and (con)fusion of forms.[16] Like the master, we couldn't always have our cake and eat it too.

It is clear that although there were important differences between the middle class–led project and folk images and attitudes in the nationalist period, these were not a sign of rigidly polarized interests and identities between the two classes. The man of speech and the village ram, who cut across class lines and showed up in politics in their various transmutations, are examples of this. The same is true of more directly "political" activities. In most territories, the labour and trade union movements, which protected the working class and which arose out of working-class action, were often part and parcel of the political movements. (Political parties had trade unions attached to them, and middle-class ideologues led the labour movements.) In some respects, the difference between mainstream and middle-class nationalist, on the one hand, and folk/working-class activist, on the other, was primarily a difference of emphasis and sometimes a difference of speech rather than of parameters.

Willy-nilly, individuals of all classes were in one way or another involved in the enterprise of self-fashioning at several levels. Individuals were members of inner communities such as the family, which depended on them for economic support, the demands of which they could not always meet but which for males especially, because of the influence of ideology and the images of political platforms, was a particularly pressing aspect of identity. Members of communities were also putative citizens of an emergent nation, to the fashioning of whose identity they were expected to contribute by way of action and discourse.

Selvon's work highlights the psychic dissonance which can result when the problem of identity becomes an immediately triangular rather than a sequential or phased project – that is, where the subject is called upon, as was the West Indian in the nationalist period, to forge simultaneous identities for self, community and nation (and even sometimes to perform these for the outsider, since England was always implied as the ghostly presence/grey eminence watching the performance). In Selvon's work, dissonance appears at the centre of representations of identity in which the projects of self-fashioning, self-representation and audience creation are simultaneously attempted and so become deeply conflicted. Again, it is the West Indian male's experience of these conflicts of identity which is represented.

Selvon's gender representations, like Wynter's, may be an important indicator of the difficulties inherent in artistic creation as a personal, cultural and literary act. I have suggested that the consistent privileging of the male protagonist is an index of the pressure that men felt nationalist politics placed on them to become visible and somehow re-created, but it also obviously helped to create and perpetuate that pressure. But the very idea of a protagonist, especially when allied to the genre of the Bildungsroman (which for obvious reasons attracted many West Indian writers) poses problems for the in-depth psychological representation of non-protagonal characters. Different writers negotiate this difficulty with different degrees of success. It may well have been a problem for Selvon, whose fictions are peopled with women, keenly imagined but from the outside as by a mystified if entertained observer looking in. The Tiger novels are marked by an ambition, not present in the London novels, to imagine a female psychology, but the effort is abortive, and this may again point to a third factor: a sense of uncertainty about the nature of female psychologies, engendered in the conflictual space of West Indian gender contention, where ideology constantly crossed swords with socio-economic reality, demonstrated abilities and self-perception.

But it is as we shift attention to the larger contexts of popular cultural expression and everyday lived experience that we begin to see how West Indian projects of identity were troubled not only by competing ideas of masculinity, but also, more radically, by the liminal category of femininity. ("Liminal" suggests that "femininity" has never been clearly defined in the West Indian context, that as a concept it inhabits a kind of ambiguous "hinterspace", as will be argued further on.) In Trinidad and the Eastern Caribbean, the calypso as a form of popular fiction continued to be an important site of men's self-representation as it had been from the last years of the nineteenth century, when female performers began to disappear from the calypso scene. Its history of suppression by the colonial establishment, especially in the late nineteenth and early twentieth centuries (modifying to censorship in the 1940s and 1950s), attests to the fact that folk masculinities, rooted in a profound relation to cultural imperatives, belonged to the political continuum of recalcitrance and subversion. But that history points also to the irony of the calypso having evolved into a male mode of expression, given its association with the "jamette" carnivals that in the nineteenth century provoked establishment fears of male-female solidarity.

It is in the calypso that ideal folk masculinity in its emphasis on the man of speech is most vividly exemplified. As Gordon Rohlehr asserts in his 1990 study of the Trinidad calypso, "Calypso grew out of . . . [a] milieu of violent self-assertiveness and rhetorical force; of a constant quest for a more splendid language, and excellence of tongue. It has been a predominantly male mode, whose themes are identity and the individual within the group" (54).

Even though the songs of the 1950s did not openly comment on national politics as did those of the earlier nationalist years, the calypso may be regarded as a counter-voice, performing in a guarded code the issues that troubled masculinity at the domestic and communal (microcosmic) levels, which were inevitably affected by the gender performances at the macrocosmic level. The calypso was the speculative mirror by which men sought to extend, (re)create and recuperate the selves under threat from national change.[17]

Recuperation of the self under threat from the recalcitrant "masculinity" and aggravating "femininity" of women was an equally important project of the calypsos. As in earlier decades, economic hardship and its threat to male sufficiency were reflected in misogynistic lyrics lambasting women's purported greed, materialism and tendency to dispense their sexual goods in exchange for unsanctioned lucre. But the representation was ambivalent.

Rohlehr's study shows the extent to which men recognized and sometimes even valorized women's exhibition of "man-like" behaviour, which they challenged with satirical self-mockery and the linguistic repertoire of the stickfighter, suggesting the recognition of an equal opponent.[18]

The emasculating potential of "woman tongue" was also recognized, this recognition a striking contrast to the occlusions of nationalist ideology, in which the female voice had no place. Many calypsos used the dramatic dialogue, or call-and-response form, to inscribe the woman's voice in direct speech, partly as an indication of her aggravating refusal to shut up, partly to enhance the demonstration of the male persona's counter-voice. The calypsonian knew women were not silent, and even the hope that they would become so was not a totally serious one, since their aggravating speech provided a space for the elaboration of men's masculine identities and a stage for the festive, linguistic performances which were both entertainment and an aesthetic means of coming to terms with pain, in this case the pain of inadequacy.

Taken together, the men's calypsos actually work to show the woman's participation in West Indian linguistic virtuosity quite clearly, albeit as a quasi-liminal category. She exists in the calypso text in the space of the unsaid – that is to say, in the lacunae of the calypsonian's complaint (for he complains against someone who most troublesomely and vociferously exists, and the complaint invites intrigued speculation as to what kind of person she might be in reality). She exists also in the calypso at the site of forced performance, where her voice is ventriloquized and distorted in the overlay of the calypsonian's ideology. In the end, she becomes most visible at the point where she troubles the representation with the questions raised by its own lacunae. In this way, she speaks with subversive paradox out of the attempt to render her speechless. Even within the text, reality clashes with ideology.

What made the calypsonian's self-appointed task impossible was this basic contradiction: that linguistic power in the mode of *picong*, subversion and hybridization was an aspect of West Indian cultural sensibility in general, non-gender-specific and produced out of the hermaphroditism of the slave collective, yet it was now the basis on which manhood was to be defined. The reification of calypso as "men's language" in this context represents an attempt to (re)claim masculine space as a male purview where it was seen as being under threat. But what then seems to become clear is that "man-ness", far from being an established category under invasion, was still in the process of being claimed. This is not the same as saying it was still in the process of being defined – its definition had been made clear, but the ground it inhabited was fraught with competing claims. It was in effect as transgressive a category as "woman-ness", the two constantly crossing each other's territorial boundaries.

The situation for men was "worsened" by the fact that some women calypsonians did exist, competing fiercely, fracturing the male attempt at monopoly. Female competition in this male arena reached a highpoint in the fiercely political decade of the 1970s. In 1977, the still famous Calypso Rose made history by winning Trinidad's Calypso Monarch crown; this made it very clear that the populace was not giving wholesale credence to narratives of male supremacy. West Indian culture, being a speech culture, has never prescribed that women should be silent. Rather, it has disapproved, applauded and been entertained by "woman tongue", a complex, paradoxical response to a complex, paradoxical construct. While being a vehicle for misogynistic attitudes (the woman as nag, and as one whose tongue emasculates men), "woman tongue" also encodes a perception that the female is endowed with a capacity to "prophesy" arcane things, even to speak them into being. On the surface, because of its threat, woman tongue – and women's speech in general – is not associated with the entertainment capacities of the male performer, but in practice, both are.

"Yard" fictions such as *Minty Alley* and Alvin Bennett's *God the Stonebreaker* (1964) illustrate this, *Minty Alley* in its celebratory staging of "tracing matches" or "mapuis",[19] *God the Stonebreaker* in its more ambiguous laughter at lower-class women's speech performance, which Bennett places in the traditions of Anancy and the apocryphal "Big Boy" narrative.[20] Bennett's text is double-framed, using parody and burlesque both through and against his picaresque main character, the redoubtable Granny B. The double frame indicates both Bennett's prejudicial attitudes and his sense of the (dangerously seductive) hilarity of Ananycism practised by his anti-heroine. These texts emphasize the entertainment quotient of women's speech and its function within the West Indian speech tradition as public spectacle, but also indicate its function as self-elaboration, self-aggrandizement and warfare, in many ways identical to the functions and expressive modes of the men's calypsos. The yard appears as the people's, but more specifically the women's, stage. It functions as a "bridging" or mediated space between the public and the domestic, showing women's influential work in both. Women's yard speech continues in transmuted form the tradition of fearsome verbality with which female slaves authorized and led resistance music on the plantations. However, in the context of "civil" society, particularly under the instress of nationalism, women's verbality becomes a threat to men's identification.

The fact that in everyday speech culture men and women routinely colluded, as on the plantation, in a shared use of speech as iconoclastic, derisory act is strikingly and uniquely illustrated in the oral poetry and performance of Louise Bennett. Bennett invents dramatic personae who speak in a merged female-male folk voice, commenting through verbal repartee, parody and satire on various matters of national, domestic and personal interest. Schoolchildren of both sexes still unselfconsciously perform her monologues, undisturbed by any suggestion that Bennett's own performances might have typecast the poems as matter strictly for women and girls.[21] Bennet's double-gendered performativity is part of the complex map presented by art culture in nationalist Jamaica, especially in the 1970s, an extraordinary period which was at once the high point of political nationalism, the high point of its masculinist representation and the high point of challenge to that representation. Practice and ideology in the dramatic arts, particularly the work of the National Pantomime and the Sistren Theatre Collective, radically challenged the nation's masculinism.[22] Since the 1930s and throughout the 1970s, Edna Manley had led the Jamaican artists' movement, inspired many of the country's male visual artists and used female representations such as her *Eve* and *Ancestor* sculptures to image the nation – these, when placed against her male representations such as *Negro Aroused,* in fact forming a double-gendered iconography of the nation that was not circulated in the popular or general political space.

The anomalies of 1970s Jamaica are emblematic of shifts that began to take place towards the end of the nationalist period, under pressure from the global and regional changes which would herald the 1980s. The shaping of nationalist politics around iconic images of masculinity was affected; Jamaica's then–prime minister Michael Manley may be considered as simultaneous example, sign, catalyst and contradiction of the change. Manley was the first West Indian leader to articulate a *counter*-rhetoric of gender within nationalist politics. Marcus Garvey in the 1920s had articulated a gender position which sought to elevate women to a place of honour in the collective. But Garvey was never really accepted as a serious political contender among the electorate; more important, Garvey was pan-Africanist, not nationalist, in his political orientation. In addition, Garvey's gender perspective was not essentially inclusive, since it iconized a particular image of women which was both class-bound and ultimately, if unintentionally, negatively nuanced against women, in ways similar to Lamming's constructions, to be discussed in chapter 4. The female Garvey icon was a "black queen" who epitomized the virtues of mothering, excluding the possibility of more diverse identities. There is a certain irony in this, given the major activist roles played by women (including Garvey's wives Amy Jacques and Amy Ashwood) in his movement.[23] In contrast, Manley's shaping of legislative and employment policy to favour women and his consistent inclusion of women in his political discourse as well as in symbolizations of nationhood, which included the creation of the Maroon Nanny as national heroine, were part of a larger praxis which sought to bring the marginalized, regardless of gender, into the mainstream of political and economic attention.

But Manley's radical departures were overwritten by a highly theatrical messianism complete with a borrowed religious genealogy by which he linked himself to the biblical leaders Joshua and Moses. Using the name of the former and a "rod of correction" whose etymology was obviously the rod by which the latter parted the Red Sea, Manley further elaborated his image by claiming that the rod had been given to him by Haile Selassie. Manley's political tools – the syncretizing of religion, the harnessing of folk sensibility and the attempt to erase gender inequalities – along with a linguistic facility which was the essence of *creólité* (Manley combined formal and folk registers in a dazzling display matched only by Eric Williams in the earlier years), paradoxically made him seem the ideal representation of how Jamaica wished to see itself, even while the image was compromised by his individualistic messianism. Significantly also, Manley became a major spokesman for the Caribbean Community in international affairs, suggesting again a general regional investment in "a certain type of man".

Nevertheless, the endemic nature of the problematizing shifts of the 1970s is indicated in two important counter-texts produced by female historians. Lucille Mathurin Mair's landmark dissertation on women in slavery (1974) and Elsa Goveia's similar documentation (1965) filled huge gaps in the information about women's involvement at the centre of political action from the very beginning of the region's history. Since then, Barbara Bush (1985, 1990) and Hilary Beckles (1988, 1989, 1998, 1999) have added important information.[24] Of major import too is Merle Hodge's *Crick Crack Monkey* (1970), one of the few novels produced by women during that period. Hodge's novel departs from the nationalist norm in creating a female protagonist, through whom the participation of women in the rabid class/colour system is explored from a first-hand point of view. The novel demonstrates the retarding influences of class snobbery and colonial education on a healthy personal identity in girls and women, but it equally paints a picture of working-class women's powers of speech, resilience and survival. Gender then emerges as a function of class, which is pegged to education and economics and which divides women in their ability to effect positive change. In Hodge's as in so many nationalist representations, the folk – but in this case particularly the women of the folk – are the radical interpreters of meaning and the source of authentic cultural personality.

Yet Hodge does not espouse a classical feminist gender ideology; rather, her narrative celebrates or criticizes relationships primarily on the basis of whether they retard or advance individual development, and no one ideologically "female" perspective goes to shape her protagonist's individuation. Hodge's text is framed in the ritual laughter of West Indian story telling, indicated in her title. Like Louise Bennett's, hers is a laughter that speaks more to a West Indian folk-cultural sensibility than to a feminist perspective. In its ultimate effect, through its emphasis on community, it shares remarkable similarities with Erna Brodber's texts, produced in the next literary generation. Even though Brodber is self-consciously ideological in ways Hodge is not, both give a similar sense of gender lines being an unsatisfactory basis for solutions; in Hodge's novel, such lines are significant only in their negative aspect.

Explaining Woman, Race, Class and Transgression

Sociologists as well as literary artists have recognized that the society's gender reality at its base was far more fluid and paradoxical than appeared in public discourse, but the tensions which militated against a rigid entrenchment of patriarchalism have been variously attributed. Commentators such as the sociologist Melville Herskovits (Bascom and Herskovits 1959; Herskovits and Herskovits 1947), who belongs to the African retention school of thought, have suggested that the primary roles played by women in West Indian society starting from slavery were a retention from African society, in which matrilineal descent and the social participation of women were major factors. Such views, while they have considerable merit, have been shown to be an inadequate explanation of the phenomenon (Besson 1995; Rohlehr 1990).

Contrary to the tendency in popular West Indian thinking to valorize West African societies as matriarchal, the truth is that these societies were at base quite the opposite, as any cursory glance at West African literary representations, particularly those by women (Buchi Emecheta and Mariama Bã, for example) will serve to indicate; the gender bias of African nationalist politics noted by Boehmer (1992) did not result from Europeanistic acculturation. While it is certainly true that the large-scale devaluation of the female and the associated feminine which marks modern and early modern European gender ideology and practice was not the case in West Africa and that women took part in public, economic and, in some cases, military life, these factors were unlikely to have been the main dynamic behind female aggression on the plantations. They more likely took second place to the immediate situation in which the slaves found themselves.

Historical evidence suggests that people reshape consciousness and strategies to deal with present exigencies of survival, so that the divisions that belong to settled society might well be erased, or at least seriously modified. Obviously, this does not mean the past has no significant influence on present or future modes of consciousness or behaviour since, after all, history consists in part of continuities within rupture. Neither does it imply a social constructionist view of society, in which practices are seen as being neatly discarded when they have outlived their usefulness. Rather, the point is that in situations where survival is at stake, the present situation takes primacy in determining the ways in which people utilize the past, both consciously and unconsciously.

The voyage traditionally known as the Middle Passage must have already created a significant rupture with the past: we have no reliable numbers or anthropologies, but it seems self-evident that the women and men who left West Africa could not have been psychologically the same when they arrived on West Indian soil. The same would have been true of the Middle Passage of the Chinese and Indian indentured labourers, though in different ways and to different degrees. Factors such as the evolution of women's central role in the use of family land after Emancipation, the inflexions imposed on gender by the peculiarities of West Indian class/colour divides, and the reconstitution of Indian and Chinese gender norms in the early indenture period under pressure of sexual and relationship needs are more tangible examples of the ways in which immediate experience may override the influence of cultural pasts. An analysis of any of these supports the view that a more cogent explanation of the fluidity of West Indian gender construction than the African-retention theory may be found in the realities of the post-Emancipation period.[25]

The period immediately following "full freedom" obviously saw the continuation of the two parallel worlds even though the ramifications of each had automatically and in some respects profoundly shifted. Certainly liminality of presence now gave way to high visibility of a particular kind, as the slave's alternative space was no longer underground or so completely enmas(k)qued. The world of overarching public institutions still belonged to the imperial patriarchy. The newly reconstituted life of the slave's freedom, though still entrapped by this context, was attuned to the consolidation of personal, familial and communal liberties and identities. At the point where the two worlds intersected, the planter sought by various strategies to refigure the newly emergent society of ex-slaves purely in terms of an inner circle of plantation society – an inner circle that was both eccentric and recalcitrant, and therefore urgently to be contained. The planter's aim was to return the ex-slave to the twilight zone of social death. This marks the planter's recognition of the slave's emergence onto an open stage in increasingly competitive terms.

As already noted, the carnivalesque/hermaphroditic challenges to the planter continued in the public spaces. But freedom (and its consolidation), rather than reply, was the ex-slave's main preoccupation. Freedom, critically, was in many instances established on family land, as has been discussed by Momsen (1998), Olwig (1995) and Miller (1991a). Family land became not only the ground of political warfare, but also the ground on which identity was shaped and represented. Family land as a political tool had to do with the fact that ownership of family land meant, first, possession of the same grounds on which the planter established economic authority and, second, greater freedom from work on the plantation, into which one could otherwise be easily forced by economic necessity. At this level, there was no division between private and public spheres, since family and family land were the signs of individual and communal identity and the space from which the planter was fought and defied.

Significantly, men and women had equal access to family land. Given the emphasis on family, as well as the continuing need for a collective front, it seems quite probable that the masculinities and femininities which may have been constructed in this new space had more to do with age and position in the family (after the African tradition of deference to elders) than they had to do with gender polarities. That is, domestic politics had more to do with necessities of governance than they had to do with sex/gender demarcations. The extended family structure (necessary African retention in the circumstances), coupled with the effects of intra- and inter-territorial migration by parents of either sex (but particularly fathers), tended to shift and diffuse authority within families, so that stable, dichotomized gender roles were not easy to maintain.

The fact that many children were born outside and prior to marriage was also a significant factor in postponing gender divisions. Children, even in the households of married parents, often belonged to different mothers and fathers, especially the latter. They were also used to seeing their mothers take part in rebellions and in economic enterprises, such as Sunday market and urban entrepreneurship, which had in fact begun in the days of slavery. Further, they may not necessarily have experienced living with their fathers prior to Emancipation, as slaves were often married across estates and children were expected to live on the estate owning the mother. Female slaves were noted by several commentators, Edward Long included, as having been more recalcitrant than males, no doubt partly because they had children, actual and potential, to defend. After Emancipation, women, again for the same reason, tended more than men to refuse waged labour on the plantations and to seek economic alternatives.

All of this meant that children's experience of gender relations and constructs were predicated on images of dominant, economically active mothers or mother surrogates, and of fathers whose authority may have been postponed or itinerant (itinerancy being caused not only by migration, but also by the search from plantation to plantation for the best conditions of waged labour when this was necessary to supplement family income). The children themselves had shared field labour, without discrimination according to sex, from as early as four years old, and for some years had no major personal experience of work differentiation according to sex.

In situations where there was no access to family land, intra-island migration swelled the ranks of the urban populace. Contributory factors included insufficient available land space in the smaller territories, restrictive land ownership laws, which curtailed access (as in Barbados), and the refusal of individuals to engage in agricultural work, which was too instant a reminder of the plantation. This, of course, not only contributed to the fluid sex/gender/age/authority scenario in the rural areas, but also replicated it in the urban centres, as adults in search of work in this context of displacement and rupture faced similar necessities of absence and delegation in the household. Throughout the twentieth century, the specifics may have shifted but the basic principle and pattern remained.

Religion, always a central aspect of West Indian culture and sensibility (see Chevannes 1995), played a role in the shaping of gender relations and identities in the post-Emancipation period as well as in the period of nationalism and beyond. Whether Christian, African or syncretic, religion figured significantly in the joint struggle of men and women towards emancipation, and in some instances arguably helped to delay traditional masculine-feminine polarities of authority and power. Popular academic discourse suggests that West Indian Christianity, with its mixture of secular patriarchy and competing biblical representations and doctrines, tended to move the society more quickly towards the traditionalizing ideologies of gender than did syncretic religion. Such a conclusion is at best equivocal. The liberationist tradition of the anti-slavery denominations (Baptist, Methodist, Moravian) is an important factor in this regard. The nineteenth-century narratives of the Hart sisters (Ferguson 1993), for example, indicate that in some churches in the immediate pre-Emancipation period, women were visibly involved in aspects of church work more traditionally associated with men. This involvement of women in pioneering activity in the church cut across racial lines, if Anne Hart's narrative, which makes mention of black women's seminal involvement in Moravian churches, is to be believed. There is no reason to believe that these relative freedoms ceased at Emancipation, though they became increasingly attenuated in the twentieth-century mainstream churches with the entrenchment of patriarchal education, which also adopted mainstream Christianity as religious emblem.[26]

Concerning West Indian Christianity generally, the taboo against premarital and extramarital sex is one factor that functions to increase women's freedom, even more than does the working-class practice of changing partners and delaying marriage. The application of the taboo to both male and female also opposes sexual double standards which help to extend the field of misogynistic discourse. Christian doctrines of humility, submission and charity, regardless of sex or gender, would also have exerted tensions against the contrary concepts of husbandly authority and rule. So would biblical figurations of the Church collectively in feminine terms, as well as the figuration of Christ as someone who in speech and practice represented what was in effect a conundrum of identity that could easily be read as a hermaphroditic gender, an unknown gender, a crossing out of genders or an amalgam of all these. The psychology of West Indian

Christianity, in the nationalist period as now, is a complex area in which biblical doctrine and representation, colonial patriarchal ideology and practice, and the wider West Indian lived experience compete in ways that render even its most conservative manifestations at least contradictory.

Several syncretic forms of religion, such as Myal, Orisha, Spiritual Baptist and Revival, which combine African and Judeo-Christian elements to different degrees, traditionally involve women in leadership positions. Present-day Revival congregations are still often de facto led by women (the "Mother" figure), though men are the de jure (iconic) heads. This is an essentially patriarchal hierarchy, but actual practice empties out much of the power of male iconization. The (male) bishops appear in the churches only on rare inspection visits, which means that what Max Weber (1947) refers to as the *charismatic* aspect of authority resides in the Mother, insofar as she is the visible power and, by extension, the visible authority where the male head may well have lost some of both, especially the former, through distancing. In other words, the bishop, in his capacity as the traditionalizing aspect of authority, has his authority delayed and, ultimately, to some extent "watered down" in a society which privileges the immediate, the charismatic and the creolizing aspects of leadership.

The situation in many extended households is parallel to that in the Revival church. Even where the male household head is present, his authority is often exercised only as a sort of final recourse, where the mother's authority is seen to be flouted or inadequate for the gravity of the offence which is to be punished. Thus the man's authority is often a latent one, concretized in the spaces left vacant by lapses of female authority. This seems to be the reverse of a classically patriarchal society. It is true that all this suggests that the mother's authority is merely delegated and is therefore an indication of bipolarities, but the point is that in their day-to-day lived experience, women do wield considerable authority, and children of both sexes, who will be the next adult generation, are influenced by this experience. Further, West Indian women across racial divides have been known to exercise domestic authority in harshly punitive ways more traditionally associated with masculinity than femininity, so that the picture is one of transgression more than polarization.

Among the influences since post-Emancipation, it would seem that family structure remained – and continues to remain – among the most powerful sites for the subversion of a male-privileged gender ideology. Within the family, male authority as a fixed, gender-specific category is often more ideological than practical. None of this necessarily supports the idea, which has achieved mythic proportions, that West Indian men are irresponsible fathers, or the theory of male marginalization offered by Errol Miller in his controversial study *Men at Risk* (1991b). Sporadic presence does not constitute either erasure or total absence, especially when the valency of psychological influence is taken into account. There is both shared and divided authority, much of it fraught with angst (high levels of spousal violence indicate, among other things, that the "merger" has not been an easy one), but there is no real evidence to suggest unequivocal loss or transferral of authority from men to women.

The scenario outlined was primarily, though not exclusively, a working-class phenomenon, at least through the first six or seven decades of the twentieth century.[27] It was obviously widespread, since the working class constituted most of the population, and, in addition, many middle- and even upper-class men had outside relationships, including children, in multiple homes while their immediate family life demonstrated a more conservative, nuclear-type structure. But obviously the situation was mediated not only by class, but also by geography and demographics. In Jamaica at Emancipation, for example, there was a large number of "saltwater niggers", that is, slaves newly imported from Africa and so not yet "creolized". (The shorter the period of exposure to slavery, the greater seemed the tendency to have recourse to violence as a means of seizing freedom.) These people were also imports from the fiercer, very militarized ethnic groups, seen as the best type of slave to manage the difficult Jamaican terrain. The militant aggressiveness traditionally associated with masculinity was a characteristic of both females and males of these groups. The relatively large land space and mountainous terrain allowed for safer escapes from the plantation as well as greater accessibility of land after Emancipation as compared to the smaller territories, and these factors combined may well have accounted for the particular forthrightness and organizing tendencies of Jamaican women in exile, represented, for example, in Selvon's *The Lonely Londoners*.

In those territories where the terrain did not so easily support escape, the slave might have been more vulnerable to the assimilationist strategies by which the planter sought to deter rebellion. We might then reasonably expect in this scenario the production of genders which were more traditional than radical, but this would by no means be an unproblematic conclusion. Janet Momsen examines the post-Emancipation case of Barbados, arguing that the male-female ratio, in which females predominated, led to the creation of a peasantry which was female-based, so that in fact conditions were created for a "masculinized" womanhood (1998, 124).

With regard to the nexus of colour and class, middle-class men and women, who up to the mid-twentieth century were mostly coloured, were closer to the traditionalizing gender polarities of European culture. This was the result of education, inclination and the traces left by differential association with the master on the slave plantation. The class/colour system was a major source of the nation's iconization in patriarchal terms. The most profound feature of the nexus between gender ideology and political government is the former's participation in a network of power relations in which the economically dominant class assumes the mantle of the colonial authority in the service of the traditionalizing ethos in society.

Yet even in the dominant class, no uniform picture can be assumed in a society produced in transgression. The narrative of Mary Seacole (1857), a coloured woman in the post-Emancipation period, may have been just one individual woman's autobiography, but there is no reason to think Seacole's paradoxical rather than orthodox gender identity, which she consciously shapes as part of her overall self-invention, was by any means an isolated type among coloureds, either then, now or in the nationalist period. Seacole presents herself as an anomalous man-woman inhabiting both traditional female roles and white male English roles denoting privilege. Not only her gender identity but her itinerant lifestyle (which took her into the heart of the Crimean War), her unconventional occupation and her strategies of self-invention are strongly reminiscent of the carnivalesque masking through which slave and working-class identities were crafted and played. All of this shows her as having much in common with the experience of black women; despite her efforts to distance herself from the "Negroes", she nevertheless shares with them much paradoxically acknowledged affinity.

Seacole's narrative highlights one side of the story. Obviously, in the same way that lighter skin and middle-class origins did not necessarily predict the nature of one's gender consciousness, working-class origins did not (and does not now) necessarily mean an absence of traditional gender norms. Factors such as economics, marriage and aspirations towards a more attractive gender identity might involve working-class persons of both sexes in various activities and psychologies of "possession" (for example, black middle-class men marrying fair-skinned women, enhancing their masculine image by an investment in colour, or black working-class women after childbearing age marrying as a sign of entry into a more respectable womanhood). In every case, gender attitudes and identities are mediated by personal, social and economic expediencies.

Research on gender in the Indo- and Sino-West Indian contexts, particularly the latter, has been sparse and slow in coming. Existing studies on Indo-West Indian gender, when taken together (Bisnauth 1977; Mohammed 1993, 1995; Moore 1984, 1995; Shepherd 1986, 1995), indicate a number of important effects that the experience of indenture had on Indian gender constructions and identities. Conditions of recruitment in the home country, as well as the Middle Passage of the journey out to the territories, began the process of deconstructing rigid caste and gender hierarchies. The process was further accelerated by the large disproportion of male to female immigrants, with women in the minority, and by the fact that most of the men who came already had wives and families in India. The operation of the laws of supply and demand, the distance from structures of the home society and the refusal to mix with Afro-West Indians meant that men often had to settle for whatever woman was available, regardless of caste or perceived level of "decency".

But it also meant that women were able to negotiate relationships with men without necessarily entering into marriage, which was seen as automatically curtailing independence. Some persons hoping to return to India entered into "legal" (Western-style) marriage since they knew that back home such unions would not be considered binding. Such marriages possibly allowed a level of psychological freedom in another direction: it became more difficult for men to impose patriarchal authority on their wives, though, even so, such authority would have been more prevalent than among Afro-West Indians, who were more removed by experience, time and distance from their original homelands. The woman's experience of freedom from the visible structures of the home society, whose authority she might have accepted, also served to some extent to loosen, if not dismantle, psychological constructs which kept women in subordinate roles.

In those territories which had relatively few Indian immigrants, more miscegenation and consequently a greater absorption of the Afro-West Indian gender ethos took place. Indian women in indenture are reported to have often practised serial monogamy for reasons of economics and personal independence. This is very similar to working-class black women's practice. It is also not surprising that the early twentieth century produced a strong entrepreneurial class comprising not only males but also females of Indian stock. Fictional representations such as Ismith Khan's Binti in *The Jumbie*

Bird (1961) take note of this reality. Khan's representation of Binti's gender identity as a self-confident entrepreneur winning her own bread is focused against the companion image of Binti's estranged husband, Kale Khan, who is unable to develop the creolizing imagination the New World demands of him and who is particularly tortured by Binti's independence, which he sees as a competing performance emptying out the powers and authorities invested in him as male and husband.[28]

In those instances where marriages were contracted according to traditional Indian custom, there was significantly less flexibility. Eventual settlement instead of the initial expected repatriation meant the stabilization of Indo-West Indian communities and the concomitant re-importation and extension of traditional gender polarities, especially in those territories such as Trinidad and Guyana where a sufficiently large Indian presence facilitated the retention of distinct traditions rather than assimilation or acculturation. In such territories, the Indo-West Indian family structure remained generally stable, an extended network similar to the Afro-West Indian system, except that at the centre of the network, one was more likely to find a nuclear unit with a visible, iconic masculinity vested in the husband/spouse, who was also father. Obviously, there were wide variations even within this norm, as V. S. Naipaul's portrayal of the matriarchal Tulsi household in *A House for Mr Biswas* (1961) indicates. Even where wives were considered subordinate, they were not necessarily subservient, and women often led complex lives, deploying their own authorities and powers.[29] Generational differences also abounded, largely facilitated by the eventual entry of Indo-West Indian children into the general education system, where contact with Afro-West Indians as well as the exposure to ideas of democracy in nationalism would have played a part.

It is important to note that gender identities and relations appeared not as isolated constructs, but as an integral part of the Indo-West Indian community's larger representation of itself. Implied in this is the suggestion that the domestic gender arrangement was also the desired public representation, a means of signalling to the larger public that "we are different". In this sense, no split appeared between the private and the public presentation: the Indo-West Indian was from this angle perhaps less subject to a schizophrenic "double consciousness" than her Afro-West Indian counterpart. (As discussed in chapter 6, the anomalies of being "insiders" perceived as "outsiders" by their Afro-West Indian compatriots may well have exerted countervailing pressures that reinscribed the potential for such a double consciousness.) Implied also is the community's sense of the necessity of protecting its cultural integrity, which as a critical foundation of identity was brought under pressure by creolizing processes in the West Indies. Many a household head, like Kale Khan, might have become more rigidly patriarchal in resistance to these pressures. Double consciousness (in this case arguably schizophrenic), the resistant effort to preserve cultural identity in a monolithic way and the extent to which this effort failed at crucial junctures are all evidenced in the existence and denial in Trinidad society of the dougla, the person of mixed African and Indian blood, almost from the first meeting of the races (see, for example, Puri 1999).

Both Khan and Selvon portray in their fictions the struggle of the working-class male of the younger generation to respond in less hermetic and exclusive ways than his foreparents, to the emergent society which in the period of nationalism increasingly demanded integration and the assimilation of discourses and representations. It could be said that in the nationalist period, while Indian gender realities were changing at a psychological level in response to the creolizing pressures that helped fuel the nationalist movement, Afro-West Indian gender identities were involved in a reverse process, in which it was they that exerted the creolizing pressure against a traditionalizing gender praxis, which in turn sought to effect their suppression.

The Chinese emigrant population was considerably smaller than the Indian, and distributed among fewer territories.[30] The Chinese came in two broad strands of migration (Look Lai 1998): as indentured plantation labourers from Emancipation up to the 1880s, and as mercantile tradesmen from the 1890s to the 1940s. The latter group were attracted by the success stories of those who had either returned home solvent after indenture or who had moved into the lucrative merchant sector. They were dispersed mainly in British Guiana, Trinidad and Jamaica, with the first wave located predominantly in British Guiana and the second in Trinidad and Jamaica. The demographics of gender were similar to those of the Indians in many respects: a preponderance of males in the first instance, and an increasing trickle of women as British government policy and familial networks combined to bring over families left behind or to import spouses to arranged marriages.

Like its Indian counterpart, the Chinese community spanned the broad spectrum from integration, creolization and intermarriage to more ethnically conservative groupings and practices. The variations were as much a function of the availability of Chinese women as they were of class (dictated by degrees of wealth or lack thereof) and location, both territorial and urban/rural. The movement of most Chinese into mercantile activity and the professions meant an increasing exposure to a peculiarly Caribbean modernity, particularly in the urban areas. Gender expectations came under the instress of that modernistic consciousness – fluid, heterodox, in many ways cosmopolitan. It was not unknown for Chinese children, like Indian ones, to experience a kind of "double consciousness", as their fathers kept multiple households even as they inhabited multiple identities. One household would be that of the black or Creole "concubine" with whom he may have formed a relationship in his bachelor days as an early emigrant; the other would be the household of his arranged marriage to the Chinese wife imported specifically for the purpose. The household head was often in his official home the traditional patriarch, shifting to a more creolized, less dominant identity in the unofficial household. The children of the official household might also be brought up by a black helper, so that their own gender experience spanned various cultural expectations.

Yet, particularly in some rural areas, that ubiquitious fixture of village life, the Chinese shopkeeper, often interacted with the community without necessarily becoming integrated with it. The Chinese shop at the centre of the village became an important index of its identity and a focal meeting point where men performed manhood in rituals of drink and repartee, within the ambit of the owner's unfailingly genial apartness. Often he went outside the village to find himself a common-law partner, who allowed him to preserve the trademark mystique of the "Chinaman", the idea of an oriental form of masculinity that could not be locally deciphered.

The complexities do not end at indenture, as the West Indian gender picture is made more fluid by factors such as increasingly diversified and gender-neutral education; the continuing migration into the region of diverse groups – Middle Eastern, European (prominently featuring Portuguese), Central American and more and more East Asian, including Indian and Hong Kong Chinese, as well as phenomenal intra-regional and cross-migration of West Indian peoples. Even in the nationalist era, the West Indian gender picture was perhaps the most heterodox in the world.

Some Conclusions

We have examined a society moving through various levels of crisis, each ultimately a crisis of self-fashioning. The periods of more extreme crisis (slavery and post-Emancipation) created radical departures from orthodox gender, as people were forcibly unmoored from normative social categories and obliged to refigure themselves in new ways as social beings, both in spite of and against the colonizer's efforts to the contrary. The period of more attenuated crisis (the nationalist period, particularly the period leading up to and after Independence) saw the unorthodox gender practices generated in the earlier crises being devalued and attenuated, though not erased.

If the discussion has shown some of the strengths of a performative praxis (the fluidity of roles, the ability to cross prescribed boundaries that inhibit positive action, to transform hostility into collusive entertainment and to empty out threat and superiority by "possession" of the threatening persona through play), it has equally suggested some of the inherent dangers. These include openness to "possession" by the part being played, which might not be a bad thing at all if men, in playing women, as in the call-and-response calypsos, develop a form of empathy with women, but clearly not such a good thing if men, playing the memory of the master's masculinity, become new oppressors in that mode. The threat of a type of "schizophrenia" (split consciousness) in which one is never quite sure who one's self is, or indeed if one possesses a "self" at all (is the self contingently produced with each performance, and therefore empty outside of performance?), is not the least of the difficulties implied.

The fact that in some territories it is men who became most visible as literal "performers" is more than a function of representational codes that sought to shift women to the private sphere or that occluded their presence in the public sphere. It is perhaps more a function of economic realities. Arguably, in a context where the household arrangement is unstable (visiting partnerships, serial monogamies) and where economic hardship is an ongoing reality, women with children find themselves playing headship and breadwinning roles more consistently and inescapably than men. "Performance" shifts its meaning, taking on a seriousness, even an edge of desperation, that quickly erases the entertainment quotient. That is, performance comes to mean "doing" instead of "playing". More than this, many women may not have felt the need to "compete" (via public representations) against men, as they were already inhabiting roles that were ideologically "not theirs"; in other words, they possessed the masculinity of role for which men were – at least ritually – contending.

If women faced the threat of psychic dislocation from the gender roles they performed, this is likely to have been the result of discursive and even economic sanctions that society imposed against female "masculinity" while exerting pressures that made its acquisition possible. Psychic dislocation may also have resulted from the mismatch between the economic roles women had to play and the ideological roles they might have wished to inhabit (arguably, the role of the delicate, porcelain female can be enormously attractive when the alternative is unrelenting hard work) or which they needed to play from time to time in order to attract the attention of men (both as partners/lovers and as potential economic sources). The capacity to juggle the two competing identities, often as simultaneous acts, may be contradictorily a source of both liberation and entrapment.

For men, on the other hand, performativity may well have become a self-protective refuge in a society which exerted enormous contradictory pressures upon the male. The ideology of the male as breadwinner and household head was set against the inability to consistently perform these roles because of economic limitations. The "village ram" ideology, with its mandatory production of multiple offspring in multiple households, compounded these limitations. The sense of a self under invasion may be increased by the fact that the designated male roles are discharged by women, both with competence and with an outrage vociferously performed, where the male was seen as failing to do his part. The reveller's mask – the ritual capacity of the performance to radically recuperate and extend the self, to create multiple selves as a shifting foil against attack, to empty out the threat of the invading other and to transform pain into aesthetics – may in such circumstances be as efficacious a defence as it had been on the plantation. And yet the empathic aspect of performance as possession, with factors as diverse as the satirical rehearsal of women's voices in misogynistic calypsos and feelings of solidarity with a "suffering" mother, might lead to conscious or unconscious internalization of the (still undefined) "feminine" against which the male persona so vociferously plays.

The West Indian polity in the ascendant years of nationalism invested hugely in masculine representations linked implicitly or explicitly to male-ness. The wider social practice, as well as competing representations in popular music, literature, legend (Nanny stopping bullets with the fullness of her female rump)[31] and myth (Anancy's linguistic cross-dressing), exhibited a contradictory identity that might be better described as still showing vestiges of the hermaphroditic. It was an identity marked by the dissolution of sex-gender links in the roles performed by women and men and by an ability to cross prescribed gender boundaries in response to the economic, relationship or entertainment demands of an essentially carnivalesque society. It was an obscured hydra head: "masculine" women "playing" feminine for social and economic kudos; men playing masculine in ritual acts of self-making, using strategies that may have caused them to inhabit the ideologically feminine at conscious and unconscious levels. For the slave in resistance, the hermaphrodite was crafted for display; for the nation in becoming, the hermaphrodite lived on, still playing but discursively denied.

Part 1

Manhood, Masquerade and Social Order

Chapter 2

Representing Exile

The Flight from Gender in Selvon's *The Lonely Londoners, Moses Ascending* and *The Housing Lark*

Between Home and Away: Gender as Social Geography in Selvon's Novels

THE SELECTION OF NOVELS EXAMINED in this and the next chapter span two distinct movements in a sustained gender discourse with which Samuel Selvon's fiction is concerned. Setting – that is, the cultural environment as physical and social geography – may be the most important variable in this discourse. The "exile" novels treated here (the first three books of the London quartet – *The Lonely Londoners* [1956], *The Housing Lark* [1965] and *Moses Ascending* [1975])[1] – present nuanced variations on a single antiphonal theme: the dissolution and reconstitution of gender as a feature of migration, or particular kinds of alien spaces. The setting described in *The Lonely Londoners* – the exilic space of London's West Indian hinterworld of the 1950s – is presented as an area on the edge of chaos, a kind of twilight zone between form and dissolution. In this twilight zone, unmoored from the structures of civil society, cast adrift from all known boundaries and landmarks, Selvon's "boys" engage in psychic rituals of survival, at the heart of which is a panicked but utterly deliberate flight from gender. In the more visible, entrenched migrant community twenty years on, described in *The Housing Lark* and *Moses Ascending,* the flight from gender simply manifests in a different form, reflecting changes in the specifics but not the principle of social conditions that had encouraged flight in the first place.

It is a flight engendered not only by the dissolution of the social world which was the colonial immigrant's lot in Britain of the 1950s, but also by the ethic of performance – that is to say, the performativity by which West Indian men had, in their home societies, confronted the invention of masculinity as a way of delaying rigidities and, ironically, certainties of self. Selvon explores the liberating and recuperative aspects of that performative ethos; however, by and large, the boys seem more trapped in its latent negativities than empowered by its positive potential. This is in itself something of a paradox given the open-ended nature of the Selvon narrative, the implicit suggestion that what appears as entrapment may in fact be a necessary space of predication for survival and growth.

In antiphonal relation to the boys' flight from gender, Selvon explores an idea of female resource, both personal and communal, that allows his women characters to reconstitute and reconfigure West Indian social structures in the exilic space and, in so doing, to both manage and transform the new environment in which they find themselves. Their modus operandi is radically different from that of the male characters, and is marked by the aggressive authoritativeness assigned to men in orthodox ideologies. Rooted in paradox, and cloaked in mystery because of the absence of any attempt to explain this male-female difference, Selvon's representation of women as an odd, consistent and feminized masculinity, both in their individual personae and in their communal strategies, is sustained not only in the exile novels, but across the entire body of his fictions.

By contrast, the masculinity of men is changeful, vulnerable and endlessly in need of rehearsal and negotiation as an aspect of performance evoked within specified, distinct geographies that to some extent compel these responses. Thus there is a marked shift from the boys' flight from gender in the exile novels, to an idea of its inescapability in the "novels of home" (*A Brighter Sun, Turn Again Tiger*) discussed in chapter 3. The difference lies in the fact that "home" is a socially structured world, whose structure presumes containment. In the world view of Selvon's texts, a simple, self-evident truth is made to do significant work: namely, that gender can be predicated only within "ordered" society – that is, where one is acknowledged and therefore implicated in existing codes of responsibility and governance. The glide between social presence as both responsibility and entrapment, in the novels of home, and social absence as both freedom and entrapment, in the novels of exile, is only one of the nuances in the amazing range that Selvon brings to his representation of gender as a form of dissonance.

This idea of dissonance arises directly out of the crises of the nationalist period: its anomalous demands; its racial and ethnic difficulties; its economically and ideologically driven migrations to a putative mother/ fatherland which in a profound sense had no space of accommodation; its strangely paradoxical regional identity that seemed to be more quickly discovered in exile, in the place of scattering, than at home. Yet in Selvon's work we see no ideological – or, for that matter, direct – engagement with nationalism, a factor for which he has on occasion been roundly criticized (for example, Birbalsingh [1977] 1988; Joseph 1992). His fictions depend on an acute observation, an almost apolitical naturalism in the rendering of lived experience – not in the sense of attempting mimesis (Selvon's subtlety as an artist precludes such simplifications), but in the sense of seriously investing in that doubly fictive construct of the realist novel: the strategy of the "absent author". (This becomes contradictory and delightfully ironic in texts totally shot through with the West Indian author's calypsonian performance.)

The issues of nationalism in Selvon's work are to be found less as overt treatment in the texts and more in the historical context (the larger field of shared texts and processes) out of which both the texts and their readers are produced. So the nationalist issues come to the fore out of the repertoire of knowledge the Caribbean reader brings to the reading, yet, as will appear, they are at the very heart of the dissonantal gender picture that Selvon paints. Outside of that nationalist history, neither the litanies of anguish beneath the texts' ritual laughter nor their carnival mas(k)querade of genders can be adequately explained.

The Lonely Londoners: Boys Fly, Women Disappear

It is in the first book of the exile quartet, *The Lonely Londoners,* that we see the most sustained reflection on the fact that gender belongs to ordered society. That is to say, gender is one strand in a wider, complex network of social identities, relations and responsibilities within which it is predicated and without which, conversely, it does not exist. The absence of society is both a precondition for and an invitation to the dissolution of gender. Selvon's West Indian men in London (to whom he refers across the quartet as "the boys", suggesting already a pre-gender category) are cast adrift in a situation in which though they are circumscribed by a social structure – that is, British society; they are not part of that structure. In Selvon's representation, absence here is twofold: not only an absence from society, but also an absence *of* it, since London as a *social* world, though peripherally implied on the edges of the boys' hinterspace, never puts in a material appearance; the reader assumes it as something that must exist, precisely because of its absence. In addition to this absence of a present world, the structures within which the boys had lived in the islands have been dissolved both materially and psychologically, so that there is also an absence of home as a recuperative resource.

Absence in the psychological sense is to be understood both as banishment – an active process of admission to consciousness followed by rejection – and as amnesia, the absolute not-knowledge which represents (deliberate) sublimation below consciousness. A sense emerges of Selvon's boys not only as victims of a social condition of structurelessness, but also as its deliberate perpetuators – that is, as colluding and investing in its continuation. The behaviours of West Indian social life are performed in their loosest, most rudimentary form, and nostalgia – the desire for home – most often appears subsumed beneath its own absence. When it does directly appear, it does so as the recalcitrance of suppressed memory and is recuperated and dismissed by a number of strategies of escape, including verbalization: "Boy, you know what I want to do? I want to go to Trinidad and lay down in the sun and dig my toes, and eat a fish broth and go Maracas Bay and talk to them fishermen, and all day long I sleeping under a tree, with just the old sun for company . . . that is the life for me, boy . . . no ballet and opera and symphony" (114). But the thought is quickly suppressed: " 'You know,' Galahad say, 'last year I had a feeling to go back too, but I forget about it. It aint have no prospects back home, boy' " (114).

The verbal strategies for escape acquire the nature of a compulsion, forming extended patterns of repetition, litany and rehearsal that give parts of the novel much the shape of a ritual performance. In the following extended sequence, the composite persona's voice inscribes both a sense of moorings lost and the evasion of an unwelcome desire for the safety of known structures:

> Hello boy, what happening.
> So what happening, man, what happening.
> What happening, what happening, man.
> What the arse happening, lord?
> Every year he vowing to go back to Trinidad, but after the winter gone . . . is as if

it still have another chance. I will wait until after the summer, the summer does really be hearts.

But it reach a stage, and he know it reach that stage, where he get so accustom to the pattern that he can't do anything about it. Sure, I could do something about it, he tell himself, but he never do anything. (124–25)

Perspective (narrative voice) is in *The Lonely Londoners* a complex construct, gliding, as in the sequence just quoted, between the inner consciousness of composite, sometimes multiple personae and the consciousness of Moses as observer-participant and as metaphor for this entire group of men unmoored. (Moses himself never becomes a narrative voice; rather, narrative is transmuted through his consciousness by an unseen speaker, a ventriloquist existing on his mind's inner edge. There is even a sense of the narrator as voyeur, or audience looking in, and out.) In the verbal strategies of advance and retreat around social memory, these unassigned narrative voices, taken together, indicate both the sense of namelessness (loss of identity) and the idea of a collective disintegration that in itself becomes identification. In London, this is what characterizes the boys as West Indians.

The effect is reinforced by the endless Sunday morning "limes" in Moses's room. These turn out to be another strategy to recuperate nostalgia, a quasi-religious ritual described in terms of church, priesthood and confession (122) but whose aimless, directionless verbal sequences of gossip and ennui indicate something else: the "limes" constitute a reduction to the most primitive kind of structure within which human intercourse can functionally exist. By their repetitiveness, their lack of variation, they also appear to be as much as the boys are willing to invest in social systemization – they are, in fact, an escape to the outer limits of society. The sense of social disjunction is heightened rather than diminished by the religious metaphor, especially when placed against the despairing cry of the anonymous narrator's "How many Sunday mornings gone like that?" It is as though Moses had become the high priest of psychic loss, in an unfunny parody of the most communal of rituals.

The life in London's West Indian underworld is a drifter's life, yet, paradoxically, these men who have been reduced to "boys" are circumscribed in work, which, again as ritual performance, is pictured in almost formulaic sequences of repetition across the novel: "Ten years, papa, ten years the old man in Brit'n and what to show for it? What happen during all that time? From winter to winter, summer to summer, work after work" (113). This is replicated across the sequences of *Moses Ascending,* but in terms of a frightening, impersonal systemization which shows the boys as cogs locked in the wheel of the vast machine that is British industry:

> What is that heavy football on the cold damp pavement before the rest of the world is awake? . . . It is the black man. He is the first passenger of the day. He is the harbinger who will put the kettle on to boil. He holds the keys of the city, and he will unlock the door and tidy the papers on the desk, flush the loo, straighten the chairs, hoover the carpet. He will press switches and stack boxes. He will empty dustbins and ashtrays and stack boxes. He will peel the spuds. He will sweep the halls and grease the engines. (6)

It becomes clear that these boys are individuals in a state of permanent social crisis.

But the experience of crisis has its most important repercussions at the psychological level. Ira De Reid, in *The Negro Immigrant* (1969), his study of black immigrants in the United States, addresses a critical phenomenon which occurs as a result of the absence of structures – social and economic – in the life of the immigrant: "The foreign born worker does not accept the necessity [of doing low-class jobs] without a struggle. His new job is seldom in his old line, it is always more hurried and harried than it was when he was a worker at home. Security on the job is relatively unknown – the job exists from week to week, and planning becomes impossible. *Yet this very atmosphere creates a new personal type. Eventually the immigrant does not worry,* because sooner or later he will either find something else, go into a business of his own, or return home" (119, emphasis added). De Reid's analysis suggests the migrant experience as a form of Middle Passage, or a crucible of opposing possibilities. The immigrant either succumbs to a passive assimilation into directionless hope, the only focus of which is the most rudimentary of survivals and which barely masks disintegration, or develops a psychological resistance rooted in a creative imaging of the future as a fluid set of possibilities which he has the power to appropriate at any given moment. In other words, De Reid's "new personal type" has learnt to live on the edge of an identity not so much already constituted as it is ready at any moment to be configured in new directions, on one side or the other of the paradox. The ground he inhabits, like the slave's, is at once a state of limbo and a foetal space.

Selvon's boys are locked on the side of limbo. For the most part, as the passages quoted above illustrate, they are involved in the harried, hurried activity surrounding work which De Reid mentions. Whether it is in search of work, escape from work or going to work, work represents the highest level of structure in their lives. It is by implication casual, directionless work, unlinked to any project of responsibility such as the upkeep of families back home or the effort to bring families left behind to England, as was common among the migrant generation of the period (R. B. Davidson 1966; Hall 1988; Marshall 1987; Richardson 1983). The exception to this pattern of behaviour in *The Lonely Londoners* is the Jamaicans, who appear as an odd subset, bringing family and social structure with them, and who therefore soon drop out of the general circle. (R. B. Davidson's sociological profile of Jamaican migrants [1966] corresponds with Selvon's portrayal, but there are many eyewitness accounts of Jamaicans going insane in 1950s Britain.) The boys' overriding concern is to escape worry – by fantasies of the type indicated by De Reid, by the verbal parodies of ritual that both function to hold them in a state of bearable stasis and to delay the necessity of confronting home or by the relation to work, from which escape is effected via immersion in sexual activity. The repetitiveness of reference to sexual activity in fact assumes the nature of yet another ritual.

Significantly, when we first meet the boys in *The Lonely Londoners,* their entrapment in crisis does not seem to involve any process of psychological disengagement from the known structures of a prior world in the islands. It is as though this conflictual process of disengagement has not taken place at all or, if it has, it has done so in a space outside the action of the novel, between shipboard and arrival. In other words, then, we encounter them as the already constituted "new personal type", frozen in the acceptance of limbo, a kind of instance of forgetting as "not-knowing", and "not-knowing" as psychic shock. It is only much later – as though the resistant residue of memory had crept up on them – that we come to realize that in fact this is the manifestation of a sense that it is futile to think about home, a banishment rather than a literal forgetting. The passages of verbal recuperation belong to these later scenes, and in these passages, what appears to be suppressed is not only the thought of home, but also the thought of structured society itself, exemplified in Moses's declaration in which marriage becomes metonymic for such society: "Boy when I see thing like that happening to other people I decide I would never married" (115).

What Selvon's text portrays is the indescribable panic of the moment of arrival, without the charts, maps or compasses, the monumental panoply of myth and monarchy with which a voyager such as Columbus could ritualize his own panic into the certainties of empire (and even Columbus's efforts were at best highly equivocal, as the confused strategies of recuperation in his diaries show [Columbus 1969; Greenblatt 1991]). At this stage in the 1950s migration cycle, the boys are also without the critical mass (the numerical power) or the absolute knowledge of having entered an enemy zone which had informed the slave from the outset that war and recovery were the only choice. The West Indian migrant, already a creature of paradox, arrives in Britain at the heart of a contradiction: to a putative parent who has issued an invitation, only to find himself abandoned. The extended moment of arrival is an extended moment of panic, a hesitation, a stammering and, finally, flight. Escape masks pain; the mask becomes a way of deflecting confrontation with the self. It is in the space left vacant by this deflection and retreat that gender is constructed as absence in *The Lonely Londoners.*

If anyone appears to perform the certainties and unquestionable authorities (including economic authority) associated with orthodox masculinity, it is the extraordinarily paradoxical city, which is also the quintessential female whore. England's presentation as masculine (paternal) authority was already established in the colonies as a kind of exotic myth. It was an exoticism based not on alienness or difference, but on an endlessly performed absence, via the products, symbols and ideas of England that were sown in the territories and took root in the colonial consciousness through the public institutional system. One was induced or forced to succumb to the imperatives produced by this paternal authority, whether by obedience, accommodation, resistance or rebellion.

An opposite, anomalous effect of this systemization of deferred signs was the breeding of a kind of pre-experiential nostalgia. England as deferred desire constantly beckoned, more as (female) siren than as father, so that the mother/fatherland becomes a kind of incestuous androgyne of the imagination. The image of England as siren is easily redrawn and reinforced on her own soil, where desire is never fulfilled though the desirer is constantly seduced. These issues are very subtle in Selvon's text, delicately placed in the subtext as nuances of suggestion, as in the remarkable stream-of-consciousness passages in which the city, both by her liminal beauties (often hidden in fog) and by virtue of the loose sexual encounters that take place within her body, transmutes into a whore the boys cannot resist (85ff, 121ff).

The irony here is the boys' acquiescence in their own seduction, born of a sense of the futility of attempting a more "respectable" relationship, in which London might have become a "woman of honour". As it is, the city's whoredom accommodates (suits with) the flight and the terror of more ordered ways – terror and flight which she herself has engendered. Not only the flight from sanctioned manhood among the boys, but the virtual absence of women except in casual sexual encounters is an immediately striking factor in *The Lonely Londoners.* This latter fact stands over against the historical data which show that by the time of the 1962 Immigration Act, the West Indian female population in Britain had almost equalled the male population. This means there was steady immigration of women over the period in which the novel is set. In a text which pays close attention to social and demographically nuanced detail, the absence of stable relationships with women appears to be more than an artistic invention – it is a portrayal of reality.

The casualness of encounters with women is linked to the dissolution of any connection between work and economic responsibility for woman or family, which are so important in West Indian gender ideology. This is graphically illustrated by the oddly rhapsodic, despairing stream-of-consciousness passage in which Moses portrays the unreal, exoticized world the boys inhabit in summer when they go in search of sexual encounters: ". . . the boys making contact and having big times with the girls working during the day and coming round by the yard in the evening for a cuppa and to hit one or two but anyone of Moses encounter is big episode because coasting about the water it ain't have no man with a sharper eye than he not even Cap . . . and one summer evening he was walking when he spot a number . . ." (87). The linkage of work and sexual escapades in the same "sentence" ("the girls working during the day and coming . . . for a cuppa") indicates their relationship as aspects of a cycle of dis-anchoring; the stream of consciousness with its dissolution of "ordered" sentence contours inscribes the dissolution of, and flight from, ordered society.

But in this scenario where the boys seem to have constructed a work/sex equation as the avoidance of gender responsibilities, both the sexual self-indulgence and the acceptance of work may be seen as a curious honouring of gender in the breach. Prolific sex with countless women (in *Moses Ascending,* Moses recalls that he had over a hundred in his *Londoners* days) makes use of the "village ram" persona but without its corollaries of prolific fatherhood or authority over women; that is to say, the construct is unravelled, stripped of its threatening systematization, which spells (paradoxically responsible) masculinity, and raided for that single aspect that will convert pain into pleasure. Sex becomes a kind of perverse aesthetic of self-unravelling.

In somewhat similar fashion, the use of work to escape the responsibilities implied in orthodox manhood indicates the knowledge of this concept as something expected by society. But this knowledge must be rejected, or negatively responded to, for the assumption of manhood in these terms becomes an intolerable burden in the situation in which the exiled West Indians find themselves. The odds are stacked against a successful appropriation of any socially acceptable form of gender that the boys might have known from home, and the psychological space to create new, healthier ones in the void seems unavailable. The freedom to create identity occupies the same psychological moment as the fear of failure; consequently, neither the fear nor the social expectation is admitted to consciousness.

This explains the boys' refusal to conceive of women as gendered individuals. The words they substitute for "woman" consistently dissolve gender and reconstruct woman as a metonym for transience, incapable of holding a man down. Woman is an activity of the moment (sport); a creature in flight (bird); an indefinite and therefore scarcely perceivable object (thing); a passing vessel in a changeful sea (craft); a manipulable cipher in the uncertainty of a gamble (number). Woman is produced in a reductive process which throws her back on her biological sex (all these terms being metaphors for sex object), and the reductive process is carried one step further by the linguistic removal of the latent threat of gender implied in biology (women want relationship; crafts and birds sail or fly away). Only in this way can the female – the incipient threat of gender and ordered society – be re-assimilated and accommodated. These casual encounters cannot be finally equated with the prodigal, prolific and promiscuous sexuality associated with the village ram in West Indian society, for they erase an audience/community of women who are to be impressed and within whose psyche the self-congratulatory masculinity must be enacted and validated.

In this context, it is significant that all encounters are with white women. Black women appear as shadows in the stream-of-consciousness celebration of sexual encounters with prostitutes, but even as prostitutes they represent the threat of responsibility, since they may at any moment decide they want to become serious. (In the economic pragmatism of these women, prostitution is clearly only an interim measure until "something better", such as an economically viable man, turns up.) Tellingly, the narrator informs us that black prostitutes are avoided on principle: "[I]t have a lot of dark women who in the racket too they have to make a living . . . but . . . a spade wouldn't hit a spade when it have so much other talent on parade" (91).

The white woman, prostitute or otherwise, poses no threat as there is little or no possibility of socially acceptable relations with her. In fact, the possibility is so remote that gender as responsibility can be admitted to consciousness in relation to the white woman, and even temporarily assumed. This is well illustrated when Cap, the Nigerian who becomes one of the boys, disrupts the trajectory by which marriage to his Frenchwoman would have inducted him into traditional roles in society. Cap is quite happy to become a husband since he intends his wife to be the breadwinner. The assumption of gender roles poses no problem because of the nature of the assumption: the roles are assumed in reversal and so effectively deconstructed.

The white woman, by her continuing *temporary* presence, helps to keep ordered society at bay. A certain amount of irony is leached out of the intersection of race and gender: the boys would like to think that they are the ones keeping the white women under containment, but a chagrined Moses discovers differently (92). Quite simply, to the women the boys are sexual exotica, neither more nor less than they themselves are to the boys. So the women become amenable to containment (if they are simply enjoying the exotica, they will not impose unwanted structures of responsibility) only because of their own agendas, and not because of the boys' actions. Any lingering idea of male superiority is levelled, and the image of masculinity is further unravelled.

Despite the boys' strenuous efforts, the threat of black women refuses to be contained. This is exemplified in the advent of family in the persons of Tanty and of Lewis and his wife Agnes – all relatives of Tolroy the Jamaican. Tanty is the type of the Caribbean "matriarch": tough, cantankerous, aggressive, supremely competent, blissfully *de trop* and therefore marvellously subversive; above all, she is possessed of a reforming zeal which is the very essence of social order, albeit social order in an iconoclastic mode. Far from being in flight from society, Tanty brings it with her, as aggression, opposition and argument against the British establishment. Tanty becomes the carnivalesque face of Caribbean ordering which is really anti-order. In short, Tanty is sheer out-of-orderness. She proceeds to attack the British system and to impose Caribbean social system on British economic activity, establishing herself as an authority in its transactions; before the Jewish shopkeeper knows what has hit him, he has begun to give "trus" (to allow goods on credit), seemingly unaware of the larger implications.

And where, for the boys, language may be considered a signifier of psychic disintegration, Tanty's non-stop clatter of tongues quickly imposes a kind of social and psychological order, signified in the changed relationships of the neighbourhood with herself at the centre. The re-speaking of the boundaries of social intercourse are tellingly inscribed: "[A]nd even the English people calling she Tanty" (62). Her management of domestic relations is equally dramatic. When she encourages Lewis's wife to leave him and subsequently take him to court for spousal abuse, Tanty is in effect not only reimposing ordered society upon the boys' experience by having recourse to the systems by which society protects its relations and institutions, she is also insisting on gender relations within guidelines that take women's equality as read.

Tanty inserts herself into the narrative even as she inserts herself into the dance against the boys' feeble, if horrified, effort at containment: she is the only female who is accorded lengthy treatment, as though the narrator had been thrust aside ("Don't push!" [98]) and Tanty had taken over to write her part of the story in her own hand. The attempt to consign Tanty to oblivion rather than to nostalgically embrace her, when placed alongside the final stream-of-consciousness expression of bewitchment by the city, inscribes an important reality: that the boys would rather live in the amorphous, disintegrative presence of the city than face the alternative of "going back home" that Tanty represents.[2] That is, the city, configured as a retreat from order, becomes a haven; women, insofar as they bring with them cultural constructs which must be escaped, represent a threat which ultimately becomes part of the condition of being "woman". Indeed, this is part of the basis on which the city may be read as the boys' ideal female, a loose woman accommodating all forms of looseness within her amorphous embrace.

The boys' effort at containment is of course handicapped by Tanty's status as an older woman. No such obstacles to the containment of the young black woman appear. As with the white woman, the attempt is made linguistically, but in a startlingly different way: black women are made to share the same designation as black men; they too are "spades". The designation removes the young black woman's sexuality, which is in this context her most threatening characteristic. The white woman is deconstructed in the space of the body; the black woman is not allowed a body at all. It is here that the significance of the fact that the boys do not have sex with black women is fully seen. It is also in the relation to women, at the intersection of race, sex and gender in *The Lonely Londoners,* that language takes on its most significant role: as an agent of unstructuring. This is diametrically opposed to its traditional West Indian role of restructuring, which is in fact imaged in the "linguistic extravaganza"[3] of the novel's narrative style.

The Lonely Londoners may be described as a text of verbal musics: ballads, movements, episodes, litanies of ritual, contrapuntal choral performances – a virtuoso calypsonian performance in a constructed Creole reflecting the Rabelaisian range of the West Indian speech-music tradition. Selvon's linguistic performance constantly reminds us of the insurrectional quotient of this speech-music tradition, of its double capacity to demolish and recreate. We have seen where it is on the demolition side – expressed in the unproductive litanies of ritual and the verbal unstructuring of gender – that the boys exhibit a memory of the tradition. Their aim is to extend a space of absence by filling it not so much with silence as with noise, a drowning out. However, the more creative possibilities of insurrectional speech are exhibited, beyond Tanty, in the fictive narrator's voice, which both systematizes the loose episodic narratives within the body of the text and provides the contrast to the repetitive fragmentation, the stunned stammer of the boys' conversations in Moses's room. It is also the voice that laughs (*The Lonely Londoners* is as funny as it is painful), invoking the comic aspect of the carnival, the ritual of transformation whereby tragedy is disguised, diffracted and diffused.

That the boys have in the extended moment of panic forgotten or abandoned these creative possibilities of their own language traditions as a way of restructuring social space is indicated in the fact that the narrative voice is always just on the edge of Moses's consciousness, never quite making the full glide to become Moses himself. (A contrast might be made with Lamming's *The Emigrants,* in which the character's stammer is the stammer of beginning self-articulation, the stringent effort to speak oneself into the terms by which "[you] make a man o' youself" in the face of exile.) Linguistic masquerade as a way of traversing the liminal space, the place of hiding, behind which the process of self-elaboration is accomplished and protected, is deconstructed and abandoned. Yet it is invoked within the text by the "masked" narrator's voice – "masked" because it refuses to reveal itself as any particular voice, except as a voice of possibility.

The masquerade is also invoked in the contrast between the boys' ritual as Penelope's skein (weaving as unravelling, and in this sense a parody of the carnival, which is a form of ritual and which constructs simultaneously as it dissolves) and in the text's use of ritual as a form of aesthetic, reinforcing the idea of performative possibilities that the boys had left behind. As will be discussed later, the major subversive implications of a novel written in (calypsonian) Trinidad Creole, open to induction into the English literary tradition of the 1950s, are taken up as a theme in *Moses Ascending,* in ways that put a more ameliorative if also more ambiguous spin on Selvon's presentation of West Indian masculinities in the space of exile.

Near the end of *The Lonely Londoners,* Moses admits ordered society to consciousness in order to reject it. It is here he contemplates the rootlessness and despair which circumscribe the boys' lives and decides "I would never married" (115). That this is more than a refusal of serious relations with women is made explicit when the narrator says, "he get so accustom to the pattern that he can't do anything about it" (125). In fact, Moses constantly links woman and home as belonging to the same untenable paradigm. The last sentence of the novel inscribes a desire for female companionship but simultaneously inscribes its negation, in the succinct use of the word "not": "[I]t was the sort of night that if you wasn't making love to a woman you feel you was the only person in the world like that" (125). The subtlety of "wasn't" is oddly reminiscent of the passages in which home is admitted and denied, so that gender and home appear as twin faces of entrapment.

Moses Ascending: In the Face of Woman and Society, a Singular Man

Where in *The Lonely Londoners* gender is configured as flight predicated upon society's absence, in the sequel, *Moses Ascending,* it is the reverse – flight predicated upon society's insistently encroaching presence – that shapes the narrative's main action. But here the flight is ambivalent, displaying signs of attraction and retreat, seeking to elaborate its terms both within and against the social frame. The context is important: this is London twenty years on; the migrants have either settled, repatriated, gone mad or continued to drift, and a new generation, signified for Moses by bevies of nubile girls sporting disturbingly sensual behinds, has been born on British soil. Moses has been around long enough and earned enough to feel that he must now make a conscious decision as to the terms of his way in this world that he has orbited for over twenty years.

Still within the mode of escape (the habits of twenty years do not disappear overnight, especially where they have brought their own, albeit dubious, pleasures) but wanting the security and above all the respectability that protects a man of advancing years, Moses embarks on a self-making performance that evokes a completely carnival laughter, shifting on the edge of hilarity and tears. His aim is to recreate himself as a completely personal kind of man, outside the control of social forces (the *mana* of the gods), particularly the West Indian ones that beat insistently at his door, threatening to undermine his strategies of escape. But the social environment proves resistant to Moses's new self-directed identity.

For one thing, it is a heterodox and therefore highly contradictory environment, in which British orthodoxy and establishment clash and live side by side with deviance, militancy and other forms of challenge from the now-intertwined Asian and West Indian communities. Moses wishes to stay on the side of British orthodoxy, which in his colonized imagination spells respectability, even while he seeks to retain a complete independence of self. His plan is to appropriate those aspects of an English masculine identity that he finds attractive and discard those that are inconvenient to the life of pleasure without responsibility which he wishes to continue to live. The contradiction between seeking to merge assimilation with total personal freedom and seeking to live a completely new life on the continuum of the old is only a small part of the complex of ironies on which *Moses Ascending* is constructed.

Further levels of incongruity arise from the strategies by which Moses seeks to construct this idiosyncratic identity. These are the strategies of West Indian performance and performativity which had appeared forgotten by the boys in *The Lonely Londoners* (though their continuing possibility had been adumbrated by Selvon's structuring of the narrative voice as a calypsonian performer drawing together and making sense of their multiple, fragmented narratives). Yet the strategies are used to construct a narrative of self that denies his West Indian connections and responsibilities: Moses wants nothing to do with West Indians lest they drag him back down to the depths of unrespectability. Moses the new man is writing his Memoirs, in the finest Victorian tradition, his perspective that of the distanced ethnographer surveying from on high those "others" (the West Indians) who must perforce be included to add "local colour".

But the subversion of Moses's project is not simply that the old ties of heart and habit draw him inexorably back into the West Indian community he seeks to avoid. It is also, finally, that he has no memoirs outside of his native culture, and more so that they are memoirs of an experience *that is in the process of being constructed* – that is to say, this new self that he declares, is being made, in the present tense, against, within and as an inextricable part of the community he denies. *Moses Ascending*, the story of Moses's attempted flight from the community, is the Memoir itself; Selvon places himself merely as ventriloquist redactor. This graphically illustrates the fact that the West Indian world Moses succeeds in describing becomes the canvas on which the picture of himself must be drawn, that is, the context of possibility for the picture's existence. The simultaneity of the constructions – the man and the cultural milieu, the Memoir and its subject matter – points to that peculiar West Indian form of dissonance in which the projects of social and personal creation must be accomplished together. In Moses's case, the self constructed as escape heightens the dissonance, since the shaping society recognized as necessity is also the society rejected, and therefore, ultimately, the self rejected.

If Moses's relation to himself as a West Indian man is fraught with paradox and contradiction, so too is his attempt to play aspects of the English lord of the "mansions" (his word for the derelict house he acquires in Shepherd's Bush, and by which he identifies himself as a propertied landlord, an English gentleman of the highest echelons, symbolized in his occupation of the attic, aggrandizingly rechristened "the penthouse"). The terms by which he appropriates an upper-class Englishman's identity are intended to exploit its privileges and refuse the concomitant responsibilities, so that his relation to English society becomes ambivalent and ultimately self-subversive. Not only does his refusal of responsibility finally cause him to lose the authority of the house to his illiterate white servant Bob, but his construction of Britain as a holding frame for his new identity is defeated by that other would-be symbol of his Britishness, the Memoirs.

The Memoirs are to serve a double function: to induct Moses into the Britishness that he claims and to prove the existence of the latter prior to induction. The test is to be his virtuoso use of the Queen's register; however, it turns out to be a glorious massacre of a range of English literary and West Indian folk registers, grammars, vocabularies and genres – in other words, a West Indian linguistic romp: syncretic, hybridic, creolizing, but royal only in its self-aggrandizing aspiration, a form of comic inversion. For Moses is not content to be just any kind of upper-class Englishman, but must be a Renaissance one, spanning ranges all the way up to kingship. He is slave owner, travel writer, owner of "mansions", gentleman of leisure, commander of servants, *seigneur du* (sexual) *droit,* colonial educator (complete with doggerel rhymes for the enlightenment of the native, Bob, once he learns of the latter's illiteracy) and, above all, linguistic monarch – an aspiration pointed in the exquisite irony of his declaration, "I am not a man of words." Subversively, the man of words is not only the idealized West Indian folk masculinity, but also the one who wins the Calypso King's crown (Moses does in fact win the Costume Band prize in the later *Moses Migrating*).

In effect, Moses's linguistic decimation of the Queen's English functions as a deconstruction of the idea of Britain itself, and removes Britain as a form of "holding society" for himself. It is easy, on the surface, to see the ironies, parodies and satirical ripostes of *Moses Ascending* purely as authorial mockery of Moses's assimilation bid, but we have here a complexly double-visioned text, which makes it difficult to assume that Moses is generally unaware of the subversiveness of his own voice. Repeatedly he insists that his text is vintage Queen's, in spite of hilarious evidence to the contrary, but the possibility of a deadpan, tongue-in-cheek aspect to Moses's declaration constantly confronts us. Any easy conclusion that he speaks out of ignorance is problematized by his highly sophisticated vocabulary, the perfect standard English of the letter he writes to Jeannie and his knowledge and use of an amazing range of literary giants and genres: Shakespeare, Wordsworth (rendered with characteristic self-aggrandizement as his "pal Billy Wordsworth"), Kipling, the ballad, the traveller's tale, the epic poem, figures of Greek myth (including, malappropriately, Eccles and Pollock), Victorian belles lettres, the autobiographical journal, the King James Version of the Bible, Augustan satire (often directed, with Anancy's forked tongue, as much against British as against West Indian). His is in effect a commonwealth of linguistic expression. Surely, as a metonym of geopolitical reach, it is the Queen's English. The Queen's English indeed stands out in delicious double subversion against the King's, for by far the majority of the genres Moses inhabits are directly associated with the narrative forms that proliferated during the colonial centuries and through which European male subjectivities as well as imperial identity were constructed.

It seems clear that the novel's double voice – the cloaked authorial double player ventriloquizing and mocking Moses's pretensions from behind, and Moses's own deliberate linguistic playing – function to erase the society he claims he wants to join, by undermining British claims to linguistic "purity". (The linguistically hybrid text exists as a "memoir" in English, Moses exists as an insertion into the British speech community, on English soil.) Indeed, language as deconstructive agency exposes the anomaly at the heart of Moses's desire: to seek to insert himself into the society is essentially to seek to change it radically, even to destroy it, so that a new, resistant order may emerge. But the new order Moses craves is one that denies all forms of socially imposed structure, as he himself informs us in his first extended diatribe against the demands of both the British and the blacks. In the end, what he espouses is a form of absence, a continued flight from society and its ideas of what a man should be: "I didn't have anything to do with black power, nor white power, nor any fucking power but my own. Why is it that a man can't make his own decisions, and live in peace without all this interference [from black and white do-gooders]?" (14).

Moses is also fully aware, as evidenced by his slippages into bitter reflection on the treatment of blacks, that he is "playing mas" on the edges of a society that neither sees nor accepts him. The house in Shepherd's Bush functions as an isolated island; when he ventures outside, he comes to the attention of the authorities in the only guise they are capable of envisaging him as – a black nuisance blot on the British landscape. In the police raids on Black Power meetings, where he inadvertently gets involved, he is forced to realize that no distinction is made between either male or female or types of man (95, 97). As on the slave plantation, a spade is a spade is a spade. Assimilation is possible only where the "receiving" society is willing to receive, and Britain clearly is not willing. But more than this, what Moses is seeking cannot really be termed assimilation. What he craves is the establishment's recognition, and therefore legitimation, of his Afro-Saxon persona, which is a radical and untenably disruptive persona. Both by his own deconstructive agency and according to British race and class mores, Moses the English gentleman is a man unmoored, without a context.

The man of pastiche – Moses's multiple playing selves – turns out to be a map of West Indian male society. The carnival masquerade of words and personae images the space of paradox within which a man could either be made or unmade in the act of performative representation. Moses's disparate ambitions and his strategies for achieving them speak to an amazing capacity for adaptability and survival, because of a willingness to become whatever is necessary in order to negotiate the lived environment. He himself points out that he had possessed that capacity even from the days of *The Lonely Londoners,* when he had been able to cross not only many roles as a man but also barriers between masculine and feminine, in order to facilitate the boys' survival strategy of flight and escape: "I have been mentor and mediator, antagonist and protagonist, father and mother too, a man for all seasons and reasons" (44).

The bid to assimilate iconic British masculine personae into himself, and particularly his love affair with the mask of the overseer/Great House owner, may be signs of the retarding psychic legacy that troubled the nationalist West

Indies, but Moses is not simply a man troubled by this legacy. He is a man who *chooses* it – that is, who gives consent to it as his guiding principle. But even here, Selvon, an invariably compassionate writer, tempers judgement with the humane quality that is perhaps his most visible form of ideology. That a new kind of man is pressured into being in the migrant context is obvious. But that Moses is not willing to consider as part of this new "original" manhood the social responsibility made so much of by the nationalist writers (although he himself is an aspiring author) is more than the sign of a colonized mentality; it is also, quite simply, the result of psychic and emotional exhaustion. As he repeatedly tells us, the role of the man for all seasons and reasons that he had played in the early migrant days has taken out of him all he felt he had to give, so that he fears he may be left destitute.

The "sheer terror" to which Moses confesses (35) might for the reader so easily have gone unremarked beneath the "kiff kiff laughter", the pseudo-carnival masquerade under which panic is disguised in *The Lonely Londoners*. Selvon here strikes a personal key, a note of private suffering, that is not always apparent in the more ideologically driven fictions of the period. In declaring the individual's need for a space of accommodation, Moses again points to the schizophrenic potential of the pressures of nationalism, which were obviously compounded for that first generation of very young migrant men, who arrived as Columbuses without landmarks and without secure boundaries or protective familial relationships.

Moses's relationship with his white batman, Bob, represents the first critical shift in his personal and social relations, and is the most elaborated aspect of his new Afro-Saxon manhood. This relationship is the first and only indication of cross-race relations among men, either in *The Lonely Londoners* or in *Moses Ascending* (and, incidentally, in *Moses Migrating* as well – that is to say, in the entire trilogy spanning the decades of Moses's life in Britain). The relationship sharply highlights the criteria for entry into the more authoritative forms of manhood. Moses's possession of money, and Bob's lack of it, overturns the unquestioned superiority conferred on the white man by race, but only where class, and particularly literacy as a feature of class, is also a factor. (Bob, being illiterate, is in Moses's employ presumably because it is difficult for him to gain employment in a white establishment.)

Moses, not only as employer but as the employer of a private factotum, is able to inhabit a form of white manhood (subversively carnivalized though that may be by his idiosyncratic rewriting of its terms and his man-of-speech performativity), while Bob is increasingly made a "lesser man" by a series of socially coded displacements. Each aspect of Moses's "superior" manhood is imagined against a corresponding image of Bob: Crusoe to Man Friday, sexual athlete to aspiring (inept) village ram, gentleman to valet, giveaway father to putative bride. In constructing his own identity against the mirror of those he invents for Bob, Moses effectively feminizes the latter – that is, allocates him the position accorded to women in the construction of masculinity. The Man Friday image implies that Bob's is a colonially inflected feminization, reversing the black-white male roles implied in colonialism. Selvon's satirical intention in the various identity reversals, in terms of gender, race and colony, is self-evident.

But the relationship is far from being a straightforward reversal of roles; rather, it is fraught with the multiple paradoxes and ironies that provide much of the text's open-endedness as well as its hilarity. Moses may be Bob's economic and intellectual superior, but their political positions are fluid, unfixed as much by Moses's expectation as by Bob's desire. On Moses's side are his refusal of the responsibilities of ownership, which he then devolves onto Bob, not realizing the concomitant devolution of enormous powers; his contradictory desire to inhabit the privileges of ownership, not realizing the extreme porosity, including openness to ridicule, of the Great House persona; his colonially conditioned idea of white manhood as an iconic single entity (all white men can read and write), clashing with his gleeful certainty that he has definitively reconstructed Bob into the form of his slave. There is also the desire for male bonding, which he had forfeited by cutting ties with the "boys" and which he now seeks with Bob the factotum; and, perhaps above all, his historically conditioned West Indian "un-surprise" at reversal. All of this allows him to traverse with equanimity a relationship that fluctuates between master and servant, comradely bonhomie, mutual respect and disrespect, and finally showdowns of power which terminate, albeit open-endedly, in his own displacement and Bob's command of the house.

On Bob's side, the relationship is facilitated by the lure of exotica in the form of black female flesh, which he hopes to access through Moses; his hunger for self-validation, which finds space in the Black Power movement; and his working-class ability to adjust to people and circumstances. All of this creates a vulnerability which gives credence to the various personae in which Moses represents him, and leads to the showdown in which his de facto rulership of the house is subverted by the underhand trick by which Moses succeeds in giving him away in marriage, as a father does a bride. But it also widens the space of power Moses's dependency opens for him, and so he is able to infiltrate Moses's domain even as he infiltrates, and by his presence as a white man modifies the Black Power movement by introducing the element of (possible) integration. The relationship marked by fluidity instead of fixity ultimately originates, however, in the (half-colonized, half-maverick) ambivalence with which the "new man", his master, is self-constructed. Moses, in his bid to demonstrate his identity as a new "Englishman with black blood in his veins", has simply demonstrated his West Indianness, both in his strategies of impersonation and the contradictions of that impersonation.

In his deliberate attempt to banish society, Moses sees the relationship as a purely personal one, even while incongruously depending on social criteria for its validation. But the relationship is as subversive in its own way as the increasing white male interest in black girls (15). The social economy based on gender, where masculinity carries more value than femininity, may in some respects be even less able to tolerate the crossing of territory by men than the exhibition of male desire for "other" women. Class is the vulnerable link in the chain of the status quo here: in a sense, it is the society's ignoring of its lower classes that allows the relationship to go uncounted. Quite simply, nobody seems to notice. The unnoticed, and therefore "unsupervised", relationship (compare the Black Power meetings, kept under constant police surveillance) in its own way constitutes an encroachment on cultural space. The extent of encroachment is succinctly double-marked in the politics of language, in Bob's assimilation of Moses's comic mode of speech: "[W]e have barely got rid of the smell of curry and joss sticks, and you want to dabble in black tragic?" (96). Moses the West Indian man of speech applauds a worthy imitator: "Were the moment different, I might have doffed my hat at that one and made a note to use it" (96). As a result then of Moses's flirtation with and flight from codes of masculinity, he and Bob come to signify lines of crossing, which represent infinitesimal but significant changes to cultural, personal and national identity.

Moses's flight from the restricting aspects of society's gender codes is evident also in his relations with women. In keeping with his more settled lifestyle somewhat inside the borders of a social structure, women have a more concrete and sustained presence, particularly in the form of Brenda, the attractive young Black Power activist, and Jeannie, Bob's wife. These are neither nebulous sexual exotica nor faceless spades, but concrete presences which force Moses to a further confrontation with gendered identity and social structure. The containment of the disruptive concept "woman" by linguistic deconstruction is carried over from *The Lonely Londoners*. The typology is identical or similar: bird; thing; piece, sleeper, chick, thirst-quencher. But such terms are only sparsely scattered within the text, and more often than not as a reminiscent commentary on the earlier days. In contrast, there is prolific use of more "gendered" vocabulary – "girl", "woman", "wife" – and an admission of the black female body in the form of rhapsodic passages on the subject of black female sexuality and radical black female behinds. Since the days of *The Lonely Londoners*, flight as a total act has become either impossible or delayed, even if it is only by the pleasures of sexual window-shopping ("It is not their [the black girls'] coming to look at, but their going. It is after they pass you and you turn your head and look that you realise what a great experience you are experiencing . . . yes, sir" [15]).

There is also a shift away from the anonymous sexual encounters of *The Lonely Londoners*. Here, young women, encountered within the context of ordered society, are not only "fecundat[ing]" (15), but, more threateningly, appearing as contenders for power. The threat perceived may well account for the peculiar way in which Moses goes about re-creating marriage as a "safe area". His devious machinations to get Bob married to Jeannie are a form of revenge against Bob for making possible Brenda's mockery of his cherished Memoirs, his ultimate proof of manhood. And she had deflated him consummately, using the terms of the Midnight Robber's challenge: "You sit down upstairs polishing and belabouring cliches, face lifting wornout phrases, and you say you are writing literature? . . . The only sentence you know, Moses . . . is what criminals get. Your conjunctions and your hyperboles are all mixed up with your syntax, and your figures of speech only fall between 10 and 20" (103–4). The energy Moses puts behind orchestrating Bob's marriage is the calypsonian's displaced retaliation against an upstart female challenger. The marriage is also a practical joke which it is difficult to imagine Moses playing on one of the boys, since the vulnerability of any one of them implies his own and leaves open to invasion his private world so carefully disjunct from that other world he wishes to appropriate on his own terms.

These Women Are too (Wo)Mannish: Moses and *The Housing Lark*

If Bob is the character who most fully represents the "advance" side of Moses's guerilla raid on British society, Jeannie is the character who most represents the "retreat" side. Together they gave a composite picture of Moses's strategy of seizure (of the codes of privilege) and flight (from the codes of responsibility). The relationship with Jeannie, defined by illicit sexual relations, serves to deflect the threat of total assimilation by keeping Moses in the same relation to women and society as he had been in his transactions with the prostitutes of *The Lonely Londoners.* Jeannie as sexual thirst-quencher, available to Moses as well as to her husband, helps to diffuse the terrors of responsibility – a form of bondage – symbolized in her position as a married woman. That is to say, their sexual relations, by crossing the boundary lines that make marriage sacrosanct, effectively dissolves the idea of marriage, of which Jeannie is a symbol.

This dissolution is particularly important because her close proximity in day-to-day interactions and her membership in the ordered society to which Moses paradoxically aspires make her a very present threat to his freedom: Jeannie is a constant and seductive reminder of the possibility that had on several occasions already occurred to him, that it might not be such a bad idea to have a female of his own around after all. There is an intimation that sleeping with Jeannie serves to "keep [such] marauders away" (125). Moreover, it possibly serves to delay a sense of the loss of (bachelor) male companionship, which he had had with Bob: if Bob is not really married, they are still two men together. In the end, Moses's relations with Jeannie expose the underlying dynamic of his sexual encounters: the fear of an invasion of psychological territory. These relations, when taken with the type of sexual encounters which occur in *The Lonely Londoners,* suggest that for Selvon's men in exile, relations with women are the most feared aspect of ordered society.

In *Moses Ascending,* as in the first novel, the black woman in the migrant context is sharply distinguished from the white woman in ways which show the former as the greater threat because of her power to order social relations. Through the character of Brenda, set against Tanty, differences between the concept of the older black woman and the concept of the younger black woman are also highlighted. Tanty is fearsome but paradoxically less threatening because she is not associated with sexuality, the trap that, as far as the boys are concerned, leads to an imprisoning sociality. The speech acts that seek to abolish this black female sexuality are fully exemplified in the composite narrator's suppression of the women's narratives of pain, which leach out of the silence about what might have driven them to prostitution. Brenda, combining Tanty's formidable spirit, energy and social efficiency with a blatant sexuality that early has Moses on the ropes, disrupts the female silence. When she goes to bed with him, Moses breaks forth into mesmerized accolade to her powers: "[W]hen I tell you that there is no business like black business, you know that I am not talking through my hat" (26).

Brenda decides the terms of her own sexual behaviour and extends this into a larger authority. She neutralizes Moses's attempts at linguistic subversion by making it clear that she sleeps with whom she wants to when she wants to, and she establishes the terms of a powerful economy based on sex when she bribes Bob with "a piece" (104) in order to get at Moses's Memoirs. Like Tanty, and unlike Moses, she confronts the establishment rather than seeking assimilation, whether partial, paradoxical or otherwise. Young, educated and bright, she is the type of an emergent species of black West Indian woman taking 1970s British social order "by the horns" in order to create what she sees as a more acceptable structure for black people. The most devastating aspect of her access to Moses's Memoirs is the opportunity it gives her to attack the self-indulgent performance of masculinity and to damage its efficacy as escape and camouflage. For though Brenda is new-generation black British, not homegrown West Indian, she has inherited the devastating linguistic capacity that renders the performer at any given moment subject to the (de)constructive power of ridicule.

Brenda, as symbolized in her speech – Queen's English with the satirical edge of the calypsonian's *picong* – represents a new kind of hybrid, a female Caliban/Anancy who is British, not West Indian, fully engaged with her present reality but equipped with the tools of her heritage. Brenda operates with ease along the entire continuum of ideologically "masculine" and "feminine" roles, and she combines this with a fearsome lack of scruples in getting her own way. An odd mixture of principle and pragmatic opportunism, she is direct and confrontational when it suits her and underhanded when it does not. But perhaps Brenda's most important quality is one that marks her (and all Selvon's women) off from Moses and the boys: she does not "play". She uses the tools of performance when it suits her, but her identity is not essentially performative. Rather than being determined by the play or in the moment of play, her action and sense of self seem to emanate from a directed, focused centre of preconstituted self-knowledge. Unlike Moses, she is not compromised in the paradoxes, contradictions and constant negotiations of an identity constituted in and through play.

Brenda's kind of hybrid, fashioned in the migrant space, is clearly able to hold its own in that conflictual environment. Neither Moses's mockery nor

Selvon's satirical exposure of the American leader of the Black Power movement as a fraud is able to faze Brenda. At the end of *Moses Ascending,* she is busy regrouping and taking over the part of Moses's house that Bob does not control. And when Moses declares that the story is, in typical West Indian style, an open-ended one (since he has an ace up his sleeve to remove Bob and reinstate himself), a clear, satirical resonance for the reader is that it may well be Brenda, the black woman, and not either of the men, black or white, who ends up in the penthouse. Symbolically, as the androgynous siren in possession of public, linguistic and sexual authority, Brenda is already the owner of the "mansions", and indeed, as a woman in masculine command of *picong,* she exceeds the authority of the male calypsonian.

In the end, woman – for Brenda is unequivocally a gendered creature – appears in *Moses Ascending* as a disruptive force that destroys all comfort zones and areas of refuge and that will not let a man be. The laughter that accompanies the portrait of Brenda as a discomforting form of masculinity mocks the associated ideological pretensions, but it also masks Selvon's attitude, which could be read as critique or collusion. One is never quite sure whether it is only Moses, or both Brenda and Moses, or masculinism as represented through Brenda and the interplay with Moses that is being satirized. For Brenda's signification in masculinity-femininity becomes a double mask, and although her satirical voice is subtended and legitimized by the narrator's, there is a sense in which her political activities are also the occasion of satirical laughter. In the end, it is Selvon the virtuoso calypsonian who eludes definition; *Moses Ascending* becomes another inscrutable text in the calypsonian's linguistic repertoire.

The idea of "woman" as a disruptive entity is even more forcefully presented in *The Housing Lark.* The central conflict is between the boys, led by Battersby, who are playing at saving to buy a communal house, and their women, led by the Tanty-like figure of Teena, who are determined that the house must be bought. The period is halfway between *The Lonely Londoners* and *Moses Ascending*: some years have passed, and increasing numbers of West Indian women have joined the stream of migrants. This is significant – here it is women, not militant black movements or the British establishment, that represent society as a form of encroachment. The narrative is full of women, not as "birds" or "pieces" but as girlfriends and wives threatening the freedom of the men, who, like Moses, are busy elaborating strategies of flight. Only Harry Banjo, Jamaican and anomalous, seems in his pursuit of the elusive Jeannie to embrace the social frames the others are seeking to escape.

The title is tellingly ambiguous: whereas in Naipaul's *A House for Mr Biswas* the possession of a house is the passionately sought consummation that signals social and psychological coherence, in this novel it is merely a "lark" – a game, a flight from real possession. "Lark" recalls the attempts to deconstruct woman as a social category by referring to her as a "bird"; the hope that she will miraculously fly away is subsumed in the vocabulary. The women, of course, represent the oppressiveness of responsibility: quite simply, they must think of the house because they have the care of the children. Although the novel ends without the house having been bought, the clear implication is that if the women have their way it will. But part of that open-endedness is also the suggestion that if the boys have their way, the purchase and its symbolism will be delayed by yet another series of diversionary plays.

The confrontation/conference with which the novel ends inscribes the insistent will of the women as a curious face-off between social ordering and its absence as represented by the boys: an absence which is not so much disorder as another kind of anti-order. Teena's organization of the conference is supremely businesslike and rational. This rationality not only traps the slippery Battersby, it also signals the loss of the boys' freedom and of the pleasures that come with freedom. For the boys in the condition of exile, the advent of social order as represented by women is always the loss of pleasure. This is comically expressed in Battersby's sad farewell to his Aladdin's lamp wallpaper at the end of the novel. (Aladdin's world is the dreamscape that substitutes for conflictual reality.)

It is in *The Housing Lark,* which offers the largest cast of female characters, that the antiphonal aspect of Selvon's representation of male and female is most pervasively highlighted. We have said that, as is typical of nationalist-era portrayals, the relation of Selvon's men to their gender identity is always conflictual. Typically also, the gender identity of Selvon's West Indian women is never in question, even in the migrant space, except insofar as the male characters attempt its deconstruction. But the very fact of the attempt points to its existence, a priori. Woman is static and stable: Selvon thus aligns the West Indian woman on the side of the gender divide in the space where classical feminism may have aligned the masculine ideal – or, rather, may have identified the masculine ideal as being aligned in patriarchal systems – and the men on the opposite side.

This treatment of female characters we have already seen in the other two novels, but here there is a crucial distinction: where in *The Lonely Londoners* and *Moses Ascending* the female's alignment with masculinity is in a heterodox

West Indian mode, in *The Housing Lark* it is more akin to the orthodox modes of Europeanist prescription. In the West Indian writer's text, where language is as much cultural ideology as it is aesthetic, this is signalled by a shift in speech: the female masculinity expressed in the command of the calypsonian's register and ambiguously admired in the inviting of the audience to ritual laughter gives way to a counterpart marked by the rational, peremptory word, which the boys find totally oppressive in its singularity and relative lack of humour. Significantly, *The Housing Lark* is pervaded by an aura of gloom quite missing from the other novels, and this seems to arise directly from the boys' sense of the women as (masculinist) oppressors.

The attenuation of the calypsonian's register in the novel is striking. Where in *The Lonely Londoners* and *Moses Ascending* linguistic play and ritual/anti-ritual are forms of masking beneath which power may be appropriated, fragile identities elaborated or their loss disguised, in *The Housing Lark* the women's speech, scalpel-like, constitutes an unmasking and a form of discordance within the London quartet. The women are not only unwilling to explore the "ameliorative" possibilities of play, but are incapable of doing so. Like Tanty and Brenda, they utilize performance strategies, but with a serious edge that displaces laughter, and without losing themselves in the performance or in aesthetic contemplation of its pleasures. Moreover, they are focused not on issues of selfhood or politics, but on material outcomes. In their use of performance strategies (subterfuge and pretence) against the men, they declare their anti-performativity; in fact, they push the envelope of performance against itself.

The Dissonance of the Spheres: Man, Woman, Nation and Migration

Taken together, these exile novels seem to suggest that it is the men who are more easily feminized in situations of crisis, possibly because of a subconscious longing for the space of femininity (not-ness, the secondary, the displaced and the marginal) which conveys the liminal freedoms in which one might more easily explore and achieve individuation. The women, on the other hand, appear to cling to their masculine identities, again perhaps because, in their experience, transgression into masculine space is what has helped them to survive in the constant crises from slavery to Emancipation and beyond. In other words, in Selvon's representation of men and women, in situations of crisis, each clings to the space which each has been ideologically denied. Women, then, become the image of patriarchal oppression/suppression of the feminine – an anomaly that perhaps could have been conceived only by a Caribbean artist, product of a society created and inured in paradox and contradiction.

Even so, the exile novels do not present the sum total of Selvon's representations of women. The characters portrayed here represent an economically driven cadre for whom migration meant first and foremost employment and the regrouping and security of their families. The novels of home discussed in chapter 3 present another view, similar but with important nuanced differences within a different social context. The importance of social context as one of Selvon's most significant variables in the construction of gender is particularly highlighted in the finale of *Moses Ascending,* where we see being suggested the possibility of an accommodation between individual desire and societal demand that is not apparent in the continuing conflict between most of the boys and the societal codes by which ideas of manhood are constructed.

Ironically, what facilitates this accommodation is the fact that Moses wants assimilation on his own terms – that is, his refusal to become a full "English gentleman". This leaves open a space of recalcitrance, or *différance,* that arguably allows the encroachment of the migrant community against which he had erected such stringent psychological and social barriers. Inexorably drawn by a series of events and seductions into the life of the community he seeks to disown, Moses begins to close the gaps between the poles of self, as indicated in his vow to "turn over a new leaf" after witnessing the sufferings of the Black Power activists (*Moses Ascending,* 117). The reconciliation is reluctant and far from wholesale, but the important development is that in making the shift, Moses also begins in effect to negotiate the space between exile and diaspora, for there is the suggestion that in finding some linkages with his true context, he has begun to dissolve the anomie in which migrancy is imagined as exile.

Further, the social and political contact across racial, ethnic and geographic communities (the Black Power leader comes from as far away as America) into which he becomes drawn are incipient signs of a diasporic imagination of migrancy and seem, when negotiated against a continuing tandem insistence on individual selfhood, to allow Moses to feel that he now has a more integrated sense of what it is to be a man in the migrant space. In other words, the Moses with whom the novel ends has again shifted his gender identity, in keeping with his changed relation to social imperatives. But at the same time that we are aware that this Moses is more in touch with himself, we are also aware of his primary investments in a model of contingency, evident in his construction of gender identity at the site of performative play. There is no certainty that the new Moses is a permanent identity or an unequivocally efficacious one. The hugely, hilariously paradoxical sequel, *Moses Migrating,* adds point to this observation.

Moses's questionable accommodations and the continuing unresolved conflict between the boys and societal expectations are, however, not merely issues of West Indian exile and diaspora. If Selvon's work can be placed within the context of nationalist thought, it is not through the journalistic approaches as a result of which critics have found him too unsatisfactory a nationalist, but rather through a deconstructive approach that draws upon the historical milieu limned not in events but in the type of personality Selvon chooses to portray. From such a perspective, his representations begin to demonstrate some of the ways in which the agonal issues of the modern democratic state are re-complicated for the West Indian, only more so in the migrant space, which is a space of double disanchoring.

The linearly imagined nation is one in which a simple divide is perceived between the individual and the collective (symbolized in the state). The accommodation demanded is simply that between two opposing ideologies: on the one hand, the allegiance owed to the collective as tradition, as stabilizing history, patrimony and ultimate context of identity; on the other, the pre-eminence of the individual, which is insisted upon as a basic article of faith. Yet the individual's pre-eminence involves alienation and movement away from the very social systems to which s/he is required to give prior allegiance; more than this, alienation is both precondition and context of possibility for the process of individuation to take place. The society is expected both to contain and to set the individual free – that is, to provide security and to allow for the risky recalcitrance of individual identity – while the individual is in turn expected to balance independence of self with responsibility towards the collective as represented in nation, community and family.

The social upheaval, even fragmentation, of the postwar and the postmodern eras in the West has been from various perspectives attributed to the increasing conflicts between these demands, as both state and individual configure and reconfigure themselves in new and complex ways. The idea of neurosis as a form of escape from these contradictions of modernity has probably been most popularly expressed by Erich Fromm (1941), for whom the separation between self and society creates in the individual a fear amounting to a horror of freedom, so that strategies of escape from freedom in particular become the sign of a modern neurosis. What is usually left out of the equation in such analyses of modernity is the double complication of gender, particularly the fact that for women in a patriarchal system, there is the added necessity of confronting the idea of woman as a secondary creature and of negotiating and articulating a response to this as part of the larger identities of self and citizenship.

The further complication of which Selvon's representations are a sign, is this: that for the West Indian who came of age in the 1950s, "freedom" meant a movement away not from social systems and authorities which conferred security, but from colonial structures which retarded individuation, without conferring the authoritative "security" which the Westerner may take for granted as being part and parcel of the retarding structures. In order not to be cast adrift at the moment of his emergence as an individual, the colonial, simultaneous with the movement into individual identity, was called upon to construct a new set of social systems and authorities within which he was to be integrated. The simultaneity of the projects (reflected in the West Indian Bildungsroman, the individual life as the story of the nation's becoming) already spawns the conditions of possibility for a dissonantal consciousness.

The migrant male colonial represented in Selvon's exile quartet experiences a re-complication of dissonance, for his problem is compounded by the peculiar circumstances of his migrancy. The circumstances create their own extraordinary terms of psychic dislocation and bring an additional dissolution of social space. His terror and his flight therefore are from both the vision of and responsibility for new structures he is being called upon to create, and without which, in dreadful paradox, he is left without a space of predication. The discordant narratives of family in *The Housing Lark* and *The Lonely Londoners*; in the latter, the absence of thought about familial and other connections left back home; across the three novels, Moses's fear of involvement, whether social, personal or political – all of this points to these variables at work in the liminal spaces of Selvon's text and in the retreat from gender as a monstrous and unbearable possibility.

In his posturings, performances and diversionary evasions, Selvon's protagonist suggests the idea that the West Indian colonial, as a creature of forced diaspora, had no unequivocal models to use in constructing the new set of relations within which he must find individual predication. His alternatives were alternatives in a constant state of flux, conflict and paradox; in fact, they arose, historically constructed, out of flux, conflict and paradox. The model that had served him best was a model of improvisation, not a model of tradition. Indeed, the model of (colonial) tradition was the source of retardation. And while the model of improvisation had its efficacies, powers and what Lamming might well term its paradoxical pleasures, in Selvon's boys it is the fragility of the model – its contingency – that seems to be more fully highlighted. By contrast, Selvon's women in exile seem to have stayed in tune with an idea of a tradition that has emerged within that same model itself, and out of this to have established places of anchoring and of definitive action that are authoritative and successful within the exilic space. In that regard, the women appear to be exporters of West Indian culture and in that sense to be diasporic consciousnesses rather than persons in exile.

Based on these differences in male and female presentation, which are products of a profoundly if paradoxically heterodox society, Selvon's exile novels leave us with questions rather than closed circles of answers. Selvon aligns the sexes with opposite stresses in the heterodox society: its traditionalizing ethos and its resistant impulse that refuses the stasis inherent in tradition. Though male and female transgress the two spaces (the women more so than the men), each tends to be more fully characterized by one side of the divide than by the other. The former ethos, a kind of unorthodox orthodoxy, is self-confident, iconoclastic, and direct in attack. The latter sidesteps, crabwise, or, where sidestepping is not possible, plays at conformity, using the appearance as a form of deflection or diversion. Lacking the imagination to conceive of itself or its traditions as inadequate in a new situation, the former appropriates power with speed and efficiency. The latter is self-protective, and looks for power in the spaces which are devalued, unseen and camouflaged. It is endlessly predicative, while the other appears more inclined to be static and fixed.

Questions such as what accounts for these differences that Selvon perceives are left unresolved, largely because of an absence of female interior psychological portraits. Also, although the women seem to accomplish more, their accomplishment is constantly questioned by Selvon's strategies of representation, both narrative voice as satire and a sense of the women's behaviours as a source of unbridgeable conflict – an impression orchestrated by the narrative voice acting as the boys' collective consciousness. Further, although the men seem to have a more complex possibility of power inherent in the latencies of their performative strategy, the hollow side of performativity as deconstructive emptying seems to hold this in permanent stasis and to question the construction of masculine selves towards which their strategies are primarily directed. Collectively, the three novels leave us with a sense that reconciliations between male and female are not able to take place in the migrant space imagined. What seems clear however, is that Selvon moves his West Indian migrant men and women in opposite yet similar circles of gender-crossing which are responses to their immediate social context and from which both in different ways seem capable of hybridizing, subverting and otherwise changing the cultural landscape in which they find themselves.

Chapter 3

Going Home

Performing Masculinity in *A Brighter Sun* and
Turn Again Tiger

Clipped Wings: An Overview

THE HOUSING LARK may be considered a halfway house between the world
of the Moses novels, which are marked by various strategies of flight from
gender, and the milieu of the Tiger novels, *A Brighter Sun* (1952) and *Turn
Again Tiger* (1959), which are marked by strategies of accommodation to
prescribed gender norms. The Moses novels explore a world in which the
boys are in flight from socially approved ideas of masculinity, this being an
element in their flight from ordered society within the context of London's
socially amorphous exilic Fourth World. In this exilic world, relations with
women remain peripheral, though to varying degrees. *The Housing Lark*
presents a movement into relations which theoretically imply a psychic
acceptance of socially approved gender constructs but still within the exilic
setting which by its nature accommodates the boys' continuing flight, at least
on a psychological level. The Tiger novels replace the exilic context with the
native environment and retain the gender-implicated relations of *The
Housing Lark* but with a new, less radically conflicted, though still problematic, set of perspectives emerging.

The Tiger novels thus provide some interesting comparisons and contrasts
to the novels of exile. Tiger's entire world is predicated upon constructions
of gender and gender relations, expressed respectively in his search for
manhood in the context of his village community and of his relationship with

his wife, Urmilla. In this regard, the essential difference between Tiger's world and the worlds of London's black migrant underclass may be described as a difference of social geography. In the London setting, the material absence of social structures that would truly embrace, legitimate but also confine/contain the boys makes it easy for them to escape the subjective internalization of such structures, or, as in the case of Moses, to "play" with them without the deconstructive nature of the play becoming societally visible and thus subject to dismantling. Tiger, on the other hand, inhabits a world which does have a recognizable structure, of which he is a part. His world is governed by norms and expectations by which, as a member of the society, he is necessarily constrained, and within which he is highly visible, so that it is more difficult to elaborate successful strategies of escape. The fact that he is a very young, untried member of an ethnic community which is more tightly constructed and more patriarchally definitive than the general society in its gender codes makes the search for accommodation rather than escape a logical response to the situation in which Tiger finds himself.

Tiger's active pilgrimage in search of masculine identity elliptically represents the transgressive complex of dilemmas represented by the threat of dissonance which we have elaborated as being characteristic of the situation faced by the West Indian colonial in the 1950s. Tiger's story also highlights the issue of racial/ethnic subculture as one of the complicating factors in a society whose fluid character includes the uncertainties of interface among very diverse groups: the Afro-West Indians who arrived as owned labour and the Indo- and Sino-West Indians who came as another kind of forced labour, each bringing a vast diversity of cultures and ideologies, each precipitated by the other's presence into a situation of suspicion and conflict but also into an irresistible process of integration, which has been traditionally described as creolization and, more recently, as a form of matrix relationality (Glissant 2000) and supersyncretism (Benítez Rojo 1996).

Thus, wide variations exist in the experience of gender across racial and ethnic lines, but, simultaneously, these lines of demarcation are cut through by the carnival ethos – the erasure of boundaries, the ritual containment of conflict through celebratory laughter on the field of play. That aspect of the latter which involves the praxis of masking and unmasking as a space for the dissolution, construction and protection of identities is highlighted in the Tiger novels. *A Brighter Sun* and *Turn Again Tiger* present two distinct acts in the play of identity, though there are points at which they blur into each other: *A Brighter Sun* may be described as a transposed audition, in which various masks of masculinity are tried on and off ("auditioned") in an attempt to find the one that "fits", *Turn Again Tiger* as rehearsal, a testing out and becoming accommodated to the mask which by the end of *A Brighter Sun* had been identified as the one that fits. The process of trial and error represents a search for security of self in a setting marked by anomaly: very definitive about the need for "man-ness" in a patriarchal mode, yet characterized by inadequate rites of initiation and an absence of unequivocal norms by which this "man-ness" is to be constituted and recognized.

Precisely because it is a search for accommodation rather than escape, Tiger's "mas" is a serious one – not so much a comic immersion in performativity as a search for the correct performance. The aim is towards the identification and elaboration of a singular self for all seasons, not towards the delay and dispersion of multiple selves in the pleasures of play. In this respect, masculine identity and performance in the Tiger novels bear some similarities to the women's performance of roles in the exile novels. There is, however, an important difference. Tiger comes to the play seeking a singular sense of self; the women come to it seemingly already invested with a sense of self that anchors the performance and in a sense limits it within bounds of control in which it becomes more conservative than exploratory, more a playing with performance than a performance in itself (their tough personalities and hard-headed Machiavellian purposes dictate and "ventriloquize" the performance). From within this anchoring sense of purpose and self, the women, though predominantly masculine, seem free to play both masculine and feminine roles. This creates a certain irony in the resemblance to Tiger, since acceptable manhood involves for the latter both an elimination of the "feminine" within himself and an identity not subject to the possibility of insecurity implied in the transgression of gender roles.

Tiger's role-playing, like Moses's, elicits comic laughter, but here, as in *The Lonely Londoners,* the narrator's voice becomes disjunct from the character's, indicating a distance between their perceptions of reality. It is the narrator who laughs, and the audience collusively joins in, but even more than *The Lonely Londoners, A Brighter Sun* is marked by a sense of tragedy subsumed and ritually dissipated. This sense of tragedy emerges both in the absence of the calypsonian's comic register and in Tiger's personality, which is almost devoid of humour. His is an extended experience of terror in the face of the uncharted quest, and the narrator's laughter is in turns subdued and striated by the parallel narrative of pain which it seeks both to illuminate and to ameliorate. The invitation to laughter then becomes the ritual invitation of carnival, to transform both tragedy and comedy by erasing the boundaries between them, but here the bare-bones linguistic strategies that replace the baroque excess of the Moses novels attenuate laughter, warn the audience that this is a different kind of play, a serious drama – that while we are playing, we are indeed not playing at all. The resolutions of *A Brighter Sun* and *Turn Again Tiger* are accomplished not in laughter but, in their own heterodox way, on the serious high note of the heroic drama.

The Tiger novels display other radical differences from the exile quartet. First, gender is much more than one among many issues of similar weight in these novels: it becomes the texts' organizing frame, evidenced in the overriding concern with domestic relations as event-source, the shaping of Tiger's Bildungsroman around the central issue of his relations with his wife, the orchestrated parallel narratives of other spousal relationships, the major concern with the treatment of women, and the direct employment of the vocabulary of gender in both novels. Indeed, the didacticism of this vocabulary, which is pervasive, insistent and unsubtle, makes its unreading even in the nationalist era remarkable.[1] There is also an attempt to develop female characters and to explore women's social and psychological worlds through various tableaux of community, as they intersect and seek accommodation with the male worlds. A more engaged and diversified focus is given to the ways in which women become implicated in the male search for identity; this involves a recognition that women have their own narratives of pain, which the texts attempt, albeit unsuccessfully, to explore.

Also, Selvon's continuing preoccupation with an idea of female psychology, which is mysteriously different from men's, acquires a new dimension as the portrayal of discomforting self-sufficiency, which we have seen across various characters – from Tanty to Brenda to Teena – is elaborated into an idea of women's community that Selvon offers as part source of this mysterious "power". Ironic disjunctions between narrative commentary and description, whether witting or unwitting, play a crucial role in Selvon's gender discourse, as these disjunctions indicate contradictory ideas about the nature of men's and women's attitudes to gender-inflected issues such as authority, power and community. In addition, this disjunction in *Turn Again Tiger* elaborates an aspect of gender relations the exploration of which had already begun in *The Housing Lark,* the only one of the exile novels in which the boys are shown in domestic relations with their women. Misogyny in *Turn Again Tiger* appears rooted not so much in ideas of women's inferiority as in the men's perception of women as competitors for masculine space. In other words, it is the fear that women may be both similar and equal that produces misogyny.

A Brighter Sun: Play Mas' Like Real Man

A Brighter Sun opens with two terrified teenagers, Tiger and Urmilla, at the beginning of a marriage arranged by their parents. Although the main point of view is the boy's, both are inscribed in the narrative as terrified consciousnesses on the edge of a rite of passage they have not even begun to understand. Tiger's sense of psychic dissolution is poignantly captured: "Unknowingness folded about him so he couldn't breathe. He was afraid" (11). Urmilla, tellingly, experiences the crisis as an invasion of her female body: "[H]er emotions were too tightly drawn, like ropes across her breasts. And she felt that if she laughed the tautness would snap and set her free" (12).

It is here that Tiger's blundering, untutored search begins, with the trying on and doffing of various masks of identity in an attempt to understand and come to terms with what it means to be a man. The one mask Tiger never puts off is the mask of the "man in control of woman"; this is the one in which he feels most secure, and so he wears it throughout. Others are simply superimposed upon it, or attached to it as accretions to a central hub. The persona this mask expresses deals with fear by various forms of spousal abuse, which deeply compromise any peace that Tiger purportedly finds with himself at the end of the novel.[2] The unswerving allegiance to this persona in an otherwise insecure becoming may well be based on the only certainties in Tiger's prior experience: gender as masculine supremacy over the subservient female might have been particularly available as an ideological model for a boy who had grown up with both parents in a traditional Indo-West Indian household. That Tiger chooses this model is paradoxically the measure of his fear and uncertainty, since obviously other models, such as those represented in Ismith Khan's images of male/female equality in the Indo-West Indian household, were also available.

Most important, the fact of the marriage thrusts Tiger into an agonal relation to himself and his wife from the outset. His is a pilgrimage based on fear, resentment and confusion: manhood is understood at this stage purely as responsibility, which is imposed at a point where he has not yet begun the normal conscious search for selfhood. The fundamental, terrifying question is how can he take responsibility for someone else, or indeed for manhood in the world of social relations, when he has not yet understood what it means to be responsible for himself:

> What had life been for him? Days in the fields, evening, playing with other children, roti and *aloo* in the night. . . . And now all that was gone. He felt a tremendous responsibility falling on his shoulders. He tried not to think about it.
>
> The third day his mind was in a riotous fever. He sat in the yard under a mango tree with Ramlal, an old Indian who often consoled him when he was beaten by his father or mother. "What must I do?" he asked Ramlal, and Ramlal laughed.
>
> "Is how you mean boy?"
>
> "I mean – I don't know what to do when I go with the girl."
>
> . . . [E]verything was a whirling, swift event, in which he was told to do this, and do that, and he obeyed. (6–7)

The irony of complete, unthinking obedience at the moment when he most feels that authority is demanded of him is surpassed only by the anomaly of his name, its aggressive declaration of male potency and concomitant masculine force exposed as pure mask, an identity made fragile by the uncertain linguistic performance of a stammer.

The third day, which should have been a day of resurrection, is a day of regression to childhood (signalled by his retreat into passive obedience); evidently the boy has been given no preparation for this rite of passage, as the parents seem to have assumed both the security of the world that is now ejecting him into manhood and its ability to sustain and receive him again. Selvon's humorous presentation of Tiger's ignorance does not mask the appalling terror and vulnerability created by that ignorance: "He would have threatened Urmilla and commanded her to bear a boy, but Joe Martin had told him that wouldn't help" (38); "Was worry one of the signs of a man?" (43).

Tiger also experiences manhood as loss and entrapment, as indicated in the long interior monologue in which, later in the novel, he reflects on his lost childhood and acknowledges his revulsion for his wife and child. This traumatic experience of gender, which is again paradoxically an experience of femininity (insofar as it is femininity that is associated with these negative aspects of engendering), is a recipe for misogyny, and so the boy's search for identity is complicated by a terror of his wife, who is a girl child but who signifies woman. This terror, which culminates in his savage physical attack on her during her second pregnancy near the end of the novel, displaces itself by various strategies aimed at silencing her. He drowns out the possibility of her critical voice by speaking first:

> He decided that he had better begin to talk freely with his wife. That way she wouldn't know he was doubtful and fearful of the future.
>
> Tiger drank tea from a large enamel cup.
>
> ". . . You must remember, first thing is that I is the man in the house, and you have to obey me."
>
> ". . . Yes, Tiger." (13)

He forces her speechlessness by refusing conversation, and most crucially, imposes the silence of not listening to her:

> "Why you stay so long, Tiger?" she asked gladly.
>
> He sulked. He was the man in the house. He could come and go as he pleased. He didn't answer.
>
> They ate in silence. (15)

Urmilla asks the question "gladly" out of her relief that he is safe, a celebration of his return to her rather than a questioning of his rights and responsibilities, but Tiger does not hear her; he hears, rather, the challenge worded by his own fear. After a while, because he does not hear her, he comes to believe that she does not speak. It never occurs to him that Urmilla may have her own dreams or her own growing-up pains. (Indeed, in order to conceive of himself as a man, he is constrained to perceive her as frozen in an eternal moment of childhood, dependent on him as the all-powerful father.) Tiger's silencing strategies are an inverse, deadpan rendition of the calypsonian's noise, the linguistic "play" by which the woman-tongue capacity to unmask is ritually deflected. Selvon's comic renditions barely recall the narrative from the edges of tragedy.

Urmilla's silencing by the authoritative speaker-persona is only the first step in a three-step process towards Tiger's masculine becoming. The second is the imposition of order on the economic world, the signature of his role as breadwinner. This is seen in Tiger's almost feverish efforts to establish some sort of income-generating activity. The third step is the acceptance of loneliness, the mask of self-sufficiency: "He was married, and he was a big man now. He might as well learn to do things without the assistance of other people" (13). The patriarchal concept that masculinity necessarily involves the isolation of the individual from community goes to the very heart of loss. The limits of Tiger's search for masculine identity are already set, existing a priori in the ideologies which shape the world in which the "new" Tiger is to be reborn.

Yet the essential schizophrenia at the core of such ideologies is exposed, for although Tiger insists that it "is just me, inside of me" that matters, he is simultaneously engaged in a search for right answers in the form of validation tests from the community. This appears in his constant seeking out of other men and other men's opinions in the rum shop, as well as in his search for models and masks. Tiger has no really organized knowledge of what a man is, so that whenever he needs a model of how a man behaves in a particular situation, he harks back to what he has seen his father and other men do. He has no alternative, as manhood was not introduced to him as process: "One day he was a little boy and the next day he was a man" (101). His insecurity in this regard is very clear from the fact that he feels threatened in the presence of older men, such as his father, who have been doing gender since even before he was born.

But the models (and masks) fail Tiger. Soon he acknowledges that he is different from most of the men around him, and that reading and writing, dismissed by his elders, are an urgent necessity with him, constituting as they do an opportunity to extend his hold on the wider world through a larger knowledge and the aesthetics of language. That is, he comes, without the models, to realize that identity involves a dimension which goes beyond socially constructed roles, to encompass that unique inner reality which differentiates one *person* in society from another, and which to that extent transcends gender roles. The models also fail Tiger in his relations with his wife, for they are unable to accommodate any idea of intimacy – beyond the physical – in his relations with her. This appears in his avoidance of a necessary self-confrontation when he beats Urmilla so brutally that she has to be hospitalized. Inured to the concept of woman as an inferior being contradictorily waiting for the slightest opportunity to get the upper hand based on any weaknesses he may exhibit, Tiger walks around in a daze during her illness, unable to bring himself to an admission of guilt or a request for forgiveness. So strong is the taboo against submission that the source of his unhappiness is not even explicitly articulated but left to be deciphered from his contrary moods in the wake of the beating.

Even so, the consequences of his action begin to force Tiger to a realization that the lived traditions of the classical Indo-West Indian household are weighed in the balance and found wanting: the husband in search of manhood must find alternatives to the solution of domestic conflict. It is these same traditions of manhood that prevent him from apologizing to Joe and Rita, though he admits to himself that "I should talk to [them . . .

But] I too shame" (204). The admission of shame is the occupation of feminine space, which, like Urmilla, must be erased by unspeaking. But unspeaking has become too uncomfortable an act, nor can the task of constructing alternatives be indefinitely evaded. The task, however, proves almost impossible for a young man with so many conflicts to resolve and no known bases for alternatives, particularly as the models which fail him are models he is just in the process of consciously discovering. The task of unearthing, wearing, judging and reconstructing the masks of identity all in the same moment is gargantuan. No wonder then that at the end of the novel we see Tiger falling back into traditional positions which he knows instinctively to be wrong.

Thus, his final assumption of manhood (for at the end of the novel he has finished with donning and doffing masks and has decided which of them he will permanently wear) is oddly conflicted. He learns a certain amount of caring, which allows him to send Urmilla home for a rest, but he remains distant from her. He says he has learnt not to invest too much emotion in anything, since "what will happen will happen", yet he gets drunk, traditional " 'man'-fashion", because peace has been declared – the end of the world war which scarcely involved him and which he scarcely understands. He considers himself a more mature man, but his traumatized consciousness continues fearfully to evade female presence: when Rita, not Joe, initiates a reconciliation, he muses, "Joe is the only one now. . . . Is only Joe next door to talk to" (206), as though Rita is simply Joe's representative and the facilitator of men's friendships.

A man, then, provides for his family and rules his household chattels and goods, including his wife. A man gets drunk and performs other acts of prowess among other men. A man learns an inner steadiness, builds walls of silence to contain the threat of woman and looks to other men for models of woman and relations with woman. A man accepts loneliness as the ground of masculine being, a position riddled with destructive contradictions. Most important, a man rigidly contains the insurrection of genders in himself: Tiger's passage from boyhood to manhood is a passage from femininity to masculinity, the former a space of "not-ness" which makes its presence known only when the thought of masculinity arrives. It is then experienced as terror of itself – that is, of unknown reservoirs of feeling which must be suppressed rather than confronted. Tiger's erasure of Urmilla and Rita, as well as his acceptance of aloneness, is part of the continuum of leaving the feminine behind.

Tiger's manhood, then, is constituted primarily of the traditional masks with which a maimed, schizophrenic ideology presents him. Even so, a fine bright thread of creative individuality runs through the picture: Tiger's sense that he is a unique individual, different from all others, possessed of an innate strength and innate possibilities which constitute the individual's most important possession in the world and which have allowed him not only to survive, but to look forward to the next phase in his life. The embracing of that individual self allows him to seed something new into the future. Tiger's open attitude to literacy is more than just a thirst for formal education: it signifies an opening of the closed frontiers of his ethnic group to the integrating forces of the society and the possibilities of the wider world. The strengths and possibilities he apprehends in himself belong to the human spirit, something eidetic that precedes gender. It is the creativity of the spirit that accounts for any heroism in Tiger, and, arguably, his willingness to confront and discharge a role and responsibility which fill him with revulsion may be accounted heroic.

There is a sense, too, in which the society has been able to provide structures of support for the young man groping towards a sense of himself: structures of community built on the opportunity for responsible work and the affections of the heart as symbolized in Joe, Rita and Sookdeo. These cut across racial, ethnic and gender lines, and in fact both the relationships and the search for work, which brings him in contact with groups from whom he was previously isolated, are an important source of the societal integration that opens up to Tiger the larger possibilities within himself as an individual. At the end of the novel we are aware that, apart from himself, these are all the securities Tiger has. These are the structures which have supported his search and which receive him back at the end of this phase of his journey. But the structures of community also encompass the elements which conflicted his search, and insofar as they have conferred on him a distorted masculinity, they leave him at the end of the novel profoundly flawed in his understanding of himself and of his relation to Urmilla.

The anomalies of Tiger's socialization as domestic tyrant and socially open individual seem to make a distinction between the search for self within the confines of a closed racial/ethnic group and that search expanded into a relation with the whole society. Retrospectively, the forces of community and integration that begin to "rescue" Tiger emphasize the denudation of the boys in *The Lonely Londoners*. That Selvon presents these forces as agents of positive self-development but stops short of allowing this development to encompass a solution to the problem of Tiger's domestic relations is more than an exercise in realism: it suggests an attempt to phase the acquisition of gender identity and gender "intelligence" (the ability to handle gender relations effectively) in an ongoing sequential process rather than as first "givens" in the project of self-becoming. It is in essence an attempt to address an aspect of the problem of dissonance, the unbearable hardship of being called upon to forge self, nation and community (social models) all in the same moment. It is also an attempt to retain a sense of the society's paradoxes and huge contradictions even while suggesting its capacity to set the individual free.

Wear Man Mask: *Turn Again Tiger*

Tiger's search for masculine identification in *A Brighter Sun* is reconstituted as a search for masculine authority in *Turn Again Tiger*. The difference between the two kinds of search has to do with the particular aspect of social direction that is emphasized: the one is directed more inwards, to the self, the other more outwards, to the community. In *A Brighter Sun,* we saw Tiger trying on, as it were, masks of masculinity – attempting to find the combinations that will fit as an answer to the question, "What is a man?" By the end of the novel he had found all the available masks, and we had a sense that he would wear them, compositely and with the greater assurance of experience. In the sequel, then, the Tiger whose reacquaintance we make is a man who is no longer uncertain about what constitutes manhood. This accounts for his air of assurance, the progression of his thought patterns by statement rather than question. He is already wearing the masks of manhood as identification, but now he is concerned to invest them with authority. This means that the status latent in his being-in-the-world as a man must be recognized by others besides himself and Urmilla. Recognition means the society's acquiescence in and submission to its twin roles as validating audience and supporting community, and it must take place in order for latent authority to become lived reality. Latency – "not-yet-ness"[3] – is still a residue of femininity, which must be erased. Authority, then, does not occur in the same moment as identification, and insofar as it must accomplish one's passage into an acceptable status in the society, it requires a wider audience.

Tiger's search for authority is expressed through his relations with a number of people and factors which he feels he must bring under his masculine control: "He upbraided himself for not knowing the neighbour-hood. The thought had a certain apprehension about it – it knocked his confidence, he began to think he wasn't sure of anything, he might lose his house and wife and child, anything was likely to happen" (46). The context is Tiger's brooding over the move to Five Rivers; the fear is that by his lack of knowledge of its inner workings, the neighbourhood could easily undermine him with its unexpected authorities. It has lurking within it the power to dislodge him from his rulership over the current symbols of his authority: in descending order, his house, his wife, his child. Not only that, it has the power to erode his sense of self ("knocked his confidence") and his authority over the universe of factual knowledge ("he wasn't sure of anything"). What this and numerous other passages reveal is that in Tiger's thinking, authority must be constantly exercised in order for masculine identity to remain a viable construct: it is under constant threat and must "keep on the move". Authority is a war zone in which the enemy must at all costs be kept under foot, and cannot be so kept if one remains in stasis. (Yet, contradictorily, paradoxically, patriarchal masculinity is an arrival at the stasis of a single extended performance over the course of a life.)

The full weight of Tiger's sense of authority denied is concentrated in his conflict with the Englishwoman Doreen. Doreen represents both the white man's historically constituted ability to divest the West Indian colonial of authority simply by being in the world and woman's ability to undermine male authority by sexual seduction. Also, in Tiger's mind, Doreen is not just a generalized racial androgyne, but specifically a stand-in for Robinson: her husband, the supervisor whose presence humiliates both Tiger and his father, Babolal. Robinson occupies the position that both had dreamt of but had been denied by virtue of the colonial economy's distribution of authority according to race.

The dissolution of sex-gender linkages in Doreen's identity as a form of transposed manhood by virtue of race and connection with a white male is aptly expressed in Tiger's thought that her clothes "looked like a man's clothing" (48) and in the labourer's taunt, "[I]s the super[visor's] wife, and you bound to do [what she tell you to do]" (62). The substitution of sex by race in the construction of gender summarily dissolves the persona Tiger had come to inhabit as his masculine self, the entire basis on which he is able to think of himself as a man: "He had run away like a little boy, scared, because a white woman had called out to him. He, Tiger, who had his own house, who had a wife and a child, who worked with the Americans during the war, who drank rum with men and discussed big things like Life and Death, who could read and write" (51).

Most devastatingly, Doreen represents Tiger's failure to properly wield the ultimate symbol of authority, the word – and not just any word but Prospero's word: that which being spoken imposes order on the world and concretizes one's authority. He attempts to speak to her in "good" English and lapses (60–63); he attempts to assert his refusal to be subservient, and instead reinforces his subservience. This importance of the word is not simply its generalized kudos in a society which accords pre-eminence to language and speech. It is at the core of Tiger's sense of himself in fundamental ways. Unlike the other indices of his identity, it constitutes not a mask but part of the ground on which he identifies himself as a unique individual: a man who thrives on words as the gateway to a philosophical understanding of the world around him (32), whose literacy and conscious attempts to educate himself have caused the other men to set him apart as unusual and different. And it has established him as a figure of authority in Five Rivers – an authority that had forced all other men into the womanish (in Tiger's terms) vestments of silence and concomitant facelessness (38).

A triple symbol of his failure of authority, then, Doreen causes a volcano of hatred in Tiger. His efforts to deny the central problem by reducing it to sex prove abortive, as is graphically demonstrated in their isolated, violently fraught coupling. The encounter, despite its surface mutuality, is an act of violence on the part of a man who is unable to eradicate history, the record of his own sense of failure. The ultimate intent (reiterated more than once throughout the scene) is murder; the fact that it takes the form of a sexual subjugation is merely an indication that what is implicated is his sense of himself as a man. The vocabulary of reasserted authority is very pronounced:

> The cause of every personal catastrophe was in his arms, and hatred and lust struggled equally in him. . . . [W]hat had tortured him had taken the form of her and that was *what he had under him* writhing and biting his arms and chest. . . . All he had to do was *fight* and *conquer* the *force* that was pulling him down against itself. . . . [A]ll the frustrations and fears would be expelled: he wouldn't run away again, because he would shed this thing from him and it would go away and leave him in peace forever. (146–47, emphases added)

Tiger triumphs in Doreen's loss of the authority of articulate speech: "She was murmuring. . . . [T]the sound came to him like moaning" (146). The moment recalls the passage in *A Brighter Sun* when he notices Urmilla's pain because she groans in a context where he has forbidden her an articulate voice. Tiger's linguistic authority is a perverse mirror side of the Londoners' fragmented stutterings in the face of the loose woman/city's androgynous and sexual authorities.

The sense of purgation Tiger experiences after this episode is not only perverse, it is based on fantasy, for the historically constituted realities of Doreen's and Robinson's being in the world have not gone away, and neither has Robinson's material authority as his supervisor and therefore over the material economy of his existence. The intersection of race and gender here continues the reflection begun in the white/black sexual encounters of *The Lonely Londoners* and elaborated in Moses's reverse colonization of Jeannie's body in *Moses Ascending* (this recurs in *Moses Migrating*). This linkage inscribes Tiger's position as a man, identified to himself as a man but with no acknowledged legitimacy in particular spheres of existence. The colonial system seeks to question, mock and feminize (relegate to a secondary or marginal/liminal space) every form of masculinity that Tiger as a West Indian male may have constructed for himself. The particular way in which Selvon deals with the race issue here also highlights the differences between the world of *A Brighter Sun* and the world in which Tiger now finds himself.

In the earlier novel, Tiger had expressed to Joe Martin his desire to learn about England and America. His encounter with the Yankees supervising the road gang had barely afforded him a glimpse of existence beyond his world. The entry of the Robinsons in his life in *Turn Again* continues his opportunity for education by bringing him face to face, for the first time, with the conflicted histories of his existence as a colonial. The world of *A Brighter Sun* had been to a large extent narrow and domestic; in this novel, the shift adumbrated in the first is reinforced: the frontiers of the wider world have been opened, and they have been opened not merely by the physical presence of the Robinsons, but also by the perspectives Tiger brings to bear on them from his expanded observation and his reading. (This is never explicitly stated but is always implied.) The latent positives implied here do not immediately come to fruition, and his inability to deal effectively with the problem of the Robinsons is expressed through those aspects of his personality which are most maimed: his relations with women. That he sees Doreen as the sum of all the other frustrations of his masculine authority suggests that Tiger indeed needs to "turn again" and create a new model of masculinity, not only to deal with the colonial issue, but also to resolve his relations with women. The problem signified by Urmilla and left unresolved at the end of *A Brighter Sun* comes back to demand attention at this stage of his development, though imbricated in the larger issue of the colonial experience.

Tiger's problems with Robinson obliquely highlight another aspect of his search for authority – a divisive, territorial approach which suggests that authority cannot be shared, that another man's possession of authority automatically robs him of his own. The historical construction of this divisiveness and the colonial system's continuing investment in it are marked in the physical spaces occupied by Robinson and the labourers respectively, and in the distance between the labourers' poverty and the symbols of Robinson's economic authority which that poverty subtends. These are Robinson's horse, his possession of the money bag, his cork hat, his fancy house and his distance. In Tiger, this idea of the closed nature of authority results in a constant distancing of himself from the other men with whom paradoxically he also seeks community.

This distancing is different from the distancing in *A Brighter Sun*: there it was felt as a necessary indication that one could stand on one's own two feet, could effectively wear the mask of aloneness. In *Turn Again,* Tiger has a pervasive sense that he is superior to the other men and that, unlike him, they do not think above the everyday world of behaviour and custom in which they are immersed in the (Schutzian) mode of the commonsense. Babolal tries to take him down a peg or two by telling him he has a long way to go before he is a man, and both Urmilla and Joe complain that he behaves as though he is the only one with a personal story of internal growth and struggle. Yet this attitude on Tiger's part is not totally the result of arrogance; it is fuelled also by the repeated frustration of his efforts to find a community of mind – what may be termed an intimacy of thought – among the other men.

In a real sense this hunger for intimacy is linked to the search for authority, and this in more than one way. First, part of Tiger's need is the need to know that the kind of person he is has validity. The individual spirit that in *A Brighter Sun* had emerged beneath the masks is in many ways a stranger to both the communities in which he has lived: the naturally philosophical turn of mind has been fed by an exposure to books which are a closed mystery to his illiterate counterparts; more, the classical English education he has received (albeit informally) from these books (Shakespeare, Plato, Aristotle) has effected a kind of psychic disjunction, a form of split consciousness, within which he is unable to negotiate the world of his lived reality and the world of his secret aspirations. Selvon's intimate over-the-shoulder narrator points this dilemma of colonial education with gentle irony: "Men who knew how to live but couldn't read and write bowed their heads in shame when Tiger passed: Tiger could read and write but he didn't know how to live" (38). The attempt to engage other men in dialogue on philosophical issues is an attempt to find connection in a world from which he is already separated by his education, but it is also ultimately an attempt to believe that this world, which has conferred his chosen masks of masculinity, is not just prescribing tradition for its own sake, but rather does have within it a deeper capacity, a thoughtful underpinning by which it is authorized.

In this context, Tiger is constantly torn between pleased shock, when the villagers utter sudden gems of folk wisdom that seem to him to hold a profound philosophical significance, and disappointment, when they fail to respond to his questions in the way he wishes, unused as they are to expressing their thought in the abstract objectified terms that come naturally to him. For Tiger, the startling insights of which the men are capable serve to validate the (male) community as a community that can sustain a man such as he is; by extension, he himself is validated. But this incipient security is constantly undermined by the men's refusal of intimacy, their unspoken view that a man keeps his secrets (Soylo: "Every man have their own life to live" [130]), and most of all by the failure of the older men either to image the purported authority of older manhood or to give the authoritative advice that will assure him of the authority of his own: "Every time I get bother and confuse . . . I want to talk to old people, because I feel they know something that young people don't know. . . . You bound to know, Soylo, and if you don't know now you is a old man, then you waste you whole life" (129–30).

Second, the search for authority in the community of elders takes on an Oedipal-type curve that is exemplified in Tiger's fraught relationship with his father, Babolal. (The relationship with Babolal is in fact the archetype for the relationship with all the others.) The significance of the title, *Turn Again Tiger*, lies in the series of circles and loops that Tiger has to make in his quest. In the earlier novel, Tiger had moved away from his parents and their world, symbolized and rooted in the cane, before he had had time to properly understand it. *Turn Again* begins with a decision to go back to that world in partnership with his father, and Tiger's own meditations point its significance (7): it is a "backward step", synonymous with Lamming's concept of the "backward glance", which Lamming argues is the task of every West Indian in the process of becoming.

This first loop is a return to a past staggered in fragments, obscurities and silences, which Tiger has to (re)construct in a process of understanding and remaking, so that the self unfolding in the present moment can itself be constructed. This is neither the linear progression of a Freudian concept of the male psychological universe nor the safe return to secure holding structures of Fromm's concept of Western individuation. Tiger's conscious entry into psychological "modernity" is a looping back to things that have not been explained – a logos that has not been uttered – and to a beginning which has to be healed and reinvented in order to be reincorporated into itself. The moment of discovering his father is a moment of simultaneous acceptance and rejection, which is also simultaneous with the moment of self-invention.

Tiger, driven by the need for security, is at first unable to accept this fact of dissonance which is also open ground of possibility for a new, untrammelled code of being in the world (this is symbolized in the fact that the return to the cane is not a return to his childhood home but to a new place, Five Rivers). The source of his rage against his father is the latter's failure to display the authority (in word and act) which he has been taught is the purview of old men, and which must be displayed in order for him to trust that that authority in himself will grow mellow with age. Every showdown Tiger has with Babolal surrounds a conflict of male authority and involves a discourse on the concept of manhood in the context of authority. Tiger takes note of his father's hunger for this authority: "Babolal was the sort of man who would say yes, yes, and nod his head vigorously, and while all the words were floating around him he would pick up [only] the ones 'supervisor' and 'in charge' " (42). The fact that he despises Babolal for his failure to appropriate authority is the measure of his recognition that Babolal's failure implicates the masks of manhood he himself has inherited from the society that had produced his father, and which has moreover instilled like a mantra the idea that the final validation of such manhood is old age, the proof that a man had been tested and tried and come successfully through (169).

Tiger is able in the end to regain some respect for his father when he sees him supervising the cane-cutting, for the first time very sure of himself, clothed in the dignity of being finally in charge in a community of respect. But the fact that it is in his role as colonial labourer that Babolal was first denuded of authority is the heart of Tiger's Oedipal crisis and renders even this ameliorative scene painful. The loop back to his father is also a loop back to the buried memories of childhood encounters with colonialism, when he had seen other overseers of Robinson's type parading the land (47). The colonial patriarchy faces him at the same moment as he faces his father, in double dissonance.

Robinson's superior position makes a mockery of Babolal's sense of himself as a man in charge and, by extension, a mockery of Tiger's also (for, as he himself anguishes when he runs away from Doreen, what price a man's authority over chattels and household goods if his sense of self is erased by a female wearing a pre-eminent masculinity, the masculinity of space shared with the white supervisor whose position usurps his father's?). It is no wonder then that the crisis precipitates a radical rejection of the most individual and paradoxically most colonially trammelled part of himself, symbolized in the books – artefacts of a colonial schizophrenia – which he burns. The burning indicates that this form of identity, too, has been questioned and found lacking in legitimacy and authority.

The abortive rationalistic search for authority within the community of elders leads Tiger to Walcott's conclusion, "there are no . . . elders, only old [men]":[4] "I got to figure everything out for myself . . . is no use asking anybody anything" (131). Yet the realization that he is not going to find anyone who will necessarily analyse the world in his terms or use the modes of expression that for him are a sign of philosophical clarity frees Tiger to hear more fully the folk voices subsumed under the cyclical patterns of daily living in which on the surface they seem to be unthinkingly immersed. Soylo's tale of horror is a kind of climax in that understanding. The structures of supportive community (the affections of the heart, the narratives of others) are represented by Soylo, and part of what Soylo's presence indicates is Tiger's need to appreciate the creative forces subsumed in the relationships the folk society offers to him. For though these had been the ground of his beginning salvation in *A Brighter Sun,* Tiger's preoccupation with the idea of masculinity as self-directed, singular quest and of knowledge as a clear-cut linear voice had limited his ability to perceive the debt he owed to the community. There had been at base an essential selfishness as well as self-centredness, which Selvon seems now to be dismantling.

Through Soylo's story, Tiger recognizes other people as more than satellites orbiting his singular self: "He didn't know what . . . to say, and in the silence now he thought how easy his own life was in comparison, and again, how you can never tell with people, you never know anything about their lives, really, not unless they tell you" (168). At another level, this thought-statement in response to Soylo's narrative suggests that Tiger is able to humble himself enough to recognize that difference does not have to mean superiority or inferiority, and that authority can be shared – for the recognition of the equal legitimacy of Soylo's story in essence displaces the pre-eminence of his own personal narrative. More than this, he comes to realize that subsuming every narrative is an individual confrontation with and response to the world which is as philosophical as the next man's, and sometimes as heroic. The philosophy may be implicit in action, or uttered in fragments, or, as in More Lazy's narratives, in parable and dream. What these differences highlight is a need to decipher the multiplicity of "languages", without necessarily losing one's own idiolect.

Whether this recognition is seen as a humanistic reconciliation of the opposing terms of democracy (individual uniqueness, which carries a certain amount of aloneness – as well as of community – which is an attitude of acceptance and cohesion), or as a suggestion that the community, despite its supportive aspects, is too striated by masculinist taboos against feeling and intimacy to bridge the gap of aloneness, or as some form of comment on the loneliness of the long-distance runner, is almost beside the point. The ability to accept this lack of full closure and to take what the community can offer may be read as a sign of Tiger's growing maturity. At the end of *A Brighter Sun,* he had thought that loneliness was a man's necessity; in *Turn Again,* the return of anguish and the absence of the friends whose help he had not fully understood or appreciated have caused him to question and unwittingly reject that same loneliness by forging new relationships with other men. The final acceptance may be ambivalent; that is, it points to the incompleteness of Tiger's movement away from the belief in aloneness as masculinist ideology ("each man [is] locked in a world where no one else [can] enter" [169]), but it also points to his growing ability to accept others as they are, which is an important aspect of community.

This humility is not the only sign of growth. Tiger comes to realize that the encounter with Doreen, effectively a kind of rape, did not solve any problems or confer any authorities; rather, it robbed him of authority: "I wasn't man enough to settle things and win. I lose respect for myself, Joe. . . . You can't see it have a principle here, man? Two things. I didn't want it to happen for myself, and I didn't want it to happen for Urmilla. Since I married I never went with another woman, Joe" (55). Tiger recognizes finally that true authority comes from the possession of one's own spirit: "But when I come a man in truth, I want to possess myself" (155). This statement is a powerful deconstruction of all the former searches for authority and all the former masks of identity explored and assumed in *A Brighter Sun*.

Not the least of its deconstructive effects is Tiger's willingness to give voice to his emotions, his vulnerability, his failure and inadequacy (surely, in his terms, the opposite of "authoritative" manhood), and to admit to consciousness his sense of human and husbandly connection to Urmilla. It is the final rejection of speech as mask, as well as a shift away from a view of life as necessarily and in all respects oppositional. The ethic of competition at the heart of authoritative masculinity is also abandoned. Again – at least potentially – the utterance constitutes a tacit recognition, subsuming Selvon's gender discourse across the two novels, that at a core level of identity, gender may be irrelevant.

Tiger's new awareness of Urmilla as a person for whom his betrayal of the marriage contract has implications is an equally important watershed, indicating that yet another piece has been dismantled from the costume of authority. A man is no longer someone who has to impose his physical will on his woman, and one gets a sense that Tiger may no longer wear this mask – an expectation borne out by the fact that later in the novel he refuses to join the other men in the wife-beating ritual. In the final analysis, Tiger's search for legitimation has been a reflexive pilgrimage, a turning again; for in testing the constructs of masculinity in the context of a project of authorization, he has in fact had to question and discard some of these constructs as elements of identity. That their authority proved to be spurious has called the bases of their constitution into question. Masculinity, then, turns out to be not a once-for-all, singular construct "for all seasons and reasons", but a process of negotiation, testing and retesting, rehearsal and change.

Significantly, Tiger does not in any major way relate his individual growth to ideas of changing the society. Such ideas emerged incipiently in *A Brighter Sun* in his nationalistic outburst after the doctor episodes, but in *Turn Again* he has apparently dealt with the dream of shaping society by shelving it until he has consolidated aspects of his individual self and has begun to deal with the logical next set of relations: his relations with his wife. This may be read as Tiger's way of coping with the threat of dissonance, rather than as the lack of sophistication in political matters of which Selvon has been accused by ardent nationalist critics. Indeed, that the political outbursts of *A Brighter Sun* had occurred in the context of Tiger's frustration and guilt over Urmilla points to the fact that his essential problem had to do with this rather than with politics, and that "politics" at that point had been a way of escaping responsibility. Its presence in his consciousness had implied that it would resurface in another phase of his development, when he was psychologically more ready.

Despite its use of circular loops rather than a linearity of progression, Selvon's extremely careful phasing of Tiger's Bildungsroman is Freudian in concept – an attempt at a developmental approach to the responsibilities of self, family, community and nation, which unravels the Gordian knot of a simultaneous approach to all of these, the heart of the dissonantal experience of manhood in his contemporary West Indian setting. The phased nature of the two-part Bildungsroman becomes clear only within the frame of a gender reading, which dispels the criticism of *Turn Again* as a mere repeat of *A Brighter Sun*. That the final issue, the issue of Tiger's development in the context of nationhood, is not pursued suggests that the two novels may well have been conceived as part of a trilogy parallel to the Moses trilogy.

It is worth noting in this context that *Turn Again Tiger* ends with Tiger being offered a position as spokesman on local concerns to the political representative of Barataria, the world of *A Brighter Sun* to which he has returned as another loop in the pilgrimage of self-making. This respect accorded by his peers tells Tiger that he has passed the test of social recognition as authority and legitimation. It allows space for him to reconcile his education into a grounded rather than disjunct relation to his environment – that is, to make it an indigenous possession rather than an alienated one. It will stand him in good stead as the community's representative, and in fact is part of the reason he is asked to fulfil this function (so that the burning of the books is not an end but a beginning). But more than this, it hints of nationalist political activity as the logical next phase of Tiger's development. Even though Selvon not does develop this issue, so grounded is his Bildungsroman in the everyday realities of the people's life that the novels may be considered an extraordinary trope of the problematics of West Indian national becoming.

In the end, then, Tiger throws off some of the crippling legacies of the society and creates new possibilities out of the dissonances of being a man in West Indian society. The note of hope which ends *A Brighter Sun* also ends *Turn Again Tiger* – a sense of continuing cycles as a principle of the universe of the land which Tiger works, and thus a sense that another phase will bring other growths: "Overhead a cloud fled the sun, moving in a swift breeze. 'Now is a good time to plant corn,' he muttered, gazing up at the sky" (*Brighter Sun,* 215).

> Tiger looked around him . . . at the land, which would sprout things when the rains came and washed away the burns of the harvest. "Soon something else going to grow here."
>
> "It just like we," Tiger said. "We finish one job, and we got to get ready to start another."
>
> He stuck his cutlass in the earth and walked away to meet Urmilla and Chandra. (*Turn Again,* 181)

Significantly, in terms of Selvon's focus, the emphasis is on the country as land, not as nation. Tiger's answers are humanistic rather than political in the narrowed sense of the term.

Transgressing Spaces: All Kinds of Woman-Man

But it would be too much to expect in such a carefully realist novel that all be made perfect. Throughout much of the novel the fundamental distance between Tiger and Urmilla is firmly in place; a meeting between man and woman as equals is not yet part of Tiger's slate of possibilities, as he had not fully come to terms with the "feminine" in himself. Indeed, he is more like a despotic slave master who magnanimously relaxes the strings of control than he is like a husband. Halfway through the narrative he is still able to congratulate himself on behaving decently to Urmilla ("He felt like a superior being meting out mercy" [*Turn Again,* 89]), and for a long time he remains impatient of displays of softer feeling. Urmilla constantly expresses frustration at his lack of interaction with his daughter Chandra; his unease with displays of affection is inscribed early on: " 'I don't remember nothing like that,' Tiger said, fighting the sentiment he felt. 'All you women always remembering funny things' " (34). His terrified seizure of Chandra from Manko's home after the nightmare of Soylo's story and the walking away "to meet Urmilla and Chandra" at the end of the novel are an open-ended indication of possibilities for growth in those relationships, not a sign of arrival, and indeed there is still enough of a sense of closedness to make this a possibility only.

Also, Tiger's continuing capacity for blindness towards his own self, which Selvon wonderfully balances against his almost painful honesty, is signalled in his failure to realize how much his own loquacious search for private dialogues and understandings is associated more with traditional femininity than with masculinity. Even the naked, triumphant declaration "I feel more like a man than when I first came" (169) is circumscribed by that ambiguity. It is not the sort of declaration that would have been made by any of the others, inured to the ideology that a man does not speak about feelings except in the performativity of play (symbolized in this novel by drunkenness, under the guise of which a man is permitted to utter anything [123–24]). The fact that this growing if extremely paradoxical tendency in Tiger is not identified as a form of femininity by the others points to the extent to which he has managed to blend this with the indices of masculinity, and ironically makes room for the imagination of a more integrated kind of self in the Tiger of the future which we imagine in Selvon's geography of open-ended personal space.

Selvon's refusal to project a singular masculine type is evident also in the variety of male characters with which the novels are peopled: each has his own peculiar sense of self, which does not necessarily conform to any societal dictates. (Tiger's attraction to the most unconventional of these and his compassion for the weakest suggest his own innate acceptance of diversity and range as part of a modern view of the world. That this exists side by side with his patriarchal rigidities is one of the paradoxes of his character.) The parade is instructive. It includes More Lazy, who does not work, who finds his legitimacy in weaving dreams and fictions and who is ultimately seduced into work not by any moral persuasion or shame associated with ideas of inadequate manhood, but by the ties of community and a sense of safety in being able to do the work of women, which is physically less demanding for a man. It includes Otto, who enters late into the discourses of masculinity and in the context of the community is allowed space to work out his relation to its codes. It also includes Babolal, who knows nothing but the cane, which is a source of retardation but which confers a moving dignity when he is able to achieve authority out of that very setting, and who depends on his son for his sense of manhood yet resents him for it. There is Soylo, who in an act of mourning for his lost woman and child removes himself from the society of others until the space of mourning is closed with healing, and who masks the process with an aggressive rage; Joe, who believes manhood is not a state to be questioned but just to be; and Boysie, who is known as a sensible man but who has to painfully negotiate the emasculations attendant upon having "foolishly" brought a white wife home from England. This range of man-selves, mixing the paradoxical, the heterodox and the conservative, links with the cultural environment, where Creole, Indian and Chinese build and participate in an integrated community whose diversity is its strength. In the end, then, masculinity is a function of the creolized society's radical heterodoxy, in which difference and glides between "feminine" and "masculine", thought and feeling, authority and vulnerability, simply exist.

A similar diversity appears in the range of male–female dyads presented in both novels. The relationships of Joe and Rita in *A Brighter Sun* and of Otto and Berta in *Turn Again Tiger* represent points on the continuum of Selvon's discourse on gender relations, forming important contrasts to the Tiger–Urmilla relationship. Joe and Rita's relationship, at one remove from Tiger and Urmilla's, represents the Afro-West Indian experience of spousal relations in the heterodox society. The union between the Chinese Otto and his common-law wife, Berta, a Creole, may be said to represent a "syncretic" possibility arising out of their different social experiences.

Unlike Tiger and Urmilla's, Joe and Rita's relationship is a common-law one entered upon by mutual adult choice. The relationship is therefore governed by a tacit knowledge that either is free to leave if he or she so desires. In addition, Rita, a type of the black working-class woman, has not been socialized into the secondariness Urmilla has been taught is her role. Rita's lived reality includes a pivotal experience of women's "masculine" roles and masculine independence, so that it is impossible for her to assume the subservient role which Joe, psychologically damaged from an abused childhood and ideas of manhood as controlling authority, needs her to assume. She is an equal in the relationship, joint breadwinner and an authority in the house. Tellingly, Urmilla is beaten by Tiger, while Joe and Rita fight (double subject, active voice).

Joe's ill-treatment of Rita does not elicit pity, as Tiger's abuse of Urmilla does, for Rita is no victim; but the net effect is the same as in Tiger and Urmilla's case: we are presented with a reinforced picture of the conflictual nature of gender relations in which men feel their roles to be in question and of contexts in which men adopt violence as a means of imposing domestic authority. Rita and Joe's relationship presents one type of black experience of gender relations as a comparison to the type of Indo-West Indian experience that Urmilla and Tiger represent: different types of social structures and social relations result in different motivations for domestic violence. Joe has been beaten by a woman (his grandmother) and seeks to regain lost face and authority by beating his woman; Tiger uses violence as a means of structural control. Both men are in search of masculine certainty, and both essentially illustrate the society's dysfunctions.

Otto and Berta are of particular interest because they represent a model potentially superior to anything the other two couples have yet achieved, and are able to do this because they start from a position of greater freedom within the social structures. We have seen that the men's relation to women in the two novels is configured in rigidly patriarchal terms. Otto is paradoxically a marginal man, outside of the ideologies created by this world. Though he is infected by the ideology of woman as subservient drudge, his lived experience has not supported the ideology, for the simple reason that he has never had a woman to rule over. (This is similar to Pinteados, the ship's pilot in Lamming's *Natives of My Person*: Pinteados's feminized image is reinforced by the fact that he has never had a wife and is sexually almost inexperienced. Yet, ironically, he is psychologically the most secure of the ship's company.)

Wherever lived experience conflicts with ideology, the former tends to supersede and subvert the latter. This is partly why Berta is able to create with Otto a completely different set of relations from that obtaining between the other men and their wives. The astute Berta starts out by appropriating the strategies men use to keep women "in their place", womanizing these strategies (that is, creating a "woman version"[5] of them) and using them to negotiate power in the relationship with Otto. The operative word is "negotiate": much humour is created by the spectacle of the evolving relationship as first one then the other gains the upper hand, their shifts of identity and role as fluid as the confrontations themselves.

The fluidity of the confrontations is the fluidity of performative play: the Otto–Berta relationship reinvokes the carnival masquerade, which in its deployment of powers is an extraordinarily ambiguous and paradoxical medium. (Berta's advent marks one of the few instances where the calypsonian's laughter returns to the novel. The calypso, product of carnival, belongs to the creolized world, with its praxis of syncretic joinings and reshapings. On more than one level, it is no accident that Berta is described as "a Creole".)[6] The equilibrium which ultimately exists despite Otto and Berta's continuing upheavals is based on a mutual recognition of each other's potential power, as well as on a mutual recognition that neither can completely predict the other; thus, projects of ownership or superior authority are effectively destabilized.

It is easier for Otto and Berta to achieve this compromise than it is for the other two couples, because they stand in the loosest relation to the traditionalizing aspects of society and so are more easily able to create new identity and relationship spaces for themselves. (Tiger and Urmilla are bound by traditional Indo-West Indian gender norms, Joe and Rita by a more "stable" home arrangement, with the expectations implicit in a spousal relationship. Otto and Berta's relationship is new and tenuous; Otto has not been fully socialized into the village norms, and Berta obviously has not yet decided whether this is supposed to be a committed relationship.) Even so, like all creative possibilities in Selvon's work, the creative possibilities in this relationship are criss-crossed and, in this case, even emptied by destructive forces. Otto and Berta fight so often, and Berta exploits Otto so much as part of a gender war, that they appear to be hopelessly locked into the society's negative codes for male-female relationships. Thus, when they achieve a measure of compromise, the tenuous nature of performative endings is highlighted.

That the Joe–Rita and Otto–Berta dyads exist in the novels and are treated at length attests to Selvon's continuing preoccupation with gender relations and to the fact that, in the novels of home, this shades into a search for equitable solutions to gender conflict. In addition, despite the larger preoccupation with the perspectives of men, *A Brighter Sun* and *Turn Again Tiger* also attempt to portray women as psychological characters. This is particularly marked in Selvon's treatment of the concept of authority in the second novel. In both books, gender is bound up with the search for social empowerment, in different ways specific to both sexes. The discussion of Tiger's pilgrimage in *Turn Again* has indicated that masculinity is seen as being expressed in authority, and that, for the male characters, authority is a vertical structure in which men, positioned by "right" at the top of the hierarchy, impose order on their women and on those symbols of culture which must be controlled in order for authority to become itself. Authority realized is the fasces of masculinity in the world.

It is interesting that even Otto and More Lazy – the most unconventional and "unthreatened" of men (unthreatened, that is, by any sense of inadequacy as men, despite their differentness) – feel it necessary to appropriate this idea of masculinity as authority once the context is relations with women. More Lazy dreams of his sexual authoritativeness subduing ecstatic maidens; Otto takes on the orthodox mantle once, and once only, to assert his right to Berta's sexual favours. It is true that both men's behaviour is governed by desire and that neither Otto's action nor More Lazy's boast is directed primarily at women. Rather, they are directed at the male audience, among whom this concept of authority is promulgated and among whom they must act or speak to save face. This serves to indicate the continuing friction between the individual sense of self and the hierarchical gender codes which transect the more equitable influences in the social world.

The women, in contrast to the men, appear to deconstruct the relationship between authority and power. For them, the issue appears to be power, in the sense of personal influence earned or granted in the context of a mutuality of relations, rather than authority, in the sense of official position conferred by right, as the essence of power. More specifically, from the women's point of view, power is vested in their ability to influence internal relations of community, as opposed to the men's perception of authority as power exerted in a vertical, externalized influence downwards. The option of power as an internal relation to the self is not explored in connection with women: Tiger's final though incomplete and open-ended arrival at a view of authority as an inward, personal possession, rather than as an outwardly constituted position in a hierarchy, is not paralleled by any female character's engagement with the issue at this level, either here or in the exile fictions.

The women's greater concern with power rather than authority is seen in *Turn Again Tiger* in the difference between their bid for their husbands' attention and the men's response to this attempt. The women have decided to stop the men going to Otto's rum shop in order to make them spend more time at home. It is important for our distinctions that they negotiate the terms of their attack in a kind of "sisterhood" relationship and that the motive is not so much authority over their men as a desire for community with them. Thus, when Selvon comments on the beating the women receive in punishment for their rebellion – "The same spirit which had strengthened the women to band together now united the men" (88) – the statement may be an attempt to suggest a gender equality, but there is a curious mismatch between the authorial (or narrational) assertion and the evidence on which the assertion is based. The disjunction points to the double-voicedness of the fictional text, the inherent gaps by which it is able to accomplish its own deconstruction.

The narrative viewpoint is deconstructed not only by the evidence of the women's dialogue in planning the attack, but by the opening paragraph, in which a comment is inserted: "That night women wailed and screamed in Five Rivers as the men *put them in their places* with blows left and right" (88, emphasis added). The hierarchical concept of "putting them in their places" is radically different from "they like to drink too much, *so they don't spend no time in the house.* . . . All the women make up a party and go to Otto, and tell him to stop trusting rum *so that the men could go home to their wives*" (81, emphasis added).

The women's action, though outwardly reminiscent of the course taken by the wives in Aristophanes' *Lysistrata,* is the resort of women who believe that in their individual selves they lack (relationship) power with their husbands – a lack which Urmilla's story in both novels graphically reveals. Underneath the acts and words of protest is the primary discourse, inarticulable in direct language or private dialogue because of the domestic silence each man imposes on his wife. In this regard it is interesting that Tiger doesn't beat Urmilla, precisely because it is this abstinence on his part that makes him feel like a superior being meting out mercy. It is interesting also that he imposes silence on her so that the other men will not know he has *not* beaten her. Thus he preserves both his authority over Urmilla and that authority in the eyes of the other men.

The beatings may be taken as a ritual re-gendering, a return of the women to their "proper" gender. The women, relegated to the private sphere, which is commanded to remain voiceless in order that the men's linguistic authority can be sustained, have made themselves agents of sedition by inserting their voice in the only place where they perceive it to be hearable: the public domain appropriated by men. The rebellion and the public appropriation of the word are, in patriarchal terms, men's strategies, and they must be recuperated by the exertion of an authority which forces the women to realize they are "not-men". The women, on the other hand, have no interest in questioning the manhood of the men, but rather in insisting on the men's responsibility to their relationships.

The discrepancy between the narrative comment and the events recounted arguably stems from Selvon's acceptance of female psychology as an a priori given. Here he presents women's community without a convincing portrayal of its sources or motivations. But he presents it in an unbroken discourse, which we see emerging from the Tanty/Agnes dyad in *The Lonely Londoners,* to the wives and girlfriends of *The Housing Lark,* to Rita/Urmilla in *A Brighter Sun,* to the wives of Five Rivers in *Turn Again Tiger.* (The discourse extends also to Tanty/Doris in *Moses Migrating,* a novel which, through Moses as a hybridic, transcontinental invention, brings the exilic and home worlds into contact with each other.) Women's community in all the novels seems to be a form of empowerment, either to challenge the men's view of things or to establish some structure which they see as necessary but which brings them in conflict with the men's view of things. Significantly, it is those women whose lives have been most exposed to the creolizing aspects of the society who confer on the group this oppositional character. Thus it is Rita who encourages Urmilla, and Berta – a picaresque version of the Tanty–Brenda archetype – who subtly catalyses the insurrection of the other wives. (Berta's influence is a kind of domino effect, arising simply from her unorthodox relationship with Otto and from her presence as a representative of the radical outer world entering the closed village circle.)

In all cases, the communality of women seems to be directed outwards, towards either the achievement of material goods or the (re)ordering of community along relationship lines. It is also generally referential, or reactive; that is, it results from the behaviour of men. In this respect it is also contingent, showing itself only as a situation arises. Invariably, it is perceived by the men as a threat to male supremacy (in *A Brighter Sun,* Tiger and Joe constantly attempt to break up the friendship between Rita and Urmilla, a relationship which no doubt saves Urmilla psychologically). The idea that power may be exercised in many forms by different people without loss is unthinkable to Selvon's men; rather, power is an exclusive category which is cancelled by sharing. This concept is the rephrasing of power as absolute authority, a competitive principle whose aim is to cancel out competition.

Selvon's idea that a community of women exists also serves to highlight the absence of a similar community between men and women, as well as the differences in his representation of women's and men's community. The latter is presented as complex and multifaceted. It is both a loose system of ideas and signs (an ideology and its symbols) and a search for and induction into this system. The system exists and is sought for primarily as a means of legitimation. The search is reflexive, that is, directed inwards to projects of self-making (or, as in the case of the London novels, self-protection or self-unravelling, which are aspects of self-making).

Both the community and the search are, however, also referential even as they are reflexive, but their referentiality seems to be more diverse than that of the women. That is to say, they constitute responses to external factors among which women are only one of several, or many. (Thus, Tiger's search for selfhood may have been triggered by his marriage, but it focuses beyond Urmilla even to national issues, albeit only incipiently. Similarly, the community of ideas of manhood involves ideas about ruling women, but also ideas about hardihood – the ability to drink – and ideas about sticking together as a sign of male identity. In the London novels, women are only one strand in the social world from which the men are collectively fleeing.)

The system of ideas and signs that constitutes male community is at once conservative and changeable, the extent of change depending on the nature of the individual search and the instress of circumstances. Tiger is arguably not very successful in his equivocal bid to force acceptance of thought-intimacy as part of the male code, but the fact that he himself invests in intimacy suggests the possibility of change in the code. The nearest approximation to a men's community of intimacy appears in the novels of exile (the Sunday-morning confessionals in Moses's room), in the liminal space where the known world is dissolved. Here the men come near to the emotional connection implied in the women's bid for closer relationships with men in *Turn Again Tiger*. The Londoners are on the edge of discovering a "femininity" of space, language and self, which might have established the principles for an alternative social structure except that constant flight freezes this possibility in stasis.

Selvon's women's community is diverse only in its strategies for male-directed attack and material survival. While the complexity of men's interactions in contrast with the singularity of women's is a direct result of the choice of male protagonist, it does point the problem of representation even in the work of this most humane and even-handed of writers. The overall side effect of the portrayal of women primarily in terms of their responses to men is that the men's view of them is supported by the narrative strategies of the text. Once they are possessed of any form of power or authority (Tanty, Brenda, even to some extent Berta) or form themselves into groups (Teena and her group in *The Housing Lark,* the women of Five Rivers), they become harpy figures who make or seek to make men's lives difficult.

But Selvon also treats the abuse of women by men, and the subtextual narratives that inscribe women's stories, as well as the overt concern with the issues of equitable gender relations in *Turn Again Tiger,* indicate a questioning of the men's gender attitudes. In the Tiger novels, the attempt at a balanced exploration is extended in the portrayal of Urmilla's inner consciousness. The female characters of the exile novels are drawn with broad penstrokes of externalized social observation, suggesting a minute eye for nuance and detail but a deliberate "hands-off" approach to psychological portrayal, so that the typical Selvon female appears somewhat in the nature of an alien, mysterious being, energized from sources not immediately available to a male consciousness. Urmilla is the one female character with whom Selvon breaks this seeming taboo of externalized representation, possibly because the circumstances in which the narrative begins imply her parallel importance to

Tiger. Thus, although Urmilla constitutes the "second sex" insofar as her thought is presented largely as either object or response in a universe bounded by Tiger's subjective consciousness, there are also snatches of narrative which seek to tell Urmilla's story outside the context of that overarching consciousness which is Tiger's.

These snatches include the vignette of the visit between Urmilla and Rita near the end of *Turn Again Tiger,* and the account of the two women's preparation of the dinner for the Yankee guests in *A Brighter Sun.* But the effort to give an internal contour to Urmilla's story is invariably uneasy and soon peters out. One telling example appears in *Turn Again,* when Urmilla, at the point where the decision to march on Otto's shop is ratified, becomes paralysed by fear of Tiger. When she confronts Tiger, she has travelled through her fear and attained a level of courage which is quite unlike the timid Urmilla and, more importantly, which is scarcely presented to the reader as the result of any convincing psychological process. We are told, "She knew he was going to beat her but she wasn't going to cringe and cower" (89), but the presentation of the movement from paralytic fear to strong courage remains fragmentary and unconvincing. Power as personal self-possession is marginally invoked but not narratively realized. Thus, in the same narrative moment in which the empowering effect of the women's community is inscribed, its representation is compromised by the artist's inability to render it in psychologically realistic terms. The same might be said of Urmilla's passage from catatonic terror to sudden sexual ecstasy on the night of her wedding to an equally terrified, fumbling stranger with whom she has made not the slightest of connections.

Selvon's attempt to create some kind of bridge between the narrative extremes of male viewpoints and suppressed female stories is not by any means a sign of incipient feminism. Rather, ironically and in a roundabout kind of way, it is part of the carefully cultivated naturalism, or realism, of his narrative stance, the fictional pretence of "letting the story tell itself" "realistically". Through this fictive construct – the "realistic fiction" – the further fiction of minimal or no authorial intervention is maintained. The attempt at balance belongs to this fiction of even-handedness, the refusal to take sides. Another aspect of it is the avoidance of the "preacherly text", which might well be the characteristic that prompted Lamming to describe Selvon as the least political of West Indian writers ([1960] 1992, 43). Yet this kind of "naturalistic", apolitical stance is already compromised, and not only because it embeds the notion of the pre-eminent authenticity (the political supremacy) of the strategically distanced point of view, which it refuses to bring to judgement.

The "apolitical" stance also empties itself out in paradox, for it is at odds with Selvon's carnivalesque West Indian sensibility, which constantly encroaches on and undermines the pretence of naturalism. So, for example, the seriousness of the women's story is only deadpan, subtended and undermined by narrative laughter. Even in the sombre *A Brighter Sun* and *Turn Again Tiger,* the calypsonian's laughter returns or is pronounced when women clash with men in the fierce contentions of the creolized Trinidad society to which the calypso belongs. In each case the political doubling, the forked tongue which curls itself beneath the seeming neutrality of Selvon's narrative style, is very present, and active. So the women who function subtextually or overtly as critiques of the men's attitudes – from the militant female group in *The Housing Lark* to Brenda in *Moses Ascending* and Berta in *Turn Again Tiger* – not only are instruments of derision, but are themselves derided. The open ending, the ending of paradox, is the moment of derision: the house not bought, the Black Power movement in (albeit possibly temporary) shambles, the sexual freedom (Berta's) curtailed and Otto's manly powers valorized in Berta's own erstwhile recalcitrant voice.

In the end also, the laughter undermines the women's critique and presents gender conflict as a form of competitive entertainment in which the women still lose because the author as master calypsonian has the last, equivocal word. This may be read as Selvon's way of insisting either on equality or on male supremacy, or again as part of the ritual delay of potential tragedy in these male-female relations. The point is that the calypsonian's laughter is ambiguous, double-faced, a Janus mask capable of any number of competing interpretations. The seriousness with which Selvon treats Urmilla is exceptional in these novels, and paralleled by his similar treatment of Sarojini in *Those Who Eat the Cascadura* (1972). It seems to be a preferential seriousness accorded to female characters whose anomaly is in their orthodoxy, their lack of masculine characteristics, which places them outside the mainstream of a combative, performative and performance-driven society. All others are stickfighters, self-aggrandizers who give and, in the texts' implied justice system, receive no quarter. In every case, Selvon's presentation of gender relations is a battlefield, albeit on carnival ground.

In the final analysis, Selvon's male-oriented gender discourse, in its carefully nuanced "naturalistic" detail, brings again a sense of a society which is complex in its gender configurations: fluid, transgressive, patriarchally and conflictually trammelled yet radically heterodox. Undeniably, there are differences in the expectations and behaviours of Selvon's male and female characters, and in the presentation strategies related to each. Even so, gender roles and identities are presented as subject to negotiation and change, and lines between manhood and womanhood, masculinity and femininity, are blurred in practice if not completely in ideology. The complex gender picture is predicated within social frames whose own flexibility is what allows for various types of masculinity and femininity to be manifested and tolerated; the flexible end of the continuum exerts a constant pressure which suggests that the conservative aspects – that is, the entrenched, essentially patriarchal ideologies – may loosen, be modified or become subdued.

Selvon seems to suggest the creolizing community as the strong ground on which gender attitudes and relations, though contentious, may be positively worked out. In this respect the Tiger novels illuminate the London group. The trauma of migrancy is understood as originating from the absence of this creolizing space, yet, paradoxically, the performative diversities learnt within it combine with the total removal of its safeties to produce new, flexible strategies of gender identification. These are as creative as they are destructive – that is, as fraught with paradox as the creolizing, colonially trammelled society itself.

It is interesting that in Selvon's fictional world, femininity is suggested not so much as a set of qualities but as a position. Femininity as presented in Selvon's texts shares this in common with Luce Irigaray's perception of womanness in Western societies: that it has not yet been (fully) described. Masculinity, on the other hand, is both a position and a set of definitive qualities, which, however, may be tested or may have to be achieved. For Selvon's men, womanhood is not synonymous with femininity; rather, womanhood constitutes both a desired ideal and aberrations from this ideal. A woman by right belongs to a secondary state in a hierarchy of authority (this is, femininity) but is known by her recalcitrance or potential recalcitrance and by her tendency to usurp male position. She is also known by her possession of qualities identified as masculine, and by her ability to force men into social relations that complicate the process of negotiating manhood. Only in Tiger's traditional ethnic setting is ideal womanhood described as a quality of silence, and this is gradually erased under the instress of Tiger's growing personal and larger cultural experience.

In the world of Selvon's men's imaginations, the ideal woman causes no trouble to men, for she knows her place; it is a question of position. The ideal woman is therefore feminine. The recalcitrant woman – which describes or, in the men's imaginative fears, potentially describes all the women in these five texts – wants to rule, overthrowing male rulership. She has linguistic powers; she is a threat both individually and collectively; she wins bread; she may manipulate sexual favours. In other words, in addition to contending for position, she has a set of qualities: she is masculine. The fact that only in Tiger's ethnic community is a definite set of qualities described for the ideal woman (silence, subservience, housewifery, chastity) suggests that in the wider society the recalcitrant woman is the norm rather than the exception.

Tellingly, no set of qualities for the ideal woman is described in connection with the women whose identities are more creolized. "Femininity" in such cases appears to be more a set of beleaguered men's wishes as to what women are but ought not to be: linguistically authoritative but ought not, prone to usurp position but ought not, discomforting but ought not – a series of implied "ought nots" that points the extent to which there is no major investment in definitions of femininity in the general social milieu that Selvon represents across the fictions. In this "ought/not" equation, femininity is both a negative and an unrealized moral conditional – a liminal, receding space that women refuse and that men inadvertently inhabit in reverse (should be but are not). Indeed, in a very real sense, it is masculinity that is elaborated as a set of qualities, and this in both male and female, though from different vantage points, and unsanctioned in the latter. Because it is unsanctioned in women, masculinity as a position (as opposed to a set of qualities) is guarded as a male purview and is endlessly contended for the very reason that its opposite has no positive (definitive) identification.

Part 2

Resisting the Voyeuristic Gaze

The Construction of Gender as Anti-colonial Discourse

Lamming's *Of Age and Innocence* and *Season of Adventure*

Lamming's Theory of Language, Gender and Genealogy

THE ISSUE OF GENDER in George Lamming's fiction is closely related to the problem of his aesthetics, which has exercised the critical academy in its attempts over time to come to terms with the significance of his work. Gender in Lamming is inseparable from a linguistic epistemology of the human and colonial subject, a metatheory of language which subsumes all his fiction and within which the problematics of his style are embedded. More specifically, we may say that Lamming theorizes gender, locating it within a wider theorization of language and the relation of the human and colonial subject to language, and that he uses his narrative style, both structure and idiom, as the metaphor in which this theory is sometimes couched and sometimes embedded. Style and gender, then, are deeply interwoven motifs of figuration across Lamming's fictions. This argument constitutes the basic frame of exploration in this and the next chapter.

My explication of the relation among Lamming's theory of language, his figuration of the human and colonial subject, and his treatment of gender begins with the recognition of Lamming's concern, across all six of his fictions, to chart a genealogy of the West Indian colonial subject. Through a combination of historical excavation, epistemological speculation and fictive mythos, Lamming constructs a genealogy of West Indian identity that will replace the colonizer's negative genealogy of the "native" as essential object, descended from nothingness, darkness or a different kind of ape.

The term "genealogy" may itself be clarified with reference to some remarks made by Lamming in the 1995 essay "Western Education and the Caribbean Intellectual".[1] Here Lamming declares that (West Indian) self-knowledge, which is the beginning of critical elaboration, must begin with a compilation of "an inventory" of that "infinity of traces" which history has deposited in the society and the West Indian person, without itself compiling such an inventory. This remark suggests that both society (nation) and individual must undertake, as it were, an archaeology of the self, locating missing acts and persons, unveiling unclarified influences and patterns and acknowledging realities which may have been known but which have remained unacknowledged. Simultaneously, whatever is found must be fitted into its proper place both in relation to those acts, persons, patterns, influences and realities already known and in relation to the social, political and psychic architecture of the subject. "Constructing a genealogy", then, ultimately has to do with recovering missing cultural and psychic inheritance or property, as the starting point by which reconstruction (in the sense of collecting, assessing and understanding) and restitution (in the sense of reclaiming and giving back what has been stolen or lost) of the self may be accomplished.

Of major importance is the fact that acceptance of this inheritance or property cannot be based on any expectation of its freedom from conflict or negativity. Further, genealogy occupies the same moment as auto-biography, both because the quest is a psychic experience and because the inheritance is already necessarily being lived. An implication is that one must, at each moment of self-discovery, make an active decision as to one's position in the genealogy, since the moment of discovery carries the burden of accepting oneself not only as offspring, but also as mother/father or other agent of psychic and cultural engendering. (The simultaneity of the projects indicates the potential for both schizophrenia and fusion, the twin poles of possibility at the site of dissonance, with which we have seen Selvon grappling in the London and Tiger novels.)

Lamming's idea of genealogy goes beyond Michel Foucault's post-modernist formulation, as the origins to be searched for are not only those constituted in discourse, but also those constituted in historical action.[2] Also, the search for and construction of genealogy on the part of Lamming's ideal protagonist has a radical relation to ontological reality: at any given moment, the protagonist has the capacity to interrupt the current of history and reformulate it in the future tense. This is in a sense what Fola Piggott does in Lamming's *Season of Adventure* (1960), when she invents a mythic origin for herself in order both to appropriate and reject society's concept of her as "bastard", and what the adolescent boys in *Of Age and Innocence* (1958) seek to accomplish by passing the mythologized history they have constructed, through multiple veils of performance that recreate the past as fluid sets of future possibilities.

Gender is foundational within Lamming's genealogy, and it is in the construction of the genealogy that the most radical as well as the most conservative aspects of Lamming's gender ideology are seen. We have said that genealogy becomes an issue on two levels: the individual and the societal (that is, the collective). In each novel, Lamming presents different casts of characters and complexes of events that speak to the issues of maternal and paternal ancestry and parentage in the context of psycho-cultural origins. The pilgrimage of individuals in search of ancestry and parentage by which they may discover self and place invariably becomes metonymic or allegorical for the ancestry and parentage of the colony as emergent nation. Gender in Lamming, then, is primarily an issue of the politics of nationhood. His formulations in this regard are major exercises in paradox and contradiction that coalesce around a number of complexly related factors: the struggle to reconcile what may be termed masculine and feminine principles in the project of national identification, the attempt to arrive at an equitable and West Indian sense of the place of men and women in the polity, and the ultimate aim to define a new concept of manhood, or a heterodox masculinity de-linked from traditional sex-gender dichotomies. This new concept of manhood elides into a definition of true self-identity; that is, manhood becomes a generic construct by which the individual and the nation's entry into self-knowledge are named.

Specifically, in *Of Age and Innocence* and *Season of Adventure,* this concept produces revolutionary explorations around an idea of a third gender, located in symbolic women and boys, who stand for the characteristics of the nation of the future that Lamming envisages. Lamming's attempt to define the nation as a heterodox form of masculinity also produces some of the most radical (and to that extent, anomalous) concepts of the feminine in West

Indian nationalist discourse. These emerge particularly in *Natives of My Person* (1972) and *The Emigrants* (1954), both when these novels are taken as separate texts and when they are read as dialogues with each other. Lamming's thought is in some ways a progression, in others a complementary treatment of threads of paradox that he perceives in West Indian lived reality. The concept of the feminine principle in national and individual ancestry and identity found in *Natives of My Person* and *The Emigrants* represents the most far-reaching development on this issue, and perhaps of Lamming's thoughts on gender as a whole. This treatment of the feminine may be seen as his most definitive break with the overt polemic of West Indian nationalism, a movement of which he was one of the most ardent proponents.

Given these revolutionary aspects of his thought, Lamming's continuing inability to break away from an essentially male-biased view of women presents one of the most striking contradictions in a range of fictions I have labelled "essays in paradox and contradiction". For, consistently throughout all his fictions, Lamming relegates the female to a patriarchally feminized space that goes beyond the imaging of historical reality to an ideology of lack, by which all females' contribution to development is ultimately aborted. In a discourse that is as much idealist as it is historicist, the marked difference between the capacity for action of male and female characters betrays Lamming's ultimate sense of the rehearsal of men's contributions as the really important utterance in the discursive genealogy of the Caribbean.

In *Of Age and Innocence* and *Season of Adventure* – the fictions which may be considered more immediately nationalist (in the sense of being directly concerned with issues of independence and representational politics, as opposed to the more generalized nationalism of *The Emigrants* and *Natives of My Person*) – it is the discovery of and relation to paternity that is the most critical factor in the nation's search for self-definition. Further, Lamming's reformulation of manhood as a gender-neutral category is undermined by the fact that it is explicitly linked to figurations in which the masculine is ultimately linked to the body of males. (Fola Piggott, who is troubled by ideas of boyhood, reinvents herself in men's clothing.) Similarly, in *Natives of My Person* and *The Emigrants,* the larger potential opened by the revolutionary concept of the feminine is subverted or left in paradoxical stasis, initially by women's absence from the centre of action and ultimately by their complete inability to effect positive action of any kind. This seems to be linked to an idea of the victim status of women in the colonial fatherlands, as well as to an ulterior ideology of woman as the weaker sex. The ideology, like Marcus Garvey's, is ironic: often it is an attempted valorization of women, particularly marked in *Natives of My Person* and *In the Castle of My Skin* (1953), where "archetypal" representations of the female are invoked as fetish.

But Lamming's West Indian genealogy goes beyond both gender and history as immediate context of production. Its stabilizing root is a universal, inviolable humanity, whose inviolability appears in the fact that it is irreducible to the categories of any known use of language. If in the beginning is the word, "beginning" is only a signifier of the point at which communication may begin; the phenomenological self (which is an *eidos* within all persons, existing even prior to the individual's ontic/historical construction of selves), is rooted somewhere before the beginning, behind the demonstrated efficacy of words.[3] At some level this is linked to an idea of the inviolability of the body, and also of the powers of the physical landscape, or the arcane life force of territory. These belong to Lamming's epistemologies of apocalypse and the body, which extend across the fictions, the latter being most fully explored in *The Emigrants.*

Lamming's belief in a universal human relation to language is documented in *The Pleasures of Exile,* and in various non-fiction writings and interviews (Kent 1973; Lamming 1958; Phillips 1997). Speaking in a 1995 essay, Lamming expresses a profound sense of language as being at the heart of power relations, which, like Fanon, Nietzsche and Foucault, he sees as in their turn constituting the human condition, not only historically, but also ontologically (15). He goes on to speak of the psychological and social aspects of language: language as being "at the heart and horizon of every human consciousness . . . the verbal memory which reconstructs our past and offers it back to us as the only spiritual possession which allows us to reflect on who we are and what we might become" (30). He speaks also of language as a function and process that needs to be reflected on as part of the discourse on regional integration and development. All of this points to what may be described as Lamming's profoundly moral concern: the recognition that the communality of language, as well as its singularity as the ultimate medium by which we know others and by which ourselves are known, may lead to its abuse and by extension to the abuse of those who through it may become known. This tendency to abuse is rooted in a false sense of the transparency of language and by extension the transparency of the human subject configured to our consciousness in language.

But this sense of the universal tendency to false-truth claims about language is in Lamming mediated by his historicist consciousness ("a profound awareness of the Caribbean nature of our relation to the world" [1995, 24]) and by his sense of political commitment as a West Indian artist organically related to his society. The construction of genealogy becomes the artist's contribution to "our discovery of the meaning of [our] severance, the conscious confrontation with the fact of our collective separations from original homes of spirit" (1995, 24). The twin problems of the colonizer's attempt to speak the "native" into a less-than-human image – that intolerable objectification of being symbolized in Shakespeare's Prospero's Caliban – and the colonized person's confused relation to self and others of like experience and skin, as well as to the products and representations of colonial power, are then the specific manifestations of the abuse of language that Lamming's genealogy addresses.

The genealogical project then becomes a search for a mode of expression so fully cognizant of the possibilities and limitations of language that it will at once be able to construct and represent unique identity and to image the ultimate opacity of the human subject – that is, the Subject's resistance to the voyeuristic gaze that seeks to reduce him/her to what is immediately accessible through language. This is both Lamming's answer to the colonizer's attempt to speak or decode the "native" into a transparent inferior object and his suggestion to the colony in search of national selfhood that it is in a particular relation to, and understanding of, language, that the search for identity will be fulfilled.

The location of the historicized West Indian nation and person within an idea of universal humanity is important: in Lamming's fictions, there are no polarizations based on race – the same sense of opacity, identity and capacity for error and self-discovery is accorded to all his characters, regardless of race or origin, even while the historical power differentials of domination and resistance represented by characters on either side of the racial divide are explored and the former rigorously judged. This sense of universal humanity accounts too for one of those elements in Lamming that is at odds with the work of many of his nationalist contemporaries: serious psychological portrayals of female characters that caused one reader in the 1980s to see Lamming as presenting the "feminine principle" as "an agency of systemic transformation" (Thieme 1984, 21, commenting on Paquet's 1982 analysis). This again exists in unresolved tension against the ulterior gender investment by which an inequitable double root, male versus female, is ultimately exposed in Lamming's genealogy.

Beyond the common human ancestry in language, Lamming's genealogy identifies the West Indies as a unique birth, unprecedented in human history and therefore scarcely to be understood by any tried methods of understanding. The point is critical: here Lamming problematizes the idea of the West Indian Subject's resistance to the voyeuristic gaze by moving him/her beyond the similarity to all other human Subjects. He suggests a double opacity arising out of the uniqueness of West Indian genesis which was in effect a disturbance – a change of direction – in the currents of history. The specific historical moment of West Indian genesis which Lamming identifies is the entry of Europe into the New World. Europe is categorically, then, the first patriarch. Here the fiction is simply another articulation of Lamming's definitive declaration that something new was begun in the Caribbean, that nothing exists in human history "quite like the meeting of Africa, Asia and Europe in this American archipelago" (1995, 25).

This historical moment of penetration is re-enacted in a variety of ways and from a variety of perspectives that image its continuing legacy and activity across time and space: *Season of Adventure* and *Of Age and Innocence,* for example, *begin* with the insertion of Europeans into the territory and life of the colony, *Natives of My Person* re-enacts only that moment of insertion, *In the Castle of My Skin*'s rituals of dialogue rehearse that moment's continuing depredations in the colonies, and *Water with Berries* stages the violent first meeting of dissonant cultures in the territorialized body of the symbolic character Myra/Miranda, who is cloned from Shakespeare's *Tempest* character and who becomes a kind of signifying crossroads of West Indian as well as female dread and possibility arising out of that encounter.

One of the questions raised by this location of Europe as patriarch is, of course, who was the original West Indian matriarch, assuming such a construct existed at the point of the colonies' birth. That in Lamming's genealogy Africa does not necessarily fill that space seems clear from the relative attenuation of references to Africa in the six novels: the few traces include the Ceremony of Souls in *Season of Adventure,* the liminal domino/Anancy figure of the African Azi and the shadowed relationship between West Indians and Africans in *The Emigrants,* and, in *In the Castle of My Skin,* an old (drunken) woman's reported declaration that the West Indies began in slavery – a declaration, incidentally, believed by no one who hears her.

Lamming's figuration of the Haitian Ceremony of Souls has, following his discussions on the subject, led to the critical opinion that the ceremony is a powerful evocation of Africa in his writing (Nair 1996; Paquet 1982; Ramchand 1970). This reading is problematic, since, apart from *Of Age and Innocence,* none of the novels in which various abstract figurations of the ceremony are subsumed makes any link between it and Africa, and even in *Season of Adventure* the link is more implied than stated. Indeed, Lamming's own reference to the ceremony in *The Pleasures of Exile* links it not to the African expression of Vodoo, but to its expression in the Haitian *tonelle,* within which it is a syncretic Caribbean form.[4] Indeed, the ceremony serves Lamming's philosophical purpose of figuring the relations between the various moments of time, history and space, as well as the need to predicate the future on "backward glances" in which reckoning and forgiveness play a major part, precisely because he de-links it from mention of Africa. This de-linking allows for its generalized deployment across the histories of Europe and the Caribbean, and implicitly any other that might play a part in his novels. (In *Water with Berries,* the ceremony appears in a transmuted figuration through the European text, *The Tempest,* which is the origin of Lamming's representation of Caribbean linguistic persona.)

Lamming's treatment of the subject of Africa contrasts sharply with his figurations of European influence on the West Indies, which is always grounded in specifically linked historical detail. Further, the de-linking from Africa situates the Ceremony on the same plane as the Tribe Boys legend which the boys of San Cristobal in *Of Age and Innocence* invent as part of the ancestral legacy they confer on themselves in their own criss-crossing of times. The Ceremony and the legend indicate the emphasis Lamming places not on Africa but on Caribbean modernity, which for him took its point of departure from Europe's entry into the Caribbean. For Kamau Brathwaite, Africa is unequivocally Sycorax, not only first mother but also definitively elder and only legitimate parent. For Lamming, the issue is not so unequivocally resolved.

Generally speaking, it is only the territories themselves that can be said to perform the role of mother in Lamming's genealogy,[5] and here "mother" is distinct from "matriarch", which suggests a level of authority, or rule, at which the territories qua territory do not aim or arrive. As presented in the fictions which I have termed "more immediately nationalist",[6] the process of collective evolution is essentially a movement from the state of being territory (female, mother and, in the discourse of these fictions, generically feminine) to being nation (masculine, father, engendering even as one was initially engendered). If the entry into nationhood is the entry into language,

Lamming's nation is definitely an entry into the logos of the father, albeit in a uniquely West Indian, creolized mode. The shift to a more nuanced conception of the feminine in *The Emigrants* and *Natives of My Person* does not essentially displace this idea of an inevitable relation among man/ fatherhood, language and national identity which for Lamming is a basic article of epistemological faith.

The idea which Lamming's treatment irresistibly if perhaps unintentionally suggests – that the colony is its own first mother – causes us to reflect on his contention that something unprecedented began in the Caribbean. The suggestion of a founding patriarch without a correspondent maternal progenitor is not merely a single-parent birth, but a birth apparently outside the womb. *Natives of My Person* establishes by allegory what the other novels only indicate: the birth of the West Indies from patriarchal Europe was a birth in a specific type of psychic space, which substituted for a womb. That this bears no equivalency to the Jovian head of Greco-Roman myth (Minerva springing fully dressed from the head of the patriarch) is clarified precisely by those liminal traces of Africa that vaguely trespass the narratives: what appears is both the possibility of the non-existence of Africa as original mother and the possibility not of her non-existence, but of her erasure. Thus the issue of a possible surrogacy is raised.

Two possibilities may be argued. The first is of Africa as original matriarch, with the Middle Passage performing the surrogate role (here the ship as womb cannot be configured as metaphor but as living reality, a physical space within which completely new psychologies were already created, as I argued in chapter 1). The second possibility, which is given weight right across the fictions by Lamming's continuing metaphorical investment in this passage as a telluric womb in which psychologies and identities are conceived, birthed or aborted, is to see the Middle Passage itself as the original mother. Both arguments come laden with paradox. For, first, on what basis can we argue Africa as a feminine rather than a masculine or even a hermaphroditic polity or set of polities at the point when the Middle Passage began? Second, if we argue the Middle Passage as original mother, we confront the problem of a demonstrably untenable identification of genesis, for the marriage of that passage with the psychology of imperialism cannot by itself account for that infinity of prior traces in West Indian history to which Lamming alludes.

But the idea of England performing the role of surrogate mother is also implied, as seen in Lamming's representation of England as both Mother and Fatherland. The most obvious example of this is Teeton's surrogate mother, the Old Dowager, in *Water with Berries.* As portrayed in the educational and administrative systems described in *In the Castle of My Skin* and in the figures of Europeans of both sexes in *Season of Adventure* and *Of Age and Innocence,* it is the image of England as Father which was constantly displayed in the political action and ritual performances of empire in the colonies. The Father, then, is constantly present as an idea, an abstraction made visible in cultural progeny and realized in the conflicted psychologies of the "native". England as matriarch is a very liminal idea, fleetingly expressed in stock phrases such as "dear Mother England" and "Britannia rules the waves", the latter owing its etymology largely to the masculinized femininity of Queen Elizabeth I, who at England's first forays into empire became a major and contradictory source of imperial iconography.

In a reversal of the usual trend in patriarchal society, then, England as mother/matriarch is the progenitor configured as absence. If, as we argue, "feminine" describes the land as territory and, further, that this is at particular points in Lamming's thought identified with the mother, then clearly it is only in the experience of the characters in *The Emigrants* and *Water with Berries,* whose stories take place on English soil, that the presence of the matriarch is ever experienced. England reveals herself in these novels as the space of the culturally powerful, which in the end is the space of masculine authority; the mother/matriarch becomes an endlessly receding category collapsed into and devoured by the image of the patriarch. England as (feminine) territory paradoxically never really appears. (Significantly, the emigrants in the book of that name arrive in England in fog, which they mistake for smoke, a double sign of obfuscation and erasure.) This collapsing and devouring, which is an anomaly rather than a creative hermaphroditism, is imaged in others of the novels, notably, in *Of Age and Innocence,* in the figures of the Englishwomen Penelope and Marcia, who simultaneously occupy the space of the dominated feminine and act as the masculine authority's representatives. In the process of imaging itself in the mutually constitutive and even indistinguishable roles of mother, matriarch and patriarch, England appears to have engendered the colony in ironically paradoxical images of itself which it simultaneously acknowledges and denies.

The West Indian territories, then, appear in a meta-analysis of Lamming's fictions as the products of an eating, erasure and surrogacy of original mothers – a process which did not simply begin and end, but is constantly being re-enacted as a psychic and cultural inheritance of grief and loss in the life of the territory and the emergent nation. In this respect, the West Indian territory, with a parent missing (in the sense of being hidden in darkness, or unknowingness), is in its representation as the offspring of a mother simply the compulsive replication of the erasure of identity which is quintessentially, historically signalled in the state of being feminine. In this sense, the state of being territory is in effect a state of being absent, so that territory becomes the constant refiguration, rehearsal and reliving of the original mother's fate, in psychic and cultural terms. Territoriality is the condition of anonymity until the father arrives to confer a name.

Lamming's figuration leads us to draw into the family tree at the point of West Indian maternal origin not a teleology of ancestors, but a trammel of possibilities which are in effect themselves the real lost ancestor(s). This birth in possibility is at one level extremely negative, specifically in the location of the female/feminine in the endless rehearsal of grief and loss. From another perspective, the inscription of possibility rather than teleology can be envisaged as the ground of the Caribbean dynamics of syncretism and creolization. It then becomes part of the extraordinary uniqueness of the Caribbean: that here it is possible to construct a genealogy of the unknown, or the unclearly known – the unknown/unclearly known in the moment of its inscription becoming the most dynamic of possibilities. This is an inscription of the Caribbean modernity that Lamming celebrates. More than this, in the thought-line between *The Emigrants* and *Natives of My Person,* it becomes the principle on which Lamming is able to rethink and recuperate the concepts of feminine and territory into his creed of inviolable humanity and, by extension, his idea of West Indian double opacity.

Lamming's representation of the father is likewise a function of the paradoxes of Caribbean modernity. It shares in many of the ambiguities of the search for the mother, albeit it arrives at a form of definition (Lamming's "masculinity" of speech) at which the search for the mother does not arrive. Europe's illegitimacy as the original known father leads inevitably to the idea of a new invention of fatherhood – that is, of the territory producing children of its own who will speak the nation definitively into being. But the nation's definitiveness of speech is hedged, for, as imaged in *Of Age and Innocence* and *Season of Adventure,* the radical way of speaking must compensate for the gaps in historical knowledge and their substitution by Prospero's duplicitous utterance. The project of speaking oneself into being then necessitates both the creation of myth as truth larger than and beyond historical fact and inventions of self which are in effect experiments in performance; these, except in an impossibly idealist world, necessarily involve struggle on the edge of a stammer. Beyond this, a masculine self spoken out of liminal and arcane realities is necessarily a self that ultimately shares the space of the feminine. This is one of the paradoxes that the discourse of *The Emigrants* begins to apprehend, and which *Natives of My Person* more clearly embraces.

Lamming's genealogy, then, involves the consideration not only of ancestries, but also of immediate progenitors, who are also descendants and transmitters of legacy. Through techniques of pastiche, such as the creation of events, political figures and geographical space in composite form to represent the islands in their collectivity, Lamming emphasizes his sense of an experience uniquely identifiable as Caribbean, over and above any particularities in the life of individual territories. The immediate fathers of the nation are the leaders of the contemporary nationalist and labour movements, who contribute to the process of liberation and oppression in the Caribbean. In his depiction of these leaders, Lamming reveals their almost helpless redistribution of the legacy of domination, oppression, violence and fear imported into the systems by which the colonies were governed. This constantly threatens to submerge the liberating possibilities evoked, in historical terms, by that very legacy of oppression and, in existential terms, by the will to power within which the irreducible humanity which is not fully knowable is framed.

The theory of language, the discourse on genealogy and the ideology of the human subject account for Lamming's radical experimentations of language, form, sequence and point of view: what these latter allow for is the competition and multiplication of perspective which demonstrate the subjectivity of knowing, the impossibility of a teleology of language or the Subject, and the implication of language use in conflicts of power. Equally, they demonstrate the artificiality, in cultural and psychic terms, of the boundaries between aspects of time, the fluid nature of identity and the search for identity, and the interconnection of public and private spheres of becoming, particularly in the West Indian context, where individual and society are called upon to construct themselves in the same historical moment.

Lamming's use of language is far from being the oddity it has been purported to be – has in fact been already recognized as participant in a tradition of Caribbean perplexity and celebration of perplexity that includes Fanon, Carpentier, Brathwaite, Harris, Glissant and Césaire.[7] Lamming's boundary-less novel, voiced in the clash, criss-cross and complement of variant forms, is, like Selvon's use of language and satirical event, best understood in terms of a carnival poetics which is Caribbean in nature. Bakhtin's idea of the novel as already, generically, an unknown form has resonances with Lamming's thought. Rooted in dialogized heteroglossia, in which part of the dialogism springs from the polysemy of language itself and part from the dynamic social context of the text's production, the novel is for Bakhtin (1981) at any given moment ready to become something new, changing form and expression at need. Beyond that generic capacity that Bakhtin describes, Lamming's fictive style emerges from the perceived, historically conditioned necessity to which Sylvia Wynter points (1971), which insists on the heterodox (liminal, carnival, contentious and contradictory) capacities that the West Indian novel, as a paradigm of the slave plot opposed to the plantation, is morally bound to explore. The novel, more than any other literary form, is the form of modernity, and indeed what some may term postmodernity,[8] within which Lamming's Caribbean is located.

Lamming's fiction is formally subversive, seeming on the surface to conform to an almost Victorian naturalism – what Paquet refers to as "British literary tradition", marked by the narration of events, a ubiquitous third-person narrator, an authoritatively controlled narrative voice and a seemingly *belles lettres* abstraction of style. Beneath this surface overlay, however, are experimentations of style and form (what Ten Kortenaar refers to as "the absence of all narrative hooks" [1991, 44]) which make Lamming a postmodern reader's dream: marriages of historiography, mythos and fiction; linearity, flash-forward and flashback; text and counter-text; omniscient narrator, dramatic prose/poetry sequence and first-person interior monologue subtly exteriorized; narrative detail and philosophical abstraction. Combinations of these often occur in the same linguistic moment. Thus, in Lamming's work we confront texts of paradox and ambivalence which deliberately resist teleology and which become the representation of the theories of the resistance of language and the human/colonial Subject to teleologization.

This linkage of the critical discourse on language with the ideology of the human subject begins in some of the fictions to embroil the artist in a perhaps contradictory double relation to his art. For in setting forth the unknowability of the human Subject, what Lamming is also setting forth is the ultimate inaccessibility of language: the space, as it were, where language denies itself. Here the writer writes against himself, deconstructs the very tools of his craft, demonstrating the impossible circularity of a task that depends on language to configure what cannot be configured in language and to make transparent through language the existentially opaque. The effect appears most powerfully in those moments of tension in the text that seem to demand a linguistic immediacy, the capability of language to express the furthest reaches of thought and emotion. In these instances Lamming's prose seems to lose itself in a wilderness of words that both declare and represent the inability of words to pin down the precise moment, to arrive, as it were, at a teleology of meaning.

Lamming's work, then, exhibits an overriding concern with theory which is over and above the general tendency, self-conscious or otherwise, of literary artists to shape their creative work in accordance with their beliefs about art. Generally in such cases the fiction, remaining primary (being simultaneously vehicle, form, meaning and voice), is still its own *raison d'être.* In Lamming however, the emphases are, if not reversed, fluidly shifting, so that often the theorization subsumes, constructs and supersedes the fiction, undermining and displacing its fictionality to a merely vehicular function. This results in that peculiar turgidity and narrative elusiveness – what may be referred to as the "stammer" – which creates so much difficulty for readers. Lamming's Caribbean perplexity manifests some of its greatest tensions at the point where the centring and identification of the gendered subject in terms of a "masculinization" of language encounters the need to reconceptualize West Indian identity as the subject of possibilities rather than teleologies. Invariably, the effort engages the writer with the endless, unknowable semiology of language, which is far more akin to its "femininity" than its "masculinity".

Among the four novels treated in depth here, *Of Age and Innocence* and *Season of Adventure,* because of their concern with the national independence movements, afford the most comprehensive focus on the problematics of the gender of nationhood in Lamming. Paradox shades into contradiction, making these novels the repositories of Lamming's thorniest and least satisfactorily unravelled conundrums of gender.

Boyz 2 Men: *Of Age and Innocence*

From the beginning, *Of Age and Innocence* grounds itself in the conflict among the various roles, contributory legacies and identifying names of the fathers of the colonial territory. The field of struggle includes the historical progenitor, the present contenders for the name of father of the nation, and the imaginary ideal of the future – the heterodox masculine nation that speaks in freedom – and is acknowledged and heard. The novel is set in the fictitious composite territory of San Cristobal,[9] symbolically named to focus the moment of Columbus's arrival which heralded Europe's invention of the territories, but also to focus a certain ironic reversal, the ongoing phenomenon of "discovery" which brings the territories into an interrogation of the terms by which the imperial fathers effected this invention. The greatest subversive potential of the name as discovery-trope is its inscription of the ability to expose/explode the sacred (San) mythos within which the discoverer/progenitor-inventor had couched his own identities. San Cristobal, then, engages our attention as the site of a linguistic contention for power and authority. The subversive potential is fixed to our attention by the fact that the current inhabitants of San Cristobal are declaring their right to self-government, in effect the right to change the course of history. This is the event around which the action of the novel is based.

In the terms explicated in *The Pleasures of Exile,* where Caliban's ordering of history involves the legitimation of language by action, we recognize that in taking political action, the people of San Cristobal are in effect re-speaking/renaming San Cristobal; the name will not mean what the founding patriarch/discoverer declared it to mean. In other words, in an act of naming (and here it is history which is to be named), the people of San Cristobal declare themselves progenitors also. At the same time, other reflexive ironies in the name cannot be ignored: the name is the signifier of an inheritance – the psycho-cultural legacy of the original father's possession, which carries the seeds of possible disjunction and failure in the liberation enterprise. This inheritance does contribute to the ending of the novel in tragedy and an open question, which interrogates the people of San Cristobal as much as it does the colonial authority, for in Lamming's moral view of responsibility and human equality, the people too are implicated in their failure to harness the possibilities of their own challenge.

San Cristobal in the midst of political upheaval, then, appears as the territory caught at what may be termed an Oedipal moment: in search of a different engendering, a movement away from the original negative paternity. The adolescence of a territory – that is, its movement towards nationhood – is by definition fraught with paradox and contradiction, for here the feminized, implicitly female territory denies and rejects the state of being female/feminine in favour of masculine becoming. This at once collapses the ideologically fixed relation between materiality and identity, by capitalizing on the fluid nature of the latter: that which is represented as generically female can become a man. But in the context of the politics of nationhood, as Lamming's fiction demonstrates, the practical application of this concept automatically divides the territory in terms of the sex of its inhabitants, so that only the males are marked for masculine possession and becoming. The category of territory is simultaneously erased and reimposed as the males in this novel stand for the nation.

That the declaration of the right to nationhood/first speech is about gender relations in the context of psycho-cultural fatherhood and sonship is made clear through Lamming's formulaic parallelization between national events, on the one hand, and filial/paternal as well as friendship relations among male characters, on the other, so that the lives of the male characters become allegorical within the nationalist discourse. The most significant of these connections are those between returning resident Mark Kennedy and nationalist leader Shephard, who have experienced conflictual relationships with their fathers; among Shephard, Singh and Lee, the nationalist triumvirate who are friends, political leaders and aspirant fathers of the nation; and among the boys in the adolescent group which includes two sons of the leaders. The boys' story counterpoints the national events, as they role-play national paternity in the secret society which they have formed. The metalinguistic discourse by which Lamming interrogates the voyeurism of language is deeply, and with rare skill, embedded in this architecture of the relation of fathers and sons.

That the psychic inheritance of colonialism will play a major part in the failure of the nationalist movement is symbolized in aspects of the portrayal of Shephard, the self-designated Father of the emergent nation. The Anancy figure Thief says of Shephard that he is "split down the middle in two" (355). This "split down the middle" describes the source of Shephard's unfitness to lead: it is rooted in the conflicted relation to his forebears, notably his biological father, who, with an evangelist's crusading zeal, passed down to his son the legacy of domination, oppression and fear behind which is the face of the colonial patriarch.

Shephard's obsessive ritual involving chairs is of critical importance on a number of levels. The words in which he addresses the chairs are the words by which his father imposed his despotic will on his Sunday School class: "Children in darkness, do not ask to change, and do not be angry that you cannot of your own accord make a change in your condition. . . . Your purpose is fulfilled in your perfect service, and the rest is my burden. Love is mine and punishment too. . . . I shall give love and punishment as I see fit, and it is your perfect service which will help to decide. Now let us stand in silence for a while, then you may sit" (109). But the words are also strongly reminiscent of the discourses (the authoritative logos) by which the empire through its representatives defined the identity and the quantity of humanity to be accorded to its colonial subjects. This confers on Shephard not simply two fathers but a *double fatherhood* – that is, an engendering by two fathers in the same linguistic moment. The word transgresses time and space: the word spoken in the past is shown to be endlessly recycled and circulated, a recycling and recirculation made possible only by the fact of memory, which is the psychic ground on which all cultural inheritance is conserved.

Significantly, not only Shephard but also Mark Kennedy remembers (for the ritual is handed down to the reader by Mark, who remembers it from being forced to participate in Shephard's frequent re-enactments, also from memory). Mark is himself the product of a traumatized memory of his own father, who died when he was young. If Shephard is an image of remembered fathering, Mark is the image of lost sonship: both, from different perspectives, are presented as inadequate men because of the unresolved Oedipal link. Further, that Mark enters Shephard's performance at a fourth remove of memory already (in the biblical terms which are part of West Indian folklore) fulfils the patriarchal curse in a complete generational cycle. The ritual is ominous with portent for the next cycle of generations, because the litany extends out the neurotic filial relation, which is essentially a father-complex, to become the expression of Shephard's own desire for offspring. This offspring is ultimately the emergent nation. Interestingly, Shephard appears to be infertile, one of the many formulaic ways in which across the novels Lamming represents the uncreative portent of the empire's legacy of masculinism.

Shephard's engagement in rehearsal and mimesis also allows for the interiorization of the colonial father's categories of identity. The liturgical rhythm connotes not only the colonizer's use of religion to expropriate consciousness, but also the myth of the sacral nature of the possession, the speaker of this word as god-father. It is what causes Shephard to feel he is completely transparent to his progenitors' voyeuristic gaze, for he realizes at some level that the language he rehearses is in essence available to him on loan, and therefore not only legally open to the owner's scrutiny, but retrievable by its owner by any means possible. Further, the original speaker's belief in his knowledge of his own word leads naturally to the belief in his ownership and understanding of anyone who has been spoken into it. Here we are speaking of language as both psychic and material property – material in the sense of the tangible connection between the authority that has been able to organize social behaviour through this medium and the economic gain that accrued from it.

But Shephard's rehearsal is also an attempt at catharsis – that is, at exorcizing psychic demons on the field of representational play. This takes on the nature of an insurrection, as the ultimate aim is to wrest power from his demons by confrontation, which has two faces: the refusal to pretend they do not exist in his psyche and the willingness to accept and deal with their consequences. Shephard himself later speaks of the ritual as a personal acknowledgement of those negative aspects of his genealogy which had made him in part the kind of man he was, and which he needed to accept in order to move on (203). In this sense, the ritual may be seen as a kind of transmuted Ceremony of Souls. Part of the problem is that Shephard's enactment of the ritual is not a totally conscious act; much of it, like his dream of eyes, has the nature of a compulsive Fanonesque neurosis, which is too deeply imbedded beyond consciousness to be easily healed. At the same time that he seeks to repossess the psychic space stolen by the colonial heritage, he is being repossessed.

That Shephard's rehearsal, as is the nature of representation, goes beyond mimesis to potentially transformative interpretation in negative and positive ways is indicated by various textual metaphors. Shephard's consciousness of his openness to surveillance is indicated in his paranoia – an absolute terror of being stared at/through, amounting, in fact, to madness. It is of critical importance to Lamming's discourse on history and resistant language that this terror is demonstrated for the first time on the plane journey out to San Cristobal with which the novel opens. One of Lamming's multiple variations on the concept of the Middle Passage, the plane journey presents complex demonstrations of motivation and relationship that recall and play out in the present moment the original passages of history, but transgress these with present-day realities. What is interesting is that although Shephard terrorizes the entire cabin of passengers because of his sense that they are staring at him, it is Penelope on whom he focuses his vituperative attack, because she reminds him of an Englishwoman who has "sucked him dry".

Shephard transmutes Penelope into the symbol of all Englishwomen, who will "suck sperm dry" "even in my island" (55–56). His language conflates his individual experience with that of the territory, and reveals an extreme anxiety concerning the vulnerability of male masculinity, which he describes in terms of sex and sexuality as weaponry. Shephard mistakes his real enemy – the imperial fatherland – and accuses instead its agent and its victim, the female/feminine concept of England as Mother, which for him is represented in Penelope, whose womb he declares barren of anything but slime. But Shephard articulates his final grievance against the mythical Mother as a disgust not with her womb but with her eyes, which are, however, only mirrors, self-reflexive. The voyeuristic eye is in fact the eye of the imperial/colonial father, the enemy within himself that is responsible for his tendency towards tyrannical behaviour. Shephard is here very similar to the Commandant in *Natives of My Person,* who replicates in his gender identity the empire whose categories he sets out to challenge. The terms by which he will father the nation become dangerously implicated.

Shephard's failure to achieve full manhood is also a failure to achieve a new relation to language. His barrenness, the inability to bring to fruition a national consciousness imbued in a language "no less immediate than the language of the drums" (85), is located not only in compulsion, but in his ritualized reproduction of the fathers' language, which Penelope, representing the masculinist colonial authority, had earlier longed to hear in San Cristobal's idiom. On the surface it seems that he has broken out of the cycle, for nothing could be more radically opposed to the ritualizing speech of the chair ceremony than the absolute insurrection of curses by which he apostrophizes Penelope. But it turns out to be the same speech, the other side of the colonial father's Manichean dialectic. In the moment that he declares his human freedom and his absolute right not to be gazed at, not to be subjected to the categorizing codes of another's language, Shephard performs his refusal of the same rights to another human being because she belongs to a particular race. What Shephard does here is to speak Penelope into the image in which he himself had been invented, as the feminine voyeurized. (Lamming's exigent integrity as artist and as theorist leads him to right the balance of mutual respect disturbed by Shephard's behaviour on the plane by later creating a space within which he and Penelope meet as equals: he rescues her from drowning, and she accepts his explanation and apology. Significantly, the chair ceremony is a pivotal factor in his explanation [203].)

It is not only speech, but also memory that betrays Shephard, as implied in his words to Penelope: "I remember" (58). The treachery of memory, "the backward glance", resides not in memory itself but in the failure to interrupt its categories, to infuse history with a vision of the future articulated in the present. The incompleteness of Shephard's rendezvous with history through memory is also the incompleteness of his language: he recognizes the flaw in the colonizer's naming ceremony but does not move forward to create his own speech. Caliban must move beyond cursing to creative idiom if he is to order history. Shephard here contrasts with Fola, in *Season of Adventure,* who invents a new name and a new language for herself. Unlike Fola, Shephard never stops feeling voyeurized, that is to say, feminized.

The imaging of the nation's destructive inheritance by the metaphors of madness, hallucination and communicative disjunction throughout the novel completes the link between Shephard and San Cristobal and indicates the source of the emergent nation's failure: the inability to understand fully the sources and terms of the discourses and acts of power and domination, and therefore to find appropriate counter-speech and to initiate appropriate counter-action. It is the same failure to perceive the real enemy, who orchestrates the policy of divide and rule, that causes Baboo to assassinate Shephard so that his Indo-West Indian colleague can have the ascendancy. Yet, paradoxically, madness – the disturbance of exteriorized syntaxes and grammars of being – doubles as a site of the successful insurrection of the colonized, as when the madman, in accidentally burning the asylum, also burns the oil which would have destroyed the anti-colonial effect of the labourers' strike. The continuing twinship of possibility, the potential to inhabit a different idiom of power, is therefore symbolized, even though in the outcome it is emptied out by failures of vision, as in Selvon's *The Lonely Londoners.*

The secret society run by the sons of Lee and Singh along with two friends forms a direct contrasting parallel with the process of flawed masculinization of the emergent nation as symbolized in Shephard. The boys, in a self-declared project to become proper men and to articulate this within the context of the secret society which functions as a microcosm of the nation-to-be, are able to approximate the unity, power and masculine authority advocated by their fathers and father-figures, both because their youth gives them an area of freedom from the negative psychic baggage which makes of their progenitors' actions at best a paradox and because these fathers, contrary to the traditional negative portrayal of West Indian fathers, have been careful to teach their sons the values of nationhood. These advantages place the boys well ahead of Shephard and the rest of the society. Critically, they are aware from the outset of the need to create a counter-history of origins. This is the basis on which they are able to capitalize on the promise of the future in ways that elude Shephard.

The boys' performance/rehearsal of genealogy and of masculine becoming involves the occupation of psychic ground by rehearsing their fathers' habits and propensities in ways that turn these into political dialogue and ideational exchange. The refrain "my father" establishes the act as ritual assumption of property, in this case transferred authority; its context as performance establishes the supplanting of identities and habitation of another's space. The performance includes the invention/rehearsal of the Myth of the Tribe Boys (for which Lamming draws on Las Casas's text discussed in Benítez-Rojo [1996, 100–104]), whose heroic stand against the Bandit Kings at the dawn of colonial invasion displaces Europe's putative fatherhood as well as Europe's version and definition of history. The displacement is imaged in apocalyptic images of flood. Although the Tribe Boys are not racially related to the current inhabitants of the colony, the boys claim their example of resistance as a right, in a sense engrafting themselves as adoptive sons in a larger family tree whose origin is human.

Yet there is a more immediate claim which the boys have on the fatherhood of the Tribe Boys: the action of the latter is engrafted in the very landscape of San Cristobal (the legend indicates that they defeated the Bandit Kings by utilizing the resources of the landscape as camouflage, guerilla-style). By engrafting political action upon landscape, the Tribe Boys rescue it from the designation "territory"; they in effect masculinize it with meaning. But the Tribe Boys inscribe the state of being inviolable Subject in another way: their guerilla tactics involved digging tunnels underground, out of range of the colonizer's voyeuristic gaze. This aspect of their resistance translates into the concept of action as language, a semiotic which is not decipherable by logocentric codes and which is a part of Lamming's problematizing of the concept "language" across his fictions. Only betrayal by the Ants from within (a prophetic comment on San Cristobal's interracial tensions) is able to undermine the revolutionary encryption.

The boys' construction and occupation of genealogy involves a series of initiation rites, each of which embeds the idea of becoming a man through right seeing/speaking and revolutionary action. Significant among these are the induction of Rowley, the white police commissioner's son, and the Ant-killing "drama" which expiates the betrayal from within by the Ants in the Tribe Boys' myth. The others' willingness to include Rowley points to their moral vision, the enabling ground of which, however, is a youthful naivety of thought and feeling – all this being part of the novel's open-ended paradox of danger and possibility. The Ant-killing, similarly equivocal, functions as an object lesson which teaches the boys a fuller humanity by confronting them with their own innate cruelty as well as taking them through a cathartic experience of what their adoptive forefathers must have gone through. The call-and-response verbalization which accompanies the act again focuses the link, mediated by language, between consciousness and action.

The extent to which the boys internalize their psychic legacy is seen at the end of the novel when they resolve to die as the Tribe Boys did if they cannot rescue the fathers unjustly accused of arson and other crimes. Ironically, but not surprisingly, the boys reach this moment of crisis because of a crisis of language: their unsolicited foray into the courthouse as witnesses for the defence is aborted by their inability to speak in the terms the court authorizes, as well as by the court's prior identification of them as "mere boys" (Shephard's "any chair is a chair"). In fact this is only one strand in the humorous, semi-satirical display of competing tongues by which the court-room plays out the ways in which justice is circumvented in San Cristobal by a political distribution of the right and formulae of speech.

Such a distribution becomes possible only because the territory does not yet fully know or own itself: the colonial judiciary by which it is judged is automatically and with willed intent inured in the linguistic categories and ways of seeing of the original patriarch. In the context of the courtroom, the body is read as a transparent sign exposing one's capabilities of vision and speech. In the same way that race as a biological feature is the ground of invention of identity (decides whether one is a feminized male or a masculine one), so the boy's adolescent body is defined as placing him in an inadequate relation to speech. His eruption into the courtroom is in effect the eruption of madness, a disturbance of grammars, an "out-of-orderness".

The trammel of possible answers to the question "Who killed Shephard and placed Lee and Singh on trial?" and the simultaneous impossibility of ascribing blame to any one person or situation or event, even while acknowledging the implication in the tragedy of progenitors, descendants and historical inheritance alike, points to the moment of chaos at which the territory has arrived. Chaos is emphasized in Lamming's characteristic use of apocalypse and in the anomalous relation to language signified in the court's response to the boys. Even so, the creative possibility of chaos is signalled in the very open-endedness with which the novel concludes: the boys plan to die only "if" the fathers are convicted. "If" becomes definitive of the genealogy of possibilities which is the Caribbean's greatest source of power and pain. The boys too are, like the women in *Natives of My Person,* "a future [the nation] must learn", a gender possibility whose time has not yet come (*Natives,* 345).

The openness to a possibility in which all must become involved and within which all must risk implication is signalled also in the absence of a single protagonist, which in its departure from traditional form is part of Lamming's Caribbean modernism: the decentring of the individual is the inscription of the idea that the entire nation's masculinization must displace that of an iconic messiah. At the same time, the close attention given to each individual's viewpoint inscribes not only the competition of voices and ideologies against which identity must be constructed, but also the necessity of the individual's emergence within the communal. The problem remains in the fact that the male body remains the semiotic of the communal.

Even so, already in *Of Age and Innocence,* Lamming's treatment of adult and adolescent males to an extent shows the concern to problematize traditional smooth demarcations by which sex decides gender. The implicit feminization of Shephard as a voyeurized male and a symbol of territory is engaged in a dialectic with the masculinization of the boys, who would in traditional terms occupy the space of the feminine, both as inhabitants of territory and as not-yet-men. The dialectic is conclusive rather than open-ended: Lamming's boys are clearly supplanting the patriarch's categories as radical agents of new engendering and becoming.

The strategic dissolution of the sex-gender dichotomy is apparent also in Lamming's presentation of Penelope and Marcia, the Englishwomen who arrive as the wife and "make-believe" wife respectively of Bill Butterfield and Mark Kennedy. Both women inhabit two spaces at once: the space of the territorialized female and the space of the empire, whose representatives they automatically become once they have set foot on colonial territory. Marcia's territorialization and female "lack" appear in her utter acquiescence to Mark's abuse, which results in her madness and death; Penelope's appear in her susceptibility to being voyeurized, her removal from the centre of political discourse despite her intelligence, and her contrived, accidental erasure in death by fire. Their contrasting implication in exploitation and rapine is noted in many ways, including the boys' unwitting irony when they comment on the size of the handbags, which look "like they going . . . touch [rob] the banks" (90). This prophetic utterance is fulfilled when the women assist in the colonization of the boys' recitation of the Tribe Boys legend.

What is interesting is that the women's conscious intentions are utterly disinterested: they are simply using radio technology to make the story available to a wide audience.[10] But it is the expatriates who in the end decide what happens to the legend. Lamming's consummate skill as an artist is shown in his manipulation of voice – the mediation of Penelope's disinterested interior monologue by the omniscient narrator's stance – to effect the text's interrogation of her actions. Here Lamming sympathetically presents and deconstructs Penelope's innocent sense of mission to extend the discourse on language and seeing. We recognize how little Penelope is transparent to herself, how large is the disjunction between what she is able to articulate and what is hidden below consciousness. Similarly, if obliquely, the interior language of Marcia's descent into madness becomes also a prophetic warning of the past: she hallucinates marauding ships which implicate her unconscious intentions as much as they image her psychic rape, which becomes the trope of female deracination under colonialism.

Like the wives in *Natives of My Person* and the central female figure in *Water with Berries,* these women become Miranda-tropes,[11] implicated in the empire's linguistic rape of Caliban, and here the dreadful paradox of claimed innocence is revealed. In Lamming's morally constructed cosmogony, there are no innocents, though there may be victims. However, the irony of a woman who rapes, even as she is raped, is more than a conundrum of genders or an indictment of colonial confusion; it is also an inscription of a belief in female inability to resist the acts of men: always in Lamming, it is women who ultimately do not resist. Ma Shephard, iconized as the quintessential grandmother, is erased by a series of masculinist coups d'état: her life's derivation of meaning and activity from her son and the company of the boys; the boys' respect for her as a generic type (that is, not for any real contribution she makes to their lives, but because she represents the culturally valorized concept of age, with a capital A); and above all, her complete removal from the site of any real engagement with transformative language. Ma Shephard is a chronicler without a sense of the future as a dimension to time; for her, the future is an apocalyptic heaven which proposes an impossible breach between eternity and time, human action and divine intervention.

In the end, it is her speech and her misunderstanding replayed in the courtroom that allow the boys' true testimony to be unheard. The authorities are eager to listen to Ma Shephard because they realize she will not rock the colonial boat. All the women, then, in their relations with the men and the boys, become the most negative image of the collusive aspect of psychic colonization, and are therefore the greatest retarding influence in personal and national becoming. (In this context, it comes as no surprise that these revolutionary adolescents appear to have no mothers.) In the *telos,* no distinction is even made between the West Indian and the European female.

Season of Adventure: A Girl May Be a Man?

At one level, the image presented by Fola Piggott in *Season of Adventure* is the opposite of the women in the earlier novel. As in *Of Age and Innocence,* the primary discourse in *Season of Adventure* is the emergent nation's search for identity through the discovery and invention of paternal ancestry and parentage. This is figured in Fola's hidden double fathering, her rejection of her two putative fathers and her invention of the biological one. In her double figuration as symbol of the lived experience of both male and female West Indians, and as a credible representation of a teenage girl at the same time that she functions as a symbol of masculine nationhood, Fola is an extraordinary literary creation. She becomes an important representation of the unique modernity of the Caribbean of which Lamming and Nettleford speak.

Yet the very success of the figuration is Fola's displacement as a woman. The insufficiently problematized substitution of masculinity as a valorized category for femininity as a degraded category confers upon the former an existentialist priority that radically questions the substitution. Lamming's construction of Fola as nation-icon is also emptied out by the failure to de-link manhood from masculinity as inhering in maleness, as indicated in Fola's various obsessions with male identification. Furthermore, Fola herself does not take any really meaningful part in the public political action which she symbolizes; her pilgrimage is entirely personal. (Her attenuated participation in the march of the drums can hardly be taken as a serious sign of her centrality in that context, as it is the men, Great Gort and the dead progenitor Jack O' Lantern, who are highlighted.)

The problem then remains of Fola as territory, within which the ideals of the nation's masculinization are to be mapped. Fola is also serially displaced by male figures who compete for protagonal space. These include Chiki, the artist-figure who becomes the focus of part 2, his musician counterpart Gort, and in a sense the men of the Forest Reserve, each of whom Lamming attempts to portray fully in symbolic terms within the context of colonial power relations. Lamming also seeks to create each character in sufficient psychological depth to avoid any diminution of that complex, unknowable humanity and individuality which is the subject of his "perpetual rage with words" (1958, 113). The treatment of Fola is reminiscent of the evolution of the hermaphrodite in classical Greek iconography, which signalled the hermaphrodite's acceptance into society by attenuating the feminine/female features in favour of the male/masculine ones (Karlen 1971).

The fathering and achievement of Fola Piggott are explicated in very methodical, strategic stages which make it clear Lamming is creating a genealogy: the branches can actually be drawn, and Lamming assists the reader with his trademark use of polemical didacticism and figurative linkages. As in *Of Age and Innocence,* a relation is posited among language, voice, personhood, genealogy and gender, but from different points of emphasis. *Of Age and Innocence* exposes limitations in language, its ability to cloak rather than to expose the human Subject, thereby preserving the integrity, the sacral nature of the Subject. In *Season of Adventure,* language as possibility of revelation that sets free, rather than as protective limitation, is staged in the context of opposition and reply, as Fola searches for, discovers and invents a new speech by which to confer upon herself a genealogy and, by extension, an identity other than those of absence and surrogacy which her mother and adoptive father have given her. Even so, the concept of the final inability of language to state the full case appears as a subtext in this novel as well.

The opening dialogue of *Season of Adventure,* staged between two Forest Reserve men on their way to the *tonelle,* turns upon two critical ideas in the novel's theoretical ideation. The first of these is the concept that the drums the men hear as they approach the *tonelle* are singing out a language, which is declared immortal because of a kind of atavistic, primal connection at the heart of humanity to which it gives voice, and because it is in touch with the true aspirations and experience of the folk. The definitive superiority of the drums over the stage of verbalization at which San Cristobal has arrived is signalled in the music's "sweeping the men's voice away" even though they speak at a level of consciousness far beyond that of the symbolic woman spoken about at the start of the conversation.

Afraid to speak lest she reveal her flaws and shatter her artificially constructed romance, this woman represents the self-sanitizing, self-deceptive romance of the relationship which the middle classes of the territories imagine they have with Europe. Their silence is the silence of shame, which is in its turn a shame of territoriality, imaged in the corporeal, female body, archetypally associated with nakedness and disgrace. The politician Baaku's later exhortation to "find a language no less immediate than the language of the drums"[12] is a comment on the way the educated classes have learnt to use the mode of verbalization bequeathed by the colonizer: the organic disjunction between life and words which merely emphasize "grammar and clause, where do turn into doos, plural and singular in correct formation" (21), as well as the disjunction among the words themselves. It is also a comment on the schizophrenia, rooted in a lack of self-knowledge and an apish fascination with things colonial, of which this obsession with correct language is a symptom.

The second related idea on which the dialogue turns is Powell's drunken, half-humorous dissertation on the concept of language "making you a man", "man" here standing for the masculinization of the human collective and the individual male person. The possession of language, Powell argues, separates man from beast, being "a question the beast ask itself", words the threshing instrument which "beat your brain till it language your tongue" (15). San Cristobal, now an "independent" republic, has not yet achieved manhood because it has not posed a question; it has simply accepted a mimetic function of speech. The quintessential example of this is Lord Baden-Semper, the pinnacle of San Cristobal's arrivant aristocracy, who remains silent, devoid of masculine authority in his own house because of what the delightfully ironic, prim narrative voice (which will soon shift into/hide behind/mediate some first-person voice, in its endless competition of perspectives) describes as certain "formal difficulties of speech" (80).

The linkage of kinds of idiom with issues of identity and ancestry is further explored in the figure of the republic's greatest living drum player, Great Gort. Identity is something of which Gort has a very good understanding, ironically because of his illiteracy: the voice of Gort's drum is authentic because it has never encountered a supplanting intermediary (the written word, which has functioned to rob the educated classes of real power) between itself and the ancestral roots from which it has been engendered. Like the voices of the Ceremony of Souls, Gort's drum instinctively knows its own genealogy, its roots in an Africanesque/folk subconscious and, more immediately, in the dreams, hopes and aspirations of the people of San Cristobal. It is this certainty of self that allows Gort at the end of the novel to defy the authorities and stage a last national convocation of the drums.

But it is precisely the instinctive nature of the drums' speaking that undermines their power. The presence of the written word in the colonial context is the intervention of the colonial patriarch's authority: it has the power to create in Gort a sense of wonder and personal inadequacy. But it also points to a need to appropriate this language as inheritance, and to recreate it with a new authority that makes its syllables mean something other than they once meant. The creation of Fola as woman and Gort as male artist in images of manhood based on their erasure of disjunctions among expression, consciousness and action indicates a socialist conferral of masculinity not only on the republic collectively, but on individual members of the society regardless of occupation, age or sex. In this sense the gender discourse of *Season of Adventure,* despite its limitations, moves somewhat beyond that of *Of Age and Innocence.*

Fola is introduced in the context of her first encounter with the Ceremony of Souls, in which the souls of the newly dead, under the convoy of the *houngan* (priest), the gods and the ancestors, are called to colloquy with the living, to state their grievances and sins and to give and receive absolution. The pilgrimage of the dead to this colloquy is a pilgrimage through the ocean, the womb of water which is also at once a grave, the hidden depository of lost inheritance, the space within which lost ancestors are to be rediscovered and the territory within which the rites of passage to the recovery and new invention of self are to be effected. This refiguration of the original Middle Passages in the context of the ex-colony's present constitutes the first stage of what the text refers to as "the backward glance" upon which any sense of the future must be predicated. Fola's season of adventure, like that of the boys in *Of Age and Innocence,* is at one level an ironic counter-play against those motivations to self-definition on the ground of the voyeurized exotic, which along with the thirst for capital, directed the first European passages of adventure in the New World.

Fola's initial resistance to the ceremony is the result both of an inculcated belief in the primitiveness of such acts and of a resentment of the voyeuristic eye of Charlot, her expatriate teacher whose ulterior motives in taking her to the ceremony she instinctively senses. She reads in him a dual attempt to colonize her response by directing its course and to diminish any aspirations she may have had to the equality invested in whiteness by insisting on her connection to these "primitive" women of the *tonelle.* In other words, she recognizes that Fola is a question Charlot has posed himself and that he expects her to assist in the answering of that question in ways which will satisfy his thirst for romance (the psychic inheritance of the Renaissance culture of wonder that defines Charlot's impotent inurement in the past)[13] and which will validate the role of (surrogate) intellectual and cultural father which as Fola's mentor he has appropriated to himself. Here Fola is the archetype of the feminine, imagined as manipulable and displaceable. But Fola siezes the right to first speech, as opposed to reply, by answering a set of questions other than those Charlot had posed, and answering them for herself alone.

Further, she makes a radical psychic break, beyond and yet totally apparent to consciousness, when she identifies with the ceremony not because of Charlot's tutelage (expressed in carefully chosen analytical syllables), but because of the passion and urgency of Liza's dancing to the drums. In that moment of rupture and connection, expressed in her seizure of the terms of speech, Fola inscribes her status as Subject. Further, at the moment when she drops her resistance to acknowledge the primal response of her body and blood to the language and epistemology of the *tonelle,* she inscribes the moment of the republic's readiness to move away from the status of territory, shamed/shameable woman, to the status of adolescent nation, on the edge of responsible manhood.

Fola's initiatory identification with the *tonelle* may be read as a reconnection with the lost legacy of the West Indian mother and the denigrated feminine, as is indicated in the symbolic event at the centre of the ceremony: the lost boy's anguished refusal to die finally because he has been rejected by his mother, whom in death he still has been unable to find. It is indicated also in Fola's recognition of an affinity with Liza and the women, who apart from the *houngan* are the only officiators in the ceremony. Yet a further indication is the link between the African goddess Oshun and the ocean which returns the boy to the reckoning. Oshun, chalice of vaginal fluids, inhabitant of marine effluvia and ocean tides, is the female/feminine/mother principle. In other words, then, this stage of Fola's connection with genealogy is a feminine connection, and in the cosmology of *Season of Adventure* therefore only a beginning. Its imminent passing is suggested in the identification of Fola with the figure of the lost boy, an identification which in its symbolism at the centre of the ritual displaces the connection with Liza. The feminine/female/mother comes to light in order to yield up what is in the womb (the masculine progeny) before being again erased. This aspect of gender ideology appears also in all Lamming's Middle Passages, in which the hidden (feminine) is dredged/milked for the production of masculine subjectivity (self-knowledge).

From here on Fola takes control of her own genealogical search. At this stage, significantly, she acknowledges her loss not of a mother but of a father: we learn that Piggott is her adoptive father, her mother having shrouded the facts about her biological father in complete secrecy and silence. She haunts the outskirts of the Forest Reserve, convinced by her visceral response to the dance at the *tonelle* that her father comes from the peasantry who live there. This is Lamming's reconnection of the nation with its folk masculine persona, the true source of its reconnection to right speech. Fola's forays into the Reserve are accomplished in the guise of a boy, partly for protection but also obviously because of her subtly expressed yearning for maleness, cryptically encoded in her repeated "It's different for a boy". Fola's transvestitism here reveals the unconscious anomaly in which masculine becoming inscribed in the female body problematizes Lamming's erasure of sex-gender boundaries and makes it more akin to Freud's concept of female penis envy than to any gender-merging such as the concept of hermaphroditism posited in chapter 1.

Fola breaks off with the "strange men" in her life, seeing them as hindrances in the way of her finding her biological father. The break with Charlot is immediate, ruthless and definitive: she dismisses him by letter, and when she accidentally breaks the frame which contains his photograph, she sees it as an omen confirming her idea of him as a spy with a voyeuristic hidden intent, of which the photograph becomes the visible sign. Piggott, the only father she has ever known, is harder to dismiss, both because she recognizes the genuineness of his devotion to her and because he is nearer to her own skin. Her severance of connection with him is therefore at first more internal – a shedding of the psychic baggage of colonial values with which his surrogate paternity has saddled her.

For Fola recognizes the common root of Charlot and Piggott's illegitimacy as her fathers: both are the embodiment, the one by direct descent, the other by proxy, of the Idea of the colonial father; through their performance of the Idea, its authority is made visible. But she recognizes also their dangerous seductiveness: the romantic myth of Europe first seduced her at the age of four or five, when she gave her allegiance to the first "strange man", Piggott, because he dazzled her with European things. Not surprisingly, she had harboured romantic feelings – not of a filial kind – for Charlot, who is described by the people of the *tonelle* as a "strange man" also, and who in terms of the semiotics of the body was no mere proxy but the very thing itself. The unusual honesty of Fola's journey into self-knowledge allows her to admit the danger of her own attraction to paternal Europe, the occasion of endlessly deferred desire whose deferral is fed by absence, mythology, surrogate performances and performers tailored to occupy the space left by that absence.

The application of Freudian terms to Fola's moment of crisis becomes complicated by the Caribbean realities of parentage and guardianship in which Lamming's ideological creation is placed. Fola's early "adoption" of Piggott had taken place at the same time as her rejection of her mother, a rejection based on a complex of reasons ranging from a sense of her mother's preferring Veronica Raymond, to her mother's failure to measure up to the upper-class women in their social circle, to resentment of her mother's silence concerning her biological father. Fola does not easily arrive at a knowledge of these factors or an understanding of the exact relation among them. She has to undertake a dredging of memory which, in a way similar to Shephard's and Mark's beginning acquistion of knowledge through the subterranean language of madness and hallucination in *Of Age and Innocence,* yields itself to her in an ambivalent space between delirium and waking during her illness after walking, symbolically, in rain.

But Fola's Oedipal moment is complicated by the fact that she must decide among fathers, one of whom is unknown and one of whom though slated for rejection has been a loving and in many ways good father. Further, her relationship with her mother is fraught with rejection and with denial of the woman she perceives as having deprived her of her father, and whose absence she "struggles to achieve". (Fola's mother as the victim first of rape and exploitation and second of concomitant rejection by the child of her encounter, expresses the ironies of territorialization.) Rejection of the mother extends into the relation with the grandmother, whom Fola vaguely remembers as a one-time visitor to whom she had reached out and who terrified her with a rat. The grandmother's shrouding in absence and a similar rejecting relationship with her own daughter locates the mother-daughter link as a representation of the feminine side of West Indian ancestry, both in terms of the legacy of erasure and in terms of the endemic attitude of shamed self-rejection and self-blame towards the slave past (shame, rejection and blame being automatically, in patriarchal terms, female/feminine possessions). This attitude arises both because the truth is not known and because the paternity of Europe has been substituted.

Both the fact of Fola's double biological fathering and the fact that it remains unrevealed to her at the end of the novel point again to the problem and promise of possibilities which not only occlude but become actual progenitors in West Indian genealogy. (Significantly, the reader, though not Fola herself, learns that Fola is the child either of an English bishop's son or of a native rapist, who had both possessed her mother in quick succession.) The problem of a double unknown fatherhood brings into focus the threat of dissonance highlighted in Selvon's novels, but in this case the confusion and occlusion of origins works as creative possibility because the free space for self-invention is seized by the protagonist, as seen in the final stages of Fola's pilgrimage.

Fola's descent into memory as a means of archaeologizing the self and its antecedents inscribes the very personal nature of her search despite its communal symbolism. This privileging of memory with its concomitant risks of forgetting and interpretation grounded in feeling moves beyond a concept of history to a concept of autobiography, which is one of the many ways Lamming is able to humanize polemic and produce a credible story. The effort of memory, although dedicated to the search for the father, leaves Fola with some very clear genealogical facts: she has a maternal ancestry (the grandmother), and the "first families" of San Cristobal who have provided the larger social context of her living are not her relatives; that is, the legacy of self-rejection cloaked in a "bastard" European identity, which they have carefully coached her to accept, now appears to her as false coin. With typical decisiveness, Fola erases this false family line by taking down their photographs from her bedroom walls.

The removal of the photographs corresponds to the erasure of false ways of seeing and being seen, and the linkage between seeing and language in the process of self-identification is made in this context not only by Fola's reception of information by means outside of ordered verbalization (memory and semi-delirium), but also in the culmination of this stage of her journey in a redefinition of her relation to verbal language. In her delirium, Fola's speech loses its standard public-persona syllables to make a radical reconnection to the Creole speech of the Forest Reserve and her slave ancestors. It is also a reconnection to the idiom of her private communication with her parents, a reconnection effected in some area of the subconscious where linkages of community are hidden and possible:

> "And it's been the same ever since", Fola was saying, "is been the same ever since, is same since, is so, same so ever since . . ."
>
> The words seemed to come like the echo of other voices from outside: "is so,

same so . . ." Syllables changed their phrasing; words showed a length that had
suffered by the roughness of an accent uttered in haste. Surfacing slowly from the
world which had [been] offered Veronica and herself at Liza's age, words seemed
uncertain of their alliance. At every stage of awareness she could feel the change,
until the rules of college speech gave way completely to the private dialect of her
own tongue at home . . . (91)

This changed relation to language, indicating a healing of psychic
disjunctions, helps to direct a complete repositioning of herself in West
Indian history. But Fola also locates herself within the human race, with an
instinctive, alogical sense of relation to eternity (92). This prepares us for her
radical reconstruction of the stigma of bastardy where her articulation of
herself as "Fola and other than" signifies an acceptance of otherness as
Shephard accepts it but moves on to *reinvent* it as an unknown quantity
beyond the definition of words, and as "other than" mere language. By the
use of the familiar conjunctive phrase in a radical new function as extensive
suffix and surname, Fola invents herself as the promise of possibilities in a
way that eludes Shephard: being younger and coming fresh to the business
of masculinity (Shephard is remaking, Fola making, masculinity), she is
better able to separate out the strands of self-acceptance and reinvention. This
signifies the possibility of an evolution of national progress. Yet this advantage
that Fola has is paradoxical: the very newness of her encounter makes her
irresponsible and dangerous. Her definition of the bastardy she appropriates
puts her completely outside the pale of "respectable" society, including its
laws: she will be neither judged nor bound by them. Fola's concept of
bastardy is more far-reaching than the traditional concept of the outlaw,
which insists on the judgement of the law against those who refuse its
sanctions. At the same time, the paradox by which she claims a total
humanity confers on her a complete slate of inherited rights for which the
correspondent responsibilities have been erased by the invention of bastardy.
What Fola in effect invents is not, as she states, "her own history" (175)
but a complete New World, a territory for which all the known landmarks
will be charted by herself. Fola's subversion of the European invention of the
New World out of the culture of wonder and in the sovereign/patriarch's
image, and her removal of all perpetuations of that image by the empire's
surrogate "native" sons, is indexed in the authorially mediated thought with
which the first part of the novel ends: "This Fola had started on a history of
needs whose details she alone would be able to distinguish: a season of

adventure which no *man* in the republic could predict" (185, emphasis added). This declaration shows Fola's sudden and pre-emptive assumption of masculinity even though she has not yet found her father. She invents what she thinks is her own version of masculinity and with it her own terms of discourse, and she engages in its ritual performance by a series of bizarre journeys and cruelties that chart the psychic refiguration involved.

The journeys are an anguished attempt to identify with the rude, crude, material body, the arcane aspects of self and culture from which her middle-class upbringing has hidden her. The cruelties are complementary, a fierce rejection of what she sees as sanitized sham. Fola destroys reputations and erases persons with the same wilful abandon with which the hunger for adventure and capital wrought depredation in the New World. Having invented a new language by which to name herself, she now proceeds to reinvent others through the same voyeuristic gaze she has herself rejected in all her thinking about herself. This reveals that Fola has not attained full self-knowledge: indeed, her contempt for her mother's (invented) sexuality reveals a level of self-contempt that Fola never really acknowledges, and in this sense her reconciliation with being female and the issue of the feminine has not been sufficiently established to allow for a healthy masculinity.

The ease, arrogance and splendour with which Fola is able to transform her anguish into an identity is possible because of her youth and consequent naivety; this capacity for abandoned and self-centred action – what Lamming describes as "the criminal indifference . . . of youth" (175) – is one of the factors that make Fola an almost wholly credible character, and adds an endearing humanness to this most ideological of constructs. But beyond all this, Fola's action speaks to a radical attempt to create what Rohlehr terms a West Indian grammar of morality. Her attempt is an exercise on the edge of a historically determined chaos, as she is caught between the twin poles of dissonance and fusion, anguish and celebration, a very carnival of curse and benediction.

Fola's invention of manhood, which by traditionalist definition can be completed only in the possession of a father, reaches its climax when, having moved from the outskirts of the Forest Reserve to the very centre of its life, she has Chiki paint a portrait of her imagined father. The portrait, illegitimate in its Nietzschean untruth but possessed of a curious legitimacy in its symbolism and its supplanting of the dissonant photographs Fola had earlier broken or erased, eventually precipitates the republic's most important confrontation with itself, for Fola announces that the face in the portrait is the face of her father and the president's assassin. As soon as she makes that announcement, Fola as person and as figuration of the republic is implicated: the act of making public a vestige of the history she had hitherto kept as a private article of faith with herself causes her to become aware of the anguish and shame such publicity will bring to her mother, and she is seized with a cathartic remorse that becomes the ground of her reconciliation with her mother. The acceptance of the shamed mother is the final sign of Fola's arrival at true manhood. The acceptance of the feminine as an aspect of individual personality tropes the need for collective acceptance of those aspects of history which have been irretrievably lost, as well the collective need to negate the ascription of shame for a history for which the territory was not at fault. This reconciliation of feminine and masculine knowledges of self constitutes Lamming's attempt to bring the nation to its "true status of personality".[14]

The portrait becomes the basis of a broad canvas of communal implication. As in *Of Age and Innocence,* the identity of the killer remains everyone and no one, even after Powell, the "real" killer, has been identified. This is the essential conundrum of Fola's multiplicity of fathers; Fola as the sign of the republic is located at the nexus of just such an infinity of traces of colonial psychic inheritance as is suggested by everyone's involvement with the portrait. The father accused of a crime he didn't commit still connotes the shadow of the territory born out of rape, violence and murder, the territory still the victim of Europe's depredations, and this by the collusion of her sons, as signified in Charlot and Piggott respectively.

The invented biological father also connotes the liminal knowledge of self, the history psychologically avoided, not yet reckoned with, as the unreflecting colonial (re)corruption of the Republic's leaders show. Here Fola signifies that blame, responsibility and exoneration can be apportioned. In a sense, Fola summons the emergent nation to another ceremony of souls, where the masculine self must be rescued from its own self-destruction (erasure). The ritual confrontation with Europe's originary patriarchy and its legacies, for which the nation is now responsible, is the necessary antecedent to the latter's fearless decision to father/re-engender itself. This alone is the arrival of independence. That Fola and Chiki together invent this mirror in which the Republic must view its own face speaks to that organic tie between artist and society which is an article of faith with Lamming. Further, by being themselves a part of the process that they stand apart from in order to judge it, they pre-empt the accusation of voyeurism with which Dixon attacks Collis in *The Emigrants.*

The sharp realism that consistently edges Lamming's vision precludes the novel's ending in a rhapsody of idealistic hope. The Eva/Camillon subplot, a Fanonesque performance of mimic masks, shadows the drama throughout, as a way of indicating that the heritage includes psychologies that may turn the outcomes towards tragedy. And although Chiki and Fola achieve the self-awareness that makes them fitting symbols of hope in the new republic, neither is presented as perfect. Fola plays a flawed masculinity, and Chiki's initial vision of past and present history as definitive is brought into question by the encounter with Fola. He has to learn from her in humility what she has already apprehended: the necessity of opening his consciousness to the possibilities of the future, including the drafting of a genealogy based not merely on an exigent archaeology of the past, but on a concept of the future in which the future is not the creature of history but rather makes history its invention.

Chiki is able to take up his art again because he finally recognizes the capacity of the people, having taken the backward glance, to decide what road the future will take. The artist is forced to abandon cynicism and engage in the inscription of hope as the only legitimate signification towards which his canvases can move. Here the artist as product and as double producer of genealogy (being both postcolonial subject and postcolonial artist) takes his place as a father of the nation. Significantly, Fola's fearless action which is the basis of this revelation to Chiki as the artist in the process of becoming is paralleled with the insurrection of the steel band players, who defy the edict of the authorities with a national carnival of music and song, a radical insertion of voices of resistance against the colonizer's first, definitive word replicated in their midst by the colonizer's proxies (bastard sons of the colonial line).

We have seen where across the two novels, contradiction troubles Lamming's vision for the healthful psychology of the nation, despite the revolutionary aspects of his thought on the nation's gender identity. Contradiction here may be described as an unsuccessful attempt to balance the terms of paradox and, in Lamming, almost invariably apparent in a disjunction between action and symbol. At first sight, and indeed from most angles, the positives are impressive. The desire to authentically represent the carnivalesque heart of West Indian culture is clear. The heterodox manhood of Lamming's nation, predicated on variations of a third gender that stand against the debilitating masculinism of mainstream nationalist represent-ation, is a conscious attempt at an inclusive figuration of West Indian identity. Its revolutionary potential in the (post)modern age is that it seeks to embrace not only women, but also children. In that respect, Lamming's thought goes far beyond the gender discourse of the present era, in which gender has purportedly come into its own as a political and evaluative paradigm.

Lamming's thought on the concept of territory in the colonial context is also important as a way of underpinning his theory of language and identity. The territorialization and feminization of the Caribbean focus the idea of the inadmissibility of the voyeur's categories and the language which constructs and expresses these categories. The representation of the feminine territory as also female tries to make a sensitive response to the fact that, although historically mapped onto male and female alike in the Caribbean context, these categories imposed on women a double suffering and a double erasure.

In the end, however, there is a level at which Lamming is unable to escape the totalitarianism of language in which the ideological category of nation comes already inured. This appears in the conjunction among a number of elements in his gender discourse: the fact that the process of masculinization is a process of acknowledging but leaving the feminine behind; the fact that femininity is represented only in its negative aspects (loss, weakness, victimization, erasure) and, ironically, in the closer identification of the feminine with women. Feminization as a political act is imposed on male and female alike by colonial discourses, which Lamming rejects. Femininity as an index of being – the inherent inability to take responsible public action (essentially the sign of a truncated self, Freud's aborted chromosome) – is the inadvertent subtext of Lamming's representation, and nowhere is this more clearly seen than in the fact that his female characters are never involved in (the masculinity of) nation-making discourse: their concerns are domestic and/or personal, linked to their men or subverted by them.

We recall that the boys in *Of Age and Innocence* radically and independently insert themselves into the public courtroom, while Fola Piggott gives way to the men of the Forest Reserve, poised in the impossible paradox of being only a symbol and catalyst for others' action. *The Emigrants,* however, shows that Lamming was already beginning to question his own gender ideologies even as he was articulating them, and, when taken with the last novel, *Natives of My Person,* begins to show more radical gender concepts emerging in a total consideration of Lamming's oeuvre, even though some anomalies remain.

Theorizing the Feminine and the Body in *Natives of My Person* and *The Emigrants*

Half of a Circle: *Natives of My Person*

LAMMING'S 1954 NOVEL *The Emigrants* and the 1972 *Natives of My Person* form closely linked strands in the speech-gender weave of his West Indian genealogy. The two texts are in some ways mirror images of each other but refracted by historical specifics – *Natives* an "eyewitness" account of the moment of West Indian "genesis" through the voyage of empire, *The Emigrants* a similar account of the colonial voyage in reverse; the one the story of the colonial patriarchs' Middle Passage to the islands, the other the story of the islanders' Middle Passage to the colonial father/motherland. The philosophical reflection on the paradoxes of language and speech in these texts represents a shift in emphasis from the preoccupations of *Of Age and Innocence* and *Season of Adventure*. Whereas the former concern themselves with the positive end of the continuum of paradox – that is, with the efficacies of verbal language even within its limitations – *The Emigrants* and *Natives of My Person* concern themselves with the radical inadequacy and primal lack that empty out its efficacies.

In Lamming's oeuvre, these two novels are the ones that take us most radically back to his beginnings. These beginnings are not only the debilitating beginnings of colony, the legacy of which trammels the project of identity presented in Lamming as the manhood of entry into free speech; they are also the existential beginnings of self beyond speech, which hold the human Subject as sacred and inviolable. In *The Emigrants* in particular, this essential humanity is explicated through what may be termed a radical epistemology of the body, which resonates with ideas of the feminine explored in *Natives of My Person.* In the later novel, Lamming's gender perspective seems to have undergone something of a sea change, opening out to a larger definition of the feminine, as well as to a far more inclusive treatment of women than had appeared in *The Emigrants* or any of the other earlier novels. But major intertextual resonances are effected by a paradigmatic connection that Lamming suggests between the feminine and the epistemology of the body, through which the idea of inviolable humanity beyond language is explored. Together the two novels speak of the possibility of a form of speech (and, by extension, identity) that closes the gaps between masculine and feminine principles of being. Lamming's West Indian Subject is invited to effect this closure by the rigorous analysis and transformation of cultural inheritance created by the circle (the reconnaissance) of the voyages of discovery.

Even though *The Emigrants* was written first, it is through *Natives of My Person* that we begin to unravel the loop in this part of Lamming's complex weave of genders, languages and genealogies. In his last novel, Lamming presents that part of West Indian genealogy which would structurally be placed first: the advent of the European patriarchs, the "imperial" founders of the New World. That this representation of advent is a statement about the nature of cultural inheritance is shown in Lamming's use of such cultural property as Shakespeare's *The Tempest,* Columbus's diaries, Caribbean planter journals and Renaissance travel narratives, as source material and for narrative form and style.[1] By these means Lamming imaginatively reconstructs the actions, thoughts, feelings, belief systems, knowledges and motivations of those men whose conflictual legacy to the West Indies must be weighed in psychic terms, as indicated in the novel's title. Through the ubiquitous third-person narrative voice which Lamming sustains in various guises throughout his fictions as a kind of masculine voice of final authority, criss-crossing and mediating the multiplicity of individual voices of his characters, this legacy is rigorously weighed and judged, and its hidden paradoxes analytically revealed.

It is also in *Natives of My Person* that Lamming most comprehensively addresses gender as overt polemic, the discourse here as explicit as the discourse on language in *The Emigrants, Of Age and Innocence* and *Season of Adventure,* and in fact almost displacing the metalinguistic concern which has superseded all other discourses in the fictions to this point. The novel explores the psychic and material cost, to European men, of Europe's construction of national identity in terms of an (autoerotic) marriage between the triumvirate authorities of conquistadorial capitalism, imperial militarism and class hierarchy, and the extension of this prototype to the construction of individual masculine identity.

The crux of Lamming's interrogation of gender identity in *Natives,* however, is his portrayal of the tragic cost of another aspect of the construction of Renaissance and by extension "New World" iconic masculinity: namely, the construction based on a displacement of women from human relations and the substitution of relations with (feminized) territories of conquest. Lamming's concept of the feminine is more fully defined in positive as well as negative aspects than in any of the previous novels. The portrayal is far-reaching, as the feminine is retrieved from obscurity to become a powerful site of subversion, insurrection and interrogation, questioning the projects of masculinity. Even so, Lamming's critique of the denigration of the feminine remains compromised by aspects of his definition of "female" virtue, which is linked to the feminine in the same way that the definition of manhood as male masculinity displayed in the body of the female protagonist compromises his treatment of woman in *Season of Adventure.*

Despite the greater preoccupation with a polemics of gender, Lamming's metalinguistic discourse remains the context within which all other discourses are made sense of: as in the other fictions, one's gender identity becomes a function of one's relation to language. In the Renaissance world of Lamming's imagination, masculine language is defined as a performative authority based on one's public role and divorced from any concept of an inner self that exists or gives integrity to the public role. The space of the inner self is taken by secrets which eventually insurrect to create a tragic denouement, signifying the subterranean unconscious whose existence is ignored in order to sustain the monolithic iconography of the public persona. In such a scenario, speech, which is order, subversively signifies disorder,[2] and the generic existential relation between silence and speech is replaced by a political one. Silence becomes an absolute necessity of self-protection (even while a self to be protected is never admitted to consciousness) and the cause of terror where the other's lack of non-threatening transparency is implied.

Language is robbed of existential significance and becomes a merely political tool.

In this context, *Natives of My Person* explores the issue of the debasement of language at the site of an absence of self which is geographically represented in the last few lines of the novel, in the dialogue sequence of the adventurers' wives unwittingly left without husbands in the territory of San Cristobal: "[T]he weather . . . it's like home . . . it is familiar. . . . The same absence that shock leaves behind. . . . Absence. . . . Like home. . . . The same sound of absence" (345). Language displaced from a connection with truth is revealed as a vast mercantile technology whose function is to commodify the human and whose power is systemic, authorized by the politico-economic directorate, as the Lady of the House points out when she declares that the relationship between husbands and wives in the fictional kingdom of Lime Stone is a relationship of whoredom, predicated on the whoredom which is Lime Stone's legal and economic policy (345).

The connection made between the crafting of private and national identities is more than a general truth, and is of a different kind from the figural connections made between West Indian national becoming and the lives of individual characters in the other novels. It speaks to the cultural realities of self-fashioning in early modern England which, scarcely emerging from the feudal categories of the Middle Ages, still effected a man's identity in terms of his public role and relation to the collective. Protestant Christianity and classical humanism notwithstanding, the concept of an individual self was at best a fledgling idea, orbiting the vast monoliths of the twin enterprises of militarist national identity and the larger continental identity in which the former was grounded and enhanced. Both these identities, emerging together (and therefore in tandem and conflict), demanded an emphasis on the collective as unitary sign, which exerted pressure against competing notions of the individual.

The very legislation of dress and occupation, obliquely alluded to in Pierre the carpenter's reference to his forebears who had always been carpenters and signified in the presentation of the characters by job title rather than name, was part of the huge systemization of persons considered necessary to preserve the unitary image of the imperial nation, which was also part of a continent of shared values.[3] These issues are explored through the medium of one imagined variation on the European Middle Passage: the colonizing voyage of the ship *Reconnaisance* to the mythical San Cristobal, early identified as the same composite territory in which *Season of Adventure* and *Of Age and*

Innocence are set and on which *Water with Berries* is predicated. The ship becomes, in the Commandant's performative phraseology, the "stage" on which the "drama" of competition is enacted to decide who best images the iconic masculinity of authority and is therefore best suited to take command.

The drama is played out primarily among the Commandant – the iconic masculine figure – and the ship's officers, most of them men of low social standing who, ironically, had been promoted by the Commandant to the same assistant authority which they later use against him. The subversive side of obedience as an aspect of the authority paradigm manifests itself, first, in the mutiny of rank-and-file ship's hands, who step out of their allotted places to assume authority over their own lives, and, second, in the revelation of the hidden authority of the officers' wives, whose behind-the-scenes orchestration of events surpasses and subverts even the Commandant's surrogate-god machinations and finally helps to effect the tragic end of the officers.

Natives of My Person is an extraordinary novel. It is stylistically the most coherent of the six works, in the sense that there is a smoother integration between theoretical polemic and narrative. In Lamming's other fictions, particularly *Of Age and Innocence* and *Season of Adventure,* his tendency towards long passages of commentary and philosophical ideation separated out from the characters' natural process is very marked; *Natives,* on the other hand, closely embeds theorization in the characters' own perspectives. Also, although the characters often explicitly speak ideology in the pontifical style of some of the other novels, this is very smoothly accommodated into the style of *Natives* – an eighteenth- or nineteenth-century kind of overlay within which diction of this type is traditional. This is particularly true of the genre of literature that purports to be based on the discovery of old letters or other artefacts left by distant ancestors. In this context, the novel's use of diaries and journals is important, as it is able to manipulate convincingly the blend of narrative and speculation which characterizes the diary as an early modern and eighteenth- to nineteenth-century literary genre.

The articulation of the novel in the various styles and genres of the colonial era and its heavy allusiveness to specific literary and historical documents suggests that Lamming is presenting the novel itself as an artefact. As artefact, the novel possesses a dual significance, being at once the source of reproduction of artefacts that are both Europe's cultural and psychic progeny and West Indian inheritance and a source itself of such progeny and inheritance. The novel speaks of its subject and becomes part of that subject.

As textual artefact, *Natives of My Person* symbolizes the fact that the cultural products of empire do become *material* property. In the end, it is because of this use of the novel as model of the thing it images and critiques that Lamming is able both to deconstruct the Renaissance gender ideology which drove the voyages and to speak about language without too overtly speaking about language: it is the book as model that allows for a narrative style which replicates the language used by actual participants in the crafting of empire. The language of the characters needs no authorial gloss since it exhibits its own ideological fissures and contradictions. The novel's mimetic aspect is what most clearly reveals its metalinguistic project, what may be described as a concern to show language as stasis – that is, its photographic or mirroring capacity, which results from the instress of monoglossia: the attempt to make language serve a monologic, authoritarian function.

But *Natives of My Person* treads a delicate boundary, for how is the charge of reverse voyeurism (which might be a kind of anthropological justice) – and therefore the questioning of Lamming's entire ideology of the human Subject – to be avoided, given the obvious question of what legitimates a representation of reality from which the author is so far removed by space, time, racial experience and orientation? For answer, it may be argued that *Natives of My Person* succeeds in preserving Lamming's ideology of the human Subject in that even within its typologies, the novel manages to present a cast of characters whose individuality is as various as the characters themselves, each given reality and voice by the in-depth psychological portraits that the diary/journal format in particular accommodates. But this is too insufficient and oblique an answer.

Natives, despite its metaphorization of aspects of the West Indies through particular characters, may be read as a historicist account of sources of West Indian gender. Its validation as an account which remains faithful to history is those sources to which we made reference above, whose content, style and language (which are a way of thinking) infuse the text. The extent of correspondence between Lamming's imaginative reconstruction and the primary sources of journal and travel narrative further validates the representation. Beyond this, Lamming's exigent application of the terms of historical analysis to himself as representative West Indian gendered Subject appears in this novel as in all the others. The "my" of his title is at once disarming and challenging: an admission that these schizophrenias which his text reconstructs have found some lodgement in West Indian social process and psychological reality (in a 1996 interview, Lamming categorically declared that *Natives of My Person* is not about England but about West Indian politicians [Birbalsingh 1996a, 19]). The novel is also a declaration of the source of impact – one's reality as a descendant in the bastard line.

It is the bastard's right to speak that is being declared, and the acknowledgement of the "thing of darkness" as "mine" that is being required. The bastard's presence and his right transgress the novel in ellipsis, in the discursive construction of the cannibals and the savage tribes on whose body the manhood of empire is erected. So, although no specific West Indian characters appear in the novel, the entire narrative is predicated on their existence.[4] Having already spoken in diverse places, particularly in *The Emigrants* and *The Pleasures of Exile*, of the organizing, inevitably ideological factor of perspective in all historical accounting, Lamming makes no concession to this question of the right to speak that for the reader inevitably arises, beyond a bare acknowledgement by the character Pinteados that an eyewitness account is at once the most authentic and the least comprehensible because it is the most difficult of accounts to communicate (316).

In *Of Age and Innocence,* Thief identifies a major part of the difficulty: it is also the least believed of accounts. (Glissant [1992] too, makes the point that traditional history suffers from a serious epistemological deficiency, in its failure to make the link between lived experience and traditionalizing moment.) The West Indian's account is that of eyewitness and victim/participant, and as such is its own validation. The only other criterion is responsibility, in the exigent terms in which the writer-figure Collis confronted it in *The Emigrants,* and it is the witness of others who stand in a similar space that will judge the extent of responsibility of the representation. We are reminded that the literary text enters into a space of endless dialogue in which it must constantly state and find its position and its voice. It too becomes a part of those power relations from which it stands aside in order to critique them.

The central problematic of *Natives of My Person* is that nearly all the officers have a tortured secret past which has to do with their relations with women and which has direct bearing, in ways both known and unknown to them, on their presence on the ship and their sense of masculine authority. The porosity of the masculine identity, its absolute vulnerability to female/feminine invasion, is set out with particular economy in two scenarios. The first is Surgeon's unwitting disclosure to Pinteados that masculin(ist) identity depends on a concept of femininity: "You have had power. . . . Everyone here has had power sometime. To have a woman is to have known some power sometime" (152). The second is Pinteados's summation of the disjunctive relation between the officers' authority and their lack of power: "They were only on the inside . . . no further. They were men who would settle for nothing else. To be on the inside was enough. To be within the orbit of power was their total ambition. But real power frightened them. . . . The women are absolute evidence of what I mean. To feel authority over the women! That was enough for them. But to commit themselves fully to what they felt authority over. That they could never master. Such power they were afraid of" (318–19).

The men in flight from their women are in effect in flight from authentic sources of power, where power means the commitment that creates influence without coercion and by implication is rooted in a willingness to confront and come to terms with one's vulnerability. Pinteados's summation is closely related to Fromm's theory of the modern male Westerner's fear of freedom. Not only the flight from women but also the inurement in secrecy begins to indicate the officers' problems: the extent to which they evade self-knowledge, the extent to which the masculine identity they strenuously perform is an essential emptiness (in the powder-maker's words, "a hole with two ends" [128]), and the extent to which they stand in danger of the substratum/subconscious as an immanent threat that may insurrect at any given moment. The fear and suspicion in which each lives and which force some of them into confession of this secret past in order to pre-empt blackmail demonstrate the ulterior authority that both woman and secret have over these men's lives of ostensible authority. This complex of secrets also ironically shows how large political enterprises are constructed out of small personal agendas – in this case, the need for exorcism and the fulfilment of discontent. This already empties out the artificial split between public and private, as well as the large claims of the masculinist empire.

The empire is to some extent symbolized in the Commandant, self-imaged as a disinterested philanthropist. The Commandant is taking the officers to San Cristobal to reunite them with their wives and to begin a new democracy outside the pernicious shadow of the imperial kingdom of origins. But he is already implicated: his confrontations with the woman he deserted for adventure on the seas, which he tried to justify by saying he was doing it all for her, have exposed his true motivation. His obsession is to prove in battle once and for all his superiority over the Tribe Boys, whose "cannibal refusal to surrender" (65) is an enigma he cannot read or allow to be, even though, ironically, it is he who has effected its linguistic construction (for the refusal to surrender can only appear as enigma in the disjunction between "human" and "cannibal").

To a large extent, this last voyage is a flight from the rigorous truths that the woman's presence inculcates. We are told that the Commandant finds a singular relief in her absence and that she pushes him towards an honest relation to speech which he finds intolerable. She makes him "the prisoner of speech" (77), entrapping him in self-confrontation to the extent that he has to seek refuge in words that "[protect] him from speech" (79) – that is, in a further dislocation of vocabulary and syntax from real meaning. The flight is essentially, then, from her usurping, subversive authority, which comes from a fearlessness of tongue and an exigent integrity which refuses anything less than the truth.

The displacement of the woman by the obsession with the conquest of lesser men is rendered in sexual terms, its autoerotic narcissism disguised as desire for the other. Language is the endless predication of desire upon which the (feminized) lesser man is constructed as a mirror image of the conqueror's sense of masculine insufficiency: "For I have seen men of the basest natures *erect themselves* into gentlemen of honor the moment they were given orders to seize command over the savage tribes of the Indies. Here is a perfect school in the arts of conquest and command" (11, emphasis added). "Erecting themselves" points both to the anticipation of fulfilled narcissistic desire and to the iconic semiotics of the conquering, masculine body, *Homo erectus* versus the savage tribes. The Commandant's linguistic naivety appears in the numerous fissures: the bringing into question of the inferiority of "the savage tribes" by the very necessity of conquest; the inadvertent admission of "base natures" among men of the kingdom; the arrival only at *erectus,* rather than *sapiens,* so that a lacuna remains between the apogee of conquest and command and the (M)an who is to wield conquistadorial authority; and the dependence of imperial authority on the savage tribes for its validation.

Yet the fissures are repaired by the Commandant's ideology of the word-spoken-in-the-imperative-mood: it is the order spoken, which mystically enshrines the power to recreate baser natures into "gentlemen of honor". The Commandant's allegiance to this ideology is absolutely consistent, as shown in later sequences where his performance of the imperative, peremptory sentence "Be rid of [any habits of division and discord] and bring to your habits the same stern discipline I saw the painter impose upon your bodies . . ." (49) images his belief in its power to change psyches instantaneously by invocation. That the Commandant wears this authority of the word as investiture, in the service of some higher masculinity whose viceroyalty he becomes, is pointed by the omniscient narrator's tandem declaration that, in moments like this, the habit of command "possessed" him, its possession branded in the agitation of his body. But the higher power which thus ironically territorializes the Commandant's body is not the House of Trade and Justice, the apogee and arbitrator of imperial manhood in Lime Stone. Rather, it is the iconic idea of masculinity as authority which, in Foucauldian terms, the House has invented and circulated/recirculated as cultural and psychic currency, and which now finds accommodation in the psyche of the man who in his intention to set up a democracy on San Cristobal paradoxically also represents a break from the imperial order. The Subject's containment in culture is another phrase for the inescapable recirculation of cultural and psychic coin when interrogation remains less than radical.

The mythic/mystical power of this authority is such that it does in fact transmute itself from the Commandant's aura into the men's consciousness. One of the most powerful dramatizations of this phenomenon occurs when Ivan, in a paroxysm of fear when the Commandant finds the men idling, begins to shout orders in the Commandant's voice and is able to motivate the men to move like automatons, bending to his will as though the Command-ant had himself been there. The biblical overtones, where the speech stands for the presence precisely because of the nature of authority, rewrite this dramatization as a reconfiguration of the sacred; that is, masculine authority vested in the word of command takes on a sacral identity whose ultimate validation and source of energy is faith, or absolute belief.

This authoritative word that the Commandant speaks has an entire tradition of meta-authorization behind it: not only the authority of cultural discourse or of his position as a nobleman, but an authorization invested in a vast technology of signification whose function is to transform the word from discourse into real economic capital. This technology is scientific knowledge harnessed into the making of ships and navigational instruments, such as maps and compasses, which will search for and deliver the goods of empire. The Commandant is the commander of all these, artefacts from which his masculine image is constructed.

In this context, the Commandant's description of the ship as "a great castle on water" (11), with its ironic reverberations against the idea of the castle of one's skin, emphasizes the idea of masculinity not as a possession of the inner self, but as a function of material possession and a reflection or transliteration of value mystically invested in the economic sign. The aura and "inherent" value of the ship transmute themselves into the image of the man. The importance of the maps in similarly charting the stable, definite geography of self is pointed by Steward's obsession with these artefacts: "The room throbbed with Steward's passion for cosmography. He had no rival to this dream that would complete his knowledge of all the globes and charts he had compiled; every item of evidence that travel and arithmetic had discovered in the four known continents of the world" (87).

This absolute knowledge is what in Steward's imagination will restore his ascendancy over the House of Trade and Justice, which had stolen his first maps and thereby set back his passage of masculine authority in the world. More critically, it will enable him to prove his masculine superiority over his wife, whose greater authority in the possession of worldly goods and connections is the source of his greatest insecurity, terror and motivation. In fact, he tells Surgeon that this is the reason for his presence on the voyage: the language of his maps at the Commandant's disposal will help to garner wealth by which to stop his wife's mouth. His wife's oppressive loquacity, which makes "the common whores [seem] dumb virgins by comparison" (179), is the sign of a rupture in a cosmic order in which the mutually constitutive authorities of economic wealth and linguistic property are generically male possessions. The wife's "whoredom", defined by a looseness of tongue which also signifies overly receptive genitalia, is cosmic chaos (chaos standing in this instance for disorder).[5]

Lamming deconstructs the signifying grapheme, showing its emptiness as a sign, the extent to which its inherent ability to confer meaning is an illusion only. The word is not transparent; language does not consist in signs, but rather inhabits them. The sign at its heart is empty. This is shown where the writing on the maps (the signs by which Steward declares his repossession of the word) becomes "a line of ants" (96), indicating the self-devouring which is at the heart of his self-construction. The image is reinforced by his relation to the rusting (unused) mirror, which he puts away, musing instead on the "screen of maps" (87). The cartographic screen is part of the extended motif of mirrors and photographs, which across the fictions expresses the failure of the voyeuristic gaze on the basis of its obsession with surfaces.

This extraordinary materialism – the belief in the aura and inherent, transmutable value of the technologically constructed sign – shows itself in Steward's rhapsodic, almost uncritical veneration of the Commandant, which amounts to the irresistible seizure of a religion: the man who is able to command both himself as the producer of these signs and the power of the signs themselves must be somewhat in the nature of a god. Yet the superior, satirically presented authority of the image of womanhood against which Steward's masculinity is even more fundamentally constructed causes him to assassinate the Commandant rather than face his wife again, when he learns that the Commandant plans to reunite him with her.

But even the ship, the maps and their mystic authority of the material are finally in the service of a higher authority whose source, nature and origin remain unknown to these men who are not in the habit of self-examination and who cannot even conceive of a self outside the visible, publicly accounted sign. This final authority, which seizes the Commandant as its possession – "The ocean had chosen him for the kingdom" (76) – is the tyrannical authority of language displaced from its proper function. In this guise it becomes Nemesis, a retributive nightmare inhabiting a delusional idea whose imposition was the cause of that initial displacement and now becomes its haunting.

Lamming represents this sense of language as a retributive Fury in a description of a party on board ship:

> [A] babel of voices arose from the mess deck, contentious and drunk with the power of their sound. They were celebrating their escape from the land, speculating on the fortunes that would reward their labors. With every league of distance, they seemed to gain fresh triumph over the silence they had endured while they waited on the coast. The darkness was restoring their manhood; and each tongue had discovered the music and speech of its Region. They were no longer fugitives from freedom, but men surprised at last by the immense and novel promise of freedom which the ocean was about to offer them. It was a delirium of the tongue which had overtaken them, spontaneous and utterly beyond their control. (16)

The equation of silence with the loss of masculinity, and concomitantly the equation of decisive speech (signified in the Commandant's order to set sail) with its reacquisition, extends into a relation with the ship, the ocean and freedom. This relation emphasizes the definition of language in a trinity in which the other two authorities are masculinity and capital – for freedom in this case means enough booty to complete the panoply of insignias of self. "Babel" and "delirium" re-mark the extent to which this concept of language as legitimated/validated in possessions is the arrival of pandemonium.

The fact that the men have been overtaken by this delirium, utterly beyond their control, is the text's re-presentation of language as Nemesis, for here not only madness, but madness as the loss of age and innocence on the ground of the very authority they revere, as well as madness located in the moment of perceived power, is signified. Language, which they had conceived as transparent, mimetic and open to colonization, subverts their power to understand themselves. In a very real sense, language has become apocalyptic. The scene achieves additional impact from its direct juxtaposition with the earlier gossip about the pilot Pinteados, a native of the rival kingdom of Antarctica and therefore a rival masculinity which they set out to diminish at all costs. Pinteados is accused of being too silent; indeed, "the enemy of sound", "[n]ot native to Lime Stone, where the word is as necessary as blood" (13). The metonymic rendering of Pinteados's foreignness as silence becomes the accusative image of the officers' fear of ambiguity. Pinteados threatens face/authority, so that even though he has never exhibited any hostility, he is constantly attacked and harried in an attempt to deconstruct his silence. Silence may house subversive plans against the enterprise – and Pinteados could do real harm, because he is, after all, the pilot, the commander of the compass, and as such the only indispensable man on board.

Lamming's satirical point is that this man (whose name identifies him as an artist-figure and therefore the thin edge of the wedge of responsible speaking in this company)[6] is the complete antithesis of the "masculine" (being speechless, foreign and without a woman – in fact, a self-confessed "semi-virgin"), yet he becomes the most powerful authority on the ship, first by his silence and later by the secrets he holds about the pasts from which all the other officers are fleeing. (Secrecy and silence cohere as twin phenomena not because their twinship is the absolute definition of silence, but because secrecy is the silence the officers need to interrogate in order to establish a right relation to the self.)

Pinteados's authority is strengthened by his connection with the wives: he has known all of them, and in a relationship of mutual respect. The relationship works reflexively to strengthen the women's positioning as subversive authorities. Pinteados is also the one man, with the possible exception of Baptiste the powder-maker, who understands the nature of power and wears it like a skin. He uses it judiciously, revealing parts of what he knows only when provoked and only in an attempt to move the hearer to self-analysis, as in the case of his cryptic rejoinder to Steward's provocation that he knows the latter's wife, both literally and biblically. Marcel the fisherman (the fisherman being another trademark Lamming trope, representing the West Indian "salt of the earth" folk) and Ivan the painter are other figurations of the destabilizing, apocalyptic power of language. Ivan becomes this figuration in his power of clairvoyant speech, as does Marcel in his silence, which in the excessively competitive arena of shipboard is also feared as "the force of a sign that none could decipher" (27) and therefore "a deformity" – a description which allies him with the Caliban figure of the colonized native.

Boatswain, the most fervent of the worshippers at the shrine of authority, recognizes the latent power in Ivan's clairvoyance even while adhering completely to the ideology of the transparent word of command. His attempts to colonize Ivan's vision by forcing him into trances out of which he is commanded to speak the foretelling he has envisioned indicate the ways in which the iconic masculinity fissures itself by its dependence on the feminizing territorialization of all others within competitive range. But it also indicates the gargantuan proportion of the project of devouring which drives the monologic enterprise. The mystic power of the prophetic word is to be collected and stored, for future consumption, into the reservoirs of authoritative command – for Boatswain plans to use the knowledge culled from Ivan to gain a competitive edge over his rival officers. Boatswain's schizophrenia reaches its logical conclusion in the madness that leads him to tear (devour) his own flesh as did the women in the lunatic asylum, yet his madness is of a different order, being the dissolution of the landmarks of authority and thus of the entire known world. The other officers' panic that Boatswain (and therefore the vulnerability of authority) "has been seen" (voyeurized, exposed) demonstrates this.

Marcel as silent, deformed territory and Ivan as Cassandra-figure occupy the liminalized space of the feminine, as do the female characters, and, like the latter, are constantly brought from periphery to centre to be staged and erased by the authorities their existence threatens. The stagings of Marcel and Ivan are done via on-board rehearsals and rituals of action and/or questioning speech; those of the women are accomplished via the flashbacks of memory, whose insurrection is rigidly controlled by the men's interpretations, which, however, are re-interrogated by the remembered actions, speech, and silence of the women.

The linkage of the women with the destabilizing power of language has ultimately to do with their occupation of an occluded space and their displacement by an ideological act. In the same way that an attempt is made to colonize language – that is, to bend it from its polyglossic/dialogic capacities to serve a monoglossic/monologic function, so that both language and its human subject are debased into a false transparency – the women are hidden away in those psychic spaces that represent the vulnerability the men want to forget. Alternatively, they are displaced by the erotics of territorial conquest. Steward and Surgeon have their perfectly sane wives consigned to the lunatic asylum, Lamming's trademark trope for the insurrection of language, its subversive ability to articulate what is true at the point where it loses authorized syntax. The Commandant seeks to make of his woman "a colony of joys", that is, to reduce her to sexual territory, beneath speech.

At one level, the women resist these inventions. In Lamming's ideology of the human Subject, they are already existentially subversive, but this subversiveness acquires a powerful, ironic signature in action. In keeping with the will of their men, they acquiesce in their own erasure: the Commandant's woman takes herself off to a nunnery and later marries into the House of Trade and Justice; the other two accept their incarceration, Surgeon's wife going so far as to agree to be blamed for her husband's crime, an admission from which her purported madness protects her but which simultaneously validates that madness. But the women use the space of erasure, hidden and unread because its non-existence is presumed, not only to assist their men to undertake the voyage on the symbolically named *Reconnaisance,* but also to organize a surprise rendezvous on the Isle of the Black Rock, San Cristobal.

San Cristobal, then, reassumes in a different context the guise it has had in the previous novels: a place of reckoning, a summit of pasts at which the present must be given account for and the future decided. San Cristobal, more than metaphorically, is rooted in apocalypse and ceremonies of soul. The landscape of the West Indies, spoken for and symbolized in Lamming's text, becomes crossroads and site of historical reckoning for every race that has encountered in it. That these evaluative and retributive functions are to be served is pointed by the women's rehearsal of the charge at the end of the novel: "Why did we follow them here? . . . Yes, why follow them here? . . . Because we are a future. . . . A future, you say? . . . A future, I repeat. We are a future they must learn" (345). That this future is not learnt is already known to the reader, who has witnessed the slayings on board ship, the outcome of the competition and fear engendered by the Renaissance masculinism Lamming represents. The women represent a language, a subconscious and an identity not entered into, the psychic loss by which the empire made itself and engendered the New World. Further, insofar as the women wield both masculine authority and the subversive power which belongs to the feminine, they begin to inscribe the possibility of hermaphroditic gender that chapter 1 suggests was the occluded legacy that nationalist discourse, in the colonizer's categories, was unable to appropriate.

But it is not the female characters who represent the most far-reaching possibility in this regard. The women's enterprise is aborted not so much by the unexpected deaths of their men, but, more fundamentally, by the quality of the virtues they display. Steward and the Commandant are paralysed by their women's impregnable virtue, the complete resistance of their selfhood to any accusation of sin that would have freed the men's consciences. This virtuousness, identified as an exigent commitment to love, even "against our interests" (328), leads them secretly to fund and organize, through the present voyage, the men's search to achieve their greatest ambitions of conquest. Yet it is the same virtue that empties their sense of self of any real meaning and, by extension, questions the quality of a love which is not merely self-sacrificing, but self-denigrating. Like Marcia and Ma Shephard, these women know no reality beyond their men; but they go even beyond this, knowing no *self* beyond their men, so that where the perceived necessity of humiliation for love's sake reaches the point of demand for the very integrity of the self, they gladly make the sacrifice. Their final accounts of the abuse and rejection that they have accepted and overlooked in the search for a renewal of relationship even though it is clear the men are not interested rival any medieval hagiographical account.

That this is not a historicist representation but an essentialist one, a definition of the female as generically self-erasing, appears both in the consistency of Lamming's treatment of the female across his fictions and in the contrasting diversity of males' images of self, even within the assimilating confines of a particular gender ideology. Inevitably, inadvertently, Lamming locks himself into that dialectic in which masculinity is something men discover, try on, perform and discard or re-perform, while femininity *when applied to the female* is an acceptance of lack which women essentially are. Women may borrow masculinity, but this is only in the service of a symbolic ideology which the lived reality of his characters eventually empties out. Lamming's cerebral ideology, in other words, has not caught up with his perhaps unconscious visceral beliefs.

The most composite and balanced representation of a gender ideal resides in Pinteados, who to some extent I am reading here contrary to Lamming's own interpretation of this character as the type of the foreign technocrat.[7] Pinteados becomes the nearest representation of the possibilities of the West Indies as a Creole society. Like the West Indies, he is voyeurized as territory, as exotic, as inferior and simultaneously threatening, but remains resistant to the voyeuristic gaze both because of the capacity for self-discovery and self-invention through language and because of a human existence beyond speech. This latter is signified in his silence, which is, first, a semiotic of the liminal, second, the silence imposed on him by the voyeur who invents the "native" in the space of erasure, but, finally and most importantly, the choice of the conscious Subject who wishes to preserve a responsible relation to speech and language.

Pinteados is able to stand as the ideal gendered Subject both because of these relations to language and humanness and because he totally accepts and integrates into himself the masculine categories of authority and power and the feminine categories of vulnerability and submission. He is able to transform these into the kind of power which he sees as being absent in the others precisely because he does not valorize or denigrate either but recognizes them as aspects of being human and aspects of negotiation in given political moments. Pinteados does not flaunt authority, but he is not afraid to use it judiciously. Neither does he feel a need to compete for or against it: his acceptance of the Commandant's higher authority is unproblematic because he is secure in his own sense of self.

He does not derive kudos from being "a man on the inside" because he recognizes the freedom of individuality invested in being on the periphery, and he is not afraid either of silence or of women because he recognizes silence as a kinetic extension of the linguistic event and because he has been configured in the same terms as the female. Pinteados is also not afraid to be compassionate: he accepts vulnerability. He makes no divisions among persons that would prevent his grieving for the loss of a man like the Commandant because he recognizes both human potential and human waste.

In his mystery, "abomination" and wholeness, Pinteados could easily be described as a man of hermaphroditic gender. Yet, as a symbol of the necessity and inability of (new) language, he indicates the inadequacy of all forms of gender in describing the human. In terms of gender, Fola comes short of the achievement which is Pinteados because she has to become (symbolically) male, because in her case the feminine is reassigned to secondariness and because in a sense she is obsessed with absolute definitions. (The latter aspect exists in tension with her intuitive understanding of the arcane underside –

the otherness – of language, which is a type of the ideological feminine and which also mirrors the inscrutable humanity it seeks to articulate.) But even Pinteados ultimately falls short, as a result of that foreign technocrat's detachment to which Lamming points. Unlike Fola, Pinteados lacks the moral fervour that would have led him to interrogate his own part in the expedition. In this sense also, he indicates the inadequacy of gender as a means not only of description, but of judgement. For Lamming, moral integrity is the bottom line.

The one person who might have displaced Pinteados at the level of gender is Baptiste the powder-maker, who plays the role of a kind of union representative of the rank-and-file crew and who with Ivan's help stages his own mutiny, deserting to San Cristobal when he guesses that the Commandant (unable to face his own woman) may have decided to turn back. The powder-maker is the quintessential revolutionary, fired with passion and the desire for equal rights. Both his rude, rough-and-ready speech, fearless in criticism of the established authorities and the establishment they represent, and his co-option of the prophetic voice suggest that he is one of the few who begin to have an acceptable relation to language. Further, Baptiste takes creative and definitive action: he will himself set up a colony, refusing the abortion of his dreams.

But Baptiste is a flawed hero, both because he is implicated in the categories of authority he is defying and because of his hostile, oppositional relation to the female and femininity. With regard to the former, as far as Baptiste is concerned, his mother's adultery, in compromising the authority of the father which he reveres like a talisman, has rendered all women generically whores. With regard to the latter, Baptiste's most exigent terror is the fear of feeling, except rage. Ivan of the artistic clairvoyant vision also falls short of the ideal not only because he joins Baptiste on a sudden impulse, without demonstrated ideation, but also because he is associated with Baptiste at all. The tragedy of the colonies is that Baptiste, the empire and the Commandant were the fathers that came. But their hopeful possibility is the space of dialogue between the figurations of Pinteados and Fola, the one a balanced, gendered individual, the other possessed of the exigent moral fervour that is the positive side of the young nation's brash, loquacious aggression.

That the ideologies and event-types displayed on the ship are inherited genealogical traces in West Indian nationalism is seen in the portrayal of the ship's boy Sasha, who learns by observation and inadvertent coaching the secret of masculinity as defined by the officers. Sasha comes to love secrets, recognizing them as the manipulative sign of power over others. He also comes to love the coercive authority of the word, hence his closeness to the seat of power, the Commandant, and his shadowing of Ivan the seer. He declares gleefully that he is learning to be a man. In the end, Sasha's innocent loyalty to the Commandant becomes the instrument by which he is inducted into the authorities of the technologies of destruction, as he shoots Surgeon and Steward in retaliation for the assassination of the Commandant. Sasha recalls Rowley, Crabbe's tortured son in *Of Age and Innocence,* and the impossibility of an equitable or neat ending to such a beginning. He also recalls Shephard, the idealistic patriot, and Fola's stepfather, both flawed examples of manhood in the colony these voyagers made. In Glissant's words used in another context, "*They sowed in the depths the seeds of an invisible presence.* And so transversality, and not the universal transcendence of the sublime, has come to light" (1992, 67).

My Other Half, The Dumb and Speaking Body: *The Emigrants*

Natives of My Person is an eyewitness account by virtue of a history whose inheritance is now being lived. *The Emigrants* is an eyewitness account in a more immediately "material" way. A representation of the experience of the first West Indian travellers to Britain, the novel bears striking resemblances of subject and treatment to Selvon's *The Lonely Londoners.* Lamming and Selvon journeyed to England on the same ship, among that first generation of travellers. They became fast friends, sharing similar experiences. Both speak at first hand, even if fictionally and in metaphor. The circumstance is important: it needs to be paid attention to as an authentic record of that beginning in exile, the anguished displacement which preceded and made possible the later celebration of migrancy in ameliorative terms as diaspora. Here too is a form of patrimony and cultural inheritance, particularly for West Indians living abroad and grappling with different issues of West Indianness in a different time and space.

The terms that drove the voyage of *Natives of My Person* are redefined in the backward glance of this reading of *The Emigrants.* The failure of language appears not primarily in its guise as Nemesis, but in its inadequacy against another form of utterance: the unreadable signification of the body. This representation of failure mocks the imagery by which the Commandant's ethic, which is the ethic of empire, had territorialized the bodies of "lesser men", using the impositions of class and race. And it does so by a peculiar form of irony – the body is accepted as territory; the charge of "mere territoriality" is embraced, not disputed. The acceptance is completely subversive, for this territoriality that is accepted already speaks its own primal language, which rejects the imposed linguistic project of territorialization. The body becomes territory in order *not* to be mere territory on any grounds. In the process, the feminine principle, denigrated by the conquistadors of *Natives of My Person,* is retrieved, defined and celebrated as an aspect of the resistant humanity of which the body speaks. Here it is mapped onto the bodies of men, the mirror side of the mapping of masculinity in the body of Fola Piggott.

This feminine principle had appeared to us in *Natives* as a contradictory matrix of political impositions and existential powers that strangely mirror the reality of West Indian consciousness and colonial history. The feminine in *Natives* is first and foremost speech that is prophetic and multiform rather than transparent and monologic. In the conquistadorial reckoning, this is abomination. It is also speech that emanates from women and "not-men" – that is to say, speech of abominable, usurping authority. And it is both silence that becomes abominable because it cannot be definitively read and silence that speaks and must therefore be definitively silenced. To be feminine is to be vulnerable, to occupy a secondary or occluded space and to occupy the space of madness – that is to say, to exist in linguistic chaos, where chaos stands for speech that defies known grammars.

In sum, then, to be feminine is to be Caliban, inventing a radical new language that seeks to remain true to *eidos* which it cannot capture; it is to be Fola and "other than"; it is to be Prospero's abomination. Language that seeks to remain true in this way is also language that is true to itself, struggling to reach the truth of its own paradoxical being, which at once allows for a clear definition of the (masculine) self and *represents* its (feminine) refusal. Prospero's voyeuristic judgement of Caliban who speaks is imaged in the latter's deformity of body, of which Marcel's deformity in *Natives of My Person* becomes a trope. The mapping of the feminine onto the bodies of men in *The Emigrants,* and its linkage to a larger, inscrutable inscription of humanity, is the celebratory recuperation of the hermaphrodite, the deformed body, even as it is the recuperation of the hybrid, transformational grammars of West Indian speech.

These recuperative projects are undertaken as a form of dialectic: the celebratory perspective is placed in answer to the perspective of negation. Negation of the body and the feminine is a transmuted legacy from the history which *Natives of My Person* records and which in *The Emigrants* is exhibited by both English and West Indian, both alike the maimed progeny of the empire. The paradox of *The Emigrants* is that, like *Natives,* it ends in an apprehension of tragedy, for the celebratory perspective which reinscribes the feminine by locating it within inviolable humanity and offering it as part of a wholeness of identity is not embraced by the characters. Celebration is instead a function of the narrative polemic, which radically judges the failure of the protagonists' ways of seeing.

Consistently, the protagonists fail to apprehend the truth about themselves, even as Selvon's boys had failed to apprehend their own language's radical powers. Indeed, part of the perspective of negation in *The Emigrants* is the threat of a tragic disconnection from the creative and liberating possibilities of language, which the novel explores with a sense of grief, angst and alienation not typical of the generality of Lamming's fiction. In the "backward" circle of glance between *The Emigrants* and *Natives of My Person,* all ellipsis is removed and the damage done through the word of the father clearly seen in its effects five hundred years after the Commandant's first putting out to sea. In the resonance between Lamming's and Selvon's portrayals, one is seized by an irresistible sense of the narratives' authenticity and their truth.

The emigrants are presented as bastard (colonial) children arriving at a rendezvous with the putative parent, whose identity and relation to them must now become fully known. (One of them, in a later conversation with the African Azi, uses exactly this metaphor of the parent-child relationship to posit his idea of the West Indian relation to England.) The prospect creates a sense of psychic terror, for suddenly – unlike Columbus armed with maps and sense of cultural "certainties" – these discoverers in reverse realize they have come unprepared. England is both an unknown and a merely putative parent. The impending confrontation with the body, as opposed to the myth (by which the parent's presence-absence had been circulated in the colony), brings this forcefully home to them. The anomaly of the relation strikes them in an even more terrifying light, for they are by their own declaration going to England to "make a man o' yuhself" (61).

The moment is Oedipal: one moves towards the father in order to find one's manhood, but theirs is a potential manhood already configured in difference. Further, they too discover the fatherland's whoredom (designated as such in *Natives of My Person*), its endless titillation and extension of desire, the cycle of proferral and withdrawal that keeps them endlessly seduced and endlessly unassuaged. The erotics of empire are replayed in the psyches of these new (world) arrivants seeking to "erect themselves" as men on English soil. Like Selvon's, the emigrants' London is an incestuous, gendered anomaly: at once putative father/motherland and devouring whore. The city's promiscuity and whoredom are aptly symbolized in the use of casual and paid sexual encounter, the dissipation and commodification of the body, as the central metaphor for emigrant-England relations. The metaphor shifts, becomes geographical: what the emigrants confront is territory without definitive landmarks (like Selvon's Londoners, they first see England through fog). It is partly in this context that the body – human and territorial – becomes the organizing metaphor of *The Emigrants.* That the body in a guise as sexual object is emphasized throughout the novel reinforces our idea of the West Indies as progeny. Its further metaphorization as territory emphasizes the economic imperative which racialized the enslaved and indentured body in the New World. These representations set up some of the paradoxes through which Lamming presents his epistemology of the body.

Here again the Oedipal crisis is Lamming's trademark catalyst for the movement into national consciousness. This appears in the feverish rehearsals by which on board ship the men seek to speak themselves into being, suddenly recognizing that all of them coming from diverse territories, with all their rivalries and mutual suspicions, are West Indians – or rather, need to become West Indians. Not English, but West Indian. The fear of the impending confrontation with the father/motherland, along with the intuitive pre-knowledge of the latter's rejection, impels the search for another self-centre: their own indigenous reality. The rehearsal is the process of movement into masculinizing self-knowledge; one ritualizes oneself into being, as it were – understands and constructs the self through a linguistic pilgrimage into one's present and past.

The term "masculinizing" here refers purely to men, for though there are women on the ship, it is clear that they are outside this search for identity or community; they take no part in the discussions and form no enclaves of their own. Here they appear as some kind of naturalistic given, outside problematization, or, if requiring problematization, only at the level of their relations with men, in whom they seem to live and move and have their being. (Apart from *In the Castle of My Skin, The Emigrants* displays

Lamming's crudest representations of women, and this despite the sophisticated ways in which the feminine is implied in the novel's posited epistemology of the body. In making this statement, we bear in mind that in these novels "feminine" is not equated with "female".)

For the emigrants generally, the rehearsal into self in the context of nationhood escapes resolution. Each is locked into an obscene privacy the totality of which is pointed by the series of bizarre coincidences with which the novel ends. One's sense of these events being intolerably contrived points to a persuasion of despair which in representation refuses to be disloyal to itself. In the end, the all-pervasive sense of dislocation is rooted in an inability to find a mode of speech, a confidence, by which to reinvent the self against England's rejection. Some do achieve a sense of community, based on the common experience of alienation, but the endless delay of a real sense of power is indicated in two ways. One is the inability of several rehearsals (in rooms, in the barber shops, on the train) to move beyond the subject of alienation and loss. The other is the poising of the dialogues on "what is West Indian" on the edge of a stammer, a reality not yet able to be spoken.

There is paradox in this, however, for the poising on the edge of a stammer is the sign that there is conversation, and that the conversation is radical, a search for new grammars within which to re-speak the self. In the same way, the metaphor of the womb suggests not that these men have died but that they are yet both to be born and to give birth. In this respect, Lamming's men-in-waiting are far more positive constructs than Selvon's boys. Even so, it is the negative side of the paradox – the stammer rather than its possibility, the round space as entrapment rather than fructifying womb – that comes to the fore in the tragic denouements of *The Emigrants*. One's sense is not that in this new Middle Passage there is a final death, but certainly that there is tragic and terrible waste in the fetid and inhuman confines of the ship's hold.

The dislocation from sufficient space within which to re-speak the self translates into a paralysis of action, which appears in the emigrants' retreat into an intense, blind preoccupation with the body. The body here becomes oxymoron and paradox: it is at once all meaning and all chaos, where chaos stands for the dissolution of signs and therefore the opening of space for re-mapping. But such re-mapping presumes an ability to see, which must in some form have existed in a time and space prior to the arrival of chaos and which is able to manipulate chaos by virtue of the adaptability immanent in the very nature of seeing. The emigrants' entrapment in the body, manifested in the multiplicity of promiscuous and economic sexual encounters, expands then into a larger discourse on the characters' psychological relation to seeing and being seen. Sex is imbricated in the dialectics of voyeurism and vision, of clairvoyance and disjunctive seeing.

The fact that real seeing, which is a right relation to language (where language includes *langue, parole* and the body's signification), constantly escapes the emigrants is metaphorized in several ways. For example, in Tornado's looking in a mirror "as though his eyes didn't really see their [own] reflection" (189); in the breakup of the writer Collis's eyesight and his confusion about whether other people's eyes are in fact eyes or just pieces of glass. England's inability to "see" the emigrants – even at the most voyeuristic moments, such as the Englishwomen's gleeful gazing at Dixon's uncovered penis – is also implied in these instances. Dixon is forced to flee naked into London's streets by the women, whose giggling, innocently confessed desire was "only to see what he *looked* like" (266). That his naked erect penis is not "he", though it is also paradoxically the sign of a larger, hidden potency, escapes the ideology of transparency in which their imaginations are inured. Collis, the writer-figure, represents the possibility the other emigrants are unable to grasp, but even he is only a possibility, dislocated as he is from an organic, symbiotic relation to a creative, developing society.

A number of discourses on the territorial body are employed as a means of interrogating these types of relation. One of the most pervasive is a warning that the body's castle of skin is constantly open to a one-sided reading as "meaninglessness". It is as though Lamming sets up landmarks in the unmarked territory to guide the unwary West Indian traveller in search of inheritance and roots. In one tableau on board ship, he prefigures the men's bodies as territory, an indication of the feminized space of erasure they will inhabit once they touch English soil:

> Collis and the Jamaican looked like shapes of land growing out of the deck. They didn't see and it didn't seem that they felt the sway that rocked them. They were asleep. Anyone could have killed Tornado or Collis or Higgins and that would have been the end of that. By interrupting a process which made them other than what they seemed sprawled on the deck it would have been possible to convert them into objects. You might even have gone on referring to the object as Collis or Higgins or Tornado. It would have made no difference at all to the heavy black flesh that lay on the deck. . . . Frustration, anger, relief, hope, triumph; these would have vanished with the process which having been interrupted left each an object. (82–83)

The body's openness to a configuration as meaninglessness is by extension its vulnerability to exploitation and rapine. This is first articulated in Collis's expression of the terms in which he desires sexual intercourse with Queenie: he wishes to erase her personality and reduce her body to "an object" even as he recognizes that it had "its own secret resources"; in voyeuristic imagination, he attempts to render her clothed body transparent, "naked under the sun before my eye" (24). Later the image is transmuted into the image of the ship's orgasmic passage through the sea, a trope of the European patriarch's arrival in the territory as marauding rapist and imperial father:

> [T]he wind came stronger and the music of the engine joined it in a savagery that knew no restraint. The surge had grown into a leap and the fall was a plunge that charged the depth of this deep and intimate darkness. The ship's pace seemed to quicken to a pace that was reckless. It cut cruelly through the water as though it had found a new pleasure in its power and possession. The rumble of the engine would not subside and the waters opened to the thrusting keel as the ship cut accurately through the receiving surface. Receptivity was strained to the utmost as though every nerve had been exposed to the invading pleasures for the ecstasy of a single moment held, and kept and squeezed till the energy had spent itself, and desire dwindled to a limp and harmless thing. (91–92)

The ship's marauding performance not only replays Europe's wanton production of the colonies as physical, economic and cultural progeny; it also prefigures the impending reproduction of that historical act on the territorialized bodies of the emigrants.

But of equal importance is the irony that as colonizers in reverse, though feminized by England as "not-men", the emigrants will subversively replicate that history and inheritance upon England's body in return. The ship's sexually represented progress is also the metaphorical statement of the sexual frenzies in which some drown their fear or persuade themselves of their masculine sufficiency on English soil. The ship's sequence ends with the comical exposure of Tornado's woman Lilian in synchronic intercourse with the "Governor", who has set himself up as the authority figure to whom all the men rally. Here and elsewhere, the Governor is revealed as the colonizer's fifth column, the traitor within. The Governor is one of the figurations by which Lamming's fictions avoid the easy polarizations of blame and race that militate against a full representation of the human Subject. Lamming's moral exigency refuses to absolve the West Indian of responsibility; if the voyage is a ceremony of soul, it must be a ceremony in which our own collusion in the problems of our history must be admitted and exposed.

The territorialization of the emigrants, male and female alike, corresponds to Selvon's "spades".[8] Here the relation between sex and gender is replaced by a relation between gender and geographical origin. The feminization of the men in *The Emigrants* brings ironic resonances to their repeated collective declaration on board ship that they are going to England to make men of themselves. It establishes one of the important terms of their sojourn in the metropole: in England's eyes, they will not arrive as fathers, that is, as masculine sowers of cultural and economic seed in the city. On the surface, this remains largely true. Their frenzied, harried labour in London's factories yields them little return; work becomes part of action as escape and paralysis. Their contribution to the city's economic re/production goes unacknowledged – the racialized labouring body remains an unidentified cog in the capitalist machine. And the enclaves in which they live are closed off from, yet penetrated by the wider London society in the form of the women who sexually voyeurize Dixon and of characters like Frederick and Peggy, new conquistadors in search of sexual potency which they feel the West Indians have and which they hope to possess vicariously.

The concept of penetration is salient: the circle of the emigrants' peregrination is at one point referred to as a womb (148), signifying their possession in feminine space. But as noted above, this too is part of the paradox in which West Indian gender is inured, for the relation is symbiotic: by their mutual desire for occluding, self-validating flesh, the emigrants penetrate England even as they themselves are penetrated. The body, like speech, becomes an agent of subversion. The identity of the incestuous mother/fatherland collapses into its bastard progeny's otherness of skin. The paid sexual encounter with native British centralizes a diachronic historical relation: that the capitalist re/production upon which England's identity rests was/is generated upon the body/sex of the slave. Their mutual "bodyness", their common blood, is revealed. "Prospero has been seen."[9]

In the double penetration, the gender of the emigrants, who had come to England to make of themselves men, becomes unfixed. The very title of the novel signifies their continuing habitation of insecure, unfixed space, unfixed identity and loss of identifying name. Identifying name is by extension language in its self-confident aspect; thus this loss is the loss of definitive speech. That this unfixing becomes despair rather than creative moment may be read as a function of the particular stress created by geographical dislocation (disconnection from body of place/original home of spirit). In this respect, *The Emigrants* contrasts markedly with the greater hopefulness of novels such as *Of Age and Innocence* and *Season of Adventure,* paradoxical even though these are. The characters in the other two novels are able to work out the issues of language, genealogy and en/gendering on their own territory, and in a sense in their own time. Their journeys of self-discovery and invention, then, take place in a context already known and therefore – at least at the starting point – capable of description in familiar speech.

But the first West Indian voyagers to London, as Selvon's novel also indicates, were lost in a completely radical relation to space. The emigrants appear to have become a new branch of genealogy, a dislocated branch whose legacy to the Caribbean must be determined at another time at which the novel does not arrive. It is remarkable that two such different writers – Lamming the cerebral philosopher, Selvon the organic observer – should in their different narratives have accorded a similar, significant place to geography and language in the construction of identity and have placed sex and gender as core dynamics of the process of self-loss and self-definition.

Territorialization of the body and erasure of identity as colonial constructions of the Caribbean are cultural and psychic inheritance which the colonial male (as much as the female) has to accept and subvert. But it is also an inheritance which he is in danger of endlessly reproducing by an acquiescence in the idea of himself as territory. He is further seduced by a masculine economy within which the body's sexual prodigality promises but never delivers manhood as secure identity (the economic spoils and the resulting kudos still belong to the mother/fatherland). More insidiously, he is in danger of accepting the idea that the struggle against territorialization defines his final state – in other words, that the circumscription of his speech in a cycle of opposition and reply (Caliban's curse) is an adequate description of his humanity. Such an acquiescence, which is a false acceptance radically opposed to the type of acceptance Lamming posits, reproduces the colonizer's idea of himself as god-father, so that the historical moment which brought the West Indies into being defines the West Indian person. The danger is in fact embedded in Lamming's locating of the beginning of West Indian history at the point of Europe's penetration of the New World.[10]

But the danger is in turn evaded by the theory of language which, as we have said, asserts, beyond Heidegger's terms, the irreducible humanity of the Subject precisely because it is beyond the construction of human language which reveals it to itself. This idea is represented in the second strand of discourses within which Lamming couches his epistemology of the body. Here the body appears to be declaring, in a kind of challenge or threat, its total opacity to the onlooker:

> The sea was very calm, almost dead but for the occasional surge of its surface. It wasn't nasty and it wasn't colourful. Just dark, and sinister and suggestively horrific. There was envy too in its darkness, as though it grudged the ship its prominence and certainty on the water. . . . I watched the sea a little excited and a little frightened for I have had strange feelings amidst such presences. Something present in the object goes beyond the properties of the thing itself, beyond the sullen ooze . . . which I now saw. . . . There was something urgent, insistent, provocative about it. It was as though the will had been focussed to the thing beyond, which had its own secret of attraction and persuasion. (6–7)
>
> When the music stopped the voices took over as strong and heaving till they tired and the music came to their relief. It was as though they had conspired against all silence or pledged to let the captain . . . feel and hear that enjoyment required no special accommodation. But it was a condition of the body, issuing from within the body whose resources were infinitely greater than the person understood. The calypso . . . was merely the signal for dancing; but the body was the dance itself. There was neither communication nor interpretation, the deliberate control of balance that makes for movement intended to attract the other's attention, call forth the other's sympathy and be measured by a sane and deliberate judgement. The other had been annihilated. . . . [The body] constituted an open secret which everyone saw but could not read. (93–94)

These passages, one on landscape as territory, the other on the human body in a similar guise, suggests an almost conscious, *speaking* agency in the physical, which has already conferred on the emigrants an identity. It is an identity that predates their own fevered search for selfhood in the confined atmosphere of the ship, even while it is the ground of possibility for that search. It is an identity that absolutely resists the colonizer's voyeuristic gaze, with its misguided view that the body of the territory or the skin/race of the colonized is a transparency that can be definitively read. The body speaks and not speaks; it is "an open secret which everyone saw but could not read"; it is a sign that questions signs, for it embeds, hides and empties out all signification. The alien landscape gives a riddling answer to the discoverer of the New World. The racialized body is a similar riddling, deconstructive space, for it houses within itself essential humanity, that which can never be definitively rendered in language yet must articulate itself in speech in order to be made available to consciousness: "There was only the body which was the dance itself, regulated, informed, nourished and dictated not only by its own blood, but by some pervasive, measureless source of being that was its own logic of receptivity and transmission, a world that could be defined only through the presence of others, yet remained in its definition absolute, free, itself" (93).

What is happening here is closely linked to what Lamming does with the *tonelle* drums in *Season of Adventure.* Here, the language of the drums, like D. H. Lawrence's sexual body, appears as a kind of instinctual and therefore unerring link to the source of life and feeling. It bears kinship too to the apocalyptic action/speech of Nature (earth, wind and fire) which Lamming deploys across several of his fictions. The connection of both drum and Nature is to a primal authority of life larger than consciousness or language but of which consciousness and language are extensions. Yet language is the only means by which either Nature or the drums come to consciousness or the possibility of creative manipulation.

In *The Emigrants,* the body joins the cosmology of the primal but brings (houses) consciousness as its unique quotient. The paradox of the body as a way of knowing is that it speaks but, until the arrival of verbal language, its speech cannot be deciphered. It is language that brings the body's intent to the consciousness of the other, who is implied in the communicative relation. Until the arrival of language as interpretation, the body which speaks is a meaningless accident of physicality. Yet this opacity points to the resistance of the human Subject to the voyeur's linguistic or other categories. And when language arrives, it speaks of the body's meaning only imperfectly, its articulation shaped like a serpent eating its own tail. "[The body's] perfection [is] its contradiction" (94), even as its contradiction is its perfection. This at a certain level empties out the women's demasculinizing voyeurization of Dixon, despite the latter's collusive exhibitionism. By extension, it empties out Europe's inventions of the Caribbean as fallen woman/not-man[11] (akin to the cannibals and savage tribes of *Natives of My Person*), even as it empties out the emigrants' self-destructive reduction of their own selves to sexual economies.

As in the other novels, style images this sense of paradox and irreducibility. The novel's discourses are couched in a range of extended dramatic monologues and dialogues where polemic shades into and structures drama. The drama is the performance of masculine/masculinizing identity, its nature as performance suggesting its open-endedness. The omniscient narrator's voice is transgressed by a liminal I-narrator who sometimes implicitly and without "logical" warning becomes identified with the writer-figure Collis, the combination managing to suggest the multiciplicity of available perspective, the fragmentary nature of seeing, the failure of the emigrants to arrive at a definitive vision of self, the collective nature of the experience and the insufficiency of answers. The inclusion of the African Azi, whose philosophical utterances link the epistemology of the body to African metaphysics, is part of Lamming's use of complicating paradox, since Azi himself, a liminal domino-Anancy figure, is perhaps the greatest betrayer of them all.

The hermeneutic relation between reader and text becomes for the West Indian reader more than merely the ground for conversation. The reader joins the artist in the project of self-fashioning, of deciphering that infinity of genealogical traces that history has deposited in us without leaving an inventory. We recognize that here too is paradox: that the body, the traditional space of the feminine, becomes central in a discourse of masculinization yet remains in the space of obfuscation and contradictory silence which accommodates all that is termed feminine. The femininity explored in *Natives of My Person* forms a loop with the epistemology of the body in *The Emigrants,* both belonging to the paradigm of the liminal and the arcane, both constructed as negative in the discourses of empire, but both transcending and subverting the impositions of such discourses.

Natives of My Person may be viewed as Lamming's furthest reach towards a reconciliation of the feminine into his West Indian genealogy. It is a reconciliation for which he had striven in the earlier novels, but less successfully, because of an inability to weave together the contradictory threads of his theory of language and the West Indian gendered Subject. In *Of Age and Innocence* (as in his first novel, *In the Castle of My Skin*), Lamming had seemed to present the feminine as something to be incorporated into the masculine, a kind of Oedipal way station in the progress of nation and self. In *Season of Adventure,* that same sense of the feminine as a way station remains, paradoxically in tandem with the dramatic attempt to erase gender polarizations in the manhood of Fola Piggott. It is in *Natives of My Person* that the feminine principle is most fully accepted as standing in its own right, a twin, tandem and mutually constitutive reality rather than a pre-symbolic stage of development. The feminine has its own speech, in Lamming the expression of the (prophetic) arcane, which is ignored at peril.

But *The Emigrants* is an important development towards the perspective of

Natives of My Person, even more so than the later *Season of Adventure.* It is true that in *Season of Adventure* Lamming celebrates the female presence where it had been denigrated both in the implicit nationalist iconography and in the projects of empire that shaped West Indian beginnings. But it is *The Emigrants* that clarifies Lamming's implicit concepts of femininity and feminization as respectively a principle and an ideological act not necessarily associated with the female, but rather with ways of being, looking and being looked at. It is also in *The Emigrants* that territory in the form of the body comes to stand in its own right as a speaking, elemental entity, rather than as the pre-symbolic, pre-language stage indicated in *Of Age and Innocence* and *Season of Adventure*; and it is in *The Emigrants* too that it is de-linked from a primary identification with the mother as the symbolic feminine.

We have seen how, in a paradoxical kind of way, the body's epistemology in *The Emigrants* questions all linguistic constructions of identity, revealing in language a loss of the primary eidetic – an inability to fully define and by extension control the human. Exactly the same questioning is revealed through the hermaphroditic figuration of Pinteados in *Natives of My Person.* Throughout, Lamming's search has been for a way of seeing and for a concomitant mode of expression that removes divisions between epistemes that shape West Indian thought and sensibility: the historical and the mythic, the rational and the religious, the spoken and the unspeakable – what appear in his implicit definitions to be ideologically masculine and feminine principles of reality.

In the dialogue between *The Emigrants* and *Natives of My Person,* the implication is that the ideal reality is a merging of these principles in the context of a larger conception of humanity which is more than the sum of their parts and which erases the view of these principles as mere opposites. The merging is not an idea of androgyny, but an attempt to define something of a larger significance than gender. For Lamming, this way of seeing, as a collective phenomenon, still belongs to the future, as his characters consistently fall short of the ideal the artist envisions, and the ideal is presented as polemic against the foil of their failures.

The tensions between Lamming's exigent allegiance to factual historicity and his West Indian apprehension of the mythic, the sacred and the arcane, as well as between, on the one hand, his nationalist commitment to the masculinity of speech and, on the other, his sense of the power inherent in the femininity of silence and his religious faith in the unspeakable, make of his epistemologies a serpent's tail in the mouth, rather than a logico-epistemic "clarification". His paradoxes and contradictions are not a failed teleology of understanding, but rather the West Indian artist's struggle of perplexity, the attempt to make sense of his diverse apprehensions of the issues he treats. We recognize that all of this might simply point to the indecipherable character of the West Indies, where gender, ancestry and legacy, like all other indices of identity, are hybrid, crablike in movement and hidden in marronage.

Chapter 6

All This, the Diasporic and the Postmodern

All This: Lamming, Selvon and the Hermaphroditic Body of West Indian Gender

THE PICTURE THAT EMERGES of the socio-cultural production of West Indian genders and their textual representations in the nationalist period is by no means an orthodox one. We see matrices of orthodoxy and transgression; dissonance and paradox; unease, accommodation and conflict, rather than a map of monolithic demarcations. Selvon's and Lamming's texts, as representations, figure gender realities in the society and, by virtue of their own narrative and gender ideologies, become certain kinds of gender identifications in themselves. Both separately and when taken together, they extend and help circulate a polyglossic representation of gender in West Indian society that is in marked contrast to the totalizing discourses of nationalism and that is more in keeping with the complex realities of the (Caribbean) experience that have been described as "supersyncretic".

Although West Indian society, then as now, was seriously trammelled by patriarchal ideologies and behaviours, neither lived reality nor the texts we have examined present a picture of complete misogyny or subordination of women. All the texts are peopled with the presences and voices of both men and women, which insert themselves whether against the grain of the text or in keeping with it. That is to say, the voices are heard even against the background of the fact that the populace of whom we speak appears both in these texts which I have examined and in my own text, at the site of forced representation. We can assert that this voicedness exists in the most patriarchal of the texts because of the double-edged nature of representation (Anancy's forked tongue, Esu's double face). We have seen, for example, the extent to which calypsonians found it important to mimic "woman tongue" in representational play in order to subordinate it in masculinist satire, making it clear that a silent/silenced West Indian woman was often no more than a figment of male imaginative desire (Rohlehr 1990, 265–70). The very extent of men's competitive voicing which appears in the (oral) literature may be an indication of the extent to which women and the feminine were owners of power in the society.

The female "silence" of which feminist discourse speaks is therefore problematic in the West Indian context. It is doubly so because the idea that one is "silent" or "silenced" is often based on whether one is represented in the public/written/academic document. But to offer these documents as the ground on which silence or not silence is to be judged is already a fallacy: though textual and social reality may be contiguous and mutually constitutive, they are not synonymous. The idea that the written text is the final arbiter of silence privileges text over social process and gives to writing the ascendancy over orality and oral culture that Caribbean theorists seek in other contexts to deplore. It is well to bear in mind too that silence is not the same as being silenced – that indeed, the latter may well be an ontological impossibility.

We consider the polysemy of silence itself, which can be *chosen* as a radical form of speech or again, in another setting, can be less reactionary than speech. An example that points the latter is the newspaper reports of the 1938 labour riots in Jamaica.[1] The socialist papers, such as *Public Opinion,* scarcely mentioned women separately in their reports. The plantocratic *Daily Gleaner,* on the other hand, gave minute details of women's involvement, making it clear that women were a separate and disruptive species. In taking the pulse of the times from the newspapers, it would be easy to conclude that the *Gleaner* was more concerned about women's rights or more responsibly gender-conscious. But the truth might lie elsewhere: in the suggestion that the presence of women as instigators of labour protest (even where they were not members of the paid workforce) was a particularly bothersome problem for an establishment concerned with the preservation of the status quo. For the socialist papers, on the other hand, there might have been nothing in this involvement to cause either surprise or anxiety, since they expected women to support the work of nationalism in all necessary ways, including public protest. Thus, one set of reports, ironically, may have assumed "a sex which is one", erasing women because it also recognized women, while the other inscribed women's action because women's seeking recognition was something to be deplored. Neither is a satisfactory response, but taken together they highlight the problem of describing what exactly is silence. And then there are those men, secure in their own sense of identity, whose voices are not heard in the performative space and who are not part of the open contention of voices. The figure of Brother Man, created by even so misogynist a writer as Roger Mais (1954), and the father figures of Andrew Salkey's children's novels are incipient indications that such men too had a major presence in the society.

Beyond all this, we witness in the work of Selvon and Lamming an intuitive recognition of the role of gender as a shaping force in all social relations. Each in his own way exhibits a groping towards an understanding of this construct as it manifests itself in complex ways in West Indian society. Their representations bring into focus the extent to which the colonial experience was constantly being recirculated in all West Indian experiences of gender in multiple and conflictual ways, as well as the extent to which masculinity was seriously invested in as an integral part of West Indian identities, both male and female. We see that women's acquisition of certain types of linguistic, familial and economic authority was a response to the socio-economic realities of colonization, from slavery through to Emancipation and onwards. West Indian women seem to have effected gender confusion by becoming "masculine", a state of affairs that mocked the nationalist icon as it did the plantation's – for here an identification is made without an identity being legitimized. The perplexities engendered by these anomalies are addressed in Selvon's fictions, particularly *Turn Again Tiger, Moses Ascending* and *The Housing Lark*.

Women's demonstration of masculinity in this mode highlights another side of the gender picture which emerges out of the colonial situation: the fact that gender is one of the constructs that has come under creolizing pressure and thus, along with race, class and general culture, must be described in terms of hybridity and syncretism which characterize the society as a whole. This process of gender creolization appears also in the multiple types of conflict apparent in West Indian men's search for masculine identity as represented in these novels. At the same time as the search was conflicted by the rigidities of colonial patriarchalism circulated through the experience of slavery and the education system, it was complicated by a principle of resistance which describes itself in Manichean terms as counter-masculinity. This imbrication in opposition and reply inevitably led to excesses of denial and self-immolation, as, for example, in the massive investment in oppositional speech which often became directed inward upon one's self and one's neighbour in a similar position, and which also too often emptied itself out as performative display rather than decisive action.

For both men and women, the cultural obsession with volubility and oppositional reply comes fraught with negatives. One troubling aspect of the representation of women in the texts we have examined is that they are never shown recognizing or appropriating the subversive powers of silence.[2] This is not to say that women do not utilize silence, but simply to point how endemic a particular perception of voice has become. Arguably, the linguistic investment in representational politics has contributed to the disillusionment so evident since the 1970s. But even despite its debilitating paradoxes, the paradigm of speech and action within the context of oppositional reply opened up creative spaces within which creolized identities, including their gender configurations, could be realized.

Beyond this, aspects of gender identity which have nothing to do with the Manichean divide but rather with the human person's capacity to respond creatively to the environment appear in the fictions. Lamming, from his ideologically driven endeavour to dismantle the more pernicious aspects of nationalist gender constructs, engages us with this issue. He takes us on a journey through various symbolic Middle Passages and Ceremonies of Soul to the imperialist-masculinist gender orthodoxies that spawned West Indian messianism and the worst and most violent excesses of native politicians' behaviour. This becomes a psycho-cultural rite of passage for the West Indian reader, the historical genealogy of whose gender identities is being charted and who then becomes implicated in Lamming's call to a reckoning between past, future and present. Lamming also calls us to an interrogation of the bases of West Indian manhood by his explorations of voyeurism, where the terror of being seen and judged inadequate by the colonial progenitor exposes the individual male's and the nation's Freudian pathology and points to the dangers of becoming locked into a recirculation rather than a reinterpretation and "remaking" of the past. The project of self-construction is aborted where the rendezvous with history ends with acceptance of the master's accusation of masculine inadequacy.

Lamming's understanding both of the political powers of language in a general sense and of the historical role of language in the oppression of Caribbean peoples in a particular sense, as well as his experience of the dynamic insurrectionism of language in the form of West Indian Creole language, leads him to conceive West Indian national and personal identity as being vested in a conscious, creative and combative relation to language, the basis for political action. In this context, we witness Lamming's growing if incomplete awareness that the gender ideology which erases women from the body politic (its voicing into being) is destructive. We see inscribed also his awareness that the West Indies has historically, through colonialism and slavery, occupied the space of the feminine and thus that a denigration of the feminine implicates the West Indian nation and the West Indian male.

The discovery/creation of new language and a new, coded name and the consequent break with Europeanist/colonialist/masculinist antecedents represent that seizure of agency, or first speech, which shows the slave's descendant as a creature capable of opposition and reply but possessed of an identity beyond that. Lamming uses the female figure as the symbol of a healthy nationalism and national identity, but also as the repository of a gender ideology in which he attempts to divest manhood of its association with maleness and to redefine it in generalized humanistic terms. Lamming's attempt highlights the heavy investment in masculinity which we have noticed as an endemic feature of West Indian self-fashioning, and his failure to achieve his objective lies in his ultimate return of masculinity to an identification with maleness.

Lamming's representation at the level of ideology speaks of a faith in the West Indian people's capacity to reorder their approaches to gender. But it is Selvon's representations at a level more nearly akin to the "naturalistic" that move the issue from mere faith to lived possibility, because much of the canvas of women he portrays becomes recognizable as images of real West Indian women with a wide range of capabilities in public and domestic spheres. If any capacity to initiate changes in gender ideology is portrayed by Selvon, it is portrayed first and foremost in his women. This is so despite the fact that Selvon does not ideologically endorse women's gender strategies. Yet Lamming's faith combines with Selvon's portrayal to create a more balanced picture than either gives individually, because Selvon's portrayal is overwritten with a certain cynicism which interprets women's behaviour as not merely masculine but patriarchal, and which prevents him from using the spaces opened up by his acute observations of gender behaviour and relations in a sufficiently creative way. Selvon is content with an implicit biological explanation for West Indian women's masculinity – women apparently have a particular character, mode of speaking and arrangement of supportive community that comes naturally to them. The impression is conveyed by a narrative style that eschews the portrayal of women's psychological space.

That this subsumed attitude of biological determinism is masculinist in orientation appears in Selvon's portrayal of his male characters, which, by its focus on inner space, allows for psychological and sociological referents in the behaviour of these characters. It is only in the deconstructive spaces of the subtext that it appears, for example, that women experience the most debilitating pressures of economics upon gender. (Women with children to feed cannot afford the luxury of flight. Similarly, it is women who become the butt of men's frustration with economic and other identity-related "failures".)

To some extent, Selvon's deployment of narrative is constrained by the structure of the traditional novel, which centres attention on a single protagonist. But the author's tentative experimentations with the character of Urmilla in *Turn Again Tiger* indicates his awareness of a wider range of possible viewpoints even within that genre. I have argued that what Selvon's prose evinces is a discomfort with the psychology of women, which he doesn't feel confident he truly understands. This inability, combined with his experience of the agonal nature of men's masculine becoming in the period in which he wrote, inevitably produced Selvon's male-centred text. Lamming's more complex struggle is perhaps evidenced in his narrative strategy, which agonizes between a rational teleology of speech (the arrival at clear statements about the Subject, which might well be associated with Dawes's and Nettleford's "masculine prose") and the endless semiology and deconstruction of speech, its ideologically "feminine" obscurity.

The accusation that Selvon did not concern himself with the issues of nationalism appears to be based in a narrowly political understanding of these issues, since Selvon, in his concern with everyday behaviour and psychology, represents the sense of angst and psychic terror with which many West Indian men addressed themselves to the search for identity in that dissonant age and which may well have become hidden in the exhortatory euphoria of public political discourse. Selvon as much as Lamming presents us with images of the real suffering arising out of the social, domestic and economic expectations invested in manhood, within the complicating context of migration. Such pictures do not so readily emerge out of demographic studies. It is Selvon too who, along with Naipaul, in the early years inscribed the voices of Indo-West Indian males, which in the spirit of the times could easily have been described as marginal. In this sense, Selvon's work is seminal in more categories than the linguistic or the representation of a generalized "folk". With regard to the latter, accepted critical opinion notwithstanding, there are no "folk" in Selvon's London fictions, but rather the loss and displacement of folkways and their attendant parameters of gender, whether positive or negative.

The canvas of various configurations of masculinity and perspectives on these afforded by Lamming's and Selvon's fictions indicates the extent to which masculinity in general, and in the West Indies in particular, is not a fixed category but a site of competing representations and identities arising out of social flux. This already begins to inscribe the problematic nature of the construct, which is rooted generically in a *principle* of certainties. This remains true of all masculinities, not only of the iconic one of Western imperialism, some of whose attributes we have outlined and to which we may add the attribute of militarized aggression. All masculinities, even the most radical and counteractive, are ultimately performances of and searches for certainty of self, role and image. The search for an identity that will subvert other identities which have been arbitrarily imposed from outside is automatically and generically a search for a presence and an idea that is contoured to stand out against the imposition; hence even maverick counter-masculinities are predicated upon the same principle of certainties.

The point I want to argue here is a crucial one, and it is that *in principle,* at generic base, whatever is labelled "masculinity" is not a male possession but appears to be a desire for definition, place, recognition, survival, law and order, which in its societal manifestations seems to transcend sex boundaries, though in Western(ized) societies its description assigns it to men. The ideological construction of gender without reference to the generic human principle upon which identity is founded results in its sex-specific allocation. Further, the failure to refer to this principle occludes its rootedness in desire, and therefore in the unconscious. Lacan's view that all language (by extension all action) is suffused in the unconscious, since desire is located in the unconscious, is connoted here. Psychoanalysts' view that the phallus, a male symbol/possession, is the object of women's desire because it signifies women's lack becomes a distortion of the principle I am discussing here – the principle of desire for definition, which manifests itself across societies and genders.

The question of why it is men who insist on sex-localizing this principle, distorting it as resistant to sharedness and rooted in competition and hegemony, is a moot point which has been exhaustively and inadequately theorized (see, for example, Miller 1991b, 103–20). The possible answers are as diverse and complex as the societies that spawn various specific configurations of masculinity. The one constant across cultures is the central role played by societies' confused readings of the semiotic of the human body. The body remains one of the profoundest of enigmas, housing what is silent and what is known. As Lamming reminds us, it confounds every palimpsest of imagination by its own unreadable signs.

The other side of the coin of masculinity is the nebulous bag of rags and patches which is designated "feminine". This term, "feminine", seems to refer to aspects of self and representation that in social and political discourse are mapped onto anyone whose inferiorization becomes the prerequisite upon which current notions of masculinity, or identity rooted in competition, are predicated. The issue of femininity enormously complicates the West Indian gender picture emerging out of the nationalist period. On the face of things, it could be argued that while economic conditions, aided by kinship relations, constantly facilitated the "masculine" side of women even in the face of misogynistic opposition, the public expression of the "feminine" side of men was by contrast delayed by the influence of the ideological-discursive field and the resistance to female gender iconoclasm. Thus, in the split which emerges, it could be further argued, the "gender-merging" shown in slavery becomes transferred from the collective to the behaviours and psychologies of women, who become "masculine" but retain their "feminine" (and feminized) characteristics.

However, whereas I have described the gender collective in slavery as hermaphroditic, in the case of the modern West Indian woman I would speak of androgyny rather than hermaphroditism. In this way I distinguish the greater contextualization of the hermaphrodite in refusal and liminality, and recognize the reality of the split between men and women in the society. But even androgyny is problematic, for it assumes a comfortable psychological assimilation between genders, whereas the truth for West Indian women might well be more an experience of schizophrenia, given the context of competition, conflict and mutual abuse within which their gender behaviour is sometimes acquired. The experience of abusing and being abused may in itself result in a double-visioned attitude to masculinity; for example, women may accept masculinity in themselves but deny or refuse it in men.

Another factor is that the definition of "feminine" is even more nebulous in the West Indies than it is in Western societies. "Caregiving" and "motherhood/mothering" are not sufficient definitions in West Indian terms, even though these activities are valorized aspects of women's roles; they cannot suffice to describe what it is that women have retained, or what men have sought in themselves to deny. Indeed, in its constitution as a foil against masculinity, femininity appears to elude a singular definition: it takes on different forms depending on the masculine turf to be recuperated. Thus it may appear as "not sexually authoritative", "not economically independent", "not linguistically competent" (though linguistically very "out of order"). In the public representations we have examined (literary texts, popular music, discourses on family and family structure) in the West Indian context, femininity in practice (as opposed to ideology) is doubly troublesome because it appears as something masculine which women should not have but do have.

At these levels – that is, the levels of definition and women's refusal of the definition – patriarchal concepts in the West Indies show femininity to be, as in all masculinist discourses, what Luce Irigaray refers to as a "lack" (1985a, 160–67) – in effect a "not-ness". Because West Indian women are represented as refusing femininity, their gender identity is then a double "not". "Not-ness" appears as the generic condition of this femininity, mothering and caregiving then being aspects of West Indian attempts to chart its specific contours. Motherhood/mothering and caregiving are often, in fact, configured as part of "not-ness". Feminist psychologist Nancy Chodorow (1978), speaking from a Western perspective, argues that males recuperate gender anxiety by refiguring woman as whore or nun. In West Indian representations, these polarities that Chodorow perceives in Western society appear conflated in the iconic image of the Mother, who is fetishized as the utterly self-erasing nurturant to the man in process of becoming and who also becomes a way of containing disruptive female reproductive potential. (Female reproductive potential poses a threat to the economic adequacy of fathering, as it might present a man with children he cannot afford.)

Rohlehr's study of the calypso extends the template created by Selvon's London quartet, as Rohlehr notes both the sexual anxiety generated by younger women's authoritative control over their sexual relations (1990, 226) and the use of exaggerated horror as a device for containing would-be sexually active old women, or "Mother-figures" (232–35). Lamming's women fissure his equalizing gender projects, as they are usually aspects of the mother-fetish: women who give up all aspects of self, submerging their entire beings in the love of their husbands and sons. The troublesome nature of the project of defining femininity in this way already appears, both in the contradiction inherent in defining what is not and in the high visibility and masculinity of much West Indian motherhood and caregiving. So the West Indian woman's femininity, like the West Indian man's, is hidden in mystery.

But this femininity is also masked in further contradiction in language as a technology of men's self-representation. Paradox, amounting to contradiction, arises between the phallocentrism of men's appropriation of the word, the attempt to erase women's equal possession of that facility, and location of West Indian folk masculinities at the site of linguistic disorder, which from several perspectives have been equated with the feminine. *Picong*, linguistic self-aggrandization, the Toastmaster and the Midnight Robber all seek to appropriate to the masculine self what the slave had possessed and what all Creole languages possess: *créolité*, the fusion of multiple ways of seeing, the principle of experimentation and hybridization, the disturbance and interruption of established syntaxes and grammars. Creole speech is, according to the nineteenth-century British observer I quoted earlier, a linguistic culture of femininity (Breen [1844] 1970). *Créolité* appears as well in what the woman possesses: woman tongue, the principle of prophecy and intuition, hybridized with another kind of disturbance – the interruption of masculinist ways of being, seeing and speaking.

The attempt to reassign the outcast, the liminal and the contestatory to the space of the (fixed, certain) dominant ideal, to take on a double identity both as ideal and as "outside the *mana* of the gods", so that one may with impunity mock and challenge idealism, is one of the unusual aspects of West Indian males' gender performance. This double identity in which men inhabit the inner/upper circle of disorder (this hierarchization already a contradiction in terms) allowed for the relegation of the female to its outer circles or, in Creole parlance, "out-of-orderness". (Of course, double identity is also an extension of cultural Creole suspicion: never put all your eggs in one basket.) Yet it is the shared colonial experience that allows women a space both to accept and to contest this designation. As parallel inheritors of the liminal, they too are able to celebrate their linguistic and other forms of "out-of-orderness". And indeed there is much – albeit sometimes grudging – male acceptance, even admiration, of female insurrection against gender lines. This extension of what in effect amounts to goodwill perhaps increases the "dangers" of spirit possession, that is, of psychological seduction by the female/feminine.

In contemplating the strange nature of a concept of masculinity which seeks to organize the liminal and the carnivalesque into hierarchical spheres, we also highlight the bases of men's real confusion about their "femininity": femininity appears as a fetish signifying that which is to be feared, that which is to be avoided, that which will rob the (masculine) self of strength and reshape it in weakness. Most of all, it signifies the robbery of Subjectness, presence and definition. Femininity becomes the enemy within that must be relegated to the unconscious (which, ironically, as we have argued, already permeates masculinity). Looked at in this way, femininity appears to belong to the circle of existence where the slave was ideologically a thing that was "no-thing" but whose no-thingness had to be endlessly reiterated in order for it to subsist. This means that like the slave's, femininity's Being is a hidden thing, which is ultimately more powerful than Prospero's word. Femininity is terribly feared because Caliban's schizophrenic entry into the word has reified even *créolité,* which in the guise of the feminine insurrects against such reification.

The feminine within the self and the other refuses the imposition of containment, which is contrary to its relationship to Being, which is beyond representation.[3] (This is why the discourse of masculinism – the reification of masculinity via the denigration of femininity – has no end: the feminine never goes away or yields to representation.) Femininity in this context may well be usefully expressed as patriarchal society's signification of a completeness of identity which is refused, not merely because it would include parts of the self ideologically considered weak, but, far more significantly, because it is unspeakable ("not-ness" inscribes the inability of language to say what a thing is). It is unknowable because unspeakable, and therefore endlessly feared. The feminine is not itself this unspeakable Being of humanity, but the fetishized and tabooed reminder/"not" signification of it – of this unspeakability of existence and identity.

Which leads me to suggest that if Being could have had a gender, it could easily be conceived in hermaphroditic terms. The hermaphrodite, being her/himself an unspeakability (though s/he cannot be a "not-ness" since masculinity is one of her/his faces), comes into her/his own when the knowable (the masculine principle in patriarchal figurations) and the unknowable (the liminal, of which what is configured as feminine and unconscious are only dim intimations – or, rather, symbolizations) are accepted within individual psyches and within cultures. The hermaphrodite, in the context of gender, is a sign that confounds signs. In its mystery and accommodation, it fuses binary significations yet empties out significations in order to become the principle of signification itself. Like Being, out of which it arrives, it speaks to something of the divine in the human.

From almost any angle from which the womb is theorized, the fact of its being a hidden place in comparison to the penis goes a long way towards explaining why patriarchal society maps the feminine onto women and erases the possibility of its allocation to "real" men. The conundrum of "hiddenness" also explains why the slave and her/his descendant, product of the Hegelian "continent of darkness", are also in imperialist practice and discourse generically feminized (territorialized). It is interesting in contemplating the ramifications of "not-ness" that men of African descent are not in imperialist articulations labelled "feminine", since that would be to suggest that they are like (white) women, but simply "not-(good enough) men", which then exposes their relegation to the feminine, what is "not".

In summarizing the characteristics of femininity which appear behind the masks of West Indian retreat and delay, then, it would seem that femininity is no one thing but a hydra-head from which we isolate four main aspects. First, it is identified with something in human personality and the possibility of human fate, which is feared, and for which "not-ness" is a symbolization. This symbolization is embodied in metonymy, which, however, is merely paradigmatic, since words and concepts are never the thing itself, either in whole or in part, but only a representation. Language stands between femininity and knowledge of femininity both because femininity cannot be adequately represented and because language creates it as a horror, which is then avoided and so remains unknown. Second, femininity, from the reification of negative attitudes to its unknowable reality, becomes also an ideology, which is mapped onto women in society. Because women in society are visible and occupy visible social roles, these roles also become identified as feminine and partake of the designation of "not-ness". The problem in the West Indian context arises as women also enter into competition for definitive space, both in political and economic arenas and, in this setting, acquire masculinities that transgress the roles and qualities designated as "not-ness", so that they are constantly fielding a masculinized femininity which redoubles men's masculine anxiety.

Third, femininity also, therefore – when we put this concept of Being and this concept of misogynistic ideology together – appears as space, in two senses: the space of its objective reality, where it is obviously "a truth" that yet remains to be known and where it functions as a paradigm of the larger reality of Being which is feared, and the space of its ideological relegation, where whatever comes to consciousness as disagreeable to masculinity or the individual male's masculinization becomes named as an aspect of femininity which is decipherable. But again, what is "decipherable" is configured in not-ness, which again returns it to the circle/cycle of the unknowable unknown. This means that, fourth, femininity becomes a curious "hold-all" for what must be avoided or postponed, so that in a sense femininity comes to be what is endlessly delayed.

The subconscious of language has been theorized as the desire for the symbolic phallus, towards which women are endlessly attracted. But it seems here that the construction of femininity is the titillation of desire (which includes fear) by an economy of endless postponement. (This endless postponement, from another perspective, is Irigaray's concave mirror, which empties out all signification, not only of itself but of masculinity, which remains troubled by the excessive recalcitrance of this Other against which its Subjectness is to be constituted.) In the West Indian context, the double problematic is that, at the level of colonial ideology and colonial experience, the male subject already has acquaintance with an even greater "monstrosity" – the hermaphrodite, birthed in the anguish and shame (but also the forgotten creative space) of slavery. At another level, perhaps the nation itself has been grieved and ashamed. The West Indian polity has been discursively and politically figured in terms of the masculine/ist construct "nation". But the history of the West Indian colony is the history of the presence of Europe's usurping "fatherhood" and of the erasure of the territories' prior histories and origins, as well as of the territories' rape – and this has also quite probably involved the physical rape of men as well as women. All of this the social evolution of the English language allows to be readily described in terms of the abuse of women and the feminization of presence (absence, loss, grief, erasure). The backward glance is as difficult for any nation to take at the level of gender as it is for anything else.

It is useful to remind ourselves in this conversation that women too have their misogynies, derived from the discursive-representational field as well as from their own lived reality. Feminists rethinking Freud see girls as retaining deep affective bonds with their mothers rather than acquiring the Oedipal mother-hatred on which Freud insists in his argument of generic male privilege.[4] But in those West Indian homes with high levels of paternal itinerancy and surrogate fatherhood, the relationship with the mother is often highly conflicted, being both a close identification born of a perceived similarity in terms of the risk of "female" fate and a resentment of the mother's perceived collusion in having deprived the child of a stable father figure. This problematizes the female-female relation postulated as "women's community", which is naively seen as completely positive. In any patriarchally troubled society, women's community is inevitably trammelled by female-female hostility born of this identification with the mother and of the perception of other women as potential competition for the attention of the iconic, fetishized male. Women's community, then, is not only a site of solidarity and psychic healing, but also the stage upon which women's own misogyny and rivalries for male attention are (often unconsciously) played out.

What can we say then? At the edge of chaos, the plantation produced a collective approach to gender that I have described as hermaphroditic, signifying both positives and negatives. Men and women joined hands in equality, despite – and indeed pooling – differences, yet their collective effort was seen as monstrous in racialized and gendered terms. Their modus operandi created them outcast, and the circumstances that necessitated the emergence of the hermaphroditic unit were utterly untenable. The agonized movement of the West Indies into civil society saw the attenuation and submersion of the hermaphrodite, to the extent that the society refused to admit its own gender complexity. The continuing signs of hermaphroditic gender in West Indian social behaviour suggest that we have some strengths on which to build. And yet indeed, in the ambit of civil society, the hermaphrodite can no longer be an adequate signification: for while as a symbol s/he re-members for us the torn history that should never be forgotten (Lamming's "backward glance"), there are aspects of the hermaphrodite that call for reinvention.

The prejudicial rootedness of the language of gender in sexuality, the inhibition of freed individuality that the suppressed side of the hermaphrodite indicates (the hermaphrodite must be brought to both separation and fusion, and there named), the association of the hermaphrodite with forced segregation from the rest of the world, and the fact that we are not here fighting the planter but dealing with ourselves – all of this suggests that there needs to be a more equitable way in which a full humanity can be made visible in the present time. A revisioning of West Indian gender involves re-finding the space inhabited by the hermaphrodite and reinventing it as personal identity and as ideological praxis. There is a need to extrapolate from the hermaphrodite those principles which may be efficacious in civil society and discarding those which would leave us frozen in the time warp of the backward glance.

The idea of a new vocabulary highlights the inability of feminist theories to encompass the issues raised by gender in West Indian society. The direction ultimately taken by Luce Irigaray, on whose vocabulary I drew earlier in this discussion, sharply focuses the problem posed by classical feminism in particular. Recognizing the lack in language in the face of femininity, Irigaray contends that only masculinity can take part in representational play (1985a, 133). This is why, in her conceptualization, all identity and Subjectness are essentially masculinist. The argument loses its deconstructive edge as Irigaray goes on to link it with an approach that preserves the negative man/woman binaries. She refuses to posit a concept of woman as separate from the feminine (1985a, 133; 1985b, 122–23) even as she posits masculinity as a male space. Her contention that woman is a concept that is "not yet" presupposes that woman can have no identity unless femininity – which she recognizes as the waste disposal of whole universes of social experience (the savage, the unconscious and the outcast join women in that category, she rightly argues) – is first defined. In the implicit (and correct) idea that femininity cannot be defined, Irigaray's contention further presupposes that any form of definition must belong to men, which then legitimates the masculinist binary that creates men and women as different species. It might even be argued that in equating woman and femininity, Irigaray confines the former to the parameters of otherness and absence set by patriarchal ideology.

The idea of a new vocabulary links us to Derek Walcott's assertion that the West Indian artist must, like Adam, assume (her) role as the namer of things. It is a good place from which to begin the charting of a grammar of morality for West Indian theory. This concept of a new vocabulary is also inherent in Lamming's theory of language and of the human person and in the terms of Erna Brodber's gender conversation, where "conversation" has its old meaning of "way of life". This too is a way of speaking. "A new vocabulary" is basic to my argument that the conundrums of "masculine" and "feminine" lose their mystique in the recognition that each has been prejudicially used to designate different aspects of human personality held in common. It necessitates reinventing words at the most basic and elementary level, where the terms "man" and "woman" will refer simply to biological and reproductive function, and their related terms (such as "mother", "father", "masculine", "feminine") will be scrutinized and reinvented in terms of roles and mutually agreed expectations rather than biological essentialisms, though these might well play a part. (Of course, in a postmodern world this return to basics may well be complicated by the advent of in vitro babies and we may need to begin to speak of types of test tube in these terms!)

Reinventing language, as we have seen throughout this book, is something for which West Indians possess an extraordinary skill. But we also recognize that changes in language and discourse are not enough: in the end, it is educational content and process and the practices of individuals in everyday relations that will decide what words come to mean, and *why* they come to mean what they mean.[5] More than this, we recognize the inadequacy of all words and by extension all theories. New ways of speaking and seeing are merely attempts to grapple more authentically with reality dimly perceived.

The Diasporic: Re/Writing, Re/Thinking Gender "after" Nationalism

Crossings – and recrossings – between the geographical Caribbean and the Western metropoles have increased significantly since Selvon and Lamming wrote their migration texts. West Indian society is mediated by these crossings and by the textual representations that have been tellingly described as "remittances"[6] – a term that suggests the troubling and unequal relations that such texts may set up between Caribbean and metropole. The crossings themselves bring their own difficulties of analysis, not the least of which is the problem of finding a vocabulary adequate to take account of the various "crossroads" identities that they have produced.

In the following discussion I use the term "migration text" to designate texts, specifically prose fictions, about migrant experiences written by West Indians in diaspora. The term "West Indians in diaspora" or "diasporic West Indians" denotes the entire range of persons of West Indian lineage who may be found in the European and North American metropoles: peripatetic visitors, binationals, recent or temporary migrants, persons of the second generation born as citizens in the metropoles. All of these, whatever their official designations, may exist behaviourally and psychologically on a continuum between nationalities and/or ethnicities. My increasing use simply of the term "Caribbean" or "Caribbeans in diaspora" as an all-inclusive term in which West Indian is implied points to the fact that linguistic categories of separation imposed by colonial owners are eroding within the cosmopolitan diasporic space which contributes to the widening of Caribbean perceptions of regional relationality. "Diasporic space", or its shortened noun form, "the diasporic", refers to the metropole and the experiences and environment it produces for Caribbeans in diaspora. "Diasporic thought" and "diasporic text", however, are distinguished from these blanket designations, as I use the two terms to indicate a celebratory attitude to diaspora, which is opposed to an attitude of mourning and loss. "Diasporic" in this sense is the antithesis of "exile" or "exilic consciousness".

Recent migration texts come surrounded by a panoply of critical and theoretical perspectives that function "naively" to produce singularized images of the Caribbean. Such perspectives erase the work of migration upon identity; that is, they suggest an unproblematic continuity of identities between the geographical Caribbean and the Caribbean in diaspora, especially in North America and Britain. The attitude is generally a celebratory one, partly encapsulated in direct critical commentaries on specific texts, partly derived, in a kind of halo effect, from the texts' being participated into the field of postcolonial inquiry. To a large extent, the celebratory ethos of postcolonial criticism marks the influence of diasporic postcolonials in the metropolitan academy: individuals whose publications and positions of privilege work to create a sense that the ex-colonial diaspora is making triumphant inroads beyond Western roadblocks to its equality and survival. Black theory – which may be seen as a branch of postcolonial theory and, in some instances, the postmodern – has made its own contribution to this singularizing, celebratory impression via studies such as Paul Gilroy's *The Black Atlantic*: (1993), positing the African diaspora wholesale as the world's foremost example of postmodernity, and Carole Boyce Davies's *Black Women, Writing and Identity*, which celebrates women's migratory travels as a way of redefining space by creating multiple global homes.[7] The global circulation of this celebratory discourse renders it hegemonic – to the extent that "other" perspectives and "other" identities articulated outside of the diasporic context (for example, in fictions produced by writers at home) are often ignored, unheard or marginalized.

But even so cursory an examination as I undertake in this section shows that both the shifting consciousness of diasporic West Indians and the different economic and cultural environments they inhabit function to produce different kinds of gendered beings and, from them, representations that re-problematize the question "What is Caribbean/West Indian?" These representations by extension become part of a new problematics of nationhood. Selvon and Lamming are part of this "textual space of migrancy" in two ways: first, as the new migration fictions join them in a body of literature identified as Caribbean; second, as both (Lamming in particular) are constantly referenced in discussions that look towards transnational or "umbrella" definitions of postcoloniality and the colonial experience. Such discussions at some level automatically shift nationalism to a secondary place. In the total scenario, issues that are at once strikingly similar to and different from those raised by Selvon's and Lamming's migration fictions are also raised. It may be that an examination of the reasons for these similarities and differences can guide us as to how we might address problems of en-gendering in the diasporic space.

We have seen where, in charting the effect of migration upon men's masculinity, Selvon and Lamming reveal how the work of colonization continually called masculinity into question. From both ends of the spectrum – the perspective on the colonizing male and the perspective on the colonized – we see the endless competition and insecurity that attend gender when a man feels called upon to "prove himself", as invariably appears to be the case when men are confronted with new territory. This is particularly true since territory carries with it not only monetary quotients but also a linguistic economy which has to do with male possession of the (territory as) generically female, so that sexual and quasi-sexual angst is also generated. In the case of the West Indian male immigrant, both writers show the experience of stress to have been compounded by his experience of feminization, inferiorization and displacement in his situation as progeny and not-progeny of the putative fatherland that he was entering. In *The Emigrants,* the acceptance of the self as territory appears in the regression to animal sexuality as a way of life: promiscuous sexual behaviour, both in the context of migration and as a tacit, double-edged criterion for West Indian men's masculinity, reflects a valorization of the descriptions by which the colonial master sought to denigrate the slave as sheer physicality and exposes some of the limitations of a praxis of opposition and reply.

The psychic loss and individual and collective anomie that Selvon's and Lamming's fictions represent seem at first glance to find no connection with the gender representations of recent migration fictions, a large proportion of which are by women. The women's fictions are marked by a fierce and committed, often single-minded search to construct and express resistant gender identities – whether against the impositions of West Indian men and male-oriented ideologies, or against colonial rapine, or against neocolonial white male abuse in the diasporic space, or simply against the debilitating circumstances of being female and Caribbean (with all its various nuances of race, colour and class) in the diasporic space. This is crucial: that their fictions exhibit a conscious and deliberate attempt not to negotiate with or to escape but to *exercise* dominance (what Lamming has referred to as "imaginative sovereignty" [D. Scott 2002]) over or within the diasporic space.

Despair is, then, not a feature of these fictions. If there is elegy, it appears more often as tribute to ancestral mothers than as mourning for the self in the current situation. Militancy is the irreducible paradigm. Performativity, if it is utilized, is the performance of the gladiator or the *retarius,* whichever persona these women may choose to inhabit as they wage war through the prism of a knowledge of self (whether pre-existent or in process of being fashioned) that becomes sovereign. While the women's portrayals of their female characters as "invincible" individuals may find resonance with Selvon's externalized representation, they go far beyond his portrayal of economic beings to encompass the range of human complexity as much as Selvon's male characters have done.

All of this produces a sense of celebration (my head is bloody but unbowed) – that is, a sense that West Indians/Caribbeans have the ability to "refashion" themselves, to constitute new "selves" or "identities" which effectively negotiate the challenges of a generally hostile metropolitan space. For example, Cliff, Brodber and Hopkinson, discussed in the introduction, in different ways present the home experience of creolization, improvisation, performativity, marronage and other forms of folk response to colonial "spirit thievery" as sources of strength against potential gender deracination in diaspora. A similar perspective may be read in the Canadian stories in Dionne Brand's *San Souci and Other Stories* (1989) and indeed even in the much earlier work of Paule Marshall. At one level, then, the fictions provide a basis for the current tendency among critics to reimagine migrancy-as-exile in wholesale terms as celebratory diaspora or diaspora-as-appropriation.

The majority of these women writers of the late twentieth and early twenty-first centuries, like their first-generation male counterparts, live either permanently or periodically in Europe or North America or visit there, so that their gender representations of diaspora are also "autobiographical". In this context, it is doubly striking that one of the most significant concepts to emerge in the women's fictions is the idea of a globalized gender identity. In her first two novels, *Abeng* (1984) and *No Telephone to Heaven* (1989), it is the development of a gendered, mixed-racial West Indian (specifically Jamaican) identity that Michelle Cliff explores. Set in the United States, the later *Free Enterprise* (1993) shifts towards the expansion of this gendered identity into what may be termed, to extrapolate a concept from Édouard Glissant, an identity of relation – that is to say, an accommodation with other cultures that are encountered globally. The protagonist of *Free Enterprise* finds selfhood in a diasporic female community dispersed from many nations and regions with similar though not identical experiences of deracination and marginalization. The community is both postcolonial and postmodern, including Jewish women, Native American women and women from former colonies. Significantly, despite Cliff's overtly feminist project, the idea of a permeability of gender roles as liberating performance by both male and female is transported as a trope of empowerment from West Indian history into this diasporic community of women; that is to say, the creolized gender performance of men also is integrated into the celebratory representation of the global female community.[8]

In similar vein, Erna Brodber's gender-inclusive healing community in *Myal* (1983), set in the West Indies, is drawn not only from the West Indies, but also from Europe and Africa, and from different religious and cultural persuasions. In the third novel, *Louisiana* (1988), Brodber shifts her focus to the global black diaspora, setting her story in the southern United States and showing diverse cultural groups of black people learning and accepting the paradox of their similarities and inviolable differences. This principle of accommodation, which is in this context a principle of relation (diasporic) rather than creolization (nationalist), Brodber extends to her male and female characters, who work through problems to a community based on mutual support and forgiveness and for whom, as for the characters in her other two novels, gender roles inhabit a liminal space where they are fluid, permeable and exchangeable – in other words, fitting totally into the context of multiplicity that marks the diasporic community.

Brodber's approach to gender, though placed within the context of a diaspora that newly and constantly refigures itself, is far from being unprecedented. For it harks back to the everyday lived reality and sensibility of West Indians that is at odds with the tenets of classical feminism, in which male and female are perceived in oppositional terms. (Recent home-based fictions by Paulette Ramsay, Merle Collins and myself share much of Brodber's perspective,[9] and it is perhaps significant that we are writers who are or have been domiciled in the West Indies – it may be that our gender representations are marked by a greater experiential closeness to the "indigenous" culture.) In a sense, Brodber's inclusive gender ideology returns us to the gender-merging of the slave collective, but her celebratory stance dispenses with the sense of being outcast that allows the slave collective to be named as hermaphrodite. A gender identification marked by the rehearsal of a history of oppression is not Brodber's interest: while her text is grounded in the realities of colonial history, her concern is to show how the strengths – not the sufferings – gleaned from that experience may affect a healthy identity, including gender, in the present day.

Brodber seeks also not so much to emphasize the effects of racial and cultural discrimination on West Indians in diaspora as to point to the efficacies of a collective black and collective male/female consciousness rooted in the openness to accommodation that has been facilitated by West Indians' history. Indeed, there is a sense in which Brodber insists on reminding us (in *Myal*) that the Caribbean itself is a diasporic space, so that the Caribbean diaspora in North America (in *Louisiana*) is simply another dimension of the same experience. Thus, for Brodber, West Indians can rise to the challenge of the newer diaspora because of their gender experiences at home. Significantly, there is no separation between racial and cultural liberation and liberation in terms of gender – all are part of a single complex of necessity.

The intersection of aspects of Brodber's ideology with some male perspectives is quite interesting. David Dabydeen, an Indo-West Indian writing out of Britain, similarly envisions West Indian capacity to manage diasporic challenges, but from an opposite direction. Dabydeen argues (Birbalsingh 1996a) that West Indians are as much outsiders at home as abroad, and insists on his own protean ability as a result to play various types of transnational and transcultural man (West Indian, British or American, as the fancy takes him) yet keep intact his individual soul. Second-generation black Briton Caryl Phillips crafts fictions that are collages of narratives of different times, races and groups; placed parallel to each other, the narratives in each novel focus the idea of a historical relationality, a connection of experience among the colonizer, the colonized, various diasporic peoples and colonial men and women. Phillips, who has always declared his own ethnic, cultural and psychological hybridity, offers the relationality of histories as a global descriptor rather than as an activist ideology for Caribbeans in diaspora, and indeed may be said to write more from a point of intersection between a generalized postcolonial angst and a postmodern "despair" than from within a Caribbean migrant consciousness. Despite these differences, his resonances with Brodber as well as Cliff and Dabydeen are clear.

If Brodber's and Cliff's diasporic answers draw on lived West Indian gender reality – a reality that is also represented in the older male-crafted fictions (though in different ways) – then it must be that any idea of a radical disjunction between male- and female-authored fictions and between the historically diasporic and the historically nationalist text must be questioned. In the same way, much of the sense of relationality with other cultures within which Cliff's, Brodber's, Phillips' and Dabydeen's gender attitudes are located, as well as much of the sense of a permeability of boundaries in West Indian culture, which appears in the newer fictions, appeared also in fiction and literary theory from the nationalist period, so that in this respect also a radical disjunction between diaspora and nationalist literature cannot be posited.

Kamau Brathwaite's postulation of a jazz aesthetic for the West Indian novel, as well as the concern of his *Arrivants* trilogy (1972) with the fortunes of black people in diasporic spaces outside the Caribbean, implies a recognition of the issues of cultural relationality, subsumed though this awareness is under his nationalist project, which moves towards definition and a certain amount of concomitant closing off, where relationality implies opening out. Lamming's fierce nationalism expressed in essays and interviews is more complexly explored through his fictions, in ways that constantly unearth the paradoxes of the West Indian negotiation between relationality and nationalism. This is also true of *The Pleasures of Exile,* an ur-narrative of relationality in which Lamming crafts an entire ideology of Caribbean linguistic identity through the pages of Shakespeare's (migrated, English) *Tempest.* (Indeed, as fictive representations of ideas in *The Pleasures of Exile* and as variations on the *Tempest* trope, all Lamming's fictions are in a sense migration fictions and fictions of relationality.)[10]

Sylvia Wynter, a nationalist who radically departed from many of the more popular tenets of West Indian literary criticism, found no difficulty in suggesting positive principles of relationality between black and white culture in the West Indies. Rather than the anguished process of creolization that some nationalist thinkers posited, Wynter (1970) referred to a period in West Indian history when a rich interaction of African cultural forms and those of marginalized groups of whites (early indentured servants, the Irish and other "poor whites") had begun to contribute to the forging of an indigenous culture. By implication, this merging had been possible precisely because the cultural forms of the European working-class people were as marked by experiences of heterogeneity as were those of the slave population.

These are not ideas that the critical academy routinely picked up or popularized. Certainly Lamming's ameliorative engagements with Europe were downplayed in favour of discussions of his "African" and peasant West Indian consciousness, and Wynter was not a popular critic until very recent times. Neither did Wilson Harris's vision of a cross-cultural relationality of arcanely perceivable deposits of world "tradition" in which the Caribbean was only one of many strands of (presumably) equal weight find much currency in the exigent self-assertion of the times. Ironically, Harris's thought might have found more accommodation among the proponents of Negritude, which, despite its white-black polarities and its influence on aspects of West Indian nationalism, was at base an ideology rooted in concepts of relationality.[11] And yet the paradox is that West Indian culture – and all of nationalist thought itself, with its idea of forging a common heterogenous culture out of plural elements – is rooted in relationality at other levels.

With regard to the idea of relationality, then, we see that its appearance in writing associated with the paradigm of diasporic thought is not new but exists in a line of continuity from concepts and representations subsumed or unread or foundational in nationalist literature and theory. The question is, is there an unproblematic junction between what the earlier writers and their more recent counterparts are representing? Are the ideas of relationality that underpin diasporic gender representations the same ideas of relationality that underpinned concepts of relationality in the nationalist era? The obvious first answer is no. While West Indian nationalists prior to the 1980s argued a principle of accommodation within their cultures, their primary aim was to define West Indian/Caribbean culture, that is, to assert its difference from other cultures, a unique kind of heterogeneity sprung from the slave/colonial plantation where the major cultures of the world met in rupture, conflict and disjunction. To put it from another angle, what nationalism sought to do was to guard the region's unique identity, not to deny relationality. Without relationality, in fact, this identity could not exist. But the nation's unique identity was uppermost.

In diasporic representations, it is often the similarity to other cultures that is highlighted and treated in celebratory terms. The movement away from discourses of self-protection – or, rather, the reinventing of the concept of self-protection – displaces the anguish of exile and perpetuates itself as its own imaginary. In other instances, as in Cliff's and Phillips's fictions, the openness of hegemonic cultures to deconstruction by West Indian and other "subaltern" cultures is also a site of triumph. And in some cases, we see an extraordinary kind of celebration by which it would seem that the West Indian experience of difference serves not to establish West Indianness, but to displace it. This appears to be the dynamic at work in David Dabydeen's assertion about his protean national selves: to psychologically and behaviourally shift nationalities at will indicates that the West Indian self is not privileged over the British or the American self.

Yet the celebratory treatments do not constitute the full picture of West Indian self-fashioning in diasporic spaces. In Brodber's *Louisiana,* the equitable working-out of gender and other communal issues is accomplished in a context almost of black isolation in the North American setting. That is to say, the frame of white society within which Brodber's black characters are circumscribed is almost ignored – Brodber tunnels inward to the processes by which the black (West Indian and southern US) communities relate to each other, as though the white context is irrelevant or does not impinge on how blacks work out their communal salvation. While this approach avoids the pitfalls of the nationalist ethic of opposition and reply, it does seem to beg the question of a form of escapism that troubles the ground of celebration.

Cliff's *Free Enterprise* too turns away from the wider society to a self-protective women's community that may have found a way to deal with psychological deracination. However, the novel avoids dealing with the practicalities of day-to-day interaction with those who own the metropolitan space. The issue surfaces also in women's fictions out of Canada; for example, in Brand's peripatetic *In Another Place, Not Here* (1997), the lesbian bonding appears predicated not on itself but on a turning away – a rejection of men's society as irredeemably destructive. Similarly, the strong female protagonists of Nalo Hopkinson's *Brown Girl in the Ring* (1998) and *Midnight Robber* (2000) are pictured in various forms of isolation in and retreat from inimical diasporic spaces whose threat circumscribes and delimits their strategies of self-empowerment, whether folk magical or carnival.[12] We are reminded that in the Caribbean carnival tradition, the Midnight Robber's toast is an escape narrative.

While the women's fictions equivocate between celebratory images of self-empowerment and stark representations of diasporic retreat, a significant body of men's fictions more directly portray triumph as shortlived, evanescent or illusory, and anomie and loss as endemic constants. Examples are Fred D'Aguiar's *Dear Future* (1996), David Dabydeen's *The Intended* (2000) and Austin Clarke's *The Origin of Waves* (1997) and *The Question* (1999).[13] Set between an England and a Guyana tragically linked by a mother's politically directed migratory crossing, D'Aguiar's text presents a negative vision of the future for Guyanese boys in the fallout from familial fragmentation, irresponsible fatherhood, absentee parenting and patriarchal-political corruption. Significantly, the presence in the Guyanese setting of a strong extended family which includes male and female role models is not enough to avert the tragedy brought on by political corruption and the breakdown at the nucleus of the family. D'Aguiar's perspective is very likely conditioned by his awareness of Guyana's isolation and other political problems at the present time, but the provocative question arises as to whether his portrayal may be overdetermined by his equal awareness of the extreme deracination of West Indian boys in Britain. Certainly his treatment foregrounds the West Indian concern about absentee fatherhood, now growing into a concern about absentee parenting through migration, and the role of the biological parent as opposed to that of the extended family.

Dabydeen's ironic, even comic, "rewriting" of Joseph Conrad's *Heart of Darkness* interrogates the idea of psycho-cultural border crossing as a form of liberation, as the transplanted Indo-West Indian adolescent protagonist fails repeatedly in his bid to both assimilate into and exercise dominance over British haute culture by rejecting his Indian and Caribbean identities. Troped in terms of the adolescent's efforts to achieve manhood by his relations with typological women (Madonna and Whore), the project is defeated as much by Lady England's corrupting underside – the libidinous subculture of unsanctioned desire – as by the emasculating images of her purity circulated via public discourse that the boy has absorbed. Dabydeen's (anti-)hero has no empowering "vision" of multiple selves able to exist harmoniously side by side: the exigent pressure of the colony in the body of the migrant insists that there can be only the one, definitive, English self. In this novel, Dabydeen's celebratory declaration of protean selfhood, like that of Brand's protagonist, seems applicable "in another place, not here". It remains fascinating, however, that the construction of England as a sexual idea continues to be a major imaginative tool for West Indian male writers.

Clarke's ironic undertone questioning the linguistic performance of their sexual exploits by two aging men in a Toronto bar in *The Origin of Waves* seems to point to a self-delusion at the heart of this performativity, recalling Selvon's masked calypsonian's commentary in the London quartet. Grief may be almost invisible in the subtext as the men's performance reveals a hilarious, self-recuperative strategy that highlights the infiltration of West Indian subjectivities on Canadian soil. Yet the performance may be as insecure and the efficacy as questionable as they were for Selvon's boys in the 1950s. For the recuperative effect of the strategy exists in dialectic tension with the fact that the men perform their exploits for each other, indicating not only that the sexual prowess enacted as history may be purely imagined or invented, but also that the performance is fuelled by competition side by side with a deep hunger for lost connection. Their "play" beats against a society that has not accepted them even though it is a society in which they have grown old and chalked up economic achievements. And if we read the novel as a reflection on the process of growing old, have the old men moved very far from the psychology of the lost boys in London? Are there indeed no elders?[14] The strategies of the carnival society appear to have their limitations.

So too do the attempts at assimilation as portrayed in *The Question*. Here the representation of anomie, alienation and, yes, sheer exile as functions of sexual and marital relations between black West Indian male and white Canadian female approaches the threnody of a tragic vision. Ironically, the gulf between is sharpened by the fact that both the protagonist and his wife/woman are hybridic subjectivities, which should have meant a space of meeting but instead becomes the very ground of their incompatibility. The differences of the West are different from the differences of the West Indies – difference is as tyrannical as oneness is hegemonic. Hope as possibility appears in the title and in fragments and slippages throughout, insistently drawn as the text's underside rather than its main frame.

Writing in 2001 about the Caribbean diaspora in Canada, Dionne Brand argues that Caribbeans abroad often retain "the most fragile diplomatic relations" with "the nations we were born in, the ones we live in, and the ones were supposed to belong to" (2001, 83). Brand suggests that this condition of placelessness is the result of ideological and cultural confusion, and, as did Kamau Brathwaite almost thirty years earlier in "Roots" (1993), links placelessness to a parading of false national/cultural identity – false because it is not based on an organic connection with the original home:

> [Caribbeans in Canada] switch from the more specific nationalisms of island and territory to region throughout their discourse with Canada. They also gesture to the continent of Africa and at times also to India and China, since there are several diasporas that come together in those Caribbean origins. They claim a Canada qualified by these tenuous origins. They quarrel with the Canadian nation on counts of racism and exclusion from kind treatment. They travel . . . back and forth from these origins to their neo-origins. They are legally embattled with the Canadian nation-state on points of physical entry into the nation. . . . The imperative for these crossnationalisms bores me. It puts into play an exhausting, stultifying set of practices which are repeated and repeated without change. It

makes people cling to the most narrow definitions of culture and identity, and deploy the most banal characteristics as exemplary. National identity is a dance of artificiality, since what it dances must be essentially unchanging. (Brand 2001, 71–72)

Brand's commentary suggests that Caribbean modes of self-identification are engaged in as strategies of recuperative self-fashioning but that in fact these strategies fail by virtue of containing the opposite of themselves: a static lack of creativity rooted in distance from the heart of Caribbean culture. Here, in providing her own answers to some of the issues concerning what is Caribbean/West Indian, Brand shows herself to be clearly not espousing any wholesale celebratory vision of diaspora. Further, she suggests by implication, as Brathwaite explicitly does in "Roots", and as Moses's shift in consciousness at the end of Selvon's *Moses Ascending* paradoxically foreshadows, that the strategies of self-fashioning do work in the right context – where there is an organic connection with the geographical Caribbean. How this is to be effected by diasporics who have been away for a long time and by what parameters they may speak of themselves as Caribbean/West Indian men and women beyond the parameter of geographical origin are among the many questions up for debate in the new frame of "What is Caribbeanness/West Indianness?"

But then there are those writers who reject the idea of "Caribbean" frames. The melancholia and continuing pessimistic world view of V. S. Naipaul who has spent most of his life outside the Caribbean, indicates that for him West Indian and other Caribbean modes of transformation are and remain fundamentally sterile. Jamaica Kincaid's strongly gendered sense of self is built on an exigent engagement with her Antiguan roots and a concomitant rejection of any solutions to the problem of identity that the Caribbean can offer her. As an article of ideological faith, Kincaid crafts gender on an idiosyncratic and individualistic world view. It may be argued with some basis (though more controversially in the case of Kincaid) that Naipaul and Kincaid invest little in Caribbean modes of being, but the point to be made is that the celebratory or politically empowered image of diaspora in some fictions and theoretical writings is by no means a universal one. Moreover, manhood and womanhood continue to be issues of conflictual and conflicting representation in which "exilic" as a way of describing some portrayals has outlived the concept "nationalist". Caryl Phillips early stated that his pilgrimage to the West Indies presented him with no guidelines by which to trace his development as a man who was black, of migrant stock and British sensibility (1987, 9). (Phillips, engaging with "global" – including non-black – diasporas, has in fact not returned to the Caribbean as a setting for his fictions since his second novel.)

At the same time, the continuing sense of a need to connect to the "home" space, or at least to "original homes of spirit" in some way, is possibly evinced in the proliferation of Afro- and Indo-West Indian fiction out of Britain that draws on the history of the slave and pre-slavery past. Fictions such as David Dabydeen's *The Counting House* (1996), much of Phillips's work, Beryl Gilroy's *Steadman and Joanna* (1991) and Fred D'Aguiar's *The Longest Memory* (1994) and *Feeding the Ghosts* (1997) may well suggest a greater ease of connection with distant, unknown and therefore more imaginatively accessible and "fixed" diasporic pasts than with the ongoing, dynamic West Indies of the present which renders efforts at appropriation open to question. Writing towards the past, one avoids the perplexities of the unknown/insufficiently known creolizing environment and its paradoxes of gender identification, as well as accusations of being "out of touch" with the present reality of the islands. The fact that writers in Britain turn so much towards the past for their West Indian linkages and at the same time profess themselves adept inhabitants of multiple transnationalities may suggest locale-specific contours to the difficulties presented by Britain as a diasporic space.

The engagement with the past and writers' more confident sense of a fluidity in their own gender consciousness intersect in a number of works by male writers who invent protagonal or quasi-protagonal female subjectivities in settings located in the past. These include Lawrence Scott's *Witchbroom* (1993), Dabydeen's *The Counting House,* D'Aguiar's *Feeding the Ghosts,* Phillips's *Cambridge* (1991) and *The Nature of Blood* (1997), and Austin Clarke's *The Polished Hoe* (2003), Commonwealth Prize winner in 2003. Not all are migration fictions in the sense of being set in the current diasporic space, but all are part of a general phenomenon and all are written by West Indians in diaspora. The intersection between writing the past and writing female subjectivity marks a paradox, for if the engagement with female subjectivity suggests a more fluent gender consciousness, the location of these in past histories suggests also a continuing tentativeness about portraying the female – that is to say, a greater ease in constructing what ultimately becomes a typological historical subject than in engaging with the more contentious project of representing the modern woman.

At the same time, the marriage of the narrative of slavery with the narrative of woman merely exemplifies the contemporary view that the slave and the female are the most fruitful subjects through whom to speak about oppression. (Clarke's narrative is the only one set in twentieth-century Barbados, so that Clarke draws on personal experience and memory as much as on history. It is instructive that his epic protagonist, Miss Mary Mathilda Bellfeels, exemplifies the West Indian linguistic performativity so evident in Clarke's male protagonists but with much more unequivocally powerful effect and with a focused knowledge and control of the outcome that at one level places her in the tradition of Selvon's "unplaying" female players.)

The seemingly greater willingness of male authors to invent female subjectivities, and to do so from a more "empathetic" standpoint, has to do with the diasporic space insofar as the focus on women's issues in North America and Europe inevitably affects both a writer's consciousness and his book sales. But a similar trend appeared in the calypso arena in Trinidad and the Eastern Caribbean beginning in the mid-1990s: not only are female calypsonians appearing on the stage to articulate radical feminist perspectives – and perhaps aesthetics – but they are being joined by male calypsonians interrogating masculinist agendas.[15] Again, feminist/womanist activism and, to a lesser extent, economics account for these changes, but certainly also I would add as a contributing factor the attenuation of the nationalist imperative and a concomitant lessening of conflict-producing stress on men. I would also add men's "acceptance" of the increasing if contradictory indices of female power through education and professional occupation[16] – another version of the stickfighter's "equal opponent".

It needs hardly be said that differences in the representation of gender in diaspora are inflected not only by discursive, biographical and economic aspects of location, but also by race, colour and class. The interplay of the struggles for inclusion by Indo-West Indian males in both Guyanese and Canadian spaces in Cyril Dabydeen's short fiction (*Berbice Crossing* [1996] and *North of the Equator* [2001]) recalls David Dabydeen's assertion that West Indians can be outsiders as much at home as abroad, and indeed suggests that for the Indo-West Indian male (though this may depend on his country of origin),[17] the psychological shift to a new transnational identity may not involve a radical reorientation at all, even while it suggests that it is pain, not the carnival inclusion of the creolizing society, that the Indo-West Indian has gleaned from home as his particular source of strength. David Dabydeen's own imagining of Afro-West Indian female slave subjectivities in *The Counting House* points as well to this sense of Indo-

West Indian fluidity. Cliff's idea of diasporic accommodation as a relatively easy possibility may be linked to the fact of being (near-)white and middle-class, which already invests her with privilege *vis-à-vis* the black working-class female immigrant. In Lawrence Scott's *Aelred's Sin* (1998), the issue of whether the white West Indian male protagonist will encounter any serious prejudice in the English monastery on the basis of cultural background is of far less import than his homosexuality.

The contrasting struggle of Brand's (*San Souci*) and Austin Clarke's working-class female immigrants (for example, in Clarke's *The Meeting Point* [1967]) bears resonances with the experience of Jean Rhys's female protagonists on English soil, suggesting that gender-specific experiences are mediated not only by shifts in time, but also by differentials in the treatment of male and female that intersect racial lines. And Brodber's celebratory vision may be of a different kind from Cliff's, built as it is on a pan-African "Ethiopianist" ideology; but it too speaks to an experience of privilege not shared across the board, and particularly not in the case of the vast new underclass of young men from the West Indian, especially Jamaican, urban ghettoes, who arrive in North America and Britain without connections to an empowering folk tradition and quickly join the ranks of the criminalized and criminal underworld, the yardie and the deportee. The strength and distinguishing feature of Brodber's diasporic community of genders, however, is its presentation as ideology – that is, not merely as history, where history means what actually happens, but as solution, the radical appropriation of strategies for freedom which changes the course of history, so that history comes to mean that which is possible. Here Brodber's thought on history shows a strong continuity with Lamming's, despite the differences between his materialist and her spiritualist etymologies.[18]

In all of this it is useful not to forget that there is a whole genre and world of performance – in dub poetry, in music, in dance – that takes place in arenas outside the main (academic) stream within which literature finds its primary audience, and which I have not dealt with in these comments on representations of gender in diaspora. These arenas include clubs, pubs, concert halls and theatres, which attract wide cross-sections of performers and audiences and which are in many cases the purview of young Caribbean men, who find in them an expressive and self-creative space not available in the world of "the book". In many cases, the energy that fuels these dynamic sites of representation comes out of the crossings, cross-fertilizations and synergies between "home" and diaspora, brought, on the one hand, by West

Indian/Caribbean-based performers who visit the metropoles on tour from time to time and, on the other hand, by West Indian/Caribbean performers in diaspora and the performance traditions of the diasporic space.

In the United States, for example, crossings among Jamaican dancehall, Trinidadian calypso and African American hip-hop are sites of production for experiments in gender identity, elaboration and resistance, particularly for young black men, in ways that may easily trouble the images produced in literature. Such crossings are of course multiplied and endlessly recomplicated via technologies such as film, the Internet and "home box offices" (television, DVD, video). In recent years also, forms of what may be termed "alternative literature" have also emerged; in Britain, for example, X Press specializes in popular literature geared towards a young black audience and is reputed to have succeeded in getting young black men to read. X Press is explicitly gender-directed, showcasing black women writers and black male writers as separate strands in its emphasis on black identity.

X Press publications fall into two distinct categories. One, which is didactically invested in a valoristic and revisionary view of black history, features reissues of well-known black classics (Claude McKay, Paul Lawrence Dunbar, Charles Chestnutt) as well as little-known writing by obscure black male and female authors, explicitly differentiated by gender and volume. The other is popular and pulp, featuring lurid sex, village-stud ideologies and swashbuckling appropriations – sometimes subversive, sometimes collusive – of European romantic traditions. The authors are generally second-generation diasporics (Britishers and sometimes Americans of West Indian lineage). In contrast to writers with a strong sense of Caribbean connection, and in keeping with the demands of the pop market, these writers portray characters whose concerns are personal rather than symbolic, even while typifying black issues. References to the Caribbean are frequent but are made either as background context, or as a way of contrasting the younger and old(-fashioned) generations, or as nostalgia for an exoticized rural paradise bearing little or no resemblance to actuality.[19]

Patrick Augustus's "Baby Father" series and Sheri Campbell's unapologeti-cally pornographic scenarios, the latter showcasing "liberated" females hungrily on the prowl for fresh and fresher sex, are indicators especially of the early (1990s) X Press pop ethos. Both revise moral positions: while the loosed female appetite is celebrated in Campbell, in Augustus's and other male-authored fictions promiscuous male sex is simultaneously bemoaned and orgasmically celebrated, irresponsible fatherhood is lambasted and made the occasion of laughter, the signifiers of material success – Porsches, bling bling (rich, excessive jewellery) and women – are valorized, and the materialistic ethos is warned against. The indicators of success are in fact held up as inspiration to ambitionless black men, both to push beyond the janitorial glass ceiling and to successfully rival white male sex appeal. The portrayal of black male criminality and violence is common in X Press's male-authored fictions; though in many cases the authorial stance is one of didactic censure, it seems that crime and violence sell black texts as much as do steamy sex and super-sexed female characters whose main role outside of the bedroom is to harry and harass men into marriage and female-biased versions of responsibility.

In the range of its publications, X Press figures the African diaspora as an entire reading community. The popular-didactic text in itself is, of course, another kind of crossing, collapsing the boundaries between "serious" and "pop", and it seems to work well, if the X Press's large following is anything to go by. At the site of this meeting of boundaries, the black popular press marshals the pleasures of reading at the same time as it presents some of the most horrendous images of black male placelessness, anchorlessness and "homelessness" that exist in literature. In case after case, deracination is as much the result of absentee or abusive fathering as it is of racial oppression. If the characters of the typical X Press novel have a "home space", it is mostly explicitly the besieged castle of the skin – race as deracinated experience in diaspora.[20]

In the end, despite the severe limitations of a purely literary survey, we are still able to recognize overall that there exists a diversity in the gender representations of diaspora that is as varied as the representations of the home space in the nationalist period. Clearly, not only is diaspora as celebration and appropriation somewhat problematized, but the celebration of different West Indians in different diasporic spaces is not of the same kind, nor is it based on the same perceptions or experiences of relationality. Diversity of experience in individual women's migration fictions makes celebration an issue for interrogation rather than a given, even though the facts that more women than men are writing fiction and that they are writing from an "imagination of sovereignty" make celebration the dominant ethos that surrounds the writing of migration fictions. Beyond this, the fact that more West Indian writers domiciled at home and abroad are writing about the diasporic space as opposed to the earlier tendency to use the diasporic space as a domicile from which to write about/(re)construct the original home space is testament to the shifts in what West Indian writers see as their location and their boundaries.[21]

It is true that many of the fictions produced by West Indians abroad are not "migration fictions"; that is, they focus outside of the diasporic space and towards the geographical West Indies – and this is an indication that despite its intersection by new currents, its attenuation even, nationalism is still a crucial dynamic in West Indian literature. But if the West continues to provide the space within which the West Indies as "home" may be visualized, critiqued and re/constructed, the West is also a space of psychological habitation and bi- or transnational consciousness that is unabashedly admitted. In several cases the writers of the present day are binationals or second-generation citizens in the Western countries, and in the case of North America and later migrants to Britain, the absence of the mother/fatherland link which had obtained for early migrants to England may allow for a less conflicted relation and thus a freer space of self-fashioning.

With regard to the women writers, the diasporic space is often the space that has clarified and recorded their strengths as women. The clarification and the record of women are the single most important change in the literary representation of gender between the nationalist period and the present time, for the women's texts are the most prominent signifier upon which a celebratory ethos has been further signified upon by critics to posit a celebratory ethos in West Indian/Caribbean diasporic writing. The facilitative role played by the diasporic is highlighted even for writers such as Olive Senior and Merle Collins, who divide their time between North America and the Caribbean home spaces yet consider themselves unequivocally Jamaican and Grenadian respectively and concern themselves with the representation of West Indian (female) subjectivities. It may be argued that such writers inhabit a paradoxical ground between an acceptance of diaspora and its rejection, as an aspect of the celebration of home.

Not only the presence of West Indians in the metropoles but also the diversity in attitude, perspective and performance among writers, which is obviously replicated and multiplied among writers from other parts of the Caribbean, gives point to Lamming's assertion that the [West Indies and the wider] Caribbean cannot any longer be conceived of in terms of geographical boundaries but rather in terms of a transnational family (Birbalsingh, 1996a). The current mapping of West Indian/Caribbean forms of gender identific-ation onto diasporic spaces and relations renders Selvon's Moses a prophetic figure and indicates an agreement with Lamming's imagination of the

Caribbean community as "an area of ground [which is the] Caribbean wherever I encounter it; it does not matter whether I find myself in Asia, Africa or wherever, it is the window through which I am looking at wherever I am" (D. Scott 2002,162). There is a sense – and this carries its own ironies – in which such an imagination applied to gender seems far easier for the diasporic West Indians of the late twentieth and early twenty-first centuries than it did for those of the nationalist 1950s. There is another sense in which it is far more complex, as for some West Indians now, West Indian–(man)ness is something one wears or performs – or not – at will.

There is irony too in the fact that while the fiction shows several pictures and ideologies of empowerment achieved through global relationality, there are far fewer pictures of empowerment through male-female bonding or through men and women seeking solutions together. That is to say, individuals and wider conclaves are portrayed as becoming more empowered, but personal relations at the very foundations where sexism and gender dissonance inhere are generally not. And those writers who raise the related issue of homosexuality, despite their celebration of the homosexual's right to be and to speak, unanimously highlight the fact that homosexuals, whether in the Caribbean or its diaspora, still have no place to call home (for example, Brand 1997; Powell 2003; L. Scott 1998). Brodber's work, in fact, stands out among migration fictions, as Lamming's stands out among nationalist ones, as an attempt to bridge these gaps of reconciliation between genders.

Many reasons could be adduced for the relative lack of portrayal of this form of communality. One of the most obvious is that the writer in diaspora inhabits realities that push more towards confrontation with other cultures than towards a foregrounding of private/personal relations. The political space of "home" and "nation" is loosened from around the writer along with the geographical removal. In the diasporic space, one's visible presence, the body, is signified upon not along these indices, but along the indices of race and differential culture. Everyday existence – the fight for sovereignty of self – becomes an unremitting battleground against these impositions. The individual inhabits an untenable paradox whereby she is isolated as individual (meaning there is no supporting collective or the supporting collective is diffused and interpenetrated by the dominant forces of the diasporic country) and is yet fixed in an eternal representation of "black/West Indian/Caribbean female" to which she must daily respond. Both the text as the story of the singular protagonist and the text as the story of the female collective are facilitated by this experience. The necessity of such texts is reinforced by the additional and shared experience of female subjugation by men on both sides of the West Indian/Western divide. The female collective and the female (protagonist's) masculine certainty of self are the West Indian woman's experience that Selvon observed as efficacious in exile and that Lamming strove to appropriate as a male symbol of national becoming.

So in looking at the female-authored texts, we see that choices about textual form are intimately bound up with choices about gender represent-ations. On the other hand, in thinking about the greater ease that some male writers portray men as experiencing when they engage in individualized "play", we are brought back to the issue of that "triple dissonance" that operates in Selvon's fiction. It may be that the diasporic space of the late twentieth and early twenty-first centuries separates out the impossibly imbricated threads of becoming individual and citizen, of inventing self and nation, both at the same time. If one is able to inhabit (and dis-inhabit) a cultural Caribbean without necessarily having to inhabit a national one, is the individual freed at last to come into his own in the space of diaspora? In these men's migration fictions that I have discussed, the absence of a male community, whose presence in Selvon and Lamming is either a feature of West Indian collective consciousness or the sign of a growing national consciousness, is quite marked. (That Clarke is somewhat of an exception is not surprising, given his experience of an older, situated West Indies.)[22]

Questions: Does diaspora sustain the kinds of literary representations that portray gaps not only between West Indian men and women, but also between men and men, precisely because of the absence of those geographical boundaries that might have foregrounded the ways in which persons with a mutual stake in the well-being of the polity come together? Does diaspora even extend those gaps of representation because more options of identity are available – that is, because in the absence of such boundaries and of nationalist pressure the individual can shift the terms "West Indian" and "Caribbean" within more fluid spaces of definition?

But what of the portrayals of popular fiction? Not everyone is able to make these "ameliorative" shifts of freedom; indeed, popular fiction seems to be indicating that one has to have a sense of belonging to some geographically experienced or imagined first polity in order to experience the pleasures of being freed from its demands. The average X Press fiction suggests that for many born or brought up in diaspora, a history of origins and a praxis of moral and familial traditions have not been transferred from the West Indies to the diasporic space and that, in the absence of these, the diasporic space is never amelioratively appropriated. The gap between the portrayals of men in serious and popular fiction is the gap between privilege and disprivilege, but certainly also often between being able to imagine West Indian/Caribbean and not being able to. The "bastard line" in the translocal Caribbean family is now redefined by this absence of genealogy within the imagination.

There are other issues. In a new-found admiration for the formidable powers of the West Indian female, Lamming has in recent times argued that it is through West Indian women that the sovereignty of the liberated imagination will be displayed in the future.[23] I cannot think of an announcement more depressing, for it simply highlights anomalies, burdens and polarizations that are far from being resolved. What, as Lamming himself recognizes in an almost-aside, is the point of the "liberation" of one-half of the population? And what of the children, that supplantive first generation that Lamming so persuasively posited in his early fictions? Many of these, left back home by migrant parents who celebrate their own diasporic consciousness, are at the mercy of less stable surrogacy arrangements that heretofore and often become known to their parents only as the receiving end of a remittance. From this new generation of "barrel children" sometimes spring the dysfunctional masculinities – the yardie and the stereotypical deportee – who function both as manufactured re-export and as tragic bodily variations on Louise Bennett's "coloniz[er] in reverse" (1966, 179).

Some parents in the diaspora in Britain are now making a conscious choice to send their boy children back to the West Indies for their basic education.[24] This sharply focuses the reality that the answers to integration have not necessarily been found in the migrant spaces or in West Indian ability to negotiate these. The education the West Indies offers to such children cannot be served up as a static across-the-board package: the introduction to new vocabularies of self and gender has to merge an understanding of history, of the present, dynamic West Indies, and of the locations to which they will return. Export-import relations might indeed take on a new meaning.

The Postmodern (Postmodernism, Postmodernity) and the Caribbean

The Caribbean and the discourses of diaspora, postmodernity and post-modernism meet at various points of intersection. Paul Gilroy (1993) put a new spin on pan-Africanist thought by including the Caribbean in his celebratory theory of the black diaspora as the dynamic source of the world's "postmodernity". And as I stated in my introduction, Caribbean/West Indian textualities and Caribbean/West Indian lived experience, particularly in the diasporic space, have led literary and cultural theorists to posit, first, the Caribbean literary text (male- or female-authored or both) as being among the most fruitful grounds for analysis through the lenses of postmodernism and, second, the Caribbean as a prototype of postmodernity. It seems easy to respond to the first of these arguments: one might simply say "yes, and no" – yes, because the grounds on which theorists such as Benítez Rojo, Glissant, Ledent and Gikandi draw the Caribbean text into a dialogue with postmodernism are, of course, quite easy to recognize; no, because of issues of history and epistemic incompatibility.

A view of the Caribbean text as a prototype of the postmodern (Benítez Rojo 1996, 21–29) is already supported by the modes of analysis utilized in this book. For the polymath picture of West Indian gender that we have seen emerges not only as a function of a historicist reading in which society and text are looked at "intertextually", and not necessarily as a function of the texts' perceived ideologies, but also as a function of what might be loosely termed the "deconstructive" strategies of reading that I have used. Such strategies exploit the polysemic/polyglossic nature of language, invested as much in its socio-cultural and political referents (Mikhail Bakhtin's "all words . . . are populated by intentions [of others]" [1981, 293]) as in its linguistic codes and associations. But, arguably, the ease with which these novels lend themselves to a deconstructive reading is attributable to more than any generic properties of linguistic utterance, fictive or non-fictive. Caribbean writing in itself is writing out of a "deconstructive consciousness", a leaning towards complications of language and ambiguity which force analyses that trouble the nature and meaning of utterance itself. If Selvon's performativity pushes the envelope of representation as a slippery, liminal and paradoxical act even as it configures West Indian gender as having the same qualities, Lamming's investments in language theory equally question certainties by pointing not only to the constructed nature of gender identity, but also to the "suspect" nature of the representational enterprise itself.

Lamming's overt-self referentiality in particular – the text asking us to question its own strategies of representation, positing its own "lack" derived in language; positing also a concomitant delay, displacement and decentred multiplicity of meaning; playing off of the conscious and the verbal against the unconscious and corporeal sources of utterance – all of this finds resonance in much of postmodern theory, particularly the ideas of Derrida, Bakhtin and Lacan. While Selvon's style is far from being so directly ideological, his masked calypsonian narrators with their ironic speaking voices achieve a similar effect of self-referentiality. The text becomes another instance of Caribbean speech in which discourse and fiction are conflated as a form of discourse. All of this points to representational paradoxes that, along with the interplay of lived experience, allows us to test the ulterior ramifications of Lamming's potentially radical gender idealism and to recognize that Selvon's "apolitical" gender stance is in fact deeply political.

Lamming's embedded linguistic theory, which provides the critical vocabulary by which his texts may be read, resonates with Gabriel García Márquez's less polemical but equally insistent way of placing in his fictions sets of Caribbean/Latin American epistemes which constituted signposts to their interpretation. The metropolitan academy, unversed in these knowledges but aware that it was being confronted by something new, gave them the name "magic realism", a distortionary translation of Alejo Carpentier's *real maravilloso.* The double-visioned, double-jointed body of the performing slave that emerges through the pages of the journals of the plantation era produces irresistible codes by which the performative praxis of West Indian gender is understood. These codes are recognized by the West Indian Subject as the outgrowth of participation in such codes within her own lived experience. Before deconstruction, Brathwaite, as a Caribbean Subject understanding and investigating the modalities of his own culture, postulated its episteme, the poetics of marronage: "The unity is submarine" (1974, 64). Before his postmodernist phase, Glissant, describing the paradoxical effects of colonization upon Caribbean culture, declared, "*They sowed in the depths the seeds of an invisible presence.* And so transversality, and not the universal transcendence of the sublime, has come to light" (1992, 67), and explicitly stated his debt to Brathwaite (66). Wilson Harris, in his early essays *Tradition, the Writer and Society* (1967) and again in *The Womb of Space: The Cross-cultural Imagination* (1983), explicated as their interpretative frame the mythopoetics of his fictive discourse.

But the problem of labelling these texts postmodern, or of creating them within postmodernist theory, is not merely that the label is anachronistic or that it imposes a false synchronicity upon asynchronous texts and discourses. Of greater import is the epistemic disjunction between postmodernism and

Caribbean poetics, which in fact in different ways is acutely recognized by Glissant and Benítez Rojo.[25] Where the endless recessive of deconstruction theory may lead towards a vacuum of meaning – a kind of cognitive black hole which some have seen as allied to despair – the West Indian and Caribbean "deconstructive" leads insistently towards a declaration of fullness that cannot be charted and a view of humanity as sacred. The idea is conveyed in Lamming's "Fola and other than" and Brathwaite's "nam", the hidden, capsule-protected name (1983), and also in the tendency of Caribbean writers towards religious language (Walcott's metaphors of sanctity and the "lost God" in "What the Twilight Says"; Brathwaite's envisioning of the search for national relation in terms of "holiness", "miracle", "grace" and "uncurled blooms of light"; Glissant's "sacrality" in *Poetics of Relation*; Lamming's decription of himself at a recent conference as an "evangelist").[26]

In many cases also, the West Indian as well as other Caribbean text (particularly the text in the nationalist mode) struggles or leans towards an idea not merely of decentring the single reader, but of creating a community of readers – by extension, the community or the nation, as shaper of the text. This is evidenced in textual strategies as diverse as Lamming's gender-composite characterizations and multiple protagonists allegorizing a national persona, as Brodber's and Collins's multiple storytellers displacing the "real" author or lowering her visibility, as the role of the gender-inclusive community in making the tale in Brodber and Collins, as Mais's choric women-sayers counterpointing the male narrative, as the frequent use of carnival as a trope for focalizing the cultural nation. Almost invariably, the carnival text at least begins to decentre gender orthodoxies as part of a strategy of instating the communal. The refusal, epitomized perhaps in Lamming and Harris, to separate the critical moment from the creative moment – that is, the praxis of conflating theory and fiction – is part of this continuum and serves to question the efficacy of a purely theoretical (essentially masculinist) frame in reading the Caribbean text. The point of divergence is, however, summed up in the concern of postmodernism with textuality and of Caribbean poetics with material history – by extension, with the material body as the site of physical and psychological experience. The seemingly deft gender performance of the slave/West Indian/Caribbean persona foregrounds this material body, the liminal hermaphrodite whose pain transcends textuality.

This leads me to the difficulties of the second argument: the use of the vocabulary of postmodernity to describe Caribbean persons and cultures.

Undoubtedly, the performativity that makes gender consciousness and identity fluid and even liminal categories, the tensions between master constructions of gender or genderlessness on the one hand and strategies of subversive engendering on the other, the paradox of collusion between systemically circulated patriarchal discourse and its antithesis in lived experience, the multiple ways in which the underbelly of lived experience becomes a problematizing "unconscious" fracturing the patriarchal discourses themselves – all of these resist closed-ended understandings and delay ideological certainties, so that Caribbean gender performances, like the texts in which they are foregrounded, easily lend themselves to a description as postmodern.

In the discourses most frequently applied to the Caribbean (and to the black diaspora), postmodernity is, moreover, a form of power: the power to straddle and effectively refashion rootless, bootless spaces such as those in which Caribbeans historically find themselves. In this context, Benítez Rojo's trope of chaos theory, which comes out of postmodernist perspectives in nuclear physics, seems very apt: "Within the (dis)order that swarms around what we already know of as Nature, it is possible to observe dynamic states of regularities that repeat themselves globally" (1996, 2). The twin ideas that West Indian gender represents circuitous routes to social ordering and that a discernible gender culture that is heterodox, dynamic and powerfully subversive exists in the Caribbean may be extrapolated from the analogy.[27]

The disjunctive underbelly of Caribbean gender experience is, however, highlighted in some of the terms I have used: "unconscious", "delay", "collusion", "rootless", "bootless". If anything is clear from the diasporic fictions I have discussed, it is that many Caribbeans in diaspora remain starkly outside the *mana* of the gods in the context of transnational dis/locations. In lived experience, the deracination, outcast and marginal positions, particularly of men and boys of minority groups in the metropoles, is grist for the mills of the mainstream media. The imprisonments, deportations and post–September 11 anti-alien, anti-refugee laws and detentions in the United States and Britain indicate the clear and present dangers of being male and ethnically or racially marked in the migrant space. The position of these males further highlights the economic quotient of global experience: globalization as capital and as controlled free market underpinned by strategic multinational resources. Here the occult underside of diaspora-as-celebration is exposed. Those who are most often discriminated against are the economically disadvantaged, and these in turn are Caribbean and other Others and their descendants, the historical victims of such discriminations. (Ironically as well in present-world dynamics, one may be discriminated against if one is possessed of capital and is racially, ethnically or religiously marked as "other" [the three may be conflated], so that again the economic quotient of global relations is foregrounded.)

To speak of Caribbean/West Indian men in such situations is to invoke postmodernity in its guise as "the postmodern condition", not in Lyotard's definition of it in purely abstract terms as the present-day condition of (Western) knowledge, in which reified, teleological positions are no longer the norm (1979), but rather in terms that refocus towards the dis/ease referents. Thus, "condition" evokes ideas of roving, placelessness and displacement, as well as the psychology of anomie, even despair, brought about by the erosion of certainties. If the particulars of the world that Selvon's boys and Lamming's emigrants encountered in the early 1950s have changed, in many cases it would seem that the principles have not, and the issue of whether one is robbed at the site of engendering remains. How women whose spouses and sons are caught in this net may be psychologically, economically and socially affected is another part of the equation. And because in the West women are often invisible – and doubly though ironically so when ethnically and racially marked – the ways in which the women themselves are directly exploited and abused is occluded in the male-dominated media. It is mainly in their own creative fiction (and quasi-fictions, such as Makeda Silvera's *Silenced* [1989]) that these factors are exposed.[28]

In contemplating the more destructive aspects of the work of translocation upon gender images and experiences, it seems clear that a definition of postmodernity in terms of celebration (whether explicit or implied), as well as postmodernism's truncation of its discourse in textuality, renders that vocabulary and episteme inadequate modes for speaking of Caribbean/West Indian cultural behaviours, gendered or otherwise. The inadequacies inhere in this case not in language, but in politico-historical referents. At the same time, as my own theoretical extrapolations indicate, the discourse opened up by bringing postmodernism and the concept of postmodernity into Caribbean discourse carries important analytical provenance that assists our search for alternative vocabularies.

The search will yield different answers for Caribbeans in diaspora and Caribbeans on "native" soil. For one thing, differentials of location bring different nuances, so that postmodernism or postmodernity as explanatory and descriptive frames might be more applicable to the Caribbean diaspora than to the geographical Caribbean, to some parts of the diaspora more than to others, and also to some persons and groups in diaspora more than to others. This is linked to another dimension of awareness: that in the same way that the boundaries of Caribbean/West Indian are changing, the frontiers of the West are also changing, and the areas of the Caribbean diaspora that "postmodern" may more fully describe may very well be not Caribbean but Western after all.[29] Differentials of territorial history might also cause some diasporic nationals more than others to see the frames of postmodernism as applicable to their narratives.[30] And then again, in the final analysis, it is a function of Caribbeanness that it is quite possible to be Eastern, Western and Caribbean all at the same time.

The difficulties of charting difference while preserving boundaries of identification are perhaps marked in Édouard Glissant's definition of relationality as a respectful understanding that the globe is made up of diverse humanities rather than the overarching Humanity of Western imperialist imagination. The postulation of diverse humanities is at odds both with Glissant's sense of respect as a form of sacred consciousness and with Caribbeans' feeling of themselves as part of a larger family of the human. Glissant's concomitant postulation of the conversation of world cultures as Babel is equally at odds with Caribbeans' and specifically West Indians' irresistible attraction to Pentecost (connoting ideas of accepting, translating and recreating all tongues, as opposed to Babel, which connotes [respectful acceptance of] one's exclusion from other tongues whose magnificence is their impenetrable difference).[31] Do such contradictions point to a postmodern anomie that is endemic, or simply to Caribbean contrarieties?

Perhaps the whole point in the context of a discussion about gender is that I must understand what I mean when I say "I am a Caribbean/West Indian woman" or "I am a Caribbean/West Indian man", and I must be sure why I choose the particular vocabularies and epistemes that I use in seeking to understand the terms of this "manness" or "womanness". I also want to be sure that such vocabularies and epistemes allow me regenerative space, and that I understand their larger political implications. "Larger political implications" includes the issue of whether I speak for myself or have the right to speak for other Caribbean persons or the Caribbean collective, and whether the terms I use violate, preserve or expand the terms of their sovereignty of self. Larger political implications inhere not only in the theories themselves, but in the socio-political space that they inhabit: all theories, in effect, are peopled with the intentions of others, and with the ghosts of the dead. We arrive yet again at the issue of vocabulary and its relation to ways of seeing and ways of being. Perhaps again the whole point is, "Let all identifications contend" – as with Babel, so with Pentecost.

Notes

Introduction

1. The exact period spanned is 1952, the year of the publication of *A Brighter Sun* to 1975, the year *Moses Migrating* was published. Lamming's fictions fall between 1953 (*In the Castle of My Skin*) and 1972 (*Natives of My Person*).

2. Paquet's *The Novels of George Lamming,* one of the earliest and most important book-length studies on Lamming, makes only brief comments on the gender bias in Lamming's work, but her remarks are important as an index of the impact of the women's movement on literary criticism at the time. Other early comments – all small insertions in the context of larger projects – include Susan Craig's mention in a 1976 review of *Natives of My Person* and Elaine Campbell's 1983 reference to gender in *Season of Adventure* in a comparative discussion with Claude McKay's *Banana Bottom.* Gikandi, in his 1992 *Writing in Limbo,* notes the unusual gender departure in the character of Fola Piggott in *Season of Adventure;* although he goes on to make the untenable claim that Lamming here blazes a trail for West Indian women writers to follow, his brief comment is important as it represents perhaps the earliest recognition of the role of gender in Lamming's nation discourse. Supriya Nair's 1996 *Caliban's Curse* recognizes Lamming's overarching concern with male struggle and his concomitant displacement of male angst onto female characters. Christine Prentice's 2000 essay "Decolonizing the Allegorical Subject" includes reference to women characters in *In the Castle of My Skin.* Kathleen Ferracane's 1987 thesis on the mother in Lamming's work was the first full-length treatment but was by no means comprehensive; it was followed in 1995 by Mary Donnelly's psychoanalytic journal article on gender in *In the Castle of My Skin.* "The Sovereignty of the Imagination", a 2003 conference on Lamming organized by the Centre for Caribbean Thought at the University of the West Indies and the Africa Studies Department at Brown University in association with the UWI Department of Literatures in English, saw papers on gender in selected novels being presented by Patricia Saunders, Paula Morgan and myself.

3. The most substantial discussion of gender in Selvon up to 1988 was to be found in Harold Barratt's essay "From Colony to Colony: Selvon's Expatriate West Indians" (published in Nasta 1988), which comments on the immature gender relations of Selvon's boys in the London quartet. Other, "throwaway" references to women and gender in Nasta's collection include an essay "Time Has Not Tarnished This Novel" by Eric Roach (116–19) and Selvon's own contradictory statement on women in a 1977 interview with Michel Fabre: "The women [in my books] are the transmitters of culture . . . they are often closer to nature" (72). In the *Ariel* interview "Christened with Snow" (Roberts and Thakur 1996), Selvon objects to feminist accusations that he does not write about women. In the composite interview "Sam Selvon: A Celebration" (also in that volume), Ramabai Espinet mentions Selvon's treatment of race/gender relations and what she sees as his "insight into the way women feel and think" (58). All the book-length studies I have listed maintain Selvon quite unequivocally within the paradigms of history, community, language and race that have been traditionally used to read his fictions; Looker, however, unlike most critics of Selvon, recognizes the political nature of Selvon's work and locates the work "at the centre of postcolonial theoretical debates" (1996, cover blurb).

4. The Organisation of Eastern Caribbean States is an economic bloc that seeks to protect and provide a bargaining base for the Eastern Caribbean States, designated "Less Developed Countries" in trade transactions.

5. Present-day West Indian critics are often hostile to the term "canon", seeing it as aligned with European monologic enterprises of literary "purity". But the fact remains that this conscious drive to define the terms of literary West Indianness did take place and is still taking place. Brathwaite used the term very specifically (1993, 207–8).

6. See, for example, Chatterjee (1990) on the Indian context and Hageman (1993) on the Weimar Republic.

7. For discussions of educational and professional inequalities between the sexes, see, for example, Miller (1991a) and Senior (1991).

8. C. L. R. James (1989) insisted on responsibility as a criterion. The idea was also implicit in the essays of Lamming and Brathwaite, as, for example, in Lamming's "The Negro Writer and His World" (1958) and Brathwaite's "Roots" ([1963] 1993).

9. It may be argued that there is a kind of neo-Romanticism in Walcott's imaginist, individualistic approach to poetry in the early stages of his career. The contrast with his historically based and far more "communal" dramas, as well as with his later historicist positions (as indicated for example in his Nobel Prize address "Fragments of the Antilles"), is quite startling. Harris's concept of the (cross-cultural) imagination too has some resonances with Romanticism, particularly with the Worsdworthian view of Nature as imbued with divine energy. This provides part of the springboard for Harris's "universal" human tradition of

cultures, which would not have gone down well with the nationalists, who were more concerned with material history as cause and event than with time and space as phenomenology or with metaphysical referents.

10. The academy was for a long time caught in an odd contradiction by which it applied historicist/cultural critique paradigms to West Indian literature but continued to read "canonical" literatures by rigidly accepted New Critical codes. Very often the fixity in New Critical modes resulted in a return to old historicist methods of reading West Indian literature; that is, the history and cultural information were treated as background while the text continued to be read substantially as text, an isolated and bounded universe. See, for example, some of the essays in L. James (1967).

11. Carole Boyce Davies and Elaine Savory Fido, in their joint preface to *Out of the Kumbla* (1990), make a distinction between the terms "feminist" and "womanist" to indicate the diverse scope of feminist theory and to distinguish West Indian and other "Third World" branches of feminism from the Euro-American branch(es). Feminism is defined as the political agenda of feminism and as a way of describing the experience of Western and white women. Womanism is seen as the cultural manifestation of feminism (for example, customs, women's talk, women's lore) and as standing in place of feminism to define the differential experience of "Third World women". The term "womanist" was previously used by Alice Walker in *In Search of Our Mother's Gardens*. Walker used the term to mean "a black feminist or feminist of color" (1984, xi) but also to suggest the rootedness of the concept in black folk tradition and to point to her idea of the qualities that should characterize the black feminist. These qualities spanned the divide between rebellion and responsibility (xi). Davies and Fido have obviously extrapolated from Walker's conceptualization. I use the two terms "feminist" and "womanist" in hyphenated relationship to preserve the sense that Fido and Boyce Davies intended and to suggest the positions of all pro-woman women, regardless of ideological divergencies.

12. Neville Dawes, in his contribution to a 1955 tribute to Mais, oddly described Mais's style as "charming . . . [without being lacking in] masculinity" (162). Interestingly, Fred Wilmot in the same tribute used the following terms to describe Mais's language: "powerful, blunt-edged, shockingly direct, full of Roger" (169). Both the list of adjectives and the use of the male author's name as the focal signifier in the adjectival phrase that climaxes the list, point to a valorization of "masculine" language. (These two articles, Dawes's under the subtitle "Black Lightning", Wilmot's untitled, were among several that formed the tribute entitled "A Green Blade in Triumph" in *Kyk-over-Al* 6, no. 20.)

13. Also, in "Western Education and the Caribbean Intellectual": "I do not think there has been anything in human history quite like the meeting of Africa, Asia and Europe in this American archipelago we call the Caribbean" (1995, 25).

14. Parallels to this refusal of British canonical criteria exist within Britain itself – for example, in the Irish Renaissance and later in the work of James Joyce – indicating that British literature itself is far from being the monolith it suited the colonial establishment to promulgate.

15. See, for example, Kirpal (1997). Several theories of the Third World novel and of Third World writing generally have been advanced. Many seem to have been influenced in one way or another by Edward Said's seminal treatise *Orientalism* (1978), and a number of quarrels have been generated. See Ashcroft, Griffiths and Tiffin (1989), Dirlik (1994), Jameson (1987), Paranjape (1991) and Prasad (1992).

16. The Organisation of Eastern Caribbean States remains a strong centre of West Indian nationalism. CARICOM (the Caribbean Community) has since its foundation been a barometer and creator of fluctuating trends in regionalist/nationalist thought. Those countries such as Jamaica which have large numbers of their populations either living or commuting regularly abroad tend to exhibit signs of a more "elastic" nationalism. Among West Indian academics living abroad, this tendency, moving towards "diasporic thought", is also evident.

17. It should be noted, of course, that V. S. Naipaul, Selvon, Ismith Khan and some less well known Indo-West Indians (see Srivastava 1989) were writing the stories of Indo-West Indians throughout the nationalist period, but either without the kind of activist ethnic frame that seems to colour these recent works or without being received among critics as primarily ethnic constructions. Fiction by Indo-West Indian women began to appear mainly in the later (post-1970s) period.

    Chen's and Lee's are among the very few literary publications by Sino-Caribbeans. Chen's book is entitled *King of the Carnival.* Lee's three volumes of poetry, much of it autobiographical, are *From behind the Counter, Heritage Call: Ballads for Children of the Dragon* and *Encounters.* These were published by Ian Randle between 1998 and 2001.

    Writers of other ethnic groups (for example, H. G. Delisser, Earl Lovelace, Olive Senior, Merle Hodge and Edgar Mittelholzer) have represented Indo-West Indians in fiction. However, writing about Sino-West Indians by non-Chinese West Indians has been very sparse. Powell's novel appears as an attempt to demystify the proverbially "silent" Chinese. However, as a work by an Afro-West Indian who has never visited China or any other Chinese society, Powell's text is problematic both as a purportedly "inside" representation of Sino-West Indian experience and as a representation of Chinese culture within China itself. On the issue of fissures of authenticity in the text, see Chang (2001).

18. Roger Mais, for example, builds his stories on juxtaposed male-female dyadic and triadic groups typically circling a male isolate whose would-be superior "difference" is quite marked. Mais's male-female groupings work in the service of a social materialist philosophy aimed at showing the depredations of poverty, ignorance

and class subjugation, so that the relationships are generally pathological; the misogyny – inflected by class bias – at the base of Mais's text is consistently foregrounded in his female characters' total and often incredible lack of agency. See K. Dawes (1994).

19. I use the term "not-man" to refer to the concept in Euro-American masculinist ideology that one has to fulfil specific criteria related to property and authority in order to be considered a man. "Not-man" obviously includes women, girls and men of "other" races but also boys. In Western thinking, boys are considered as potentially masculine rather than as having arrived at masculine identity. Freudian psychoanalysis, with its location of heterosexual identity (which to Freud is the legitimate identity) in puberty, supports this view. The Renaissance practice of dressing children of both sexes in similar clothing except for the addition of a sword (symbol of the potential phallus) to the boy's regalia is one example of this view of children. Also see Walters (1993) for a discussion of the historical construction of boys' genderlessness.

20. "Postmodernism" refers to specifically Western theories/epistemological frames that have arisen in the postmodern age to explain various aspects of reality – most often textual – in ways that reflect the increasing insecurity and contestation but also the recalcitrance of traditional unitary (essentially hegemonic and imperialist) ways of seeing. Perhaps the major difference from "postcolonialism" is that the latter refers to the epistemological frames and theories that are brought to the analysis of these factors by the peoples of the former colonies of the West, and that postcolonial approaches are based in examinations of the specifics of colonial history. (Postmodernist Michel Foucault's discourse theory draws on history, but Western history, and in a more diffused form.) "Postmodernity" refers to a way of being-in-the-world and a mode of consciousness that reflects both a sensitive engagement with and a contribution to the changes that demystify traditional hegemonies and lead to more flexible and equitably empowering relations. It also has a negative edge – often underplayed in discourse – as it connotes an obverse side of rootlessness, anomie and dissonance.

21. West Indian taboos against homosexuality are very strong and previous treatments were often either veiled or censorial. Smith (1999) identifies Selvon's *The Lonely Londoners* as one such veiled treatment.

22. See, for example, Ashcroft, Griffiths and Tiffin (1989). Two recent volumes of *Ariel* include essays that use Caribbean/West Indian as springboards for evolving theory. See, for example, Deloughrey (2001), Ledent (2001), McCarthy and Dimitriadis (2000) and Prentice (2000).

23. See, for example, the special issue of *Ariel* called "Postcolonialism and Its Discontents" (January 1995), as well as the July 1995 issue.

24. Barry Chevannes has done important work in sociology, and Graham Dann in history. Feminist sociologists Dorian Powell (1986) and Christine Barrow (1998)

have also moved towards a less polarized view of the concepts of feminine and masculine as they operate in West Indian culture. Historian Janet Momsen (1998) has also recognized the transgression of gender spaces in post-Emancipation land arrangements. Literary work in the area of men's studies includes Michael Bucknor's "Staging Seduction: Masculine Performance: The Art of Sex in Colin Channer's Reggae Romance *Waiting in Vain*" (2004) and his "Troubled and Troubling Representations of Caribbean Masculinities Abroad: Austin Clarke's *The Origin of Waves*" (2001).

25. Selvon's *Moses Migrating* (1983), not treated in this book since it falls outside the selected period, is also, as its title indicates, a migration text. Here Selvon looks at the emigrant returning home.

Chapter 1

1. For example, *Jane's Career* (DeLisser 1914); *Becka's Buckra Baby* (McDermott 1903).

2. Hilary Beckles (1998, 1999) sees these instances as examples of gender differentiation, which I argue is not possible in a context where the slave is chattel and excluded from society. Other commentators who have noted the construction of genderlessness as a function of race and/or slavery include Spivak (1987) and Moglen (1993).

3. Augier and colleagues, in *The Making of the West Indies* (1960, 80–81), refer to plantation records that listed slaves along with cattle and horses as "livestock".

4. In Lorraine Hansberry's *A Raisin in the Sun* and James Baldwin's *Going to Meet the Man,* African-American usage of the term "the Man" designates the iconization of white middle-class masculinity, by which the American socio-political machinery is governed.

5. The colonial authorities in the West Indies, for example, were known for their elaborate Empire Day parades (treated with wonderful irony in Lamming's *In the Castle of My Skin*) and governors' military progresses reminiscent of the "royal progresses" of Elizabeth I. Elizabeth, a major author of the English nationalism that later translated into imperialist culture, was fond of parading herself in the provinces and city streets, in elaborate theatrical processions calculated to awe her subjects into submission. In a socio-political climate fraught with tension, riot and the constant threat of revolutionary insurrection, it was an astute political strategy, which actually seems to have helped to keep rebellion in check. (See Bristol 1998; Manning 1988; Mullaney 1988.)

6. The extent to which the more esoteric masks of the slave's gender representations confused and destabilized the master, who had no terms by which to read such unlooked-for manifestations, appears in narrative traces from the period in many

ways. Lewis (1861), for example, recounts a scene starring himself as the benevolent distributor of largesse to a group of slaves, who surprise him by not begging him for anything. Old women in the group apostrophize him as "my son" "my husband" "mi massa, mi *tata* [father]". In another episode, a seemingly unteachable slave, Strap, wakes him from slumber in the night to force him to admire his (Strap's) twin daughters, and in yet another, a woman insists on her child being baptized into the name "Shakespeare". Lewis is condescendingly amused by all of this ostensibly childlike behaviour, completely unaware of the subversive underside whereby the slaves undermine his position as colonial patriarch and exalt their own by vicarious possession.

7. Of course, it is useful to bear in mind that Prince could not read or write; her narrative is mediated by the British abolitionist perspective of her redactor as well as by the goals of the abolitionists who produced the narrative as a weapon in their anti-slavery campaign. Even so, the story is not negated as an example of the collective slave voice.

8. For a discussion of Esu's ambiguous gender, see Gates (1988). Brathwaite, interestingly, highlights the more general aspects of Esu's prototypical ambiguities as a figure of (Caribbean) re/presentation (1983, 41).

9. See Kumari (1988), Scholz (2001) and Stephen Feldman, "Collected Information about the Eunuchs of India Known as the Hijra", http://androgyne.0catch.com/hijrax.htm.

10. The terms "traditionalizing", "individualistic" and "charismatic" in reference to types of power and authority are based on Max Weber (1947).

11. See, for example, the discussion of early modern English constructions and punishments of female loquacity in Boose (1991).

12. *Samfie* (pronounced with the long *i* sound, as in "pie") and *mamaguy* (*v.t.*) are Jamaican and Trinidadian respectively for "to trick, to fool, to take for a ride".

13. Gordon Rohlehr (1992) has already argued that a West Indian morality, by virtue of the region's unique history in oppression, must be a unique invention, not based on any known tenets by which the conventional (implied Eurocentric) world judges itself.

14. Although women have always been involved in Rastafarianism, up to the 1950s it was the men who were visible, for a number of reasons. One was the violent ("racial-war") rhetoric associated with some of the leaders; another was their sudden influx on the streets of Kingston of the 1950s after police raids demolished their separatist settlement. This in the volatile socio-economic climate made the Rastaman a kind of symbol of working-class threat, particularly because of his radical dress. But also quite probably this higher visibility was because there were then many fewer women than men, and, in addition, Rastafarianism outlined misogynistic taboos that might well have kept the female members in the "private" sphere.

15. Reggae was not, however, a primarily Rastafarian phenomenon but a grass-roots, urban proletarian one. The erroneous tendency to identify the music with Rastafarianism resulted from a combination of the fame of Bob Marley, who was Rastafarian, the proliferation of Rasta artists on the reggae scene and the fact that many non-Rasta artistes presented themselves as Rasta in order to capitalize on the Marley connection.

16. I extrapolate this meaning of the term "*créolité*" from some underlying principles in the treatise *Éloge de la Créolité* by Jean Bernabé, Patrick Chamoiseau and Raphaël Confiant (1993). The authors "invented" the term to encompass a complex range of concepts of fusion, diversity and polysemy which they use to describe Martinican and, by extension, Caribbean identity. Aspects of their theory are controversial, but the basic principles of fusion, diversity and dissolution of boundaries are what I wish to highlight here.

17. "Speculative mirror" references Luce Irigaray's concave mirror/speculum trope, which she uses to describe the inferiorizing male gaze trained on the female and the feminine. Inevitably, the mirror in which the "other" is constructed trains the gaze back on the self, showing it to be utterly dependent on the "other" for its existence, its "superiority" and its validation. Indeed, the mirror reveals the self in the other.

18. Women participated in stickfighting during the nineteenth century.

19. "Tracing match" and "mapuis" are Jamaican and St Lucian respectively for "yard quarrel", which typically involves "tracing" the opponent's questionable (read "disgraceful") antecedents/ancestry for the benefit of the audience – that is, for the crowd that invariably gathers to watch and listen. Quarrels may begin as serious private affairs, but once they reach the space of the yard, the impetus to competitively entertain the crowd often displaces the original acrimony. To lose the tracing match is a serious disgrace, an unbearable form of defeat.

20. In Jamaica, "Big Boy" stories are apocryphal funny stories based on the legendary stupidity of Big Boy, a kind of transmuted country-bumpkin figure. Big Boy's stupidity is genuine but often subversive. The Barbadian equivalent is Ossie Moore.

21. The traditional image of the oral storyteller as female does not hold true for the Caribbean. Men as well as women perform this role, which is succinctly recalled by Bennett's merged dramatic personae.

22. During the 1970s, the National Pantomime, governed by a fiercely nationalist agenda, featured productions dominated by strong female characters leading communal recovery against the work of destructive male forces. The pantomime consistently staged women not only as political restorative, but also as the nation's conscience and moral voice. Sistren, a feminist working-class group which also emerged in the 1970s, evolved out of the "crash programme" initiated by Michael Manley to provide employment for the endemically un(der)employed. The programme had a notorious reputation, and Sistren is seen as one of its few

positive results. The collective uses drama to portray women's problems, such as sexual abuse and domestic violence, and to image possible solutions. All roles, including male ones, are performed by the all-female crew. Scripts are not pre-written but worked out in a workshop/rehearsal/audition setting in which the entire group has an input. The group's democratic and gender-crossing modes of performance, production and script-writing, as well as its social interventionist programme, have rendered it a kind of distilled representation of West Indian heterodox gender culture. Under the leadership of director Honor Ford-Smith, the group has acquired an international reputation and disseminates its work via international tours, videos, a magazine and the seminal text *Lionheart Gal* (Sistren 1986), a collection of the first-person narratives of the group members, radically told in their own voices and Creole language.

23. On women as "founding fathers" in the Garvey movement and on Garvey's essentially sexist allocation of "queenship" to women, see Ford-Smith (1988) and Martin (1988).

24. Prior to the emphasis on gender, most of the research on women in West Indian history tended to emerge via studies of family structure, as in pioneering works such as Blake's (1962) and Clarke's (1957). In most cases, it was the woman in the domestic setting who became visible.

25. Conclusions regarding the reconstitution of Indian gender norms as a result of "Middle Passage" and plantation experiences are extrapolated from historical discussions by Bisnauth (1977), Moore (1984) and Shepherd (1986).

26. Some of the newer evangelical and Pentecostal denominations which have emerged in the last few decades are an interesting mix of Afro-West Indian forms of worship, inherited patriarchalism and North American (neocolonial) influences. In many cases there is constant tension between the numerical dominance, volubility and activity of women on the one hand, and the ideological and practical dominance of men at the level of leadership, on the other.

27. A number of factors have combined to create a more fluid class/colour profile than existed during the nationalist period. In some countries, IMF/World Bank structural adjustment programmes have resulted in economic hardships for all social classes. This in turn led to a kind of "levelling down" among social classes. Migration to North America has increased opportunities for the working classes to acquire wealth. In an economically driven age, parental migration has also exposed more children of all classes to unorthodox family structure and familial experience. The removal of structural barriers to types of education across gender lines has also served to expose more originally working-class women to education and its concomitant ideologies, which are associated with middle-classicism. The political orientation of the 1970s has also allowed working-class subgroup voices and influences to permeate the societies. In short, West Indians have been exposed to similar experiences across the class divide.

28. In her survey of images of women in Indo-Caribbean literature, Aruna Srivastava finds such diversity that she concludes, "The unrelenting fragmentation and fluidity I encountered in trying to come to terms with the categories . . . 'Caribbean', 'Indian' 'feminist' – caused the playful theorist in me to dub this experience quintessentially postmodern" (1989, 114).

29. See Pat Mohammed's interview with V. S. Naipaul's mother (Mohammed 1993), and Lakshmi Persaud's novel *Butterfly in the Wind*.

30. I am indebted to Victor Chang of the University of the West Indies, Department of Literatures in English, for anecdotal information on the Chinese in the West Indies.

31. The Maroon heroine Nanny is widely reputed to have displayed supernatural powers, such as catching and neutralizing British bullets with her buttocks.

Chapter 2

1. The fourth of the exile novels that make up the London quartet is *Moses Migrating* (1983).

2. Brathwaite, in his 1957 essay "Sir Galahad and the Islands: The Folk in Caribbean Literature", sees a folk ethos in *The Lonely Londoners*. My own reading is that it is precisely the absence of a folk ethos that Tanty represents: her very singularity in the context of the boys' London experience suggests Tanty as an inscription of absence rather than presence.

3. "Samuel Selvon's Linguistic Extravaganza" is the title of a paper presented by Maureen Warner Lewis at the University of the West Indies, 1982.

Chapter 3

1. An example of this blatant unreading appears in Birbalsingh ([1977] 1988, 144), where he reads Tiger's outburst at the doctor's office as a sign of Tiger's desire for racial and cultural unity in the context of discourses of national identity. As discussed in this chapter, the incident is much more clearly linked to Tiger's guilt about his beating of Urmilla.

2. See, for example, the argument by Ramchand that at the end "Tiger has come through" despite the "areas of darkness currently being offered to West Indian society by its new academic doctors and historical pundits" (1988, 172).

3. My use of this term is an extrapolation from Irigaray (1985a). See chapter 6 for discussion.

4. Paraphrase of "There are no more elders / Is only old people", from Walcott's poem "The Saddhu of Couva" (1986, 373), originally published in *The Star-apple Kingdom* (1979).

5.   From the title of Evelyn O'Callaghan's book (1993).

6.   "Creole" has several meanings: it may refer to a person of European descent born and raised in the Caribbean, to the new languages forged in the Caribbean by the hybridization of European and African and/or indigenous languages, (as an adjective) to the hybridized nature of Caribbean society, or to a person of mixed European and African blood. Berta is in this last category.

Chapter 4

1.   In *Coming Coming Home* (1995, 12); Lamming is here quoting from Antonio Gramsci, whose words form the epigraph to the essay. Lamming speaks specifically of the West Indian intellectual but is clearly also referring to West Indians as a whole.

2.   Foucault's discourse theory (as in *The Archeology of Knowledge* and *The History of Sexuality*) is based on historical analysis but focuses more on how occult discursive systems are deployed in the shaping of corporate consciousness. What one might refer to as the more "concrete" factualities of history do not play a large part in his theories, in contrast to the emphasis given to these by West Indian nationalists and postcolonial theory in general. See chapter 6.

3.   Lamming's human being renders my use of the term "Subject" in this chapter somewhat problematic, as his concept is not synonymous with the usage of this term in current discourses, whether postcolonial or postmodern. Some theorists use "Subject" rather than "self" or "person" to negate the idea of a unitary or universal self or identity, as well as to convey the idea that the Subject is constituted in language. Others – deconstructionists in particular – ultimately do not believe in the factual existence of the Subject, seeing this as an endlessly reduced/delayed/deferred category formulated out of the reader's perception. Lamming, while sharing the view that one may inhabit multiple, dynamic identities, obviously also believes in an essential humanity, which is not adequately described by any vocabulary I can use here. The term *eidos,* used by the German phenomenologist Edmund Husserl, best describes this essentiality on which Lamming sees the diversities of Subjectness as being predicated. Martin Heidegger's *Dasein* – Being-as-consciousness-in-the-world (extrapolated from Husserl) – implicitly presupposes *eidos* as the very ground on which *Dasein* is possible. The discussion of the epistemology of the body in chapter 5 explains Lamming's concept, which fuses *eidos, Dasein* and Subjectness together.

4.   Lamming's comments in his 2002 interview with David Scott (111, 122–25) support my reading: here he very explicitly distances himself from a cultural Africanness and iterates his commitment to a Caribbean national selfhood.

5.   In speaking of the territories as being their own mother in Lamming's

representation, I refer to the fact that the concept is usually invested in the mother of one or more of his symbolic protagonists within the territory itself, such as Fola's mother in *Season of Adventure* and G's in *In the Castle of My Skin*. The protagonist, representing the adolescent nation, moves away from the mother and towards the father in order to find selfhood. In *Of Age and Innocence,* this process of erasure is taken to its logical conclusion, as the boys in whom the hope of true nationhood is invested do not seem to have any mothers at all. Interestingly, only in Europe (and this includes ancient Rome and Greece) does it seem conceivable for societies to be born without a female progenitor. As Joseph Campbell notes in his 1964 work *Occidental Mythology: The Masks of God,* other societies enshrine the maternal principle in their creation/genesis myths. Campbell argues that Judeo-Christian traditions enshrine the idea of a single patriarchal progenitor, but it seems clear that the Jews saw the maternal principle embodied in the figure of Eve. Further, the Old Testament representation of God (see, for example, Exodus 3:14, 20:1–4 and 33:17–20), as well as the representation in the Gospels (as in Luke 24:39; John 1, 4:24 and 6:46), indicates that God as Creator was originally seen as outside the social/material construct of gender. The patriarchal slant of Western religious discourse cannot be satisfactorily accounted for by recourse to the actual stories of origin, but rather to other aspects of gender representation in the Bible and in Western culture itself.

6. *Of Age and Innocence* and *Season of Adventure* are more immediately nationalist only in the sense that they deal directly with (albeit fictionalized) independence movements that did take place. But all Lamming's fictions are nationalist in intention.

7. Norval Edwards (1995) points to this aspect of West Indian hybridity. Critics who have commented negatively on Lamming's style include fellow writers Brathwaite, Harris and Naipaul, as well as Boxill (1973), Chukwu (1992), Marshall (1961), Van Sertima (1968) and Wickham (1961). A few among the first generation of critics, such as Stuart Hall (1955), John Thieme (1984), Sandra Pouchet Paquet and Gordon Rohlehr, did pay attention to the issue of a different aesthetics operating through Lamming's fictive style, but it is only in the last two decades that this has been given extended treatment, particularly by Gikandi (1992) and Edwards (1995).

8. On the concept of postmodernity, see the notes to the introduction. In David Scott (2002), Lamming indicates that he has not returned to the novel form as his published medium (since 1972) but is now substituting the direct "statement" as he feels it reaches more people (195–99).

9. The fictional(ized) events in San Cristobal are based on Guyana's struggles into republicanism. Lamming spent time in Guyana and was deeply interested in the political events.

10. Penelope's and Marcia's dissemination effort recalls Henry Swanzy's *Caribbean*

Voices, the radio programme that made West Indian writing available to the general – including the West Indian – public during the 1950s. Lamming was among those featured on the programme. Perhaps what is also recalled is the work of the multinational organization through which primary goods from the "Third World" are exported, transformed into manufactures in the metropoles and re-exported (as "made in England/USA") to their place of origin.

11. I am indebted to Norval Edwards for this insight.

12. Bhaku is based in part on Kofi Baako, a member of Kwame Nkrumah's government in 1960s Ghana, and partly on Eric Williams, prime minister of Trinidad in the 1960s and 1970s. San Cristobal in *Season of Adventure* is aligned not with Guyana's but with Trinidad's political history. But here again, San Cristobal represents the entire West Indies.

13. Greenblatt (1991) provides a cogent discussion of the role of the Renaissance (early modern) culture of wonder in the ideological construction of the "New World".

14. Lamming, in *The Pleasures of Exile,* spoke of the West Indian novelist as having "restored the West Indian peasant to his true and original status of personality" ([1960] 1992, 39).

Chapter 5

1. In an interview with George Kent (1973), Lamming notes his debt to Hakluyt's *Voyages,* particularly the voyages of Drake and Hawkins; and in *Coming Coming Home* (1995) he cites also Kidd, Las Casas, Montaigne and Esquemaling.

2. On the public regulation of personal life in that period, see, for example, Greenblatt (1980) and Manning (1980).

3. The idea of Europe as a continental community was itself a fledgling idea that emerged simultaneously and symbiotically with the Renaissance and the invention of the "New World".

4. Here Lamming parodies the eighteenth- and nineteenth-century travel narrative's propensity for dehistoricizing the landscape by speaking of it in romantic terms as virgin territory (to be conquered) and excluding all mention of the "natives". See Pratt (1992).

5. The idea that women who spoke "too much" were also sexually loose was common in early modern England (Boose 1991).

6. The Spanish "Pinteados" can be translated to mean "painted [man]", suggesting the inscrutability of a mask or of representation, or "[man of] paintings/painted things", suggesting an artist.

7. In his interview with Kent (1973), Lamming explained Pinteados as the type of the detached foreign technocrat, who does his job and refuses to "get involved".

Pinteados, by virtue at least of his detachment and probably of his foreignness, would not in Lamming's terms be a desirable figuration of the ideal West Indian man, whom Lamming sees as organically involved with his society. Pinteados's lack of involvement, however, is relative, and also paradoxical. His stance proceeds from a careful, principle-driven (and therefore ultimately morally driven) analysis which makes it clear to him that the crew's and officers' performances are hollow at the core and therefore not worth his participation. Detachment then becomes involvement, of the most responsible kind. Pinteados's relationship with the "mad" wife also speaks to this involvement which is also detachment. Where his detachment is more unequivocally seen is in his willingness to work for the Commandant, untroubled by the (im)moral aspects of the expedition. This flaw in Pinteados is what illustrates clearly the inadequacy of gender either as a means of description or as a means of judgement.

8. "Spades" refers to the spade in the deck of cards: black, and therefore undifferentiated – faceless, genderless – as well as lifeless.

9. "Prospero has been seen" is Lamming's own phrase, used in *The Pleasures of Exile* (for example, 158) to convey the idea that the West Indian writer ("the native") in the era of nationalism has come of age, in that he has recognized the colonizer's fraudulence and weakness.

10. This location of the beginning of West Indian history tends also to contradict Lamming's location of existence in *eidos,* beyond the historical construction of selves. His viewpoint contrasts with those of Brathwaite, who begins with "Sycorax's" history in Africa, and of Wilson Harris, who roots history in a concept of metaphysical connections manifested in a human collective unconscious symbolized in myths and archetypes.

11. European iconography from the sixteenth century onwards represented the Americas as a naked or semi-naked woman baring herself voluptuously to the conquering (European) male gaze. See Pratt (1992) and Montrose (1993).

Chapter 6

1. See the *Daily Gleaner* reports on the Jamaican uprisings, 2 May–30 June 1938. The constant refrain "men and women" – as in "men and women . . . smashed windows" ("Fatal Riot in Westmoreland", 3 May), "men and women writhing in pain" (ibid.), "crowds of workmen, women . . . preventing all business places from opening" ("The Strike So Far", 26 May), " a gang of . . . both sexes stopped work on the dam" ("Strike Now Hydra Headed", 14 June) – clearly indicates the extent to which the conservative *Gleaner,* like the *Trinidad Gazette* commenting on post-Emancipation carnival, felt the status quo to be threatened by the political involvement of women. Not only *Public Opinion,* but also the left-leaning *Jamaica*

Labour Weekly and *Plain Talk,* being arguably more ready to take women's participation as a given, made fewer gender descriptions, and these usually were made for heightened drama more than anything else, as in "labouring men and women and their children were willing to die" (*Plain Talk,* 4 June). Other historical documents reinforce the evidence that by the 1880s, not only were the people seeing themselves as an important part of the political process, but women were involved from the leadership downwards. (Examples include the 1844 riots in Dominica and the Morant Bay Rebellion in Jamaica.) See Heumann (1995) and S. Wilmot (1995).

2. Marlene Nourbese Philip is one critic who has been exercised a great deal by the issue of women's "silence". Several of her publications seek to dismantle this silence, which she sees as having been laid on women of the African diaspora by the removal of original (African) languages. It is precisely this idea that the black woman was/is silenced as the colonial master intended that I am questioning. See Philip's 1991 novella *Looking for Livingston: An Odyssey of Silence* and also the poetry collection *She Tries Her Tongue: Her Silence Softly Breaks* (1989).

3. I am using "Being" here in its meanings as *eidos* and *Dasein.*

4. See, for example, Chodorow (1978). Also, Nourbese Philip's *Looking for Livingstone* and Michelle Cliff's *Free Enterprise* are fictions based on strong feminist assertions of a healing female community. Negative aspects of female community based on childhood cathexes are by contrast presented in (Haitian) Edwidge Danticat's *Breath, Eyes, Memory* and Patricia Powell's *Me Dying Trial.*

5. Perhaps there is need to radically question the praxis of performance itself – not only its generic nature, but also its motivations and emotional sources in West Indian cultural behaviour. This kind of educational endeavour works best when undertaken by small community and non-governmental groups. On that note, it is worth mentioning that sociologist Barry Chevannes has, since the 1990s, been engaged in such interventionist work via his involvement with fathers' groups in working-class Kingston, Jamaica. However, the process may well include public policy informed by research from various disciplines and perspectives; people may need to go to school to learn parenting, healing speech and silence, drawing on the modes without necessarily the antagonisms of our speech culture; as a workshop and forum, we may well recreate Eric Williams's University of Woodford Square in diverse forms responsive to locale and other specifics of situation. Such a proposition of corporate acknowledgement that there are problems that need corporate solutions possibly returns us to a nationalism that is "anachronistic", and there is indeed the danger that in seeking to solve problems, we run the danger of singularizing an enormously rich and diverse cultural practice.

6. The term was first used by Kezia Page (1998). See also Burman (2002).

7. Although Boyce Davies recognizes and alludes to "horror stories" that indicate Caribbean women's suffering in the diasporic space, her overall stance is one of

celebration, indicated in the introductory statement by which she puts her book into perspective: "My mother's journeys redefine space. Her annual migrations, between the Caribbean and the United States, are [acts] of persistent re-membering and re-connection. She lives in the Caribbean; she lives in the United States. She lives in America. She also lives in that in-between space where her children, grandchildren, family and friends reside" (1994, 1). Boyce Davies refers to each of these places as "home spaces", arguing that her mother is able to critique each of these, and that "the re-negotiating of identities is fundamental to migration as it is to Black women's writing in cross cultural contexts" (3). She goes on to show how black women's migration texts are a positive indication of this. Gilroy too recognizes black suffering but sees the "restlessness" of blacks in diaspora not as a negative but as the crucial ingredient that makes diaspora culture "vital" (1993, 16). Gilroy further argues that the "black" challenge to modernity's totalizing ethos is relevant not only for black advancement, but also for a general world politics of "just, sustainable development" (223). For other discussions foregrounding black and postcolonial contribution to postmodernity and postmodernism, see Anzalduá (1987), Basch, Schiller and Blanc (1994), During (1985), Hanchard (1990), Hutcheon (1989), Said (1990) and Slemon (1989). See also Kenneth Ramchand's editorial in the January 1993 issue of *Ariel,* in which he voices his objectons to the terms "postmodernism" and "postcolonialism" as descriptors of Caribbean literature and theory.

8. In Cliff's narrative, the male slave Barabbas – who, as his name suggests, represents unsanctioned, subversive power – works undercover and weaves cloth like a woman.

9. Paulette Ramsay, *Aunt Jen*; Merle Collins, *The Colour of Forgetting*; Curdella Forbes, *Songs of Silence.* For an interesting discussion of Collins's gender inclusiveness in *Angel,* see Lima (1993).

10. The entry of Shakespeare's text into the West Indies is in itself a form of migration. Lamming's deployment of different tropes from the play into each of his fictions represents reverse migratory journeys for the play, both because Lamming's texts are "repatriated" to England for publication and because the constructed worlds of the texts span Europe and different parts of the Caribbean and perambulate freely among different time periods in history.

11. Despite its polarization between affective, intuitive and artistic aspects of knowledge (as distinctively African) and the scientific, analytical aspects (as distinctively European), Negritude aimed in essence to emphasize that all belong to a common humanity to which each culture had brought its unique offerings. Negritude envisaged a "Utopian" age when there would be mutual understanding and acceptance of each other's cultures by black and white. Jean-Paul Sartre, one of the champions of Negritude, in fact referred to it as "an anti racist racism" (1964–65, 18).

12. In *Brown Girl in the Ring*, Ti-Jeanne lives in a liminal ghetto that has been apocalyptically cut off from community by some technological and sociological upheaval. Here she is constantly harassed by denizens of a sinister underworld; the only attempts at contact by the world of the white and the powerful are exploitative in nature. In her guise as usurping female King of Carnival, the protagonist of *Midnight Robber* subverts male power, appropriates carnival texts across cultures and times, and traverses planetary spaces in her wide-ranging discovery and elaboration of spaces – but only at the cost of forcible retreat from the diasporic space in which she was born and the exilic one to which she is condemned, and always her retreat is a struggle to the death with a sexually abusive father.

13. D'Aguiar has said that the major influence on his writing, both poetry and fiction, has been his consciousness as a black male growing up between England and Guyana over two decades, in the 1960s and 1970s (Slade 1999).

14. Clarke uses the phrase "There Are No Elders" (Walcott) as the title of his short fiction collection *There Are No Elders* (2000).

15. Such female calypsonians include Singing Sandra and Denyse Plummer in Trinidad, and Jany Williams, Lady Leen and Lady Spice in St Lucia. Williams and Spice have been calypso monarchs. See also the column "Beat People" (18–20) and the article "Crossover Rhythms" (37–43) in the July/August 2003 issue of BWIA's in-flight magazine *Caribbean Beat*; both discuss "crossover" collaborations between male and female artistes at home and abroad.

16. Statistics from the University of the West Indies and other sources indicate that West Indian women surpass men in education and professional qualifications (tertiary-level education in Jamaica, for example, exceeds a 2:1 ratio across the board and, in individual programmes and institutions, may rise above but never fall below this ratio in favour of women). Yet claims about women's increasing psychological enfranchisement remain questionable. See, for example, Leo-Rhynie (1984) and Senior (1991).

17. Guyana and Trinidad have the largest Indian populations – in both, roughly half of the total population. Though Trinidad has had its share of race problems between its Afro and Indo populations, this has been far less than in the case of Guyana, which remains the least racially integrated of the West Indian territories. Both Dabydeens are from Guyana.

18. Michael G. Cooke (1990) has noted the close similarities between Brodber's and Lamming's work.

19. Other black presses, such as Fourth Estate, circulate similar representations. See, for example, Rocky Carr's *Brixton Boy* (1998).

20. This is true even of revisionist portrayals of black men at work and in relationships, as in Peter Kalu's *Lick Shot* (1993) and Michael Maynard's *Games Men Play* (1996).

21. Gilroy (1993), by contrast, rejects the concept of family as a description of diasporic black relations, seeing these as rooted in essentialisms rather than history.

22. Clarke is an older West Indian who lived in the region until his mid-twenties. He would then be very familiar with these types of normative behaviour on West Indian soil.

23. See, for example, *Coming Coming Home* (1995, 37). At a 2003 conference, Lamming reiterated these views in reference to the women writers.

24. Prestigious Jamaican high schools, including Wolmer's Boys School and Munro College, an all-boys' boarding institution, have been receiving such pupils from England since at least the late 1990s (see Mike Baker, "British Pupils Sent to Jamaican School", BBC, 11 March 2002, http://news.bbc.co.uk/1/hi/education/features/1863104.stm). In some cases, the children were actually born in Britain. In 2001 and again in 2004, delegations of British teachers visited Jamaican schools and interviewed teachers in the hope of finding solutions to the "problem" of teaching children of West Indian origin or descent.

25. Benítez Rojo's vision is not a wholesale embracement of postmodernism; rather, it is complex and marked with his own "double-visioned" sense of the problematics and pitfalls of reading the Caribbean through postmodernism. Similarly, Glissant's postmodernistic viewpoint in *Poetics of Relation* (2000), which addresses global relations, exists in tension and tandem with his more nationalistic *Caribbean Discourse* (1992). For a discussion, see Forbes (2002).

26. Final address at 2003 Conference, "The Sovereignty of the Imagination".

27. My use of chaos as trope throughout this book is based on a concept of liminal space – space that is "uncreated" and tensile between the imminent/immanent possibilities of creation and destruction. This is akin to the idea of chaos founded in creation stories such as the Greek and Hebrew. It is not linked to chaos theory in physics.

28. Makeda's text collates the stories of abused West Indian domestic workers in Canada. The stories are told in the women's own voices with Makeda as redactor, in the vein of Honor Ford-Smith's *Lionheart Gal,* the redacted stories of crash programme workers in 1970s Jamaica. I refer to such stories as "quasi-fictional" since the redactor's task of organization and editing, as well as the fictive devices associated with autobiography, inevitably mediates the "factuality" of any account. This is in no way meant to suggest inauthenticity but simply to highlight the problematics of representation that always call any claim to unmediated factuality into debate.

29. This is not to suggest that Caribbeanness should be externally decided or legislated, since obviously identity is a matter of choice and consciousness. But this is precisely the point: often descendants of Caribbeans in the West are refused recognition as nationals, even after generations (they may receive or be born into official recognition [citizenship] but not into the recognition of the community).

The question becomes not "When does one stop being Caribbean?", but rather, "When does one start being English or Canadian or American or . . .?"

30. It might not be surprising, for example, that an imagination of globality comes attractively to Benítez Rojo and Glissant, not only because of their positions within metropolitan academies, but also given their national histories: Martinique's continuing position as a département of France and the critical role played by Martinican intellectuals in the shaping of Negritude philosophy; the intersection of Cuba's revolutionary politics by its beginnings as a settler colony (in cultural terms more integrally, less combatively linked to the continental father/motherland as well as to South American counterparts than the West Indian colonies might have been). The fierce assertiveness of Cuba's political nationalism from its beginnings might also account for the central role unique identity plays in Benítez Rojo's globalism, as opposed to Glissant's greater emphasis on a pluralistic relationality. At the same time, a Cuban living in present-day revolutionary Cuba, for decades ostracized by and isolated from the West, might not necessarily embrace Benítez Rojo's American-influenced globalism.

31. For original constructions of these two terms, see Genesis 11 and Acts 2.

References

Anderson, Benedict. 1991. *Imagined Communities: Reflections on the Origin and Spread of Nationalism.* London: Verso.

Anzaldúa, Gloria. 1987. *Borderlands: The New Mestiza: La Frontera.* San Francisco: Spinsters/Aunt Lute.

Ashcroft, Bill, Gareth Griffiths and Helen Tiffin. 1989. *The Empire Writes Back: Theory and Practice in Post-colonial Literatures.* London: Routledge.

Augier, F. R., S. C. Gordon, D. G. Hall and M. Reckford. 1960. *The Making of the West Indies.* London: Longmans.

Bakhtin, Mikhail M. 1981. *The Dialogic Imagination: Four Essays.* Translated by Caryl Emerson and Michael Holquist. Austin: University of Texas Press.

Balutansky, Kathleen, and Marie-Agnes Sourieau, eds. 1998. *Caribbean Creolization: Reflections on the Cultural Dynamics of Language, Literature and Identity.* Gainesville: University Press of Florida.

Barrow, Christine. 1998. "Caribbean Masculinity and Family: Revisiting 'Marginality' and 'Reputation' ". In *Caribbean Portraits: Essays on Gender Ideologies and Identities,* edited by Christine Barrow, 339–58. Kingston, Jamaica: Ian Randle.

Basch, Linda, Nina Glick Schiller and Cristina Szanton Blanc. 1994. *Nations Unbound: Transnational Projects, Postcolonial Predicaments, and Deterritorialized Nation-States.* New York: Gordon & Breach.

Bascom, William R., and Herskovits, Melville J. 1959. *Continuity and Change in African Cultures.* Chicago: University of Chicago Press.

Bayley, F. W. N. 1830. *Four Years' Residence in the West Indies.* London.

Beckles, Hilary. 1988. *Afro-Caribbean Women and Resistance to Slavery in Barbados.* London: Karnak House.

———. 1989. *Natural Rebels: A Social History of Enslaved Black Women in Barbados.* New Brunswick, NJ: Rutgers University Press.

———. 1998. "Centering Woman: The Political Economy of Gender in West African and Caribbean Slavery". In *Caribbean Portraits: Essays on Gender Ideologies and Identities,* edited by Christine Barrow, 93–114. Kingston, Jamaica: Ian Randle.

————. 1999. *Centering Woman: Gender Discourses in Caribbean Slave Society.* Kingston, Jamaica: Ian Randle.

Benítez Rojo, Antonio. 1996. *The Repeating Island: The Caribbean and the Postmodern Perspective.* 2nd edition. Translated by James Maraniss. Durham, NC: Duke University Press.

Bennett, Alvin. [1964] 1973. *God the Stonebreaker.* London: Heinemann.

Bennett, Louise. 1966. *Jamaica Labrish.* Kingston, Jamaica: Sangster's Book Stores.

Bernabé, Jean, Patrick Chamoiseau and Raphaël Confiant. 1993. *Éloge de la Créolité.* Bilingual edition. Translated by M. B. Taleb-Kyar. Paris: Gallimard.

Besson, Jean. 1995. "Land, Kinship and Community in the Post-Emancipation Caribbean: A Regional View of the Leewards". In *Small Islands, Large Questions: Society, Culture and Resistance in the Post-Emancipation Caribbean,* edited by Karen Fog Olwig, 73–99. London: Frank Cass.

Birbalsingh, Frank. [1977] 1988. "Samuel Selvon and the West Indian Literary Renaissance". In *Critical Perspectives on Sam Selvon,* edited by Susheila Nasta, 142–59. Washington, DC: Three Continents Press.

————, ed. 1996a. *Frontiers of Caribbean Literature in English.* London: Macmillan Caribbean.

————. 1996b. "Sam Selvon: A Celebration". Interviews with Austin Clarke, Jan Carew, Ramabai Espinet and Ismith Khan. *Ariel* 27, no. 2: 49–64.

Bisnauth, Dale A. 1977. "The East Indian Immigrant Society in British Guiana 1891–1930". PhD dissertation, University of the West Indies.

Blake, Judith. 1962. *Family Structure in Jamaica: The Social Context of Reproduction.* In collaboration with J. Mayone Stycos and Kingsley Davis. New York: Free Press of Glencoe.

Boehmer, Elleke. 1992. "Motherlands, Mothers and Nationalist Sons: Representations of Nationalism and Women in African Literature". In *From Commonwealth to Postcolonial,* edited by Anna Rutherford, 229–47. Sydney, Australia: Dangaroo Press.

Boose, Lynda. 1991. "Scolding Brides and Bridling Scolds: Taming the Woman's Unruly Member in Early Modern England". *Shakespeare Quarterly* 42: 179–213.

Boxill, Anthony. 1973. "San Cristobal Unreached". *World Literature Written in English* 12, no. 1: 111–16.

Boyce Davies, Carole. 1994. *Black Women, Writing and Identity: Migrations of the Subject.* London: Routledge.

Boyce Davies, Carole, and Elaine Savory Fido, eds. 1990. *Out of the Kumbla: Caribbean Women and Literature.* Trenton, NJ: Africa World Press.

Brand, Dionne. 1989. *San Souci and Other Stories.* Toronto, Canada: Women's Press.

————. 1997. *In Another Place, Not Here.* New York: Grove Press.

————. 2001. *A Map to the Door of No Return: Notes to Belonging.* Toronto, Canada: Doubleday–Vintage Canada.

Brathwaite, Kamau [Edward]. [1957] 1993. "Sir Galahad and the Islands: The Folk in Caribbean Literature". In Kamau Brathwaite, *Roots,* 28–54. Ann Arbor: University of Michigan Press.

———. [1963] 1993. "Roots". In Kamau Brathwaite, *Roots,* 28–54. Ann Arbor: University of Michigan Press.

———. 1967. "Jazz and the West Indian Novel". *Bim* 11, no. 44: 275–84.

———. 1971. *The Development of Creole Society in Jamaica 1770–1820.* Oxford: Clarendon Press.

———. 1974. *Contradictory Omens: Cultural Diversity and Integration in the Caribbean.* Mona, Jamaica: Savacou.

———. 1983. "Caribbean Culture: Two Paradigms". In *Missile and Capsule,* edited by Jürgen Martini, 9–54. Bremen, Germany: University of Bremen.

———. 1993. "The African Presence in Caribbean Literature". In Kamau Brathwaite, *Roots,* 190–258. Ann Arbor: University of Michigan Press.

Breen, Henry H. [1844] 1970. *St Lucia: Historical, Statistical and Descriptive.* London: Taylor and Francis.

Bristol, Michael D. 1998. *Big Time Shakespeare.* London: Routledge.

Brodber, Erna. 1980. *Jane and Louisa Will Soon Come Home.* London: New Beacon.

———. 1983. *Myal.* London: New Beacon.

———. 1988. *Louisiana.* London: New Beacon.

Bucknor, Michael. 2001. "Troubled and Troubling Representations of Caribbean Masculinities Abroad: Austin Clarke's *The Origin of Waves*". Paper presented at the Twentieth Annual Conference on West Indian Literature, St Augustine, Trinidad. 1–3 March.

———. 2004. "Staging Seduction: Masculine Performance: The Art of Sex in Colin Channer's Reggae Romance *Waiting in Vain*". *Interventions: The International Journal of Postcolonial Studies* 6, no. 1: 67–81.

Burman, Jeremy. 2002. "Remittance: Or, Diasporic Economies of Yearning". *Small Axe* 12: 49–71.

Bush, Barbara. 1985. "Towards Emancipation: Slave Women and Resistance to Coercive Labour Regimes in the British West Indian Colonies 1790–1838". In *Abolition and Its Aftermath,* edited by David Richardson, 27–54. London: Frank Cass.

———. 1990. *Slave Women in Caribbean Society 1650–1838.* Kingston, Jamaica: Heinemann.

Campbell, Elaine. 1983. "Two West Indian Heroines: Bita Plant and Fola Piggott". *Caribbean Quarterly* 29, no. 2: 22–29.

Campbell, Joseph. 1964. *Occidental Mythology: The Masks of God.* Harmondsworth, UK: Penguin.

Chang, Victor L. 2001. "Uncertainties of Self: Patricia Powell's *The Pagoda*". Paper presented at the Twentieth Annual Conference on West Indian Literature, St Augustine, Trinidad. 1–3 March.

Channer, Colin. 1999. *Waiting in Vain.* New York: Ballantine.

———. 2002. *Satisfy My Soul.* New York: Ballantine.

Chatterjee, Partha. 1990. "The Nationalist Resolution of the Women's Question". In *Recasting Women: Essays in Colonial History,* edited by Kum Kum Sangara and Sudesh Vaid, 233–53. New Brunswick, NJ: Rutgers University Press.

Chen, Willi. 1988. *King of the Carnival and Other Stories.* London: Hansib.

Chevannes, Barry, ed. 1995. *Rastafari and Other Afro-Caribbean Worldviews.* The Hague: Macmillan.

Chodorow, Nancy. 1978. *The Reproduction of Mothering: Psychoanalysis and the Sociology of Gender.* Berkeley: University of California Press.

Chukwu, Austin. 1992. "Mad-Men and Sane Boys". *Commonwealth Novel in English* 5, no. 2: 49–65.

Clarke, Austin. 1967. *The Meeting Point.* Toronto, Canada: Vintage.

———. 1980. *Growing Up Stupid under the Union Jack.* Toronto, Canada: McClelland and Stewart.

———. 1997. *The Origin of Waves.* Toronto, Canada: McClelland and Stewart.

———. 1999. *The Question.* Toronto, Canada: McClelland & Stewart.

———. 2000. *There Are No Elders.* Toronto, Canada: Exile.

———. 2003. *The Polished Hoe.* Kingston, Jamaica: Ian Randle.

Clarke, Edith. 1957. *My Mother Who Fathered Me: A Study of the Family in Three Selected Communities in Jamaica.* London: Allen & Unwin.

Cliff, Michelle. 1984. *Abeng.* Trumansburg, NY: Crossing Press.

———. 1989. *No Telephone to Heaven.* New York: Vintage.

———. 1993. *Free Enterprise.* New York: Dutton.

Cobham, Rhonda. 1990. "Women in Jamaican Literature 1900–1950". In *Out of the Kumbla: Caribbean Women and Literature,* edited by Carole Boyce Davies and Elaine Savory Fido, 195–222. Trenton, NJ: Africa World Press.

Columbus, Christopher. 1969. *The Four Voyages of Christopher Columbus.* Edited and translated by J. M. Cohen. Harmondsworth, UK: Penguin.

Cooke, Michael G. 1990. "The Strains of Apocalypse: Lamming's *Castle* and Brodber's *Jane and Louisa*". *Journal of West Indian Literature* 4, no. 1: 28–40.

Covi, Giovani. 1990. "Jamaica Kincaid and the Resistance to Canons". In *Out of the Kumbla: Caribbean Women and Literature,* edited by Carole Boyce Davies and Elaine Savory Fido, 345–54. Trenton, NJ: Africa World Press.

Craig, Susan. 1976. "A Ruthless Rootless Enterprise: Notes and Impressions on Reading George Lamming's *Natives of My Person. Kairi* 8–9.

Cucchiari, Salvatore. 1991. "The Gender Revolution and the Transition from Bisexual Horde to Patrilocal Band: The Origins of Gender Hierarchy". In *Sexual Meanings: The Cultural Construction of Gender and Sexuality,* edited by Sherry B. Ortner and Harriet Whitehead, 31–79. Cambridge: Cambridge University Press.

Dabydeen, Cyril. 1996. *Berbice Crossing and Other Stories.* Leeds, UK: Peepal Tree.

———. 2001. *North of the Equator.* Vancouver, Canada: Porcepic.

Dabydeen, David. 1996. *The Counting House.* London: Jonathan Cape.

———. 2000. *The Intended.* London: Vintage.

D'Aguiar, Fred. 1994. *The Longest Memory.* London: Chatto and Windus.

———. 1996. *Dear Future.* New York: Pantheon.

———. 1997. *Feeding the Ghosts.* London: Chatto and Windus.

Davidson, Basil. 1984. *The Story of Africa.* London: Mitchell Beazley/Channel 4.

Davidson, R. B. 1966. *Black British.* London: Oxford University Press.

Dawes, Kwame. 1994. "Violence and Patriarchy: Male Domination in Roger Mais' *Brother Man*". *Ariel* 25, no. 3: 19–49.

Dawes, Neville. 1955. "Black Lightning", tribute to Roger Mais, in "A Green Blade in Triumph". *Kyk-over-Al* 6, no. 20: 161–62.

Deloughrey, Elizabeth. 2001. "Caribbean and Pacific Archipelagraphy". *Ariel* 32, no. 1: 21–52.

De Reid, Ira. 1969. *The Negro Immigrant: His Background, Characteristics and Social Adjustment 1899–1937.* New York: Arno Press.

Dirlik, Arif. 1994. "The Postcolonial Aura: Third World Criticism in the Age of Global Capitalism". *Critical Inquiry* 20: 328–56.

Donnelly, Mary. 1995. "Mother Country, Father Country: George Lamming's *In the Castle of My Skin* and Oedipal Structures of Colonialism". *Ariel* 26, no. 4: 7–20.

During, Simon. 1985. "Postmodernism or Postcolonialism?" *Landfall* 39: 366–80.

Edmondson, Belinda. 1999. *Making Men: Gender, Authority and Women's Writing in Caribbean Narrative.* Durham, NC: Duke University Press.

Edwards, Bryan. 1801. *The History, Civil and Commercial, of the British Colonies in the West Indies.* London.

Edwards, Norval. 1995. "On the Edge of Writing and Speech: Towards a West Indian Ethnopoetics". PhD dissertation, York University.

Ferguson, Moira, ed. 1993. *The Hart Sisters: Early African Caribbean Writers, Evangelicals and Radicals.* Lincoln: University of Nebraska Press.

Ferracane, Kathleen. 1987. "Images of the Mother in Caribbean Literature: Selected Novels of George Lamming". PhD dissertation, University of New York at Buffalo.

Forbes, Curdella. 2002. "The End of Nationalism? Performing the Question in Benítez-Rojo's *The Repeating Island* and Glissant's *Poetics of Relation*". *Journal of West Indian Literature* 10, no. 2: 2–19.

———. 2003. "Resisting the Voyeuristic Gaze: The Construction of Gender as Anti Colonial Discourse in the novels of George Lamming". Paper presented at the conference "The Sovereignty of the Imagination", in honour of George Lamming. Centre for Caribbean Thought, University of the West Indies, Mona, and Department of Africana Studies, Brown University, in association with the Department of Literatures in English, University of the West Indies, Mona, Jamaica. 5–7 June.

Ford-Smith, Honor. 1988. "Women and the Garvey Movement in Jamaica". In *Garvey: His Work and Impact,* edited by Rupert Lewis and Patrick Bryan, 73–83. Mona, Jamaica: Institute of Social and Economic Research and Department of Extra-Mural Studies, University of the West Indies.

Fromm, Erich. 1941. *Escape from Freedom.* New York: Discus Books.

Gates, Henry Louis, Jr. 1988. *The Signifying Monkey: A Theory of Afro-American Literary Criticism.* New York: Oxford University Press.

Gikandi, Simon. 1989. "Narration in the Postcolonial Moment: Merle Hodge's *Crick Crack Monkey*". *Ariel* 20, no. 4: 18–30.

———. 1992. *Writing in Limbo: Modernism and Caribbean Literature.* Ithaca, NY: Cornell University Press.

Gilroy, Beryl. 1991. *Stedman and Joanna, a Love in Bondage: Dedicated Love in the Eighteenth Century.* New York: Vantage.

Gilroy, Paul. 1993. *The Black Atlantic: Modernity and Double Consciousness.* London: Verso.

Glissant, Édouard. 1992. *Caribbean Discourse: Selected Essays.* Translated by J. Michael Dash. Charlottesville: University Press of Virginia. Original published in 1981.

———. 2000. *Poetics of Relation.* Translated by Betty Wing. Ann Arbor: University of Michigan Press. Original published in 1990.

Goveia, Elsa. 1965. *Slave Society in the British Leeward Islands at the End of the 18th Century.* New Haven, CT: Yale University Press.

Greenblatt, Stephen J. 1980. *Renaissance Self-Fashioning: From More to Shakespeare.* Chicago: University of Chicago Press.

———. 1991. *Marvelous Possessions: The Wonder of the New World.* Oxford: Clarendon.

Hageman, Karen. 1993. "Men's Demonstrations and Women's Protests: Gender in Collective Action in the Urban Working Class Milieu during the Weimar Republic". *Gender and History* 5, no. 1: 101–19.

Hall, Stuart. 1955. "Lamming, Selvon: Some Trends in the West Indian Novel". *Bim* 6, no. 23: 172–78.

———. 1988. "Migration from the English Speaking Caribbean to the United Kingdom 1958–1980". In *International Migration Today,* vol. 1, *Trends and Prospects,* edited by Reginald Appleyard, 264–310. Paris: UNESCO and University of Western Australia Centre for Migration and Development Studies.

Hanchard, Michael. 1990. "Identity, Meaning and the African American". *Social Text* 24: 31–42.

Harris, Wilson. 1967. *Tradition, the Writer and Society: Critical Essays.* London: New Beacon.

———. 1983. *The Womb of Space: The Cross-cultural Imagination.* Westport, CT: Greenwood.

———. 1999. *Selected Essays of Wilson Harris: The Unfinished Genesis of Imagination.* Edited by Andrew Bundy. London: Routledge.

Henriques, Fernando. 1974. *Children of Caliban.* London: Secker and Warburg.

Herskovits, M. L., and Frances S. Herskovits. 1947. *Trinidad Village.* New York: Knopf.

Heumann, Gad. 1995. "Post-Emancipation Resistance in the Caribbean: An Overview". In *Small Islands, Large Questions: Society, Culture, and Resistance in the Post-Emancipation Caribbean,* edited by Karen Fog Olwig, 123–34. London: Frank Cass.

Hodge, Merle. 1970. *Crick Crack Monkey.* London: André Deutsch.

Hopkinson, Nalo. 1998. *Brown Girl in the Ring.* New York: Warner.

———. 2000. *Midnight Robber.* New York: Warner.

Hoving, Isabel. 2001. *In Praise of New Travelers: Reading Caribbean Migrant Women's Writing.* Stanford, CA: Stanford University Press.

Hutcheon, Linda. 1989. "Circling the Downspout of Empire: Post-colonialism and Postmodernism". *Ariel* 20, no. 1: 149–75.

Irigaray, Luce. 1985a. *Speculum of the Other Woman.* Translated by Gillian G. Gill. Ithaca, NY: Cornell University Press.

———. 1985b. *This Sex Which Is Not One.* Tranlated by Catherine Porter with Carolyn Burke. Ithaca, NY: Cornell University Press.

James, C. L. R. 1936. *Minty Alley.* London: Secker and Warburg.

———. 1965. "A New View of West Indian History". Lecture delivered at the University of the West Indies, Mona, Jamaica, 3 June.

———. 1989. "A New View of West Indian History". *Caribbean Quarterly* 35, no. 4: 49–70.

James, Louis, ed. 1967. *The Islands in Between: Essays on West Indian Literature.* London: Oxford University Press.

Jameson, Fredric. 1987. "World Literature in an Age of Multinational Capitalism". In *The Current in Criticism: Essays on the Present and Future of Literary Theory,* edited by Clayton Koelb and Virgil Lokke, 139–58. West Lafayette, IN: Purdue University Press.

Joseph, Margaret Paul. 1992. *Caliban in Exile: The Outsider in Caribbean Fiction.* New York: Greenwood.

Karlen, Arno. 1971. *Sexuality and Homosexuality: A New View.* New York: Norton.

Kent, George. 1973. "A Conversation with George Lamming." *Black World* 22, no. 5 (March): 4+.

Khan, Ismith. 1961. *The Jumbie Bird.* New York: Longman.

Kirpal, Viney. 1997. "George Lamming's *In the Castle of My Skin*: A Modern West Indian Novel". *Ariel* 28, no. 2: 103–14.

Kumari, Ranjana. 1988. *Female Sexuality in Hinduism.* Delhi: Banhi Series Joint Women's Programme.

Lamming, George. [1953] 1987. *In the Castle of My Skin.* London: Longman.

———. [1954] 1997. *The Emigrants.* Ann Arbor: University of Michigan Press.

———. 1958. "The Negro Writer and His World". *Caribbean Quarterly* 5, no. 2: 109–15.

————. [1958] 1981. *Of Age and Innocence*. London: Allison and Busby.

————. [1960] 1999. *Season of Adventure*. London: Allison and Busby.

————. [1960] 1992. *The Pleasures of Exile*. Ann Arbor: University of Michigan Press.

————. [1971] 1972. *Water with Berries*. 1971. New York: Holt, Rinehart and Winston.

————. [1972] 1992. *Natives of My Person*. Ann Arbor: University of Michigan Press.

————. 1995. *Coming Coming Home: Conversations II*. Introduction by Rex Nettleford. Translated by Daniella Jeffry. Philipsburg, St Martin: House of Nehesi.

Ledent, Bénédicte. 2001. "A Fictional and Cultural Labyrinth: Caryl Phillip's 'The Nature of Blood' ". *Ariel* 32, no. 1: 185–96.

Lee, Easton. 1998. *From behind the Counter*. Kingston, Jamaica: Ian Randle.

————. 2001a. *Encounters*. Kingston, Jamaica: Ian Randle.

————. 2001b. *Heritage Call: Ballads for Children of the Dragon*. Kingston, Jamaica: Ian Randle.

Leo-Rhynie, Elsa. 1984. "The Status of Women in Education in Jamaica, Midway in the UN Decade for Women 1975–1985". Paper presented at the symposium sponsored by the Women's Studies Working Group, Kingston, Jamaica. 13 December.

Lewis, Matthew Gregory. 1861. *Journal of a Residence among the Negroes in the West Indies*. London.

Lewis, Maureen Warner. 1982. "Samuel Selvon's Linguistic Extravaganza". Paper presented at the Inter-Departmental Conference of the Departments of English, Mona, Jamaica, University of the West Indies. 19–21 May.

Lima, Marie Helena. 1993. "Revolutionary Developments: Michelle Cliff's *No Telephone to Heaven* and Merle Collin's *Angel* ". *Ariel* 24, no. 1: 35–56.

Lipsitz Bem, Sandra. 1993. *The Lenses of Gender*. New Haven, CT: Yale University Press.

Looker, Mark. 1996. *Atlantic Passages: History, Community and Language in the Fiction of Sam Selvon*. New York: Peter Lang.

Look Lai, Walton. 1998. *Chinese in the West Indies 1806–1995: A Documentary History*. Kingston, Jamaica: University of the West Indies Press.

Long, Edward. [1774] 1970. *The History of Jamaica*. 3 vols. London: Frank Cass.

Lovelace, Earl. 1982. *The Wine of Astonishment*. London: André Deutsch.

Lyotard, Jean-François. 1979. *The Postmodern Condition: A Report on Knowledge*. Translated by Geoff Bennington and Brian Massumi. Manchester, UK: Manchester University Press.

Mair, Lucille Mathurin. 1974. "A Historical Study of Women in Jamaica 1655–1844". PhD dissertation, University of the West Indies.

Mais, Roger. [1953] 1970. *The Hills Were Joyful Together*. Kingston, Jamaica: Sangster's Book Stores/Jonathan Cape.

————. [1954] 1970. *Brother Man*. Kingston, Jamaica: Sangster's Book Stores/Jonathan Cape.

————. [1955] 1970. *Black Lightning.* Kingston, Jamaica: Sangster's Book Stores/
Jonathan Cape.

Manley, Norman Washington. 1971. *Norman Washington Manley and the New Jamaica:
Selected Speeches 1938–1968.* Edited by Rex Nettleford. London: Longman Caribbean.

Manning, Roger B. 1988. *Village Revolts: Social Protest and Popular Disturbance in
England 1509–1640.* Oxford: Clarendon.

Marshall, Dawn. 1987. "A History of West Indian Migration: Overseas Opportunities
and 'Safety-Valve' Policies". In *The Caribbean Exodus,* edited by B. B. Levine,
15–31. New York: Praeger.

Marshall, H. 1961. Review of *The Pleasures of Exile,* by George Lamming. *Bim* 8,
no. 32: 59–290.

Martin, Tony. 1988. "Women in the Garvey Movement". In *Garvey: His Work and
Impact,* edited by Rupert Lewis and Patrick Bryan, 67–72. Mona, Jamaica: Institute
of Social and Economic Research and Department of Extra-Mural Studies,
University of the West Indies.

McCarthy, Cameron, and Greg Dimitriadis. 2000. "Art and the Postcolonial
Imagination: Rethinking the Institutionalization of Third World Aesthetics and
Theory". *Ariel* 31, nos 1–2: 231–53.

McKay, Claude. 1933. *Banana Bottom.* New York: Harper Brothers.

Meeks, Brian, and Folke Lindahl, eds. 2001. *New Caribbean Thought: A Reader.*
Kingston, Jamaica: University of the West Indies Press.

Miller, Errol, ed. 1991a. *Education and Society in the Commonwealth Caribbean.* New
York: Institute of Social and Economic Research, University of the West Indies;
Institute for the Study of Man.

————. 1991b. *Men at Risk.* Kingston, Jamaica: Jamaica Publishing House.

Moglen, Helen. 1993. "Redeeming History: Toni Morrison's *Beloved* ". *Cultural
Critique* 24: 17–40.

Mohammed, Patricia. 1993. "Structures of Experience: Gender, Ethnicity and Class in
Trinidad". In *Trinidad Ethnicity,* edited by K. A. Yelvington, 208–34. London:
Macmillan.

————. 1995. "Writing Gender into History: The Negotiation of Gender Relations
among Indian Men and Women in Post-indenture Trinidad Society, 1917–47". In
Engendering History: Caribbean Women in Historical Perspective, edited by Verene
Shepherd, Bridget Brereton and Barbara Bailey, 20–47. Kingston, Jamaica: Ian
Randle.

Momsen, Janet Henshall. 1998. "Gender Ideology and Land". In *Caribbean Portraits:
Essays on Gender Ideologies and Identities,* edited by Christine Barrow, 115–32.
Kingston, Jamaica: Ian Randle.

Montrose, Louis. 1993. "The Work of Gender in the Discourse of Discovery". In *New
World Encounters,* edited by Stephen Greenblatt, 197–217. Berkeley: University of
California Press.

Moore, Brian. 1984. "Sex and Marriage among East Indian Immigrants in British Guiana during the Nineteenth Century". Paper presented at Third Annual Conference on East Indians in the Caribbean, University of the West Indies, St Augustine. 28 August–5 September.

———. 1995. *Cultural Power, Resistance and Pluralism: Colonial Guyana 1838–1900.* Montreal: McGill-Queen's University Press.

Morgan, Paula. 2003. "As It Was in the Beginning: Originary Violations in *Water with Berries* and *Natives of My Person*". Paper presented at the conference "The Sovereignty of the Imagination", in honour of George Lamming. Centre for Caribbean Thought, University of the West Indies, Mona, and Department of Africana Studies, Brown University, in association with the Department of Literatures in English, University of the West Indies, Mona, Jamaica. 5–7 June.

Mullaney, Steven. 1988. *The Place of the Stage: License, Play and Power in Renaissance England.* Chicago: University of Chicago Press.

Naipaul, V. S. 1961. *A House for Mr Biswas.* New York: McGraw-Hill.

Nair, Supriya. 1996. *Caliban's Curse: George Lamming and the Revisioning of History.* Ann Arbor: University of Michigan Press.

Nasta, Shusheila, ed. 1988. *Critical Perspectives on Sam Selvon.* Washington, DC: Three Continents Press.

Nettleford, Rex. 1971. "Introduction". *Norman Washington Manley and the New Jamaica: Selected Speeches 1938–1968,* edited by Rex Nettleford. London: Longman Caribbean.

Nourbese Philip, Marlene. 1997. *A Genealogy of Resistance and Other Essays.* Toronto: Mercury Press.

Nugent, Maria. 1839. *Journal of a voyage to, and residence in, the island of Jamaica, from 1801 to 1805, and of subsequent events in England from 1805–1811.* London: T. and W. Boone.

O'Callaghan, Evelyn. 1993. *Woman Version: Theoretical Approaches to West Indian Fiction.* New York: St Martin's Press.

Olwig, Karen Fog, ed. 1995. *Small Islands, Large Questions: Society, Culture and Resistance in the Post-Emancipation Caribbean.* London: Frank Cass.

Page. Kezia. 1998. " 'Send It Western Union': The Remittance Text from Exile: Jamaica Kincaid's *My Brother*". Paper presented at the Annual West Indian Literature Conference, University of the West Indies, Mona, Jamaica. March.

Paquet, Sandra Pouchet. 1982. *The Novels of George Lamming.* London: Heinemann.

———. 2002. *Caribbean Autobiography: Cultural Identity and Representation.* Madison: University of Wisconsin Press.

Paranjape, Makarand R. 1991. "The Ideology of Form: Notes on the Third World Novel". *Journal of Commonwealth Literature* 26, no. 2: 71–84.

Patterson, Orlando. 1982. *Slavery and Social Death.* Cambridge, MA: Harvard University Press.

Pearse, Andrew. 1956. "Carnival in 19th Century Trinidad". *Caribbean Quarterly* 3–4 (May/June): 175–93.

Pereira, Joseph. 1998. "Babylon to Vatican: Religion in the Dancehall". *Journal of West Indian Literature* 8, no. 1: 31–40.

Phillips, Caryl. 1987. *The European Tribe*. London: Faber and Faber.

———. 1991. *Cambridge*. New York: Vintage.

———. 1997a. "George Lamming Talks to Caryl Phillips". *Wasafiri* 26 (Autumn): 10–17.

———. 1997b. *The Nature of Blood*. London: Faber.

Porter Poole, F. J. 1991. "Transforming 'Natural Woman': Female Ritual Leaders and Gender Ideology among Birmin-Kuskusmin". In *Sexual Meanings: The Cultural Construction of Gender and Sexuality,* edited by Sherry B. Ortner and Harriet Whitehead, 116–65. Cambridge: Cambridge University Press.

Powell, Dorian. 1986. "Caribbean Women and their Response to Familial Experiences". *Social and Economic Studies* 35, no. 2: 83–130.

Powell, Patricia. 1999. *The Pagoda*. San Diego, CA: Harcourt Brace.

———. 2003. *A Small Gathering of Bones*. Boston: Beacon.

Prasad, Madhava. 1992. "On the Question of a Theory of (Third World) Literature". *Social Text* 31–32: 57–83.

Pratt, Mary Louise. 1992. *Imperial Eyes: Travel Writing and Transculturation*. London: Routledge.

Prentice, Christine. 2000. "Out of the Pre-texts of Imperialism into 'a Future They Must Learn': Decolonizing the Allegorical Subject". *Ariel* 31, nos 1–2: 203–29.

Prince, Mary. [1831] 1997. *The History of Mary Prince: A West Indian Slave, Related by Herself*. Edited by Moira Ferguson. Ann Arbor: University of Michigan Press.

Puri, Shalini. 1999. "Canonized Hybridities, Resistant Hybridities: Chutney, Soca, Carnival and the Politics of Nationalism". In *Caribbean Romances: The Politics of Regional Representation,* edited by Belinda Edmondson, 12–38. Charlottesville: University of Virginia Press.

Ramchand, Kenneth. 1970. *The West Indian Novel and Its Background*. London: Faber.

———. 1988. "A Brighter Sun". In *Critical Perspectives on Sam Selvon,* edited by Susheila Nasta, 160–72. Washington, DC: Three Continents Press.

———. 1993. Editorial. *Ariel* 24, no. 1.

Ramraj, Victor J., ed. 1995. "Postcolonialism and Its Discontents". Special issue, *Ariel* 26, no. 1.

———. 1996. "Tribute to Sam Selvon (1923–94)". Special issue, *Ariel* 27, no. 2.

Reid V. S. 1950. *New Day.* London: Heinemann.

Richardson, B. C. 1983. *Caribbean Migrants: Environment and Survival in St Kitts and Nevis*. Knoxville: University of Tennessee Press.

Roberts, Kevin, and Andrea Thakur. 1996. "Christened with Snow: A Conversation with Sam Selvon". *Ariel* 27, no. 2: 89–115.

Rohlehr, Gordon. 1990. *Calypso and Society in Pre-Independence Trinidad.* Port of Spain, Trinidad: G. Rohlehr.

———. 1992. "Possession as Metaphor: Lamming's *Season of Adventure*". In Gordon Rohlehr, *The Shape of That Hurt and Other Essays,* 66–96. Port of Spain, Trinidad: Longman.

Said, Edward. 1978. *Orientalism.* New York: Vintage.

———. 1990. "Reflections on Exile". In *Out There: Marginalization and Contemporary Culture,* edited by Russell Ferguson, Martha Gever, Trinh T. Minh-ha and Cornell West, 357–66. Cambridge, MA: MIT Press.

Salick, Roydon. 2001. *The Novels of Samuel Selvon: A Critical Study.* Westport, CT: Greenwood.

Sartre, Jean-Paul. 1964–65. "Black Orpheus". Translated by John MacCombie. *Massachusetts Review* 6, no. 1: 13.

Saunders, Patricia. 2003. "The Privileges/Pleasures of Exile: Lamming's *Water with Berries* and the Sexual Politics of Caribbean Nationalisms". Paper presented at the conference "The Sovereignty of the Imagination", in honour of George Lamming. Centre for Caribbean Thought, University of the West Indies, Mona, and Department of Africana Studies, Brown University, in association with the Department of Literatures in English, University of the West Indies, Mona, Jamaica. 5–7 June.

Scholz, Piotr O. 2001. *Eunuchs and Castrati: A Cultural History.* Princeton, NJ: Marks Weiner.

Scott, David. 2002. "The Sovereignty of the Imagination: An Interview with George Lamming". *Small Axe* 12: 72–200.

Scott, Lawrence. 1993. *Witchbroom.* Oxford: Heinemann.

———. 1998. *Aelred's Sin.* London: Allison and Busby.

Seacole, Mary. 1857. *The Wonderful Adventures of Mrs Seacole in Many Lands.* London: Blackwell.

Selvon, Samuel. [1952] 1994. *A Brighter Sun.* Essex, UK: Harlow.

———. [1956] 1972. *The Lonely Londoners.* London: Longman Caribbean.

———. 1959. *Turn Again Tiger.* New York: St Martin's Press.

———. 1965. *The Housing Lark.* London: MacGibbon and Kee.

———. 1972. *Those Who Eat the Cascadura.* London: Davis-Poynter.

———. [1975] 1984. *Moses Ascending.* Oxford: Heinemann.

———. 1983. *Moses Migrating.* Harlow: Longman.

Senior, Olive. 1991. *Working Miracles: Women's Lives in the English Speaking Caribbean.* Cave Hill: Institute of Social and Economic Research, University of the West Indies.

Shepherd, Verene. 1986. "The Dynamics of Afro-Jamaican East Indian Race Relations in Jamaica 1845–1945: A Preliminary Analysis". Paper presented at the Eighteenth Conference of Caribbean Historians, Nassau, Bahamas. 20–25 April.

————. 1995. "The Indentureship and Post-indentureship Experience of Indian Females in Jamaica, 1845–1943". In *Engendering History: Caribbean Women in Historical Perspective,* edited by Verene Shepherd, Bridget Brereton, and Barbara Bailey, 233–57. Kingston, Jamaica: Ian Randle.

Silvera. Makeda. 1989. *Silenced: Talks with Working Class Caribbean Women about Their Lives and Struggles as Domestic Workers in Canada.* Toronto: Sister Vision.

Simoes da Silva, A. J. 2000. *The Luxury of Nationalist Despair: George Lamming's Fiction as Decolonizing Project.* Amsterdam: Rodopi.

Sistren. 1986. *Lionheart Gal: Life Stories of Jamaican Women.* Edited by Honor Ford-Smith. London: Women's Press.

Slade, Ted. 1999. "The Poetry Kit Interviews Fred D'Aguiar". http://www.poetrykit.org/iv/dguiar.htm.

Slemon, Stephen. 1989. "Modernism's Last Outpost". *Ariel* 20, no. 4: 3–17.

Smith, Ian. 1999. "Critics in the Dark". *Journal of West Indian Literature* 8, no. 2: 2–9.

Smith. M. G., F. R. Augier and Rex Nettleford. 1960. *The Rastafarian Movement in Kingston, Jamaica.* Mona, Jamaica: Institute of Social and Economic Research, University of the West Indies.

Spivak, Gyatri Chakravorty. 1987. "Imperialism and Sexual Difference". In *The Current in Criticism: Essays on the Present and Future of Literary Theory,* edited by Clayton Koelb and Virgil Lokke, 319–37. West Lafayette, IN: Purdue University Press.

Srivastava, Aruna. 1989. "Images of Women in Indo-Caribbean Literature". In *Indenture and Exile: The Indo-Caribbean Experience,* edited by Frank Birbalsingh, 108–14. Toronto, Canada: TSAR Publications.

Ten Kortenaar, Neil. 1991. "George Lamming's *In the Castle of My Skin*: Finding Promise in the Land". *Ariel* 22, no. 2: 43–53.

Thieme, John. 1984. Review of *The Novels of George Lamming,* by Sandra Pouchet Paquet. *Wasafiri* 1, no. 1: 21.

Van Sertima, Ivan. 1968. *Caribbean Writers: Critical Essays.* London: New Beacon.

Walcott, Derek. 1974. "The Muse of History". In *Is Massa Day Dead? Black Moods in the Caribbean,* edited by Orde Coombs, 1–27. New York: Anchor/Doubleday.

————. 1985. "Ti Jean and His Brothers". In *Plays for Today,* edited by Errol Hill, 21–72. Harlow: Longman.

————. 1986. *Collected Poems, 1948–1984.* London: Faber and Faber.

————. 1998. "The Antilles: Fragments of Epic Memory". In *What the Twilight Says,* 65–86. New York: Faber and Faber.

Walker, Alice. 1984. *In Search of Our Mothers' Gardens: Womanist Prose.* San Diego, CA: Harcourt Brace Jovanovich.

Walters, Jonathan. 1993. "No More Than a Boy: The Shifting Construction of Masculinity from Ancient Greece to the Middle Ages". *Gender and History* 5, no. 1: 20–33.

Weber, Max. 1947. *The Theory of Social and Economic Organizations.* Translated by
A. M. Henderson and Talcott Parsons. Illinois: Free Press.

West and Zimmerman. 1991. "Doing Gender". In *The Social Construction of Gender,*
edited by Judith Lorber and Susan Farrell, 17–37. London: Sage.

Whitehead, Harriet. 1991. "The Bow and the Burden Strap: A New Look at
Institutionalized Homosexuality in Native North America". In *Sexual Meanings:
The Cultural Construction of Gender and Sexuality,* edited by Sherry B. Ortner and
Harriet Whitehead, 80–115. Cambridge: Cambridge University Press.

Wickham, John. 1961. Review of *Season of Adventure,* by George Lamming. *Bim* 9,
no. 33: 67–72.

Williams, Eric. 1993. *Eric E. Williams Speaks: Essays on Colonialism and Independence.*
Edited by Selwyn Cudjoe. Wellesley, MA: Calaloux.

Wilmot, Fred. 1955. Tribute to Roger Mais, in "A Green Blade in Triumph".
Kyk-over-Al 6, no. 20: 166–70.

Wilmot, Swithin. 1995. "Females of Abandoned Character: Women and Protest in
Jamaica 1838–1865". In *Engendering History: Caribbean Women in Historical
Perspective,* edited by Verene Shepherd, Bridget Brereton and Barbara Bailey,
279–95. New York: St Martin's Press.

Wyke, Clement. 1991. *Samuel Selvon's Dialectal Style and Fictional Strategy.* Vancouver,
Canada: University of British Columbia Press.

Wynter, Sylvia. 1962. *The Hills of Hebron.* London: Jonathan Cape.

———. 1970. "Jonkonn in Jamaica: Towards the Interpretation of Folk Dance as
Cultural Process". *Jamaica Journal* 4, no. 2: 34–48.

———. 1971. "Novel and History: Plot and Plantation". *Savacou* 5 (June): 95–102.

———. 1990. "Afterword: Beyond Miranda's Meanings: Un/silencing the 'Demonic
Ground' of Caliban's Woman". In *Out of the Kumbla: Caribbean Women and
Literature,* edited by Carole Boyce Davies and Elaine Savory Fido, 355–72. Trenton,
NJ: Africa World Press.

Index